Barbra Streisand
THE MUSIC

REVISED & UPDATED

Barbra Streisand
THE MUSIC

REVISED & UPDATED

MATT HOWE

FOREWORD BY JAY LANDERS

TUCKER DS PRESS

Barbra Streisand: The Music, the Albums, the Singles Revised and Updated

Edited for content by Scott Ryan
Copy edited by David Bushman
Book designed by Scott Ryan
Cover design by Matt Howe
All album art and promo photos are courtesy of Columbia Records
Some album cover scans by Kevin Schlenker
Front cover photo: Columbia Records/Kevin Mazur
Back cover photo: Columbia Records/Firooz Zahedi
Special thanks to www.barbra-archives.info
Some photos from the collections of Matt Howe and Scott Ryan

Hank Parker/Columbia Records: 10, 16 with feathers, 30, 31 (studio shot by Don Hunstein), 41 (Streisand and Harold Arlen), 47 (recording with Michele Legrand), 51 (pictured with Columbia-head Goddard Lieberson). Columbia Records/Sony: ii, 4, 7, 11 (color photo, Marty Erlichman & Streisand: Russell James); 21 (Matz and Barbra by Mark Sennet); 178-179 "Back to Broadway" alternate, photo: Firooz Zahedi; 180 (Crawford, Foster, Streisand) photo: Jeffrey Mayer; 191-192 (photo of Celine Dion & Barbra Streisand): Firooz Zahedi; 195 (Jay Landers and Barbra at Scoring Stage) photo by Kevin Mazur; 198 photo by Jim Shea; 200, 205, 208, 223, 225, 277 photos by Firooz Zahedi; 212 "Movie Album" photo by Terry O'Neill; 215-217 "Guilty Pleasures" photos by Alberto Tolot; 224 Diana Krall photo: John Clayton; 226 Barbra and Sammy photo by Russell James; 241-243 "Back to Brooklyn" concert photos: Russell James; 246 Barbra in her back yard, photo: Russell James; 247 at microphone, photo: Jason Merritt; 259, 264 photos by Russell James; 260 Barbra in her garden, photo by Kathryn Boyd Brolin; 273, 275 Barbra and Paul McCartney and Mariah Carey photos by Kevin Mazur; 274 Laufey and 13-year-old Barbra courtesy official Barbra Streisand YouTube; 275 photo of Ariana Grande and Barbra by Jay Landers; 276 Sting and Barbra, photo by: Sting Instagram;

Published in the USA by Fayetteville Mafia Press
Columbus, Ohio

Contact Information
Email: fayettevillemafiapress@gmail.com
Website: TuckerDSPress.com
Instagram: @Fayettevillemafiapress

"With all there is,
why settle for just a piece of sky?"

- Alan and Marilyn Bergman,
Yentl

CONTENTS

FOREWORD BY JAY LANDERS

On February 9, 1964, the Beatles made their first appearance on *The Ed Sullivan Show*. I was eight years old and fell hard. Seeing the long-haired lads from Liverpool was my "big bang" moment. Armed with an old tennis racket for a faux guitar, I mimed along to their records until I'd memorized every lyric, bass run, drum fill, and vocal harmony by heart.

After high school, I tried every way I could to turn my passion for music into a vocation. I managed aspiring record producers and artists, published songs by unknown writers, and knocked on every door imaginable trying to convince established artists to record the songs. Each modest success gave me more confidence that I'd chosen the right career path. Still, it was slow going.

My lucky break finally arrived when I started working as a song plugger for Charles Koppelman—a golden-eared music industry titan who could spot a hit a mile away. Among his many illustrious credits: a quartet of multiplatinum albums he executive produced for Barbra Streisand—*Superman*, *Songbird*, *Wet*, and the 1980 global chart-topper *Guilty*.

In the summer of 1981, with *Guilty* zooming toward five million sales in the US alone, Columbia Records was eager to capitalize on its success by releasing a new Streisand album for the holidays. However, she was deeply ensconced in the development of *Yentl*, which she'd been nurturing for over a decade. After many false starts, there was finally a green light at the end of the tunnel, but Barbra knew her duties as lead actress, director, producer, screenwriter, singer, and soundtrack album producer would barely leave her time to breathe, much less create a worthy follow-up to the best-selling album of her career.

As a stopgap measure, the ever-intrepid Mr. Koppelman proposed that Columbia release a new Streisand compilation, featuring some of her best-known seventies-era love songs, like "The Way We Were," "My Heart Belongs to Me," "Evergreen," and "You Don't Bring Me Flowers." To make the package extra special, he would try to convince Barbra to set aside a day or two to record a few new songs. When she tentatively agreed, Charles issued an all-points bulletin to his small but mighty staff: "Need best songs for Barbra."

Behind every song lies a story. That same summer, when my dad and I saw the West End production of Andrew Lloyd Webber's *Cats*, the musical was over a year away from opening on Broadway. The moment Elaine Paige performed her eleven o'clock showstopper "Memory," I knew it had Barbra's name written all over it. I put it on my short list to send to Charles. He loved the idea and thought he might be able to get Webber himself to produce it.

Back in LA, I was having a friendly meeting with an old-school Polygram Records executive named Russ Regan. Earlier in his career, Russ had signed Elton John to his first recording contract with MCA Records. He was a world-class schmoozer and always willing to share a few great showbiz war stories. As our fun chat was winding down, he handed me a plastic cassette box (remember those?) bearing a dozen titles by a little-known Chicago-based writing team—Richard Wold (aka Richard Parker) and Bobby Whiteside. Russ couldn't recall who'd sent it to him, but he said, "I think these guys have some pretty good tunes. Unfortunately no one here gives a shit." He nonchalantly added, "You can give it a listen or just toss it." Later that afternoon, I slipped the cassette into my trusty Ampex tape machine. The first two songs on it were "Comin' In and Out of Your Life" and "When the Lovin' Goes Out of the Lovin'." I listened to both about twenty times, imagining how Barbra would relate to the lyrics, how she'd soar with the melodies, and especially how she'd phrase each line in her inimitable style. Satisfied they ticked all the boxes, I sent them to Charles. A few days later, I was happy (make that relieved) when he confirmed that all three songs I'd pitched were good candidates. The next day, he took the three-and-a-half-hour Concorde flight from JFK to London Heathrow to meet with Barbra.

I don't actually know how many other tunes Barbra and Charles reviewed at their listening session, but afterward, he called me to say the only ones she'd liked were the three I'd suggested! While she was working in London, Barbra wound up recording "Memory" (produced by Andrew Lloyd Webber), "Comin' In and Out of Your Life" (credited to Webber but, in truth, produced by Barbra and Charles when Webber was a studio no-show), and a work-in-progress take of "When the Lovin' Goes Out of the Lovin'" (also produced by Barbra and Charles). The first two songs became the singles from her *Memories* album. Although Barbra's vocal on "Lovin'" was well sung, the arrangement was lacking and was left on the proverbial cutting-room floor.

When Columbia released *Memories* in early November '81, it was an out-of-the-box smash—selling a whopping five million copies in the US and another five million internationally. In the UK (where *Memories* was retitled *Love Songs*), it topped the charts for nine weeks and was awarded a platinum certification as the best-selling album of 1981. From a sales perspective, *Memories* turned out to be just as successful as *Guilty*.

As for "When the Lovin' Goes Out of the Lovin'," soon after Barbra's *Memories* was released, an executive at Columbia named Mickey Eichner asked Charles if he could find one song to complete a new Johnny Mathis album titled *Friends in Love*. Since Barbra's version of "When the Lovin'" had been relegated to her vault, I asked Charles what he thought about submitting it to Johnny (who happens to be Barbra's favorite singer). Johnny loved the song and agreed to record it, with Charles supervising the production.

In 1984, Barbra was back in the studio with Charles recording the pop album *Emotion*. While it had some lovely songs on it, the overall collection lacked a certain cohesiveness. Maurice White, the trailblazing founder of Earth, Wind & Fire, had been asked to produce a few songs. To my surprise, Charles told me Maurice wanted to revisit "When the Lovin' Goes Out of the Lovin'." However, despite everyone's best intentions, the master tape was, once again, returned to the vault.

Forty years later, in August 2021 to be precise, using the same original vocal, Barbra finally released her third version of "When the Lovin' Goes Out of the Lovin'" with a revamped arrangement and mix by Jochem van der Saag. It was included as a bonus track on the Target exclusive edition of *Release Me 2*.

If you're wondering how I'm able to reconstruct the minutia of these particular forty-year-old recordings when I can barely remember what I had for breakfast this morning, the answer is I turn to Matt Howe and his brilliantly informative website, barbra-archives.info. For all things Barbra, Matt has the passion of a superfan, the detective skills of Sherlock Holmes, and the dedication of a research scholar. Now, in his book, *Barbra Streisand: The Music, the Albums, the Singles*, he's gathered all of the salient information concerning the historic albums Barbra made long before she and I met, as well as equally compelling facts about the many recording sessions I've attended with her.

Matt knows who produced and arranged Barbra's first single of "Happy Days Are Here Again" . . . and the second version, for *The Barbra Streisand Album* . . . and even the third version (Barbra's favorite), from *A Happening in Central Park*. He knows how many copies were pressed and sold of each. If you're curious about where the celestial photograph adorning Barbra's *A Christmas Album* was taken, ask Matt. He can also tell you the hour of the morning and location where photographer Don Bronstein shot the iconic Grammy-winning "back to the camera" cover photo of the *People* album. With his unerring attention to detail, Matt leaves no Streisand stone unturned!

Having been present at every Barbra Streisand recording session since 1989, I can only look back in amazement at the countless times I've witnessed how a true musical genius can bend, shape, and will a song to life. With little concern for what is or isn't deemed "commercial," Barbra has had one overarching goal: to create music of lasting value.

Anyone wishing to take a deep dive into the remarkable catalog of the most celebrated female singer of all time should look no further than to *Barbra Streisand: The Music, the Albums, the Singles*. It's a fascinating exploration into the who-what-when-where-and-how the "Greatest Star" has assembled her unparalleled body of work.

Jay Landers
A & R/Executive Producer
September 2022

INTRODUCTION

"Sing, sing a song
Sing out loud, sing out strong ..."

Publishing *Barbra Streisand: The Music, The Albums, The Singles* in April 2023 was immensely gratifying for me—I'd never written such a comprehensive book before, and its reception was exciting and humbling. Now I am delighted to update it—it's a great chance to correct some things and expand on what I'd written two years ago.

Barbra, meanwhile, has been busy since we first published: She released more albums (now included in this book), and she finally published her autobiography, *My Name Is Barbra*, in November 2023. I've added some important quotes from that book to this one. Also, shortly after my hardcover book was released, Sony added the two Streisand digital holdouts to streaming services—the soundtracks to *Nuts* and *Funny Lady*. I'm proud that I helped bring this to their attention. Now we can stream Barbra's entire official discography on our favorite devices.

When we first released the hardcover book, my publisher, Scott Ryan, and I publicized it by doing a series of YouTube videos in which we covered five albums (or so) each episode and spoke extemporaneously about our one favorite track—we only allowed ourselves the choice of one (although we both cheated on a couple of occasions.) We had guest stars too. The "Baron of Broadway," Richard Jay-Alexander, played along with our format on one early episode, then came back for another. Randy Waldman, Barbra's 2016-2019 concert conductor, enthralled us with his stories. And the generous Jay Landers joined us several times, always with great stories and behind-the-scenes info that our YouTube audience ate up (some of the exclusive information he shared on those videos has been added too). We even enticed Lauren Frost, who played "Young Barbra" in the *Timeless* concerts, to come on the show. Scott and I persisted on camera with our funny chemistry for over a year; we Zoomed over twenty episodes and developed a fun fan following. I just added it up: we had over 71,000 views combined on all the episodes. I'm so glad you all enjoyed it. The videos are still streaming over at the Barbra Archives YouTube channel and are a great extension to this book.

This all began with my website, Barbra Archives. For over twenty years I have collected facts, photos, and interviews about Barbra's career. The website covers her movies, TV shows, awards, live performances, and more. Around 2010, Barbra's team began consulting me for information and photos about Barbra's career. Whenever she would appear on a TV interview, release a compilation album, or go on a concert tour, I was asked to contribute photos or check the facts. Like Barbra, I just want it all to be *right*. I will never forget the joy I felt when Barbra first sent me a note thanking me for "caring about the truth" (I framed it).

Back to this book. The art of album making isn't the same as it was for the first thirty years of Streisand's recording career. With vinyl, we had two sides—you'll notice I list the early albums by sides in this book because it matters. Sides were abandoned when CDs became the disc of choice around the world. Luckily, vinyl has had a resurgence, and some of Streisand's latest albums are being released in that format, gratifying many old-school fans. For newer fans, I'm trying to convey that buying a Streisand album wasn't only about the music . . . we also had a sexy printed product to hold in our hands. Sometimes we even got the complete lyrics to all the songs, printed on the album insert!

I wrote this book by taking a deep dive into Barbra's discography starting back in 1955, when her miraculous voice was first recorded. I listened to each and every album from the first to the last track. And then, because I was feeling nostalgic (and because I was housebound due to the COVID pandemic), I listened to Barbra's vinyl records. My collection of bootleg tracks informed the book too.

I was able to include new interviews with Streisand associates like Bill Ross and Richard Jay-Alexander. Jay Landers filled in some gaps of information about many of the albums he produced with Barbra. Then I included quotes from earlier interviews I had conducted for my website with the Bergmans, Phil Ramone, Rupert Holmes, and others. They're all here, illuminating Barbra's creative process when she records her albums.

I was encouraged by my publisher to be critical and share my opinions of Barbra's work, which I always shied away from on my website. Apologies to David Foster. And shame on you, Grammy Awards—Barbra hasn't been awarded since 1987!

My goal for this book? That it inspires fans, new and old, to listen to Streisand tracks or albums that maybe they haven't considered in years. *Barbra Streisand: The Music* is best experienced while listening to whatever Barbra Streisand album you're reading about.

Some disclaimers: I use Columbia Records and Sony interchangeably, both referring to Barbra's record label, which, for a time, was also called SonyBMG and CBS Records. Oh, and don't forget their catalog division, Legacy Recordings.

Apologies to my European friends, but this book focuses completely on Barbra's US releases for the very practical reason that I don't collect the EU albums. I do mention a few important European releases, though.

Mostly, I hope this book *lights the corners of your minds*, because Barbra's music is so impressive: a discography spanning studio albums, live albums, soundtrack and cast albums, and a box set. There's so much to discuss. We best get started.

Matt Howe
www.Barbra-Archives.info
November 2025

YOU'LL NEVER KNOW

The earliest known recording of Barbra Streisand was made when she was thirteen years old, on December 29, 1955. Her mother paid for a recording session at Nola Recording Studios in New York (at twenty-five dollars an hour, a fortune for the family).

Nola was located on the second floor of a large building at Fifty-First Street and Broadway. Barbra and her mother had met a piano player while they were in the Catskills on vacation, so they recruited him to play for them on the recording. This scene was dramatized in her 1999 *Timeless* concert with Lauren Frost playing and singing as young Barbra.

But Barbra had to give the pianist direction. "My mother went first, but she could hardly get a chorus in edgewise," Barbra wrote in 1991, "because the piano player kept launching into endless, elaborate refrains. As soon as he started that with me, I told him, 'No, no, we'll just do a little interlude and then I'll come back in.'" (Streisand, *Just for the Record* liner notes, 1991)

Streisand recorded two songs at Nola Studios, which were cut onto an acetate record: "Zing! Went the Strings of My Heart" and "You'll Never Know." The latter was included on her 1991 retrospective box set, *Just for the Record*. "Zing!" was never officially released, although Barbra allowed a few seconds of it to play during an Australian television interview in the 1990s.

THE 1960S

EARLY RECORDINGS

Barbra Streisand was next recorded by her friend and collaborator Barry Dennen when she was putting her act together in New York nightclubs around 1960.

After Barbra and Dennen appeared together in an off-Broadway play called *The Insect Comedy*, she reached out to him for a favor. According to Dennen's recollection, Barbra wanted a recording of her singing to give to Eddie Blum, the casting director for Rodgers and Hammerstein. Barbra recalls that they recorded the songs "A Sleepin' Bee" and "A Taste of Honey" and that she "mailed it off to some important agent, who promptly lost it and sent me back an empty tape months later with a note: 'Sorry. Here's a replacement'" (Streisand, 2023).

"She had a voice the microphone loved—and everybody else loved it, too," Dennen wrote (Dennen, 1997). Dennen recorded many of Streisand's engagements during this period, including her live performances at the Lion and the Bon Soir nightclub and her radio performances in Detroit in 1961.

I've heard three of the songs that Dennen recorded at the Bon Soir. They have historical value but ultimately are eclipsed by the amazing restoration job that Jochem van der Saag did on the 2022 *Live at the Bon Soir* album.

These tapes caused bad feelings between Streisand and Dennen for many years. Dennen put them up for auction in 2009 for $1 million, but they did not sell. He passed away in 2017, and in 2021 his estate reached out again to sell them back to Streisand's team. No word on if that sale took place.

Marty Erlichman, Barbra's stalwart manager, who has represented her for decades, arranged for Streisand to record demo albums and audition discs for the record labels he was trying to sign her to in 1961 and 1962. These acetates featured Streisand singing in the studio accompanied by a piano. On the demo for RCA Records, Streisand recorded the songs she was already singing in her club act: "Sleepin' Bee," "Have I Stayed Too Long at the Fair," "When the Sun Comes Out," "A Taste of Honey," "Lover, Come Back," "Bewitched," "I Had Myself a True Love," and "Soon It's Gonna Rain." On this demo was a song Streisand talked about recording for her 2003 *Movie Album*, but didn't: "At the Codfish Ball." Barbra turns this cutesy song, originally performed by child star Shirley Temple in the 1936 movie *Captain January*, into a swinging showcase for her wry interpretation. After all, the song is about fish attending an underwater ball. In fact, Barbra goes up on the lyric to "Codfish Ball" on take one. "What? I forgot the words," she exclaims. Take two went much better. She also asks for a retake on "Lover, Come Back," snapping out the tempo for her pianist. Marty Gold accompanied her here. Besides playing piano, he was a composer and arranger at RCA. The man on the studio microphone telling Barbra to try another take on these recordings is unidentified.

There was another ten-inch demo acetate, recorded at Fine Recording on West 57th Street in New York, which went up for sale in 2007 by Heritage Auctions and contained two Streisand vocals accompanied by what sounds like a trio backing her: "Come to the Supermarket in Old Peking" and "Have I Stayed Too Long at the Fair." According to the auction website, the demo was "one of only ten that were manufactured in the early sixties; eight were sent to record companies and are no longer believed to exist, one went into Barbra's vault, and this one was given by her to a friend who's kept it in pristine condition for the past four decades."

That "friend" was Don Softness, who did publicity for Streisand around 1961. Heritage Auctions' website indicates the acetate demo did not sell.

There's one more early Streisand recording I should mention. This one was shared with me by a fan. It features Barbra rehearsing "Have I Stayed Too Long at the Fair" in 1961 during her run on Broadway in *I Can Get It for You Wholesale*. She's accompanied by Peter Howard—one of the arrangers on *Wholesale*. There's a funny bit on the recording at the bridge of the song ("Oh, daddy, dear...") where Howard plays a wrong chord and Barbra immediately reacts: "No. No. No."

Meanwhile, Columbia Records finally signed a contract with Barbra Streisand on October 1, 1962. That initial contract was reportedly for five years (one year guaranteed, with four annual options) and gave her a royalty of 5 percent against 98 percent of the records she sold (paid after recording costs).

Erlichman stated that Streisand received a cash advance with the label. "It was small—twenty thousand dollars, I believe. We weren't interested in big front money. We waived that for other considerations such as creative control, no coupling, and the right to choose her own material" (the coupling clause gave Streisand the right to refuse to be placed on a compilation record with other artists). (Considine, 1985)

Erlichman, always looking out for Streisand, insisted on "an album within the first six months. The wording was that twenty sides [songs], which meant two LPs, had to be recorded and released at six-month intervals that first year," he said. "I wanted to be sure that in the event she was dropped by the label, she was first given every opportunity to succeed—our way, not theirs." (Considine, 1985)

Before Columbia Records recorded Streisand's premier album, it teamed her with producer Mike Berniker and conductor/arranger George Williams and released four Streisand songs as singles. "I don't know why I was chosen," Berniker said. "I met with Marty, then with Barbra. I sent her a copy of a Tammy Grimes album I had just done. She listened to the album and said, 'Yeah, let's go.'" (Considine, 1985)

"Happy Days" and "When the Sun Comes Out" (Columbia #4-42631) were paired for Barbra's first seven-inch single release in early November 1962, with only five hundred copies pressed on vinyl. Because these were recorded first, they have different arrangements from the versions heard on *The Barbra Streisand Album*—George Williams, not Peter Matz, orchestrated these singles. A second single was sent out later: "My Coloring Book" b/w "Lover Come Back to Me" (Columbia #4-42648).

"It was a rush session," said "Coloring Book" arranger Bob Mersey. "We were doing an album with a group called the Arena Brass. So we sneaked Barbra in on that session, for the one song, and I will never forget it." (Considine, 1985) Streisand was late to the "My Coloring Book" party, though. *Cabaret* songwriters Kander and Ebb said they wrote "Coloring Book" for comedienne and nightclub star Kaye Ballard, but it was Sandy Stewart who ended up singing it on a Perry Como television show, and it became a big hit for her. George Chakiris (Bernardo in the *West Side Story* film) also recorded it, for Capitol Records; Kitty Kallen sang it too. "We got screwed," Erlichman said. "Columbia never told us of the other versions." (Considine, 1985)

Meanwhile, in 1962 Barbra became a Broadway star in the musical *I Can Get It for You Wholesale*, appearing as the secretary Miss Marmelstein. In November that year, she taxied over to the Bon Soir after the show and performed her nightclub act. Columbia sent a remote recording crew to the Bon Soir to record four of the shows, believing that capturing Streisand live would be a dynamic first album to release. Columbia publicist Peter Reilly (who worked with Streisand in her early years at the record label) sent out invitations to Columbia executives, guests, and members of the music trade. The invitation read: "Miss Marmelstein invites you to a party for her best friend BARBRA STREISAND to hear her sing a few tunes which will be recorded (on the spot) by Columbia Records." Barbra's A & R (artist and repertoire) man David Kapralik was another early supporter of Streisand's talent. He introduced Barbra to the crowded club, saying "For me and everyone at Columbia, she's a singular artist. You can't put her in any category." Ultimately, Columbia decided not to release *Live at the Bon Soir* (until 2022). Instead, Barbra recorded her first album in the studio with Peter Matz arrangements.

Released: April 10, 1962
Produced by: Goddard Lieberson
Music and lyrics by: Harold Rome
Musical direction and vocal arrangements by: Lehman Engel
Orchestrations by: Sid Ramin
CD released: October 1993
CD restored by: John Arrias at B&J Studio using the C.A.P. System
CD remastered by: Bernie Grundman

Catalog Numbers:
KOS 2180 (LP, 1962 w/gatefold)
KOL 5780 (mono LP w/gatefold)
KOL 5780 (LP, Columbia Masterworks)
AKOS 2180 (LP, Columbia Masterworks reissue)
CK 53020 (CD)
Stage Door 990 (2022 2-CD set)

Side One:

1. Overture 2. I'm Not A Well Man (Kruschen, Streisand) 3. The Way Things Are (Gould) 4. When Gemini Meets Capricorn (Cooper, Gould) 5. Momma, Momma, Momma (Gould, Roth) 6. The Sound Of Money (North, Gould, Monte, Reilly, Verso) 7. Too Soon (Roth) 8. The Family Way (Roth, Gould, Cooper, Lang, Linn, LeRoy) 9. Who Knows? (Cooper)

Side Two:

1. Ballad Of The Garment Trade (Streisand, Cooper, Linn, Gould, Lang, LeRoy and Chorus) 2. Have I Told You Lately ?(LeRoy, Linn) 3. A Gift Today (Gould, Roth, Linn, LeRoy, Cooper and Chorus) 4. Miss Marmelstein (Streisand) 5. A Funny Thing Happened (Cooper, Gould) 6. What's In It For Me? (Lang, North) 7. Eat A Little Something (Roth) 8. What Are They Doing To Us Now? (Streisand, Brown, Hickman, Turner, Lisa, Curley, Bond)

I Can Get It for You Wholesale was the first commercially released album that Barbra Streisand appeared on—and it was released before she signed her contract with Columbia.

Wholesale was also Barbra Streisand's first Broadway musical, its tunes written by Harold Rome. It opened on March 22, 1962, and Barbra was a big hit in the musical, garnering a lot of press for her portrayal of the put-upon secretary Miss Marmelstein. *Wholesale*'s director was Arthur Laurents, the man who wrote the book for Broadway's *West Side Story* and *Gypsy* and the screenplay for the movies *The Way We Were* and *The Turning Point*. Laurents wrote that Streisand's voice "was a perfect match for the plaintive Jewish wail in [Rome's] tunes." (Laurents, 2000)

On a Sunday a week after opening, the cast assembled at Columbia Record's Thirtieth Street studio to record the cast album. Columbia's president Goddard Lieberson was present at the session as the album's producer. Streisand had already auditioned for Lieberson, but he had not made up his mind whether to sign her to Columbia Records. Lieberson sent a note to Arthur Laurents: "Barbra Streisand is indeed very talented but I'm afraid she's too special for records." (Laurents, 2000)

Barbra elaborated in her memoir: "Goddard thought my voice was 'too Broadway' for middle America . . . that I was too specialized a taste and wouldn't get the kind of airplay you needed to break through, now that rock and roll was all the rage. He didn't think there was an audience for a girl who sang ballads . . . and obscure ones at that."

Barbra expanded on this notion by writing: "It also probably didn't help that one of his associates, John Hammond, was dead set against me. Hammond had recorded Count Basie and Billie Holiday, and when he first heard me he wasn't sure if I was black or white. Apparently he didn't want any competition for Aretha Franklin, whom he had just signed to the label . . . or at least that's what Marty [Erlichman] heard through the grapevine."

There were some changes made to the *Wholesale* cast album that should be noted:

- The "Overture" on the album is actually the "Prologue" music. *Wholesale*'s true overture was not included on the album, and it's unknown if it was ever recorded.
- The songs were resequenced for the album, and the CD keeps the same order.

Here's the in-show order of songs as they were sung onstage:

Overture*/ Prologue/I'm Not A Well Man/The Way Things Are/When Gemini Meets Capricorn
Momma, Momma, Momma/The Sound of Money/The Family Way/Too Soon /Who Knows?
Have I Told You Lately?/Ballad of the Garment Trade/Finale Act I: Fashion Show*

Entr'acte*/A Gift Today/Miss Marmelstein/Reprise: The Sound of Money*/A Funny Thing Happened
What's In It For Me?/What Are They Doing To Us Now?/Eat A Little Something/Curtain Calls; Exit Music*
**These songs are not on the cast album; it is unknown if they were recorded.*

Wholesale will forever be known as the Broadway show that Barbra Streisand stopped when she sang "Miss Marmelstein." We've all heard about performers who "stop the show," but when you think it through, it must have been incredible to witness. Imagine being in the theater, and at the top of the second act of *Wholesale* Barbra wheels herself on stage in an office chair and sings this comedic song. The audience was so charmed and impressed with Barbra that after she sang "I could bust" they clapped and cheered so long and so enthusiastically that the entire company of *Wholesale* held the show while this happened. Legend has it that the ovation lasted three minutes.

Since the closing of *Wholesale* in the early 1960s, Barbra has performed the song only once in concert (she complained that her fancy *Timeless* tour sequined outfit made it hard to sing the song "in character," since Marmelstein was a *mieskeit*). The song is forever connected to her, and even though there is no video or film of the showstopper, we have plenty of iconic photos of Streisand wheeling herself around the stage in 1962 singing the song. Barbra fought director Arthur Laurents for the chance to sing it sitting in a secretarial chair—and her instincts paid off—literally! When quizzed in 2016 whether the ovation was really three minutes long, Streisand demurred. "All I know is that my salary was $175 and the next day it went up to $350," she said. (Morning, 2016)

Matt on *Wholesale*

I Can Get It for You Wholesale is a long-forgotten gem. It's rare that I'll sit and listen to the album from start to finish, and while writing this book I gave it several listens. Almost every song is melodic, catchy, and beautifully ethnic. One reviewer during the Philadelphia previews wrote: "Harold Rome has dipped into Jewish musical sources for his score—a fröhlich, a chant of sorrow, even a bar mitzvah ceremony; but he has successfully transplanted these into the musical comedy idiom." (Gahan, 1962)

The *I Can Get It for You Wholesale* album is also historic. It wasn't revived until 2023, when Jerome Weidman's son, John, retooled the script for a production at Classic Stage Company. The *New York Times* review explained that John Weidman "restored some of the novel's first-person narration—Weidman has cut a song, moved two, added three from Rome's archive and trimmed several others. He's excised any hint of redemption at the end." The original, 1962 version featuring Streisand was labeled a cynical show, criticized for being a downer, with hardly any likable characters. Also, Jerome Weidman's novels (and therefore this show) have been criticized for decades for being anti-Semitic, even though Weidman was a New York Jew.

Be sure to relisten to Barbra's delightful vocals on "What Are They Doing to Us Now?" and "Ballad of the Garment Trade." She's given the opening verse to sing on each song, and no wonder. Her clear, bell-like voice was special enough to spotlight on more than just her comedic character song, "Miss Marmelstein."

Did you know that Barbra recorded a song from *Wholesale* in 1988 when she was laying tracks for a version of *Back to Broadway* that she ended up abandoning? Barbra and her conductor/arranger Rupert Holmes ("The Piña Colada Song") recorded "A Funny Thing Happened," which was originally sung in the show by Marilyn Cooper. Streisand's 1988 recording is fantastic—she has sped up the tempo so the song sounds more like her version of Stephen Sondheim's "Putting It Together" or other tongue twisters that she's sung. I have always imagined that Barbra was backstage in 1962 listening to Cooper onstage and thought to herself, "This tempo is too slow! One day, I'll record that song better."

STREISAND COLLABORATORS

MARTY ERLICHMAN

Marty Erlichman has managed and represented Barbra Streisand in all matters of her show business career for over sixty years. Theirs is an artist-management relationship as important and iconic as Elvis and the Colonel, René Angélil and Celine Dion, or Brian Epstein and the Beatles.

Born in Brooklyn in 1929, Marty Erlichman was the son of a bakery businessman. Erlichman attended Drake University in Des Moines, Iowa, before moving to New York, where he worked in the mailroom at CBS-TV. On Saturdays, Erlichman read interoffice memos and contracts, gaining knowledge about the legalities of show business.

In 1960, Erlichman, who was producing jazz and folk music concerts at the time, went to see a comedian friend perform at a little club in Manhattan called the Bon Soir. "I went to check out his material," Erlichman recalled, "but out walked this eighteen-year-old singer as his opening act. She sang five songs and I had chills through all of them." Erlichman went backstage to meet Streisand. "I told her, 'Barbra, the first time out of the box, you're going to win every award that this business has to offer—the Tony, the Emmy, the Grammy, the Oscar.' She looked at me and said, 'The Oscar?' and I said, 'That's going to be the biggest one, because you're going to be the biggest movie star of them all.' She giggled and said, 'I think I'm going to be a star too.'" (Spada, 1983)

Streisand wrote in *My Name Is Barbra*: "I felt comfortable with Marty from that first moment. He was like a guy from my old neighborhood . . . dark hair, glasses, kind face, a bit chubby. Turns out he grew up near me in Brooklyn. We spoke the same language."

Besides negotiating Streisand's record contract with Columbia Records and her multiyear deal with CBS Television—both of which accorded her creative control—Erlichman has been an executive producer on all of her TV shows. Erlichman produced her film *For Pete's Sake* as well as *Coma* with Michael Douglas and *Breathless* with Richard Gere. Besides Streisand, he managed the "Ernest" comedy franchise for Walt Disney as well as the "Where's Waldo?" franchise, negotiating books, television shows, and movies for that character.

"We started together and grew together," Marty said about Streisand. "To me Barbra was always like a live Erector set: Whatever you could think of, she could make happen. It's one thing to say, 'Central Park,' it's another to get 150,000 people there." (Grein, Erlichman Back as Streisand's Manager, 1986)

Barbra has said she worked so closely with Marty because of their "soul connection." Erlichman attributes their long professional relationship and friendship to their honesty. "We haven't always agreed, but that's the strength of our relationship. I'm not a yes guy. I'm a recommender with a good, objective view." (Drake University, 2007)

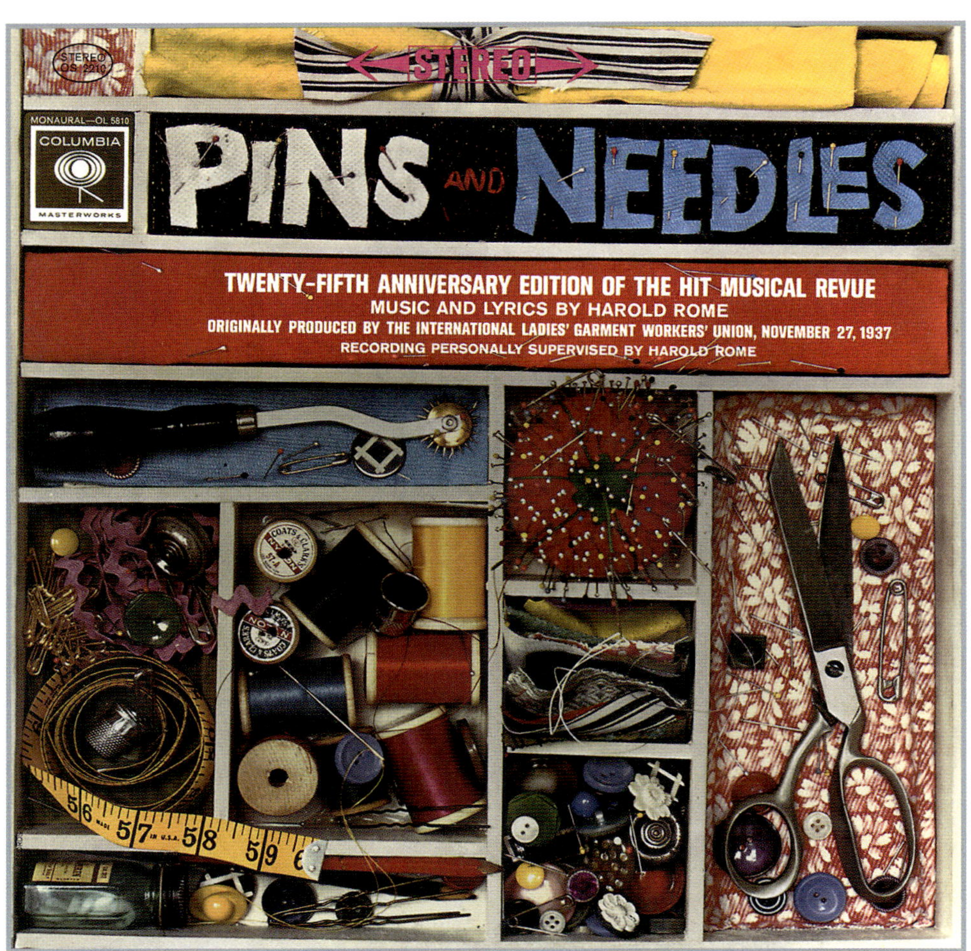

Released: May 1962
Produced by: Elizabeth Lauer and Charles Burr
Supervised by: Harold Rome
Music and lyrics by: Harold Rome
Original recording engineer: George Knuerr
Cover art: Antonakos
Back cover photos: Hank Parker
CD restored by: John Arrias at B&J Studio using the C.A.P. System
CD remastered by: Bernie Grundman

Catalog Numbers:
OS 2210 (LP)
OL 5810 (LP, mono)
CK 57380 (CD)

Side One:

1. Sing Me A Song With Social Significance (Jun) 2. Doing The Reactionary (Streisand) 3. One Big Union For Two (Carroll, Jun) 4. It's Better With A Union Man (Rome) 5. Nobody Makes A Pass At Me (Streisand) 6. I've Got The Nerve To Be In Love (Carroll, Jun) 7. Not Cricket To Picket (Streisand) 8. Back To Work (Carroll and Chorus)

Side Two:

1. Status Quo (Streisand) 2. When I Grow Up (The G-Man Song) (Rome) 3. Chain Store Daisy (Jun) 4. Four Little Angels Of Peace (Rome, Carroll, Streisand, Sokoloff) 5. Sunday In The Park (Carroll) 6. What Good Is Love? (Streisand) 7. Mene, Mene, Tekel (Rome and Chorus)

Pins and Needles is an album from 1962 that paid tribute to a 1937 Broadway revue that ran for four years. *Pins and Needles* was an album of nostalgia, for sure, and as *Audio* magazine wrote, "The show is an extremely lively museum piece that throws a vast quantity of new light on the talents of composer-lyricist Harold Rome." (Santon, 1962)

To explain this anachronistic LP, Gary Marmorstein revealed that Columbia Records was motivated to record it because it wanted to release the cast album of Rome's *I Can Get It for You Wholesale*. "As an inducement to Rome," Marmorstein wrote, "[Goddard] Lieberson offered to record the twenty-fifth anniversary version of his International Ladies' Garment Workers' Union show *Pins and Needles*." (Marmorstein, 2007)

Does a modern audience need to understand the roots of an album to enjoy it? Sure, *Pins and Needles* has good ballads and catchy up-tempo numbers, but what does it all mean? In 1937, *Pins and Needles* had the distinction of being the only hit Broadway show to be produced by a labor union. This show reflected the times: Roosevelt's New Deal, the recession, Hitler's dictatorship in Germany, unemployment, and the battling of labor unions. "Where was the joke in the AFL-CIO split? Who was laughing at the headlines about Hitler? What's funny about a strike, class struggle, appeasement of Fascists, or the exploitation of workers?" wrote Charles Burr in the album's liner notes.

To answer, Harold Rome wrote fifteen charming, comedic, sophisticated but biting tunes with great melodies that addressed the issues. Since Streisand had already made her mark in Rome's musical *I Can Get It for You Wholesale*, it was no stretch that he requested that Barbra participate in Columbia Records's anniversary recording of the revue. Rome also recruited Jack Carroll, Elise Bretton, Stan Freeman, and Rose Marie Jun to perform the songs on the record. Album producers Charles Burr and Elizabeth Lauer arranged for piano, guitar, bass, and drums to accompany the singers.

Harold Rome was impressed by Streisand. "She's nineteen years old, for heaven's sake!" Rome exclaimed about Barbra's grasp of the older material. "She's not a history student. She doesn't know about the period, and yet she gets into the songs as if she'd been born to them. I don't know where it's coming from." (Morgenstern, 1983)

Just for perspective, you should note that although *Pins and Needles* was with Columbia Records, Streisand had still not signed a contract with the label at this point. It wasn't until October 1993 that Columbia finally released *Pins and Needles* on CD—restored and remastered by John Arrias. The only noticeable change was that Columbia added "Featuring Barbra Streisand" and an extra row of ribbon on the bottom of the CD cover.

"What Good Is Love?" is a solid ballad sung by Streisand. It's a most excellent antilove song that's in the same league as "Down with Love" or "Love Is a Bore." "What Good Is Love?" even has a humanist lyric: how can you experience love when you don't have the basic things in life to take care of yourself? "Doing the Reactionary" needs a retro dance video! I'm picturing Fosse-esque choreography. It's also a sly, political lyric, chastising reactionary politics in 1937, especially "the best dictators," Henry Ford, J. P. Morgan, and "the 400"—a list of high-class New York society members. But if you ignore all that, you can still boogey to the tune.

The Barbra Streisand Album

Released: February 25, 1963
Produced by: Mike Berniker
Arranged and conducted by: Peter Matz
Original recording engineers: Fred Plaut, Frank Laico
Liner notes: Harold Arlen
Art director: John Berg
Cover photo: Hank Parker
CD released: October 1993
CD restored by: John Arrias at B&J Studio using the C.A.P. System
CD remastered by: Bernie Grundman

Catalog Numbers:
CS 8807 (stereo LP)
CL 2007 (mono LP)
CQ 592 (reel-to-reel, 7 ½ ips, 4-track stereo)
7-8807 (7-inch "stereo 33" jukebox record; 5 tracks)
PCA 166 (8-track)
PCT 8807 (cassette)
PC 8807 (LP, reissued)
CK 8807 (1987 CD)
CK 57374 (1993 Remastered CD)

Side One:
1. Cry Me A River
2. My Honey's Loving Arms
3. I'll Tell The Man In The Street
4. A Taste Of Honey
5. Who's Afraid Of The Big Bad Wolf?
6. Soon It's Gonna Rain

Side Two:
1. Happy Days Are Here Again
2. Keepin' Out Of Mischief Now
3. Much More
4. Come To The Supermarket (In Old Peking)
5. A Sleepin' Bee

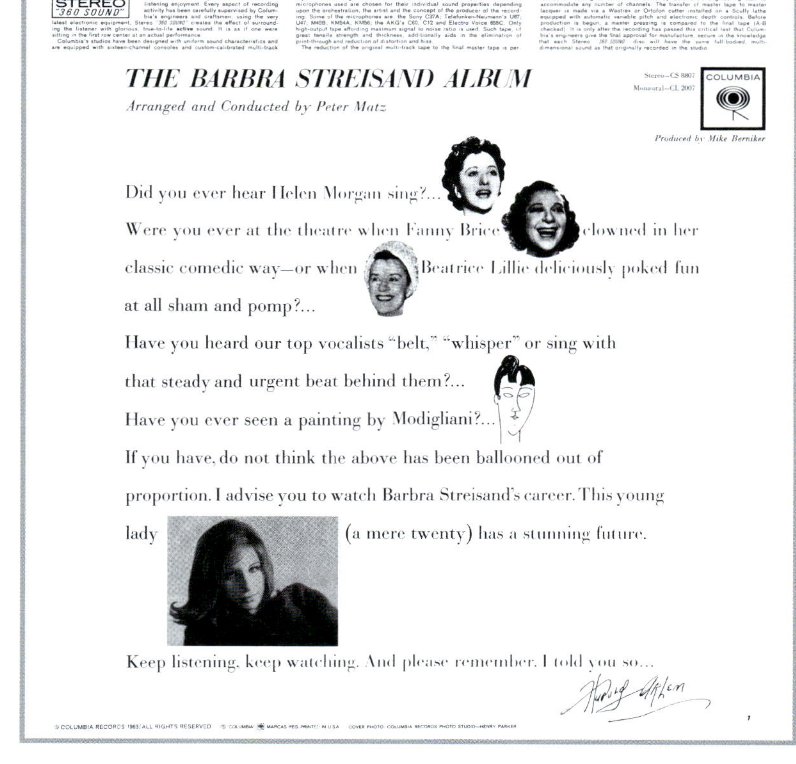

STEREO "360 SOUND"

THE BARBRA STREISAND ALBUM

Arranged and Conducted by Peter Matz

Stereo—CS 8807
Monaural—CL 2007
COLUMBIA

Produced by Mike Berniker

Did you ever hear Helen Morgan sing?...
Were you ever at the theatre when Fanny Brice clowned in her classic comedic way—or when Beatrice Lillie deliciously poked fun at all sham and pomp?...
Have you heard our top vocalists "belt," "whisper" or sing with that steady and urgent beat behind them?...
Have you ever seen a painting by Modigliani?...
If you have, do not think the above has been ballooned out of proportion. I advise you to watch Barbra Streisand's career. This young lady (a mere twenty) has a stunning future.

Keep listening, keep watching. And please remember, I told you so...

Harold Arlen

After *Live at the Bon Soir* was scrapped, twenty-one-year-old Barbra Streisand went into the studio to record her first album. In 1963, most record buyers chose vinyl monaural LPs over stereo—America hadn't upgraded to a new stereo record player, which sold for anywhere from $50 to $300 for a console model.

Sixty-plus years ago, Columbia Records was willing to spend only around $18,000 on Barbra's entire first album. These days, big recording stars (Rihanna, Beyoncé, Lady Gaga) have spent upward of $1 million to develop and record *one* song.

Team Streisand (at this point: her manager, Marty Erlichman; her record producer, Mike Berniker; and Peter Matz) didn't try to reinvent the wheel with this first album. Streisand had honed her act as a cabaret singer in small nightclubs for over a year before going into the recording studio—these songs were already "up and running." Matz has admitted that his arrangements really built on what Barbra and her concert pianist, Peter Daniels, had already established on the road.

Streisand said that she and Marty met with Peter Matz at a restaurant to discuss orchestration of the album. "I remember walking in and seeing this nice-looking guy with dark curly hair and a warm smile . . . He'd worked with Marlene Dietrich and Noël Coward on their nightclub acts . . . I thought he was sophisticated, charming, and very attractive in that Jewish intellectual way" (Streisand, 2023).

What Matz did expertly for Streisand was support the dramatic song stories she was singing with orchestral embellishments or cutesiness that called attention to itself. Listen to his Asian music quotes on "Come to the Supermarket (in Old Peking)" or the beautiful string arrangement on "Soon It's Gonna Rain." Matz provided musical character by using a flute (for the pigs), an oboe (for the wolf), and even a slide whistle on "Who's Afraid of the Big Bad Wolf?"

"I was at his apartment on West End Avenue almost every day, so we could go over each song I planned to do. Peter would sit at the piano and play for me as I sang. And I'd tell him what I heard in my head, because his job was to take these songs, which I was used to doing with just a piano, guitar, and bass, and expand them by writing parts for other instruments in the orchestra," she wrote.

The Beatles wouldn't touch down in America until February 1964, and the British Invasion would follow, making rock music very popular among American teens. On this album Streisand was singing songs that were very popular at the time—ballads from America's rich theater songbook and standards from some of the great popular song composers. The songs were curated by Streisand herself because she had creative control written into her record contract. Isn't it interesting that both the Beatles and Barbra recorded the song "A Taste of Honey" on their 1963 debut albums?

There's also the matter of the vinyl record, which had two sides. Albums were sequenced and planned around flipping the record over. It was an art, mostly lost or unconsidered over the last forty-something years due to CDs and endless playlists. So Streisand fans got out of their chair after "Soon It's Gonna Rain," flipped the LP, then "Happy Days Are Here Again" began the second side. Like a Broadway show, the LP had a built-in intermission. Everyone could have a bio-break, snack, or drink refill.

Even the way *The Barbra Streisand Album* was recorded must be admired. Again, with such a small budget, the album couldn't afford big orchestras or fancy production. "Maybe thirty pieces, if that," Barbra stated. Until the Beach Boys and the Beatles revolutionized multitrack recording, making an album in 1963 was simple: Barbra recorded in the studio onto analog tape using a three-track system. Her vocal was recorded on a dedicated track, while the band used the remaining two tracks, which also provided full stereo. There was no layering or "punching in" of vocals—Streisand's 1960s albums are essentially live recordings. She's singing in the studio with a band or orchestra, and if no major mistakes were made (wrong notes, ambient sound from the musicians), they picked the best take and that was that.

In the studio, Streisand was surrounded by sound baffles—acoustic walls. Engineer Frank Laico confirmed the baffles were meant "not to close [the singer] in, but so they could hear themselves better while singing. I always set the vocalists right close to the rhythm section; they needed that. We didn't use headphones in those years, so the closer to the orchestra, the better." (Frank Laico: Anatomy of a Session Pt 1, 2008)

They also recorded fast! *The Barbra Streisand Album* was recorded in New York at Columbia's Studio A over *three* days. Each session lasted about three hours, and they recorded about four songs per date. "Imagine the intensity," Barbra wrote, "when you've got a whole studio full of people concentrating on the same page of sheet music. The adrenaline kicks in, and it feels amazing. I thrived on that sense of excitement … and danger, because it could go wrong at any moment" (Streisand, 2023). As for the title of the album, Barbra was now working for one of America's most important record labels, and Columbia had already released albums with a creative array of titles: *The Electrifying Aretha Franklin*; *Irish . . . and Proud of It—Ruby Murray*; *Sincerely Yours . . . Robert Goulet*; and *Helen Shapiro: A Teenager Sings the Blues*.

Sweet and Saucy Streisand was Columbia's idea for the album's title. Barbra wanted to call it *The Barbra Streisand Album*. "I thought, well, people would have seen me a bit on TV, and they'll go into a record store, and they'll say, 'Give me that new girl. I forgot her last name, but she came out with an album.' 'Oh, you mean Barbra Streisand?' 'Yeah! I'll take that album.'" (SiriusXM, 2014, 2016)

For the album cover, Streisand posed for Columbia's staff photographer Hank Parker. In one photograph she is peering out from underneath an ostrich-feather boa. But Barbra ended up choosing one of Parker's photographs from her Bon Soir shows. She's wearing a herringbone vest in the picture, and she also chose the typeface—*DeVinne Italic* —for the album. John Berg, the Grammy-winning art director for Columbia Records who designed many iconic album covers over the years, confirmed Barbra chose the cover photo and that Barbra "also wanted to make sure that her first name was spelled correctly. And she chose the typeface. That was the first logo ever done for a recording artist, and she used it for years to come," Berg said. (Considine, 1985) Streisand trivia: She has used the typeface on twenty of her album covers since.

In the spring of 1963, *The Barbra Streisand Album* ranked in the Top 100 Albums with other popular LPs, including the movie soundtracks of *Lawrence of Arabia*, *Gypsy*, and *West Side Story*; albums by male crooners Steve Lawrence and Andy Williams and folk group Peter, Paul and Mary; and Eydie Gorme's *Blame It on the Bossa Nova*. The Album peaked at number eight on the *Billboard* 200 Albums Chart, selling over 500,000 units. "It's a wild kind of thing," Streisand told columnist Leonard Feather. "It proves my point that anything that's truly real, musically genuine, is commercial. Hip people dig it, but the people in Arkansas dig it too, because the songs are beautiful. And I can get additional groups of people interested by doing unexpected pieces of material, like 'Who's Afraid of the Big Bad Wolf?'—which I did just because it's the last kind of song you'd expect to hear in the sophisticated settings where I work." (Feather, 1963)

Matt on *The Barbra Streisand Album*

The Barbra Streisand Album won the 1964 Grammys for Album of the Year, Best Female Vocal Performance, and Best Album Cover. In 2006, the album was inducted into the Grammy Hall of Fame. It's hard to top "Cry Me a River" by Streisand. That simple bass line gives us a stark beginning; then the strings come in to support Barbra's revengeful vocal. She sang it live in the 1960s and again in the 2000 *Timeless* shows, but this original recording is raw, which is why I love her so. *The audacity to open the album with this song*!

Barbra explained: "This girl is angry at being jilted . . . it nearly drove her mad. And if I'm going to express those feelings, I couldn't stay in tempo" (Streisand, 2023).

"Soon It's Gonna Rain" is such a perfect combination of musical arrangement and Barbra's vocal performance. The song is from *The Fantasticks*, which Barbra auditioned for when she was sixteen years old. She was not cast. Instead, she just sang most of its score on her early albums! "Feel how the rain is falling now"—I feel it when Barbra sings it! Barbra wrote that this song was "simple, innocent . . . sung by two young people who are falling in love and looking forward to the rain so they can go inside and be together. But I interpreted it in very personal terms. I identified with that girl. In the beginning, she's shy . . . tentative . . . but when the rain comes, I chose to have the music build . . . the drums roll . . . as her emotions build. It's her sexual awakening."

Cole Porter's "Come to the Supermarket" is the most amusing song on the album next to "Big Bad Wolf." Have you tried to sing along? It produces lots of dopamine. When Barbra used to sing this song in her act, she would comically take a hurried breath between verses and say, "Breathe!"

SIGNATURE STREISAND

"HAPPY DAYS ARE HERE AGAIN"

"Happy Days Are Here Again" appeared for the first time on *The Barbra Streisand Album.* Barbra Streisand has sung the song on record, on television, and in concerts her entire career. It will always be associated with her, even though it is also associated with the Democratic Party in America, first adopted by Franklin D. Roosevelt during his 1932 presidential campaign. Streisand, of course, is a proud and active Democrat who has sung "Happy Days" for three US presidents: Kennedy, Johnson, and Clinton.

The prototype of "Happy Days Are Here Again" appears on this album, but fans will notice that the song's arrangement and Streisand's vocal interpretation of it would change over the years. Barbra's association with the song began in May 1962, when she was nineteen years old and sang it on TV on *The Garry Moore Show.* Moore had a feature on his show he called "That Wonderful Year," where his weekly cast would sing songs from a notable year. Streisand's episode concentrated on 1929—the year of the stock market collapse (also the year "Happy Days" was first published). Streisand maintains that Ken Welch, Moore's music director, played the song slowly during rehearsal so she could learn it. Streisand elaborated that "the lyric took on new meaning—became ironic and dramatic. So, Ken and his wife, Mitzi, wrote a verse for it [I'm broke, I'm poor, I'm back where I started . . .] and created a scene about a woman who has just lost all her money in the crash." (Streisand, Just for the Record liner notes, 1991)

The original, 1963 recording on *The Barbra Streisand Album* frustrated Streisand because "I wasn't happy with the ending. I'm *geshreying* (yelling, in Yiddish), getting so emotional that it's embarrassing."

Barbra told The Hollywood Reporter in 2018 that when she recorded the song in 1963, "It was a few months after the Cuban Missile Crisis, and the country had just averted an unimaginable catastrophe. So my concept for the ending was almost like saying, 'My God, we nearly came to the end of the world!' But when I heard the playback, I didn't like it. It was too traumatic. I wanted it to be more symphonically traumatic, like Mahler, with beauty in the chords. Unfortunately, we ran out of time and money to redo it. I changed it immediately for my live performances." (Malkin, 2018) Barbra's discography supports this statement—seven years after this record came out, she substituted a live version of the song on *Barbra Streisand's Greatest Hits.*

My favorite recording of "Happy Days"? I can't help but love the live version sung in 1986 for the *One Voice* concert. That evening she said she was singing it with "hope," and you can hear it in her interpretation. How can you not plotz when you hear Barbra's thrilling vocal on the line "All together SHO-OUT it now!"

The Second Barbra Streisand Album

Released: week of August 31, 1963
Produced by: Mike Berniker
Arranged and conducted by: Peter Matz
Additional material by: Peter Daniels
Cover photo: Woody Kuzoumi
Miss Streisand's coiffure by: Fred Glaser
Liner notes: Jule Styne
Remastered CD released: October 19, 1993
CD restored by John Arrias at B&J Studio using the C.A.P. System
CD remastered by: Bernie Grundman

Catalog Numbers:
CS 8854 (stereo LP)
CL 2054 (mono LP)
CQ 607 (reel-to-reel, 7 ½ ips, 4-track stereo)
PC/KCS 8854 (LP, reissue)
PCT 8854 (cassette)
CK 8854 (1987 CD)
CK 57378 (1993 Remastered CD)

Side One:

1. Any Place I Hang My Hat Is Home
2. Right As The Rain
3. Down With Love
4. Who Will Buy?
5. When The Sun Comes Out

Side Two:

1. Gotta Move
2. My Coloring Book
3. I Don't Care Much
4. Lover, Come Back To Me
5. I Stayed Too Long At The Fair
6. Like A Straw In The Wind

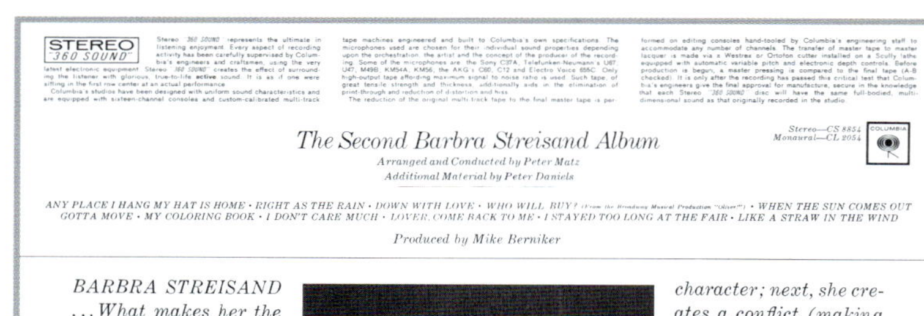

STEREO 360 SOUND

The Second Barbra Streisand Album

Arranged and Conducted by Peter Matz
Additional Material by Peter Daniels

ANY PLACE I HANG MY HAT IS HOME · RIGHT AS THE RAIN · DOWN WITH LOVE · WHO WILL BUY? · WHEN THE SUN COMES OUT · GOTTA MOVE · MY COLORING BOOK · I DON'T CARE MUCH · LOVER, COME BACK TO ME · I STAYED TOO LONG AT THE FAIR · LIKE A STRAW IN THE WIND

Produced by Mike Berniker

BARBRA STREISAND ...What makes her the unique and ingenious talent that she is? Listening to this album again and again, I have reached one conclusion: besides possessing a God-given singing voice, Barbra is the first girl I have ever heard who is a great actress in each song. Barbra makes every song sound like a well-written three-act play performed stunningly in three minutes. Although the same Barbra Streisand, she takes on an exciting new characterization for each song. At its beginning, she establishes her

character; next, she creates a conflict (making all the lyrics mean so much more than they seem to), then she reaches a tremendous conclusion—so that, even after hearing only one song, lasting only a few minutes, one is completely overwhelmed.

Barbra knows what she is singing, knows what lyrics mean. I was one of the early, early Barbra Streisand fans and in all my years of writing songs and being associated with top singers, I have never been as thrilled as I was listening to this new album. JULE STYNE

Columbia Records released *The Barbra Streisand Album* in late February 1963, then put out *The Second Barbra Streisand Album* just over six months later, in September. As the second album was released, the first album had been on the Top 10 popular albums lists and sold over 100,000 units.

The Second Barbra Streisand Album included more songs from Barbra's nightclub act. Five of the eleven songs were written by Harold Arlen. "Most of the material was songs we had been doing for two and a half years," her accompanist Peter Daniels said. "It was a big compliment to me when Peter [Matz] took our arrangements and expanded them for an orchestra. The collaboration was incredible." (Considine, 1985) Matz added that for the second album, "[Columbia] gave us a little more money, so I had a more luscious orchestra to arrange for. But in terms of studio time, they continued to short her." (Considine, 1985)

Streisand and orchestra logged time at Columbia's Studio A in New York on February 8, 1963, then June 3, 6, and 7, with Matz again arranging and conducting and Mike Berniker producing. But Matz was correct—*The Second Album* sounds lusher and more sophisticated. Remember, Columbia Records didn't have a hit with Streisand quite yet and was proceeding cautiously. In fact, one of Matz's original compositions landed on this album: "Gotta Move." He recalled: "I wrote it for [Barbra] to do at the Blue Angel. She complained that she didn't have anything to get off with. I did the song, using her speech patterns . . . she started using it as her closing theme." (Considine, 1985) The song was used in a 2022 Bud Light beer commercial—"Not my usual demographic . . . but I'll take it!" Streisand joked in her memoir.

Matz's arrangement for "My Coloring Book" is superior to Bob Mersey's arrangement on the 1962 single. Mersey's arrangement reflects a more mainstream sensibility—there's a backup chorus singing "oohs," and the entire track has more tempo than Matz provided. For *The Second Album*, Matz instead created a melancholic violin intro and a waltz tempo for the song. The violin plays during the entire song, reminding us that these are poignant and burnished mem'ries . . . that light the corners of our minds.

Larry Verdugo, in the 1979 fan magazine *Barbra*, best explained Matz's importance to Streisand during these early days. "The contribution that the arrangements of Peter Matz made to the effectiveness of Streisand's first recordings is important and should be noted. Matz understood exactly what Barbra wanted to do with these songs: her desire to tell stories, create specific moods, and most importantly, portray characters. His arrangements, therefore, emerge as models of support."

Matz created dramatic bookends for this album. Harold Arlen's "Any Place I Hang My Hat Is Home" opens the LP, and Matz interpolated quotes from that song into the last song—Arlen's "Like a Straw in the Wind."

Kander and Ebb's "I Don't Care Much" is a standout on the album. The song started as a Kander and Ebb "trunk song," unattached to any musical. They tried inserting it into *Cabaret* during its 1966 Broadway run, but it was cut. Then they added it back to the 1998 Broadway revival. Barbra's interpretation of the song is fresh and unburdened by the *Cabaret* pedigree. Matz gives her a German song setting, incorporating an accordion and then a driving, oompah tempo that reveals the lyrics' singlemindedness.

Three songs that Barbra sang often in her live act appear on this album: "When the Sun Comes Out," "Lover, Come Back to Me," and "I Stayed Too Long at the Fair." When Barbra dusted off the introspective song "Too Long at the Fair" to sing it during her 2006 concert tour, she explained how she used to perform it in the 1960s and that "perhaps I was too young to sing it then." Streisand recorded a song for this album that remains unreleased—Cole Porter's "Who Would Have Dreamed?" from the 1940 Ethel Merman Broadway show *Panama Hattie*.

By December 1963, *The Second Barbra Streisand Album* was hanging out at the top of the album charts with such other albums as *The Singing Nun*, *Joan Baez in Concert*, two albums by Peter, Paul and Mary, and *Surfer Girl* by the Beach Boys. *The Second Barbra Streisand Album* peaked at number two on the *Billboard* 200 album chart.

Streisand chose a photograph by Woody Kuzoumi as the cover of *The Second Barbra Streisand Album*. Barbra's Chicago-based hairdresser, Fred Glaser, explained that "I had a photographer [Kuzoumi] living rent free in the top floor of my building. He photographed most of my clients as I worked on them. I insisted on that. A mirror can show so much, but a photograph tells all. We had many sessions with Barbra. It went beyond just doing her hair. I wanted to stylize her, to get a definitive look for her, which we eventually did through a long process of elimination." (Considine, 1985) Streisand hated the cover photo. "When I look at [it] now, I think, *Ugh. It's terrible . . . taken from the wrong angle*. (I didn't know better then.) The only thing that looked good was my hair!"

For the back cover, Jule Styne—who was writing the score for the upcoming debut of *Funny Girl*—contributed the liner notes, in which he declared Barbra "the first girl I have ever heard who is a great actress in each song."

Later editions of the album added an extra sentence to Styne's notes: "The only thing I can imagine exciting me more is hearing Barbra sing the score from the new musical by Bob Merrill and myself based on the life of Fanny Brice. We can't wait for that first rehearsal!" He must have written the notes before *Funny Girl* had been titled. And the sentence must have been left out originally because Barbra's casting wasn't announced until July 1963. Streisand opened in *Funny Girl* on Broadway in March 1964.

There is a remarkable difference between the original, 1963 LP cover and the 1993 remastered CD cover. The LP photo was highly contrasted, with Streisand's features practically bleached away. Fans were surprised to see the same photo on the 1993 remastered CD restored in glorious gray tones, not retouched.

Streisand's engineer, John Arrias, remastered *The Second Barbra Streisand Album* in 1993, working from the three-track masters. "I'm re-EQing and cleaning up the tape hiss as well. We're using analog filters to bring out the best quality. I'm blown away, hearing all the little nuances that you couldn't hear before."

Arrias further explained: "There's not one overdub on the first three albums; she sang live, it was one take, surrounded by the orchestra, and that was it. You feel the room, the atmosphere, the energy level, and her vocals are just spectacular." (Streisand Catalog Overhauled, 1995)

Matt on *The Second Album*

You've gotta love "Gotta Move"—this is the stripped-down version with bongos that Barbra sang on *The Bob Hope Show*, but it's also very different from the sexy-orchestrated 1966 *Color Me Barbra* version.

"Lover, Come Back to Me" is another stellar arrangement for Barbra, and it's fast and fun. She's practically spastic performing it live on *The Ed Sullivan Show*, especially when she sings, "I remember every little thing you used to do," then giggles almost inappropriately. We can only use our imagination.

"Down with Love" is so clever and quotes many love song standards.

- "I don't stand a chance with a ghost like you" is a quote from a popular Bing Crosby tune.
- "The promised kiss of spring is here" references the Kern/Hammerstein song "All the Things You Are."
- "Why does my heart go dancin' overhead/On the ceiling near my bed" quotes the Sinatra song "Dancing on the Ceiling."
- "I talk to the trees" is a line from the *Paint Your Wagon* musical by Lerner and Lowe.
- "You say either, I say either . . . Let's call the whole thing off" is from the famous Gershwin song.
- "Down I go, around and around I go" is from "That Old Black Magic."
- "What is this thing called love?" is the Porter song that Barbra sang during her 1994 concert tour. Although that version was not released on the CD, it can be heard on the Las Vegas DVD.

STREISAND COLLABORATORS

PETER MATZ

Peter Matz began his long association with Barbra Streisand on her first album. Columbia and Barbra hired him to arrange *The Barbra Streisand Album*'s songs, and Matz was recommended by Barbra's new admirer, the illustrious Harold Arlen. Matz started as a rehearsal pianist for Arlen on his Broadway show *House of Flowers*; later he wrote arrangements for Arlen's show *Jamaica*. Then Matz accompanied the British star Noël Coward when he came to America, and he moved on as musical director for the Richard Rodgers's Broadway show *No Strings*.

Matz aided tremendously in Barbra's first few albums. His arrangements were witty and sleek. "We had very small combinations, just four or five instruments," Matz said. "That was because Mike Berniker, the producer of the album, said, 'Look, we can't spend a lot of money on this; we don't know if this woman is going to sell records.'" (Spada, 1983)

Streisand said, "Peter was so attuned to the actress in me and the drama of each song, which made it fun to work together" (Streisand, 2023). Barbra wrote about Matz's "particular sound . . . his distinct way of writing for horns and strings. He also was known for using various instruments to comment on a lyric, in a delightfully funny way. It's a bit like one of those old cartoons where whistles and drum rolls anticipate a pratfall. I'd call it a kind of musical filigree."

Matz contributed his amazing arrangements of songs for Streisand over the years on albums like *Color Me Barbra* and *The Broadway Album*. Barbra said in the documentary of the recording of *The Broadway Album*, "It was great working with Peter Matz again, who did my first few albums." He was the music director for Barbra's television special *My Name Is Barbra* and her live show *Funny Girl to Funny Lady*.

Barbra revealed in her autobiography (and shocked us all!) that she and Peter Matz had an affair in the early 1970s. "I was crazy about him," she wrote. Streisand explained that at this time, Matz "wrote me wonderful letters, declaring his love and confessing that he had wanted to get involved with me for a long time, but had always pulled back." Streisand and Matz corresponded with each other about salary differences and his devotion to his family. "Peter was such a good father," she wrote, "and ultimately he felt he couldn't just walk away from his kids." They put aside their breakup for *The Broadway Album* and produced an amazing record— "our affair ended, but we remained friends," Barbra explained.

Peter Matz received a Grammy Award for Best Accompaniment Arrangement for *People*, an Emmy for the TV special *My Name Is Barbra*, and an Academy Award nomination for Best Original Song Score for Barbra's 1975 film *Funny Lady*. Peter Matz will always be an integral part of Barbra's career. His orchestrations are a vital part of Streisand's musicology.

The Third Album

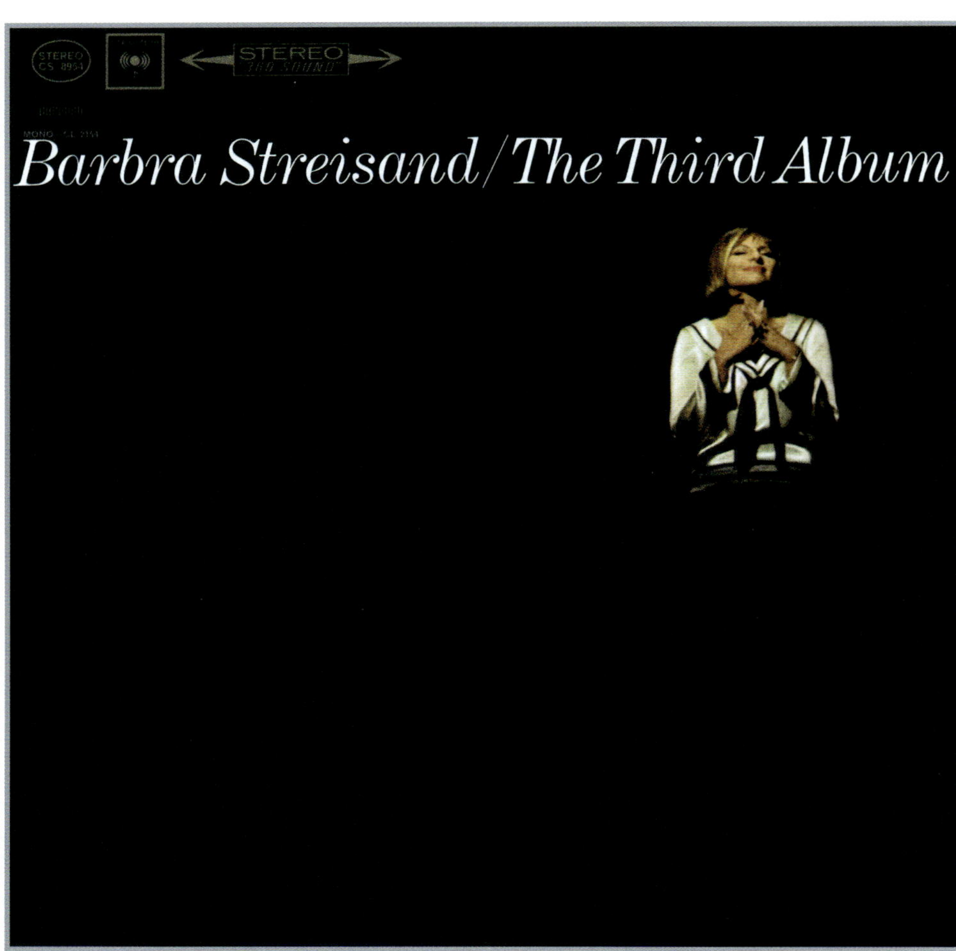

Released: February 1964
Produced by: Mike Berniker
Liner notes: Sammy Cahn
Cover photo: Roddy McDowell
Original recordings engineered by: Frank Laico and Ted Brosnan
Restored by John Arrias at B&J Studio
Remastered by: Bernie Grundman

Catalog Numbers:
CL 2154 (mono LP, 1964)
CS 8954 (stereo LP, 1964)
CQ 624 (reel-to-reel, 7 ½ ips, 4-track stereo)
CS 7-8954 (7-inch "stereo seven" jukebox EP)
CT 57379 (cassette)
PCA 206 (8-track)
PC 8954 (LP, reissue)
CK 8954 (1987 CD)
CK 57379 (1993 remastered CD)

Side One:

1. My Melancholy Baby
2. Just In Time
3. Taking A Chance On Love
4. Bewitched (Bothered And Bewildered)
5. Never Will I Marry

Side Two:

1. As Time Goes By
2. Draw Me A Circle
3. It Had To Be You
4. Make Believe
5. I Had Myself A True Love

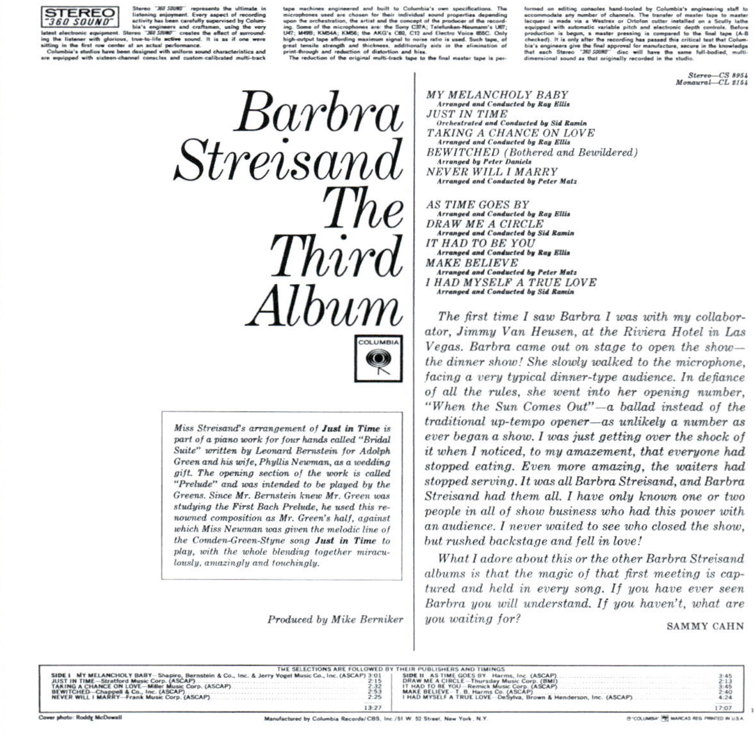

The Third Album was the third album that Mike Berniker produced for Barbra Streisand at Columbia Records. He explained how, in just a few short years, Streisand had grown as a vocalist: "There used to be an edge on the top of her voice," he said, "but now that edge is gone. She's still pushing just as hard, but it's not as evident as it used to be. In her third album, her new one, there's a real serenity—at least, for Streisand it's serenity." (Wilson, J. S., A Kook from Madagascar, 1964)

Released in February 1964, *The Third Album* had a different tone from the first two Streisand albums. "Here Barbra forgoes her larger-than-life-size approach and turns more introspective, allowing her innate musicality to help her make her points," Larry Verdugo wrote. (Verdugo, 1979)

Some fans thought the album was too subdued and undramatic. Others said it was boring. Streisand admitted to *High Fidelity* that she had matured. "I'm not a rebel anymore," she said. "I'm not a crazy kid who has to be heard. That fight is over because I don't have to work so hard to get my point across. As I go along, I feel the need to express is much less. I want less of an emotional thing now." (Wilson, 1964)

At this time, Barbra married Elliott Gould and finished a series of West Coast concerts. She was a guest star on television specials with entertainment icons Bob Hope and Judy Garland. And by January 1964 she was trying out *Funny Girl* in Boston. She recorded *The Third Album* in New York City in the fall of 1963 in three recording sessions. This time she employed two new arrangers—Sid Ramin and Ray Ellis. Ramin had already worked with Streisand when he orchestrated her first Broadway show, *I Can Get It for You Wholesale*. As for Ellis, Streisand was a teenager when she first heard Billie Holiday's album *Lady in Satin*. "I remember buying [the album] off the rack in a supermarket for $1.98. It was extraordinary," Streisand said. "I don't recall if I even knew who she was at the time . . . maybe it was something about the album cover . . . the lavender color . . . the gardenia behind her ear." Streisand also enjoyed the orchestrations on that album. "Ray Ellis' arrangements made such an impression on me," Streisand recalled. (Housman, 2003)

As for the album's title, Streisand told the Columbia Records art department: "It's my third album, so let's just call it what it is: *The Third Album*. I guess I like straightforward titles even though the songs are less than straightforward songs." (SiriusXM, 2014, 2016) The songwriter Sammy Cahn contributed gushing liner notes that appeared on the album's back cover.

About the cover: actor and photographer Roddy McDowell (you'll know him as the man beneath the ape makeup in the 1960s *Planet of the Apes* movies) took the striking photo of Streisand as she sang on *The Judy Garland Show*. "Looking at it now," Streisand confessed in her memoir, "I wonder why. Maybe I just wanted something different from the close-ups on the previous two albums."

The Third Album was, unfortunately, underpublicized. Instead, the saga of *Funny Girl* occupied the entertainment columns, with Streisand's name appearing almost daily with rumors and reports on the Broadway musical and the behind-the-scenes struggles. Columbia may have torpedoed *The Third Album* when it released the seven-inch single of "People" in January 1964—a month before this album. None of the *Funny Girl* songs were on *The Third Album*. Wanting to cash in on the Broadway buzz, Columbia released Barbra's *People* album a mere seven months after the third one.

Ultimately, *The Third Album* was eclipsed in 1964 by Capitol's original Broadway cast album of *Funny Girl*. Still, *The Third Album* rose as high as number five on *Billboard*'s Top LPs chart and managed to stay in the top ten during the summer of 1964, with *Funny Girl* always besting it.

Then there were the Beatles, who in early 1964 represented the emergence of rock and roll and a new era of music. Their albums *Meet the Beatles* and *Introducing the Beatles* hovered at the top of the charts, but Barbra Streisand remained true to her muse. "I just sang whatever interested me, and somehow my kind of music was able to coexist with the Beatles, the Rolling Stones, and all those other groups that kids were listening to," Streisand shared. "I was surprised by that, but also delighted." (SiriusXM, 2014, 2016)

It's hard to pick favorites from this album because I believe Streisand sang so many of these songs better live! The album versions sound too cold and measured to me. "Melancholy Baby" is perfect on *The Belle of 14th Street* TV show; "Bewitched" is flawless on *The Judy Garland Show*; "It Had to Be You" is sung with such passion while Barbra reclines on a bench on *Color Me Barbra*; and "Make Believe," once again, is beautifully vocalized while Barbra reclines on a tête-à-tête sofa on *My Name Is Barbra*. And to beat this dead horse a little more, I prefer the live version at the Bon Soir of "I Had Myself a True Love."

Released: April 1964
Album produced by: Dick Jones
Music by: Jule Styne
Lyrics by: Bob Merrill
Conducted by: Milton Rosenstock
Orchestrations by: Ralph Burns
Photography: Henry Grossman
2014 reissue producer: Frank Collar
2014 reissue liner notes: Jay Landers
2014 reissue mastering: Robert Vosgien

Catalog Numbers:
SVAS 2059 (stereo LP, 1964)
VAS 2059 (mono LP, 1964)
STAO-2059 (stereo reissue)
YIT 2029 (reel-to-reel, 7 ½ ips, 4-track stereo)
8XO 2059 (8-track)
4XT 2059 (Capitol cassette)
EG 64661 (Angel cassette)
Capitol CDP 7 46634 2 (CD, 1987)
Angel 64661 (CD, 1992)
513656K—Musical Heritage Society (CD, 1994)
Capitol B0019958-02 (CD/Vinyl, remastered 2014)

Side One:

1. Overture
2. If A Girl Isn't Pretty
3. I'm The Greatest Star
4. Cornet Man
5. Who Taught Her Everything?
6. His Love Makes Me Beautiful
7. I Want To Be Seen With You Tonight
8. Henry Street
9. People

Side Two:

1. You Are Woman
2. Don't Rain On My Parade
3. Sadie, Sadie
4. Find Yourself A Man
5. Rat-Tat-Tat-Tat
6. Who Are You Now?
7. The Music That Makes Me Dance
8. Don't Rain On My Parade (Reprise)

The Broadway musical *Funny Girl* opened on March 26, 1964, at the Winter Garden Theatre. Ten days later, on Sunday, April 5, the cast assembled at Manhattan Center studios on West 34th Street to record the cast album for Capitol Records, and that was released about one week later.

Why did Capitol Records release *Funny Girl*, and not Streisand's record label, Columbia Records? Barbra's manager, Marty Erlichman, explained: "We knew Barbra was set for *Funny Girl* before we signed with Columbia, and we wanted to be sure she was able to do it. Capitol got the album because of an overall Broadway and picture deal between Ray Stark's Seven Arts concern and Capitol." (Rolontz, 1964)

The only records in Streisand's recording career not released by Columbia Records are the Broadway *Funny Girl* album and the soundtracks to *Hello, Dolly!* and *Funny Lady*.

Capitol reportedly invested one-third of *Funny Girl*'s final cost of production. It's also said Columbia president Goddard Lieberson heard the score while the show was in early development and passed on the cast album. For Capitol's use of Barbra Streisand, however, Lieberson required the right to have her record four singles from the show. Only "I Am Woman" and "People" were released (single #4-42965); "Who Are You Now?" and "Cornet Man," both orchestrated by Peter Matz, remain unreleased.

Originally, the *Funny Girl* cast album was released as a vinyl disc, then in 1992 as a CD on Angel Records. In 2014, Capitol Records released a fiftieth-anniversary version that was remastered and contained a large booklet of rare photos—I provided some of those photos and helped the reissue team with some research too. That is why my name appears in the album credits, which was a thrill. The 2014 *Funny Girl* is a handsome package and contains not only a CD but also a vinyl version of the cast album. *Funny Girl Original Broadway Cast* was inducted into the Grammy Hall of Fame in 2004.

Matt on *Funny Girl* (Broadway)

I tend to listen to the movie soundtrack of *Funny Girl* over the Broadway album. So the cast album almost always sounds fresh to my ears. First, there's the amazing "Overture"—this has got to be one of Jule Styne's greatest, right up there with *Gypsy*. It's so good that Barbra and her codirector Richard Jay-Alexander used it as her overture during her concert performances in 2006.

"I'm the Greatest Star" doesn't quite compare to the movie version for me. The tempo on the cast album is much slower, and Streisand hadn't quite mastered the song. In merely a year, Streisand's performance of this song changed greatly. You can listen to the live version of "Greatest Star" on *Just for the Record*, recorded in 1965 at the final performance—She performs it effortlessly and with speed. The movie version, for me, has a better arrangement and an almost spontaneous vocal from Streisand, despite the medium. It helps greatly that the film sped up the song's tempo; the jokes land better when they're not so belabored.

But the cast album wins bonus points over the movie soundtrack with the songs "Cornet Man" and "Who Are You Now?"—both cut from the movie. I've always wondered why Streisand never resurrected "Who Are You Now?" for one of her recent concerts. It's a lovely, touching song.

"The Music That Makes Me Dance" is a chestnut too, with a moody trumpet duetting with Barbra and a big, Broadway climax to the song. Barbra recorded "Music" again on her 1999 *A Love Like Ours* album, this time with saxophonist Kenny G providing the accompaniment.

When this album was made, audio engineers were still discovering how best to use stereo on records, which had been in monaural sound since the beginning of the format. *Funny Girl* contains several tracks in which the sound is "panned." The track "People" is a good example. Streisand's voice begins in the right speaker on "we travel single-o," and by the time she sings "people, people who need people," the engineers have centered her vocal. "Cornet Man" is another example in which the trumpet is placed left at the beginning of the song, with Streisand singing in the right channel. On "stay, sweet man, stay," they pan her vocal center, although the trumpet is still in the left speaker. Halfway through "Cornet Man," Streisand's vocal moves right again, duetting with the trumpet, which is still far left. Perhaps the technicians were trying to suggest stage movement to at-home listeners? It's an extreme version of stereo that sounds somewhat crude to modern listeners. That's why I recommend the mono version

of *Funny Girl*. The mono version, which you can still find on eBay, is an interesting and better listen—none of those panning effects exist on it. And there's an alternate version of "Cornet Man" on it too! "We're goin' home," Streisand exclaims to the band near the end of the song.

SIGNATURE STREISAND

"PEOPLE"

"People" is probably Barbra Streisand's most well-known signature song—when she's announced at awards shows or live appearances, the orchestra almost always plays her onto the stage with "People." It's the big ballad from *Funny Girl*, and it's been closely associated with Streisand for her entire career. The song's lyrics express a desire we all have to connect to people, and Barbra has always sung it with a vulnerability and a universality. No matter what's going on in the world when she's touring, she seems to find a spoken introduction to make the song timely: natural and nuclear disasters, as well as political causes. Streisand stated in her book, "When I sang ['People'] onstage, it was a love song for a character who didn't have a partner in her life. The meaning changed as I got older and took on a broader point of view. But the essence of the song's underlying message remains the same . . . We all need each other."

It's funny, but Streisand confessed, "When I first heard the song 'People,' I said to Bob Merrill and Jule Styne, 'Shouldn't it be "People who *don't* need people are the luckiest people in the world?"' But if you can be vulnerable enough to need people, you're open to more love in your life." (CBS, 2004)

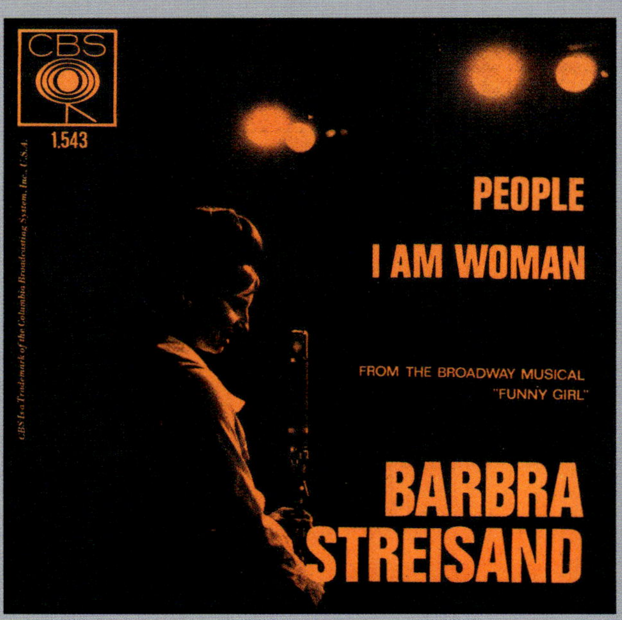

The single version of "People" became the most utilized version in Barbra's discography, appearing on five greatest hits albums. The single peaked on the Hot 100 *Billboard* chart at number five in 1964 and spent nineteen weeks on the chart. There have been at least eight live versions released over the years.

On the flipside of "People" is the playful single "I Am Woman," arranged by Peter Matz. The song is not only renamed ("*You* Are Woman" is the title of the song), but also has a new set of lyrics—written so Streisand could sing it as a solo.

I am woman, you are man/I am gentle, so you can be barbarian
I'm all pleats and pins and rouge/Mostly sham, but man,
I love the subterfuge

It's truly unfortunate that "I Am Woman" (and other rare singles) has never been released in the digital age. It exists on 45-rpm vinyl only save for a 2002 European CD of the *People* album, in which it was included as a bonus track. If you're a fan with an internet presence, you'll know that savvy acolytes have used music software to remaster some of these vinyl rarities over the years and shared them with others.

Columbia released another rare single in the summer of 1964. "Funny Girl," backed with "Absent Minded Me" (#4-43127), which is curious because neither song was in *Funny Girl*. This single of "Funny Girl" was an up-tempo song supposedly written for and cut from the show. It is not the same tune or lyric that was written for the movie version, by the way. It has never appeared on a Barbra Streisand album. "Absent Minded Me" ended up, two months later, on Barbra's album *People*.

Finally, the cast-album version of "People" is the bastard child of Barbra's many recordings of this song. Totally forgotten and seldom played, the Broadway version is one of the few to include the lovely introduction verse ("With them just let one kid fall down and seven mothers faint"). The movie version and Barbra's 2006 live recording are the only other albums to include the verse. The original cast "People" was orchestrated by Broadway stalwart Ralph Burns and has a lovely string section, finishing with a big Broadway climax. Streisand's vocal is beautiful too, especially at the end of the song. Can't we start including *this* version on future Streisand compilations? I'm convinced if I did an informal poll, I would find that most fans have rarely listened to the Broadway recording of "People." Listen to it again . . . it's Broadway Barbra, unconcerned with a number-one radio single, singing in character as Fanny Brice.

Barbra summarized: "Even though I get bored singing the same old material over and over, I will never stop singing this song, and appreciating it, and loving the man who wrote it. Thank you, Jule" (Streisand, 2023).

Barbra won a Best Vocal Performance, Female, Grammy for the song in 1965. And "People" was inducted into the Grammy Hall of Fame in 1998, established by the Recording Academy "to honor recordings of lasting qualitative or historical significance that are at least 25 years old."

All the "Peoples"

Barbra Streisand's best-known song has been recorded live and in studio over the years. Here's a list of all the commercially released versions of "People" over the years.

- Seven-inch Columbia single (1964) (otherwise known as the "single version")
- *People* album (1964—the above seven-inch single version is the same as this track)
- *Funny Girl—Original Broadway Cast Recording* (1964)
- *My Name Is Barbra* (TV program 1965, sung live)
- *Funny Girl—Original Soundtrack Recording* (1968)
- *A Happening in Central Park* (TV program/album, 1968, sung live)
- *Barbra Streisand's Greatest Hits* (album, "single version," 1970)
- *Live Concert at the Forum* (album, 1972, sung live)
- *Barbra Streisand . . . and Other Musical Instruments* (TV program/album, 1973, excerpt)
- *The Stars Salute Israel at 30* (TV program, 1978, sung live)
- *One Voice* (TV program, 1986, and album, 1987, sung live)
- *Just for the Record* (box set, 1991, "single version")
- *Highlights from Just for the Record* (album, 1992, "single version")
- *The Concert* (TV program/two-CD album, 1994, sung live)
- *The Concert: Highlights* (album, 1994, sung live—same version as two-CD)
- *Timeless—Live in Concert* (concert/album, 2000/TV program, 2001, sung live)
- *barbrastreisand.com* (Madison Square Garden last song, 9/28/00, streamed, sung live)
- *The Essential Barbra Streisand* (two-CD, 2002, "single version")
- *Streisand Live in Concert 2006* (two-CD, 2007, sung live)
- *Super Hits* (album, 2007, "single version")
- *Barbra: The Ultimate Collection* (album, 2010, "single version")
- *Back to Brooklyn* (TV program/album, 2013, sung live)
- *Partners* (album, 2012, duet with Stevie Wonder)
- *Barbra: The Music . . . The Mem'ries . . . The Magic!* (TV program/album, 2017, sung live)

Released: September 1964
Produced by: Robert Mersey
Miss Streisand accompanied by: Peter Daniels
Cover photo: Don Bronstein
Back cover photos: Hank Parker

Catalog Numbers:
CS 9015 (stereo LP)
CL 2215 (mono LP)
CQ 686 (reel-to-reel, 7 ½ ips, 4-track stereo)
CK 9015 (1987 + 1994 remastered CD)
PCA 00020 (8-track)
PCT 00020 (cassette)
PCT 9015 (cassette—"Best of Times" series)
KCS 9015, PC 9015 (LP, reissue)
CK 86103 (2002 remastered CD)
CK 5063572 (2002 UK remastered CD with bonus track "I Am Woman" (Single Version)
N/A—mastered for iTunes (2015 digital download)

Side One:

1. Absent Minded Me
2. When In Rome (I Do As The Romans Do)
3. Fine And Dandy
4. Supper Time
5. Will He Like Me?
6. How Does The Wine Taste?

Side Two:

1. I'm All Smiles
2. Autumn
3. My Lord And Master
4. Love Is A Bore
5. Don't Like Goodbyes
6. People

People was Barbra Streisand's fourth studio album for Columbia Records, and it contained "People" (the single) from *Funny Girl*. Mike Berniker, who produced Barbra's first three albums, wasn't available for this one, so Bob Mersey assumed the role. "Not to minimize the importance of the record producer in those days, but at least in my case, they were usually assigned by the label to organize the sessions, book the studio, and make sure no one went over budget!" Streisand said in an interview with the Library of Congress in 2019. "I don't recall a lot of creative involvement from Bob. I found the songs, and then I worked with Peter Matz and Ray Ellis to come up with interesting arrangements. Columbia had great recording studios and wonderful engineers, like Fred Plaut and Frank Laico. The engineers captured the sound, the arrangers conducted the orchestra, and I sang . . . so there wasn't a lot of 'production' like there is today." (Streisand, 2019)

The album's arrangements were almost evenly split between Matz and Ellis, with Matz orchestrating seven out of twelve songs. Peter Daniels, from Barbra's early club dates, was back on *People* too. Although he received an album credit for piano ("Miss Streisand accompanied by Peter Daniels"), he was also busy behind the scenes helping with the selection of songs.

One of those songs, "Absent Minded Me," was first recorded by Julie London for her 1962 album, *Sophisticated Lady*. What's curious is that the only writer credited on that album was Bob Merrill. On Streisand's album two years later, the song was credited to Bob Merrill (lyrics) and Jule Styne (music), published by Chappell-Co. What changed? Jule Styne wrote a new melody for Streisand, "but the lyrics were recycled from an earlier song by Bob Merrill that I didn't even know existed until recently," Barbra revealed in her memoir.

Another interesting song on the *People* album is Sammy Cahn and Jimmy Van Heusen's "Love Is a Bore." It was utilized in the 1964 World's Fair show *Les Poupées de Paris*. Produced by Sid and Marty Krofft (see *H. R. Pufnstuf*) and billed as a marionette extravaganza, *Les Poupées* was a French musical revue for adults performed by 240 string puppets on elaborate sets. Cahn and Van Heusen's songs were prerecorded by such famous performers as Gene Kelly, Frank Sinatra, and Liberace, then performed by the marionettes in the show. Pearl Bailey sang "Love Is a Bore," which, lyrically, is the same as the version Streisand sang, complete with the opening verse. Cahn and Van Heusen are on record saying that they tried out "Love Is a Bore" for Streisand backstage at the Cocoanut Grove, which would have been back in 1963—a year earlier than *Les Poupées de Paris*. So . . . which came first, Streisand or the marionettes?

Streisand recorded the *People* album in four sessions in July and August 1964 while she was appearing in *Funny Girl* in New York.

"In those days we worked fast!" Barbra stated. "It was typical for artists to record two albums per year. I'd listen to the playbacks and pick the best takes. If there were mistakes, or if the tempo felt too fast or slow . . . too bad . . . you were basically out of time, because there was always someone watching the clock!" (Streisand, 2019)

People was a big hit for Barbra Streisand and Columbia Records. After its release in September 1964, the album went to number one on the October 31, 1964, *Billboard* Top LPs chart and stayed there for five weeks. Barbra battled the Beatles (*A Hard Day's Night*) and the Beach Boys (*All Summer Long*) as well as the legendary Dean Martin (*Everybody Loves Somebody*) for her position. Most importantly, *People* was Barbra's *first* number-one album!

The cover photograph is iconic. Barbra was photographed while she was in Chicago performing at Mister Kelly's. She posed at dawn at Michigan Avenue Beach near the famous Drake Hotel for photographer Don Bronstein. Streisand recalled the experience herself in 2019: "When I first came [to Chicago], I was enchanted by how beautiful the beach was. So one night after the show at Mister Kelly's, I went with a photographer, who had been hired to shoot a magazine article about me, down to [Oak Street] beach. We took a bunch of shots there, and then we waited for the spectacular postcard-ready sunrise." (Reich, 2019)

Matt on *People*

Who could resist the catchy and cosmopolitan Cy Coleman and Carolyn Leigh song "When in Rome (I Do as the Romans Do)"? They wrote it for the 1962 musical *Little Me*, although it was not used in the show.

Barbra's Italian-spoken section in the song goes something like this:

E molto difficile resistere agli uomini di Italia
Per esempio, per esempio i biondi,
I biondi di Firenze, di Venezia
E i bruni di Palermo, di Milano

Roughly translated: "She can't resist Italian guys, nor the blonds of Florence or Venice, nor the brown-haired men from Palermo or Milano . . . Do ya know what I mean?" This spoken section also gave Barbra the chance to show off—she studied French and Italian during these years while she was waiting around for her evening supper club shows.

"I'm All Smiles," with its lilting tempo, was the first song Streisand recorded from the musical *The Yearling*, with music by Michael Leonard and lyrics by Herbert Martin. *The Yearling* was based on the Pulitzer Prize-winning novel about a boy and his pet fawn by Marjorie Kinnan Rawlings. Streisand recorded several numbers from the show, which closed after only three performances. Barbra also recorded "My Pa" (which was cut out of town), "Why Did I Choose You?" and "The Kind of Man a Woman Needs."

Barbra takes a very confusing point of view when she sings "My Lord and Master." She presented herself at this point as a feminist. The song, from the musical *The King and I*, is in essence a character song sung by Tuptim about her master, the King of Siam. Certainly, Streisand was attracted to it because of the drama: the singer has a secret ("He'll never know I love another man").But the lyrics betray the headstrong and feminist posture that Streisand projected early in her career. A critic sometimes says it better than I can, and Andrzej Lukowski, who reviewed the 2018 revival wrote: "Like an elderly relative who you make allowances for on grounds of age, classic musical *The King and I* is kind of racist, but difficult to entirely hold to modern standards" (Lukowski, 2018).

In 2017, "People" was deemed worthy of preservation as part of America's heritage by the Library of Congress. Added to the Library's National Recording Registry, "People" was singled out as "culturally, historically, or aesthetically significant" by the Library of Congress. Streisand responded: "I believe 'People' touched our common desire to relate to others with love and caring, and I've always tried to express this in my renditions of this magical song."

My Name Is Barbra

Released: May 1965
Produced by: Robert Mersey
Arranged and conducted by: Peter Matz
Cover photo: Sheldon J. Streisand
Back cover photos: Peter Oliver

Catalog Numbers:
CS 9136 (1965 stereo LP)
CL 2336 (1965 mono LP)
CQ 725 (reel-to-reel, 7 ½ ips, 4-track stereo)
PCT 00168 (cassette)
CK 9136 (1987 and 1994 remastered CD)

Side One:

1. My Name Is Barbara
2. A Kid Again/I'm Five
3. Jenny Rebecca
4. My Pa
5. Sweet Zoo
6. Where Is The Wonder?

Side Two:

1. I Can See It
2. Someone To Watch Over Me
3. I've Got No Strings
4. If You Were The Only Boy In The World
5. Why Did I Choose You?
6. My Man

My Name Is Barbra was the companion album to Barbra's first network television special, also titled *My Name Is Barbra*, which aired on CBS television April 28, 1965. The music—so intrinsic to a Streisand appearance—was handled by Peter Matz, who continued his excellent work with Streisand as the TV show's musical director.

Let me highlight some impressive things about this Emmy- and Peabody Award-winning show:

- Barbra signed a $5 million contract with CBS to produce specials for the network.
- Marty Erlichman once again negotiated creative control for Barbra—she could essentially make any type of special she wanted and was free to succeed (or fail) on her own merits.
- Barbra prepared and taped *My Name Is Barbra* while she was appearing on Broadway in *Funny Girl*.
- Joe Layton conceived the show, and Dwight Hemion directed it for the cameras.

Barbra's special was taped in New York in March and April 1965, and Columbia Records was running newspaper ads for the companion album, which hadn't been completed yet. "Place your order now for Barbra Streisand's exciting new Columbia album," the ads announced.

In fact, the album barely made it into record stores on time. Streisand booked the studio to record songs for the album two days before and two days *after* the TV show aired on CBS. Columnist Earl Wilson told his readers, "Barbra Streisand's album, *My Name Is Barbra*, is a rush job—it hits the stand a week after being recorded." (Wilson E. , 1965) Wilson's column was accurate—ten of the songs were recorded the week before the album came out. On Saturday and Sunday, May 1 and 2, Columbia's engineers edited the album. Demo copies were messengered to Streisand on Monday morning, May 3. Upon her final approval, the albums were rushed to record stores later that day.

"We truly set a record for speed on that album," said Warren Vincent, Columbia's editing supervisor. "We worked nonstop for seventy-two hours." (Considine, 1985) Streisand apparently did not envision the album as a song-by-song audio version of the TV show. Out of the thirteen tracks on the album, only seven appeared on the show.

Two of the new songs were from Leonard and Martin's upcoming musical, *The Yearling*. Streisand had already recorded their song "I'm All Smiles" for *People*, but when Erlichman asked them to contribute material for the TV show (and when Barbra heard the tunes), she recorded them all!

"Why Did I Choose You?" was sung as a duet in *The Yearling* ("Why Did You Choose Me?"), so Leonard and Martin altered the lyrics to serve Barbra's solo rendition. Barbra also requested switching two words at the song's climax. The original lyric was "And when I lost my heart so many years ago, I lost it willingly and lovingly. . . . " Leonard explained that "'willingly' is a closed sound, a very difficult word to sing up high; so she said, 'It's too hard, it'd be better if I switched the words and sang "lovingly" at first.' And that's the way she did it." (Considine, 1985)

Another *Yearling* song on the album was recorded by Barbra twice under two different titles with the same melody—"My Love" and "My Pa." The song was cut from the show during out-of-town tryouts, but Barbra was drawn to it, probably because her father had died when she was fifteen months old. On the album, Barbra sings "My Pa" as a child would sing about her father. But the 7-inch single (#4-43248) was released as "My Love" with new lyrics that universalized the song. You can only hear "My Love" on vinyl; it's never been released on another album or in digital format.

In fact, before the age of CDs and digital music, *My Name Is Barbra* the LP was more like a musical in that side one contained songs of childhood, then there was an "intermission" when the listener had to flip over the record, and side two featured six songs an older girl/woman would sing.

The song that opens the album (and the TV show) is "My Name Is Barbara"—and, yes, "Barbara" is spelled correctly because it wasn't written for Barbra. Streisand sang "My Name is Barbara" in her nightclub act for two years, but this was the first studio recording she made of it. Leonard Bernstein wrote the song as part of his 1943 cycle *I Hate Music: A Cycle of Five Kids Songs for Soprano and Piano*. Streisand also sang another song from that cycle in her act and on two other albums— "I Hate Music." Let's talk about Leonard Bernstein.

Bernstein wrote those songs that Barbra sang in her early career. Later she sang live at a couple of political concerts with him. Decades later, of course, she recorded Bernstein classics like "Somewhere," "Make Our Garden Grow," and "Take Care of This House."

Enter Bradley Cooper. He portrayed the Kristofferson part in the remake of *A Star Is Born* (2018), which he also directed.

Then, Cooper portrayed Leonard Bernstein in the 2023 movie he also directed about Bernstein's life, *Maestro*. (Streisand's career is so long, there is bound to be several "six degrees of separation" along the way. This is definitely one of them.)

"I Can See It," by Tom Jones (lyrics) and Harvey Schmidt (music), was from the long-running musical *The Fantasticks*. Streisand liked that score and recorded four songs from it—"Soon It's Gonna Rain" and "Much More" on *The Barbra Streisand Album* and a phrase from "Try to Remember" on *Color Me Barbra*.

Streisand included the Gershwins' standard "Someone to Watch Over Me" as well as the Disney song from *Pinocchio* "I've Got No Strings" on the album—both were new songs to her, not from the TV special.

The album's cover photo was of Streisand as a child. Barbra's brother, Sheldon J. Streisand, took the photo. Both Robert Cato (Columbia Records's graphic designer) and Sheldon were nominated for a Grammy Award for the front-cover photograph. "I was too lazy to take another picture [for the cover] . . . I remember pulling a squashed magenta bow off a box of candy and sticking it on my dress, because I wanted to perk it up for the picture" (Streisand, 2023).

The back-cover photos are in contrast to child Barbra on the front. She is sexy and sleek in a green dress, and those photos were taken by Peter Oliver.

Matt on *Name*

For me, "Jenny Rebecca" is a lost gem on this album. Barbra didn't sing it on the show, although thematically it could have fit into the format she used. Songwriter Carol Hall wrote "Jenny Rebecca" as a gift for a friend who had just had a baby. The song has a tidy structure, with a bookend quality to the intro and outro verse. But mostly, Barbra sings it so sweetly, and the song's middle section has such movement—you can imagine Jenny Rebecca swinging on swings, sliding on slides, and climbing trees.

"I've Got No Strings" has a delightful 1960s arrangement and contains a bridge that was cut from Disney's *Pinocchio* film.

SIGNATURE STREISAND

"MY MAN"

"My Man" was the song Barbra sang at the end of the *Funny Girl* movie—and the performance that probably won her the Oscar for best actress that year. Because of that moving, emotional performance, in which she cries on camera, then pulls it together for an amazing final note, the song has been associated with her for her entire career. Barbra has always acknowledged that "My Man" was Fanny Brice's song, the Ziegfeld Follies star in the 1920s whom Barbra portrayed on stage and film. Brice recorded it in 1921, based on the French song "Mon Homme" (Channing Pollock provided the English lyrics). The movie version is sung without the bridge, meaning that Barbra sings the same verse twice . . . and yet she imbues the second part with such emotion that you'd swear they were different lyrics.

Barbra first sang "My Man" on her TV special in 1965 and a studio recording appeared on the *My Name Is Barbra* album. She also sang it to the closing night audience of *Funny Girl* on Broadway, which can be heard on *Just for the Record*. For these recordings, as well as all her live performances of "My Man," Barbra sings the bridge—"It cost me a lot but there's one thing that I've got . . . "

During *The Concert* tour, Barbra introduced "My Man" as a "classic victim song," which is one way of looking at it. Jule Styne, *Funny Girl*'s composer, is on record as hating the addition of "My Man" to the movie, despite it being Fanny's signature song. He thought it undermined Fanny's enduring single-mindedness with tragedy.

I'll never forget those last concerts Barbra performed in 2019 when she sang the song strongly and passionately. Barbra was particularly effective singing "My Man" at Chicago's United Center where she held that long final note, and we all melted in our seats.

Barbra may have decided at one point that "My Man" was a "victim song," but I'm pretty sure we all love to hear her sing it because of the journey we took with Barbra in the *Funny Girl* movie. She is so vulnerable on screen, with tears rolling down her cheeks. Barbra's truthful and honest performance moved us all … forever more.

My Name Is Barbra, Two

Released: October 1965
Produced by: Robert Mersey
Arranged and conducted by: Peter Matz and Don Costa
Cover photo: Roger Prigent/courtesy of *TV Guide*

Catalog Numbers:
CS 9209 (stereo LP)
CL 2409 (mono LP)
H2C4 (reel-to-reel, 7 ½ ips, 4-track stereo)
CK 9209 (1987 CD and 1994 remastered CD)

Side One:

1. He Touched Me
2. The Shadow Of Your Smile
3. Quiet Night
4. I Got Plenty Of Nothin'
5. How Much Of The Dream Comes True?
6. Second Hand Rose

Side Two:

1. The Kind Of Man A Woman Needs
2. All That I Want
3. Where's That Rainbow
4. No More Songs For Me
5. Medley: Second Hand Rose, Give Me The Simple Life, I Got Plenty Of Nothin', Brother Can You Spare A Dime?, Nobody Knows You When You're Down And Out, Second Hand Rose, The Best Things In Life Are Free

My Name Is Barbra, Two . . . was released in October 1965 to coincide with the second broadcast of Barbra's first television special on CBS. *Two* followed the trend set by the previous *My Name Is Barbra* album—a majority of its songs were not on the TV special—only "Second Hand Rose" and the poverty medley, which closes the album, were sung by Streisand on TV. The medley was a big selling point for the second album—the back cover features photos of Barbra in the Bergdorf Goodman department store. The back cover also declares that *My Name Is Barbra* was an Emmy-Award winning TV show (Barbra won the Emmy the previous month, September 1965). Composer Neil Wolfe wrote "All That I Want." The song was originally recorded by Wolfe as a 45-rpm single for Columbia titled "Barbra" (Columbia #4-43291). Later, Francine Forest wrote lyrics to the melody. Wolfe and his band opened for Barbra at Forest Hills in 1965. He also recorded a Columbia Records tribute album called *Piano for Barbra* (# CS 9600) in which he covered Streisand's best-known songs of the time. Barbra, who tends to form strong bonds with people she likes, first met Wolfe at the Caucus Club in Detroit in 1961. "Between sets, I also hung out with Neil Wolfe, who played piano in the cocktail lounge," she recalled. "He was a very sweet guy with thick, wavy hair who was madly in love with a blond girl who looked like Kim Novak, and he talked about her constantly. He was really nice to me, and we became fast friends."

Matt on *Two*

The standout song on this album is "He Touched Me," in which Barbra soars and reaches the stratosphere. Barbra's husband at the time, Elliott Gould, was starring in the 1965 musical *Drat! The Cat!* with Lesley Ann Warren. *Drat!* had a book and lyrics by Ira Levin and music by Milton Schafer. In it, Warren portrayed a cat burglar who was plundering 1890s New York society. It was Gould who sang the song in the show, where it was titled "*She* Touched Me." Barbra's favorite television talent, Joe Layton, directed the show, which was a tongue-in-cheek spoof of melodramas from that era. It's too bad it ran for only eleven performances.

Streisand recorded two songs from *Drat! The Cat!*'s score—"He Touched Me" and "I Like Him" were released as the A and B sides of Columbia single #4-43403, which came out about a month before *My Name Is Barbra, Two*. "He Touched Me" is the same recording on both single and album, whereas "I Like Him" has never appeared on a Streisand album.

"He Touched Me" fits beautifully into Streisand's repertoire, because the song and her performance illustrate exactly what the director and choreographer Bob Fosse meant when he allegedly said that in a musical, "when words aren't enough, sing . . . "

Streisand sings gloriously what it feels like to be in love. She repeats "He touched me" twice, then states to the universe: "Suddenly nothing, nothing, nothing is the same!" Streisand explained that "Don Costa did the arrangement . . . He was shy and quiet, but his work was amazing, and he used chords that were so unexpected."

Although "He Touched Me" probably qualifies as a Streisand Signature Song, she didn't perform it that much. She's captured on television singing it in Central Park in 1967—and that version is a doozy, with Streisand finishing the song with head thrown back and arms spread wide as a throng of fans applaud her genius! But she dropped the song from live performances in the 1970s and 1980s. Barbra did include "He Touched Me" in her triumphant 1994 concert tour—and it always prompted a standing ovation, because she was still *that* good singing it. But '94 was the last time she sang it live, and that's too bad.

Released: March 1966
Produced by: Robert Mersey
Art director: Bob Cato and John Berg
Graphic artist: Elinor Bunin

Catalog Numbers:
CS 9278 (stereo LP, 1966)
CL 2478 (mono LP, 1966)
CK 9278 (CD remastered)
CQ 810 (reel-to-reel 7 1/2 ips, 1/4" 4-track stereo)
PCT 9278 (cassette)

Side One:

1. Yesterdays
2. One Kiss
3. The Minute Waltz
4. Gotta Move
5. Non C'est Rien
6. Where Or When

Side Two:

1. Medley: Animal Crackers In My Soup, Funny Face, That Face, They Didn't Believe Me, Were Thine That Special Face, I've Grown Accustomed To Her Face, Let's Face The Music And Dance, Sam, You Made The Pants Too Long, What's New Pussycat?, Small World, I Love You, I Stayed Too Long At The Fair, Look At That Face
2. C'est Si Bon (It's So Good)
3. Where Am I Going?
4. Starting Here, Starting Now

Color Me Barbra was a third television-special soundtrack album. It was released to coincide with the airing of her second CBS special in March 1966. Local newspaper ads read, "Watch Barbra Streisand's *Color Me Barbra* tonight on TV . . . Play her new album tomorrow!"

Unlike the two *My Name Is Barbra* albums, *Color Me Barbra* contained all the songs she sang on the TV special—no additives or filler. The album was recorded in three sessions, and there are only three songs that remain unreleased: an orchestrated version of the Harold Arlen song "Napoleon," "Nobody's Heart Belongs to Me," and a version of "When Sunny Gets Blue" that she remade later for her *Simply Streisand* album. She intended to sing these songs during the concert portion of the show.

The two French songs that appear on *Color Me Barbra* ("Non C'est Rien" and "C'est Si Bon") were recorded during sessions with Michel Legrand in November 1965 and January 1966 for Barbra's forthcoming French album, *Je m'appelle Barbra*. Legrand arranged and conducted the French songs; Peter Matz arranged everything else on *Color Me Barbra* except "Where Am I Going?" which Bob Mersey handled, and "Starting Here, Starting Now," for which Don Costa did the arrangement.

Columbia packaged the original vinyl album with a four-page, twelve-inch, full-color pullout that was not duplicated for the CD release. The pullout has many photos from the TV special, including one page dedicated to Barbra cavorting with the animals in the circus segment of the show.

When Grammy time came, *Color Me Barbra* didn't win, but garnered nominations for Album of the Year and Best Female Vocal Performance, plus one for the artists who put together the packaging—Elinor Bunin (she created the cover drawing), Bob Cato, and John Berg.

The highlight of the album and the show was the second-act circus medley, which Barbra performed on a pink-colored set that looked like a three-ring circus complete with animals including penguins, a llama, and an aardvark. The medley, however, was edited for the album. For completists who want to know what was left out, here is a list of all the songs as they were sung on the TV show, including the writing credits, with the edited songs notated:

Animal Crackers in My Soup (Caesar/Henderson/Koehler); Funny Face (G./I. Gershwin); That Face (Bergman/Spence); They Didn't Believe Me (Kern/Reynolds); Were Thine That Special Face (Porter); I've Grown Accustomed to Her Face (Loewe/Lerner); Let's Face the Music and Dance (Berlin); Sam, You Made the Pants Too Long (Lewis /Young /F. Whitehouse); What's New Pussycat? (Bacharach/David);* Who's Afraid of the Big Bad Wolf? (Churchill/Ronell);** Small World (Styne/Sondheim); Try to Remember (Schmidt/Jones);** I Love You (Porter); Have I Stayed Too Long at the Fair (Barnes); Look at That Face (Bricusse Newley)

* On the album, Barbra's sassy "What's New Pussycat?" phrases are cut out. The album simply cuts to the "ballad" version.

** "Wolf" is cut completely; Barbra sings "Try to Remember" to the elephant on the TV show. The album cuts it but keeps a bit of the instrumental.

Matt on *Color Me*

There are two outstanding Peter Matz arrangements of songs on this album. First, "Gotta Move": it's the second time Streisand recorded this Matz-penned song—the first time was on *The Second Barbra Streisand Album*. On that disc, it was a sparse arrangement with bongo drums (that same track was included on *Barbra Streisand's Greatest Hits*). This 1966 arrangement is fantastic and dynamic, with driving strings, syncopation, and a hot horn section. In fact, the drag queen comedy movie *To Wong Foo, Thanks for Everything! Julie Newmar* used it to underscore a scene in which the ladies rebelliously drive out of town. "Gotta Move" is a hot, hot song, and Streisand sang this arrangement live during her 1966 concerts. Oh, to have been there!

The other song is "One Kiss," and I feel it's been overlooked in Streisand's repertoire all these years. With only a piano and cello as accompaniment, Streisand's vocal is simple, pure, and striking. Streisand knew the song from 1955, when her mother recorded it at Nola Recording Studios. Barbra's mother, Diana Kind, sang "One Kiss" in her operatic contralto voice, which matches the style in which it was written—an operetta with music by Sigmund Romberg and book and lyrics by Oscar Hammerstein II. Streisand, however, eschews the opera affectations and performs it more like an art song—still singing those long phrases, supported by the excellent breath control that she is known for.

STREISAND COLLABORATORS

HAROLD ARLEN

Harold Arlen is one of the great American composers of the twentieth century. He wrote some of the most cherished songs from the 1930s and 1940s, including the score to *The Wizard of Oz* and songs for Judy Garland's *A Star Is Born*.

"Ever since I was 18, when I discovered Harold Arlen, it's like he's my guy," Streisand told the *Chicago Tribune* in 2006. After listening to his repertoire, Streisand thought, "This man is a genius. His music seemed to capture all the angst I felt inside. It had real emotional substance because, as I again discovered, so much of it was also written for Broadway shows" (Streisand, 2023). "Stephen Sondheim—who I think is so brilliant—when he came to see me in New York, he said to me, 'God, what is it about you and Harold Arlen that just fit together like a glove?'

"Maybe our roots," Streisand answered. "Jewish, [and] identifying with the black soul, you know?" (Reich, *Barbra Today*, 2006)

Harold Arlen contributed to Barbra's early career by suggesting she work with arranger/conductor Peter Matz for her first album. Arlen also provided the liner notes for Barbra's first album: "I advise you to watch Barbra Streisand's career," he wrote. "This young lady (a mere 20) has a stunning future. Keep listening, keep watching. And please remember, I told you so. . . . "

For Harold Arlen's centennial celebration in 2005, Barbra wrote on her official website: "His melodies hit you in the gut . . . soulful, almost painful, moving. When I got to duet with him singing 'Ding Dong! The Witch Is Dead,' I came to know the little-boy part of Harold," she stated. "We had fun being kids together on that recording. I believe that decades from now, people will be as affected by his music as I've been. Thank you, Harold."

Harold Arlen songs recorded by Barbra Streisand:

- Any Place I Hang My Hat Is Home
- Come Rain or Come Shine
- Ding-Dong! The Witch Is Dead (with Arlen)
- Don't Like Goodbyes
- Down with Love
- House of Flowers
- I Had Myself a True Love
- I Never Has Seen Snow
- It's a New World
- It's Only a Paper Moon
- Like a Straw in the Wind
- Man That Got Away, The
- My Shining Hour
- Napoleon (*Studio version unreleased)*
- Over the Rainbow
- Right as the Rain
- A Sleepin' Bee
- That's a Fine Kind o' Freedom
- When the Sun Comes Out

Released: October 1966
Produced by: Ettore Stratta
Arranged and conducted by: Michel Legrand
Cover photo: Richard Avedon
Liner notes: Maurice Chevalier, Nat Shapiro

Catalog Numbers:
CS 9347 (stereo, LP)
CL 2547 (mono, LP)
CS 7-9347 (7-inch "stereo seven" jukebox EP)
CK 9347 (CD remastered)
CQ 862 (reel-to-reel 7 1/2 ips, 1/4" 4-track stereo)

Side One:

1. Free Again
2. Autumn Leaves
3. What Now My Love?
4. Ma Première Chanson
5. Clopin Clopant
6. Le Mur

Side Two:

1. I Wish You Love
2. Speak To Me Of Love
3. Love And Learn
4. Once Upon A Summertime
5. Martina
6. I've Been Here

Produced by Ettore Stratta
Arranged and Conducted
by Michel Legrand

Stereo—CS 9347
Mono—CL 2547
COLUMBIA

Je m'appelle Barbra

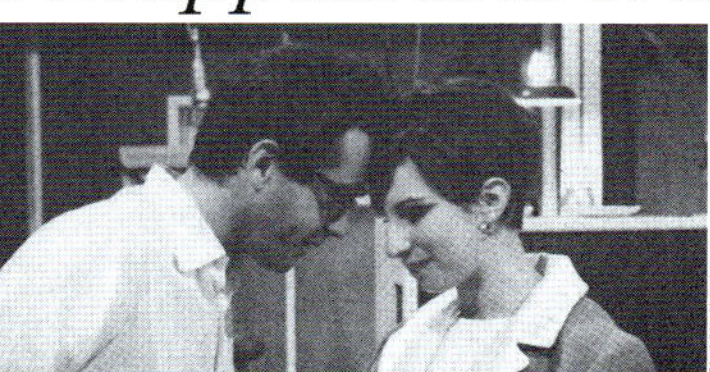
PHOTO: BRYAN DALY

Michel Legrand and Barbra at the recording session

I Wish You Love
Speak to Me of Love
Love and Learn
Once Upon a Summertime
Martina
Le Mur

Free Again
Autumn Leaves
*What Now My Love**
Ma Première Chanson
Clopin Clopant
I've Been Here

Consult label for correct sequence.

**Arranged and Conducted by Ray Ellis*

Barbra Streisand is one of those miracles which comes along once in a lifetime, even in America where the sensational apparently never ceases to flourish.
She is mad with talent and more gifted than any human being should be permitted to be.
She sings Les Feuilles mortes*—among other songs—with the voice of an angel and gives the French words a poignancy that they have never had before.*
This very young American girl is enchanting the whole world with an artistry that is new, impulsive and staggering.
We bow to you, "grande petite Madame." We embrace you, Barbra Streisand.

Maurice Chevalier

When handled with affection, care and respect, superb French songs, like some of the finer French wines, travel well. The flavor, the bouquet and, most important, the afterglow somehow survive the perilous journey between cultures and languages and remain to sharpen our tastes and enrich our lives.

In all, the program is a heady, potent mixture of both the old and the new: Speak to Me of Love (Parlez-moi d'amour) *by Jean Lenoir, with English lyrics by Bruce Sievier, was introduced in France in 1930.* I Wish You Love (Que reste-t-il de nos amours?) *is from the pen of that charming troubadour, Charles Trenet, and the tender English version was written by Albert Beach. One of France's greatest contemporary poets, Jacques Prévert, wrote* Les Feuilles mortes *shortly after World War II to music by Joseph Kosma. As adapted by Johnny Mercer, it became* Autumn Leaves *and turned up in the United States in 1950.* What Now My Love (Et maintenant) *is by Gilbert Becaud who, like Trenet, sings only the songs he composes. The English lyrics are by Carl Sigman.* Clopin Clopant, *with French words by Pierre Dudan and music by Bruno Coquatrix, is presented here in its British rather than its American-lyric version. The English lyrics are by Kermit Goell. Michel Legrand, who conducted and arranged this album, wrote* Once Upon a Summertime (La Valse des lilas) *in 1954 at the age of twenty-two. The French lyrics are by Eddy Marnay, and the adaptation is by Johnny Mercer.*

Of the new songs, I've Been Here (Le Mur) *was written for Edith Piaf who did not live to perform it. When informed that Miss Streisand was planning an album of French songs, the composer, Charles Dumont, and the lyricist, Michel Vaucaire, withheld the song from French singers for more than a year in anticipation of her debut on records in France. Following traditional Gallic procedures, the English-language version by Earl Shuman was written specifically for Barbra Streisand.*

Non c'est rien, *which was introduced on the "Color Me Barbra" television show, has words by Michel Jourdan to music by Armand Canfora and Joss Baselli. The French version, along with its English-language counterpart,* Free Again, *by Robert Colby, was also written especially for Barbra Streisand.*

Love and Learn (Qui es-tu) *and* Martina (Les Enfants qui pleurent) *are by the aforementioned Michel Legrand and Eddy Marnay. The English lyrics were written by, respectively, Norman Gimbel and Hal Shaper.*

Ma Première Chanson (My First Song) *was composed by Barbra herself. She asked her friend Eddy Marnay to write the lyric which says:*

"One finger on a piano, my voice around some words,
I played with your name and a song was born.
In my hands your heart and mine…
That old piano takes me back to the first day of my first love
When each second held your name…
And then I found…My First Song."

The refreshing irreverence that Barbra Streisand has shown toward the moldy concepts of "accepted" popular singing is once more demonstrated in her choice of, and approach to, this group of songs adapted from their French originals. Ever unafraid of open emotionalism and yet wondrously aware of subtleties and characterization, this amazing young woman points the way toward the day when American popular music will reach a new level of intelligence and artistry. May her courage, talent and enormous popularity continue to stimulate and inspire the creation of new songs of beauty, wit and power.

Nat Shapiro

COVER PHOTO: RICHARD AVEDON

Michel Legrand appears through the courtesy of Philips Records

Je m'appelle Barbra was created during a particularly busy time in Barbra's career and personal life—between television specials, the *Funny Girl* play, and the birth of her son. The album also marked the beginning of a highly creative and enduring collaboration with French composer, arranger, and conductor Michel Legrand.

It's also the second time Barbra named an album of hers *My Name Is Barbra*—except this time, it's in French!

Nat Shapiro was the director of artists and repertoire for the international department of Columbia Records in 1965 and had spoken with Barbra about expanding her popularity in Europe. "She agreed with me that French was classier than Italian," Shapiro recalled. "They had more sophisticated songs and songwriters. Also, we had a much more active company in France [Disques CBS]. Another strong factor was Michel Legrand. He was one of the best composers and orchestrators in the world. He had just written the music for *The Umbrellas of Cherbourg* . . . That appealed to Barbra." (Considine, 1985)

Ettore Stratta was manager of international A & R and creative services for CBS Records International (Columbia Records's international organization for distribution). "I was producing recordings by American artists singing in foreign languages for the foreign markets," he recalled. "And the idea [came] that we would do an EP—four songs—with Barbra in French" (Jacobs, 2003),

Michel Legrand flew to New York in the spring of 1965. "I met Barbra at night after a performance of *Funny Girl*," he wrote. "She had a little piano, you know, in her dressing room. Every night we worked after her performance, you know, until four or five in the morning in her dressing room." (*Michel Legrand Anthology* [liner notes], 2013) Streisand agreed. She wrote in her memoir: "After a few minutes of conversation, I was completely charmed. Michel was so warm and engaging, with a shock of dark wavy hair, glasses, and a tie that he quickly loosened so we could get right to work. He sat down at the little upright piano in my dressing room and started to play. That became our routine. Luckily he was a night owl like me! He would come to the theater after the show at midnight, when everyone else had gone home and we had the place to ourselves."

Nat Shapiro commissioned songs for Barbra's EP from contemporary French songwriters he knew. But Streisand began collecting more French songs, utilizing a French tutor to learn the language. She was also coached in French by Legrand and Stratta.

The material they initially chose was recorded at Columbia Records on November 16, 1965. Streisand sang eight songs with Michel Legrand arrangements. The session was produced by Stratta. The eight songs were:

- "Clopin Clopant"—written by Bruno Coquatrix, Pierre Dudan. English lyrics written by Brooklyn-born Kermit Goell. Johnny Mathis and others recorded this English-language version. "Clopin Cloplant" roughly means "hobbling along." Streisand must have liked Goell's lyric better—there is another English version of the song that changed the title and lyric to "comme ci, comme ça," which translates as "so-so."
- "Speak to Me of Love"—written by Jean Lenoir. English lyrics by Bruce Sievier.
- "Non, C'est Rien"—written by Armand Canfora, Joseph Baselli, Michel Jourdan.
- "Martina" and "Les enfants qui pleurent"—music by Michel Legrand. Barbra recorded the same song twice—the French version with lyrics by Eddy Marnay as well as the English lyrics by Hal Shaper.
- "Look" and "Et la mer"—again, the same song sung in English and French. Music by Michel Legrand; English lyrics by Earl Shuman; French lyrics by Eddy Marnay. "Look" was actually released as the B side of Barbra's "Stout-Hearted Men" seven-inch single in June 1967.
- "Le mur"—As Nat Shapiro explained in his liner notes, Vaucaire and Dumont wrote this song for the French chanteuse Edith Piaf, who died before she could record it. They withheld the song from being recorded by other artists when they heard Streisand was working on an album of French songs. The original French lyrics for "Le mur" (or "The Wall") were about the Berlin wall—roughly translated: "They built a large gray wall . . . a wall of hate, a wall of fear . . . " The English lyrics changed the meaning of the song from the Berlin wall to a song of empowerment: "And so I live to have my say /To get and give each burning day/And if in time I find my love/He'll find that I'm no frightened dove."

On January 13, 1966, Streisand returned to Columbia Records's Studio A with Legrand to record more songs—her EP was expanding into a full LP. From this session, "La Valse des Lilas" (the French language version of "Once upon a Summertime") remains unreleased.

Legrand told a story about how it took Streisand multiple attempts to record "Autumn Leaves," accompanied on viola by Emanuel Vardi. "So, in a corner I said to Barbra, 'I'm sure you're aware that the first take is the best?' She said, 'Oh yes, I know.'

I said, 'Why?' She said, 'Just for the *pleasure* of it.' I loved her attitude of redoing it for pleasure." (Jacobs, 2003)

CBS Records released in February 1966 the EP titled *Barbra Streisand: En Français* (#EP 6048). On this two-sided seven-inch record were four songs:

- Non . . . C'est Rien
- Les enfants qui pleurent (available only on this EP)
- Et la mer (available only on this EP)
- Le mur

By the end of March, the EP was a hot seller in Belgium, and by June it was number ten on the top ten EP charts in Great Britain.

But Streisand wasn't done with her French album yet. Ten days before *Color Me Barbra* aired on CBS, she reserved Columbia's Studio C on March 20, 1966, in order to record two more songs: "Free Again" and "I've Been Here"—the English-language version of "Le mur." Side one ends with the French version, side two with the English version. Earl Shuman wrote the English lyrics. "My approach to writing a lyric to a foreign song was to ignore the original lyric and just get infused with the melody," Shuman stated.

Listening to Charles Dumont's stately melody, Shuman explained, "My plan was to write something very much for Barbra's personality and vocal technique. The song built beautifully—it kept modulating, and had a wonderful, fierce ending." (Shuman, 2013)

Next, Streisand jetted to London, where she opened *Funny Girl* at the Prince of Wales Theatre in April 1966. She returned to America in mid-July to complete some concert dates before she gave birth to her son, Jason, in December. At those four shows, Barbra began performing the French material.

"For your entertainment pleasure," Streisand announced from the Philadelphia stage, "I should very much like to do three songs which are not yet released on a new album of mine called *Je m'appelle Barbra*. Actually, there are two albums. One I did completely in French and the other I did in English and in French . . . and I should like to do them for you now—if I can remember the words."

Barbra sang "What Now My Love?" "Autumn Leaves," and "I Wish You Love" during her 1966 concerts. It is interesting to note that during those shows, Barbra sang the complete French verse of "Autumn Leaves" before singing the English lyrics. On *Je m'appelle Barbra*, it is obvious that after the fifteen-second viola intro, Columbia has edited the vocal. Barbra begins in the middle of a phrase. Take a listen now—after the viola, you can hear the cut before Barbra sings the line "Et le vent du nord les emporte."

Columbia released "Non, C'est Rien" b/w "Le mur" as a single (#4-43739) in July 1966. It followed that with "Free Again" b/w "I've Been Here" (#4-43808) in September.

Pregnant with her son and done with her concert minitour, Streisand returned to the recording studio on September 14, 1966, and sang seven French/English songs. From those sessions, several songs remain unreleased: I Wish You Love/Qui Es-Tu (Love and Learn)/Et Maintenant (What Now, My Love?)/Parlez-Moi D'amour (Speak to Me of Love)/Que Reste-T-Il De Nos Amours (I Wish You Love).

This September session was very special because Barbra recorded the first song for which she'd written the melody. She remembered, fondly, "The *Je m'appelle Barbra* album—oh, I love that because I had written my first song, called 'Ma Première Chanson,' and since I was working with them for my French album . . . Eddy Marnay, a dear, dear person—he was doing the lyrics—so I asked him to write a lyric to my melody." (SiriusXM, 2014, 2016)

Writing the song enabled Barbra to join the American Society of Composers, Authors and Publishers (ASCAP). She published it on September 28, 1966, via her publishing company, Emanuel Music Corporation. Barbra resurrected "Ma Première Chanson" during her 2006 concert tour, and she even played the piano to demonstrate her original melody to her audiences.

Barbra spent four more hours on October 14, 1966, recording songs. The final album version of "What Now My Love?" was probably from this session, with an arrangement by Ray Ellis. Two songs from this session have not been released, both sung in French: "Clopin Clopant" and "Les Feuilles Mortes" (Autumn Leaves).

Je m'appelle Barbra was released by Columbia Records in late October 1966, and in 2006 Barbra said it was "the most unpopular album I ever made" and joked about how long it took to go gold. She was right. It wasn't until Columbia Records's audit of the album in 2002 that the Recording Industry Association of America certified *Je m'appelle Barbra* as a gold record, having sold 500,000 units.

"Better late than never," Barbra mused. "And even though it wasn't a great commercial success, I always thought it was a creatively adventurous project, so I loved it!" (SiriusXM, 2014, 2016)

The debonair Maurice Chevalier, the French entertainer best known for his role in *Gigi*, wrote the album's back-cover notes. He gushed: "She is mad with talent and more gifted than any human being should be permitted to be."

Matt on *Je m'appelle*

First, I must mention the gorgeous, striking cover photo in beautiful black and white by the iconic photographer Richard Avedon. This was Streisand's first sitting for Avedon, and he managed to take many beautiful photographs of her that day, including several rolls with Streisand wearing the papier-mâché bracelets; some of Streisand bare shouldered, touching her nose; and about four rolls of Streisand wearing a wide-brimmed Spanish-styled hat. A photo from this shoot was published in her 1991 *Just for the Record* booklet.

This has to be one of Streisand's best album covers, no? Streisand loved posing for Avedon. "His studio was simple and spare, just like his aesthetic," she wrote. "He often preferred to photograph people against a sheet of white paper . . . no props, nothing to distract from his subject. And he knew exactly what angles would work for my face. I didn't have to say a thing. He didn't waste time fooling around with lights. If he was photographing me from the left, the hot light would be on the left. I remember he used a strobe, with a white umbrella reflector to diffuse the light."

The experience of listening to this album always feels like a warm croissant with a strong coffee, maybe with some escargots in garlic and parsley butter on the side.

Je m'appelle Barbra is a salubrious collection of Gallic tunes—cosmopolitan, grand, and elegant. For me, there's not a miss on the album's twelve tracks. The only irksome arrangement is that 1960s rhythmic tempo on "What Now My Love?" . . . but that's a stretch. For years I disliked "Clopin Clopant," I think because it has such an irregular melody, with Streisand singing notes that were surprising, not where I thought the song was going to go. "Clopin" has turned into one of my favorite songs lately. Once my ears adjusted to the unexpected intervals, I grew to love it. Michel Legrand decides to "swing" the song a little more than halfway through on "love is a dance, and one must learn it."

The song "Once upon a Summertime" is absolute perfection. The arrangement. Barbra's vocal. When she sings in French. My god, to hear her sing "*N'en finiront, n'en finiront jamais* . . . ." There's really nothing better. Except coq au vin or maybe bœuf bourguignon.

"Martina" breaks my heart. What a melancholic and beautiful song. Hal Shaper wrote the English lyrics from Eddy Marnay's original, French ones.

Streisand's take on "I've Been Here" is epic. Shuman's English lyrics are truly tailored to her talent—this song would have been a fantastic encore during her 1960s concerts. The way the song keeps modulating is very exciting and recalls Ravel's "Boléro," which has a similar structure in which the piece builds excitement until it finally releases tension. In "I've Been Here," that happens when Streisand announces, "the world will know that I've been here!"

I love Barbra's singing-acting on "I Wish You Love," which she performs as a revenge song! Barbra's position is *not* one of forgiveness, as illustrated by the dripping sarcasm we hear when she sings the word "sincerely" with great irony. I also enjoy her Machiavellian enactment of the line "a lemonade to cool you in some leafy glade"—she poisoned that drink and is going to watch her ex-lover die! To "cool you"—she's talking death! This song and Barbra's interpretation of it are so much fun.

STREISAND COLLABORATORS

MICHEL LEGRAND

Michel Legrand and his sweeping melodies and beautiful arrangements have complemented Barbra Streisand's voice and musical sensibilities for years. Legrand's music inspired Streisand's passion yet also tickled her musical wit. He is a clever melodist whose songs are drenched in sensual grandeur. Legrand enjoyed a decades-long career as a pianist, composer, arranger, and performer. Probably Legrand's most enduring work with Streisand is on the soundtrack to her movie *Yentl.* His melodies for "Papa, Can You Hear Me?" and "The Way He Makes Me Feel" gush with feeling and sensuality. "I wanted to do *Yentl* because I loved Barbra," he said. "I admired Barbra very much. I wanted to do *Yentl* because I love the Bergmans; I love to work with them," he stated. (Jacobs, 2003)

The feeling was mutual with Streisand, who was more than just a musical associate with Legrand and the Bergmans—they were family. Marilyn Bergman described Legrand's work with Streisand more succinctly: "I think Michel, first of all, writes very lyrical, vocal music. And he also understands Barbra's voice very well, so I think he writes the kind of melodies that really utilize the range and the strengths of her voice and stretches her and the interesting intervals she likes to sing. I think from that standpoint he knows how to write for that instrument that is Streisand very well." (Jacobs, 2003)

Legrand and the Bergmans created a bespoke album for Streisand in the early seventies. "The album concerns a lifetime," Michel Legrand told Joyce Haber in 1975. "The first song deals with birth, the last with death. In between are songs about childhood, adolescence, a first love at age 16, marriage, motherhood. The songs are intense." (Haber, *The Goings-on of Jon and Barbra*, 1975) "We never finished it," Marilyn Bergman told Barbra Archives in 2007. "I think we all got busy."

"I don't think Michel, Marilyn and Alan had fully mapped out their concept yet, except for the basic 'womb to tomb' idea," Streisand said. "The only two songs I didn't relate to musically or lyrically, at the time," she added, "were about birth and death. They didn't want to change them, and then we all became involved in other projects, so the idea lost momentum." (Vincentelli, 2017) Retired opera singer Natalie Dessay finished the album with Legrand in 2017, and it was certainly an impressive oratorio for voice and orchestra. *Between Yesterday and Tomorrow: The Extraordinary Life of an Ordinary Woman* was released in 2017.

Legrand and Streisand first met back in the sixties when she was appearing on Broadway. They collaborated on her French album and became close friends. There's a hysterical video of Streisand and Legrand on YouTube from a 1984 appearance on the French TV show *Champs-Élysées*. The host explains to the audience that she is there to promote her film *Yentl*, "but maybe she can bless us with something else too?" The audience begins clapping in unison, so Legrand and Streisand are forced to walk over to the piano, with Barbra demurring: "Hum? You want me to hum?" After Legrand plunks out the correct key for the song, they engage in a sweet duet of "What Are You Doing the Rest of Your Life?" with Legrand harmonizing with Streisand.

Legrand passed away in 2019 at the age of eighty-six. Streisand tweeted about it but didn't give away her feelings about his death. "His beautiful music will live on forever. I will treasure the memories I have of working with him," she wrote.

In 2022, Alan Bergman revealed that he had written English lyrics for two Legrand songs composed for the French play, *Bistro,* that Barbra intends to record on her next album. The songs, titled "You" and "We," are "maybe the two best melodies Michel ever wrote," Bergman said to the San Francisco Classical Voice website. We can't wait to hear them.

Released: October 1967
Produced by: Jack Gold and Howard A. Roberts
Arranged by: Ray Ellis
Conducted by: David Shire
Engineering: Frank Laico, Ray Gerhardt
Cover photo: James Moore, courtesy CBS television network
Liner notes: Richard Rodgers

Catalog Numbers:
CS 9482 (stereo LP)
CL 2682 (mono LP)
CQ 966 (reel-to-reel)
PCT 9482 (cassette)
CK 9482 (CD)

Side One:

1. My Funny Valentine
2. The Nearness Of You
3. When Sunny Gets Blue
4. Make The Man Love Me
5. Lover Man (Oh, Where Can You Be?)

Side Two:

1. More Than You Know
2. I'll Know
3. All The Things You Are
4. The Boy Next Door
5. Stout-Hearted Men

Produced by Jack Gold and Howard A. Roberts
Arranged by Ray Ellis
Conducted by David Shire

COLUMBIA

Stereo CS 9482
Mono CL 2682

Nobody is talented enough
to get laughs,
to bring tears,
to sing with the depth of
a fine cello or the lift of a climbing bird.
Nobody, that is, except Barbra.
She makes our musical world
a much happier place
than it was before.

Sincerely,

Richard Rodgers

BARBRA STREISAND
SIMPLY STREISAND

Side 1

MY FUNNY VALENTINE (2:20)
(From "Babes in Arms")
THE NEARNESS OF YOU (3:28)
WHEN SUNNY GETS BLUE (2:55)
MAKE THE MAN LOVE ME (2:25)
(From "A Tree Grows in Brooklyn")
LOVER MAN
(Oh, Where Can You Be?) (2:50)
(Arranged and conducted by David Shire)

Side 2

MORE THAN YOU KNOW (3:28)
I'LL KNOW (2:46)
(From "Guys and Dolls")
ALL THE THINGS YOU ARE (3:34)
(From "Very Warm for May")
THE BOY NEXT DOOR (2:50)
(From "Meet Me in St. Louis")
STOUT-HEARTED MEN (2:42)
(From "The New Moon")

The selections are ASCAP.
Engineering: Frank Laico, Ray Gerhardt

Manufactured by Columbia Records/CBS, Inc./51 W. 52 Street, New York, N.Y. / ® "Columbia," Marcas Reg. Printed in U.S.A.

Simply Streisand was the first album released after Barbra and manager Marty Erlichman renegotiated her contract with Columbia Records's Clive Davis—the administrative vice president and general manager, appointed in 1965 by president Goddard Lieberson. "Back then," Clive Davis wrote in his memoir, "an established label like Columbia had a carefully defined set of parameters regarding the kinds of contracts it could offer . . . . The label's standard royalty rate was five percent. Based on the success they had already demonstrated, [Andy] Williams and Streisand were both asking for more than a million dollars." Davis explained that the deal he made with Streisand was for fifteen albums over a five-year period for reportedly just under a million-dollar guarantee. (DeCurtis, 2012)

In her memoir, Barbra confesses she didn't remember much about this album. It was right before she was due in Hollywood to film the *Funny Girl* movie. She fit the recording sessions into her schedule for Marty Erlichman, who loved the standards she sang on it.

Simply Streisand did not achieve gold status (five hundred thousand units) until 2002, and Barbra noted in her book that Marty told her this album was an outlier "because all of your first seven albums went Gold almost immediately," he said. Streisand disclosed: "I broke that streak with *Simply Streisand*, which I did for Marty, and the album right before it, *Je m'appelle Barbra*, which I did for me."

By the numbers, then, *Simply Streisand* was Barbra's ninth studio album, her first time working with Jack Gold and Howard A. Roberts, and the second album not to be certified gold by the RIAA until 2002, some thirty-five years later. Despite Marty Erlichman's efforts and Columbia Records's publicity, *Simply Streisand* was simply not a chart-topper. Instead, *Diana Ross and the Supremes' Greatest Hits* and the Beatles's *Sgt. Pepper's Lonely Hearts Club Band* were the big sellers on the *Billboard* charts for the rest of 1967.

Jack Gold was Columbia's West Coast A & R chief, and he shares a producing credit on *Simply Streisand* with Howard Roberts. Roberts produced records at Columbia for Tony Bennett and Diahann Carroll and was also musical director for Harry Belafonte.

Streisand was able to record all the songs for the album in March 1967, before she began work on her third CBS television special, *The Belle of 14th Street*. Only Barbra's 1967 recording of "Spring Can Really Hang You Up the Most" remains unreleased from these sessions. Streisand used to sing the song in her nightclub act, but this was the first time she recorded it for Columbia. Most know that Streisand rerecorded the Fran Landesman/Tommy Wolf tune forty-two years later, in 2009, for her album *Love Is the Answer* because she thought her 1967 unreleased recording was "lousy."

The first US pressings of *Simply Streisand* included a rare, illustrated ten-page foldout pocket catalog that listed all of Streisand's albums up through 1967.

Six of the ten songs on *Simply Streisand* are show tunes. Just like for her first few albums, Streisand attracted a famous composer to write the album notes. This time it was Richard Rodgers, the man who wrote the music with Oscar Hammerstein's lyrics for *Oklahoma* and *The King and I* and who had collaborated with Lorenz Hart earlier in his career.

SONG TITLE	ALBUM TITLE	ALBUM AND TAPE NUMBERS
Keepin' Out of Mischief Now	The Barbra Streisand Album	CL 2007/CS 8807 CQ 593/18 K0 0166 TC8 14 K0 0166 TC4
Kid Again, A	My Name Is Barbra	CL 2336/CS 9136 CQ 725/H2C 4 18 K0 0168 TC8 14 K0 0168 TC4
Kind of Man a Woman Needs, The	My Name Is Barbra, Two . . .	CL 2409/CS 9209 H2C 4/18 K0 0102 TC8 14 K0 0102 TC4
Le Mur	Je m'appelle Barbra	CL 2547/CS 9347 CQ 862/18 K0 0134 TC8 14 K0 0134 TC4
Let's Face the Music and Dance (Medley)	Color Me Barbra	CL 2478/CS 9278 CQ 810/18 K0 0044 TC8 14 K0 0044 TC4
Like a Straw in the Wind	The Second Barbra Streisand Album	CL 2054/CS 8854 CQ 607
Look at That Face (Medley)	Color Me Barbra	CL 2478/CS 9278 CQ 810/18 K0 0044 TC8 14 K0 0044 TC4
Lord's Prayer, The	A Christmas Album	CL 2757/CS 9557
Love and Learn	Je m'appelle Barbra	CL 2547/CS 9347 CQ 862/18 K0 0134 TC8 14 K0 0134 TC4
Love Is a Bore	People	CL 2215/CS 9015 CQ 686/18 K0 0020 TC8 14 K0 0020 TC4
Lover, Come Back to Me	The Second Barbra Streisand Album	CL 2054/CS 8854 CQ 607
Lover Man (Oh, Where Can You Be?)	Simply Streisand	CL 2682/CS 9482
Make Believe	Barbra Streisand/The Third Album	CL 2154/CS 8954 CQ 624/18 K0 0206 TC8 14 K0 0206 TC4
Make the Man Love Me	Simply Streisand	CL 2682/CS 9482
Ma premiere chanson	Je m'appelle Barbra	CL 2547/CS 9347 CQ 862/18 K0 0134 TC8 14 K0 0134 TC4
Martina	Je m'appelle Barbra	CL 2547/CS 9347 CQ 862/18 K0 0134 TC8 14 K0 0134 TC4
Minute Waltz, The	Color Me Barbra	CL 2478/CS 9278 CQ 810/18 K0 0044 TC8 14 K0 0044 TC4
Miss Marmelstein	I Can Get It for You Wholesale	KOL 5780/KOS 2180
More Than You Know	Simply Streisand	CL 2682/CS 9482
Much More	The Barbra Streisand Album	CL 2007/CS 8807 CQ 593/18 K0 0166 TC8 14 K0 0166 TC4
My Coloring Book	The Second Barbra Streisand Album	CL 2054/CS 8854 CQ 607
My Favorite Things	A Christmas Album	CL 2757/CS 9557
My Funny Valentine	Simply Streisand	CL 2682/CS 9482

CL, OL, KOL—Monaural/CS, OS, KOS—Stereo/CQ, H2C—4-Track Stereo Tape
TC8—Continuous Loop 8-Track Stereo Tape Cartridge
TC4—Continuous Loop 4-Track Stereo Tape Cartridge

SONG TITLE	ALBUM TITLE	ALBUM AND TAPE NUMBERS
My Honey's Loving Arms	The Barbra Streisand Album	CL 2007/CS 8807 CQ 593/18 K0 0166 TC8 14 K0 0166 TC4
My Lord and Master	People	CL 2215/CS 9015 CQ 686/18 K0 0020 TC8 14 K0 0020 TC4
My Man	My Name Is Barbra	CL 2336/CS 9136 CQ 725/H2C 4 18 K0 0168 TC8 14 K0 0168 TC4
My Melancholy Baby	Barbra Streisand/The Third Album	CL 2154/CS 8954 CQ 624/18 K0 0206 TC8 14 K0 0206 TC4
My Name Is Barbara	My Name Is Barbra	CL 2336/CS 9136 CQ 725/H2C 4 18 K0 0168 TC8 14 K0 0168 TC4
My Pa	My Name Is Barbra	CL 2336/CS 9136 CQ 725/H2C 4 18 K0 0168 TC8 14 K0 0168 TC4
Nearness of You, The	Simply Streisand	CL 2682/CS 9482
Never Will I Marry	Barbra Streisand/The Third Album	CL 2154/CS 8954 CQ 624/18 K0 0206 TC8 14 K0 0206 TC4
Nobody Knows You When You're Down and Out (Medley)	My Name Is Barbra, Two . . .	CL 2409/CS 9209 H2C 4/18 K0 0102 TC8 14 K0 0102 TC4
Nobody Makes a Pass at Me	Pins and Needles	OL 5810/OS 2210
No More Songs for Me	My Name Is Barbra, Two . . .	CL 2409/CS 9209 H2C 4/18 K0 0102 TC8 14 K0 0102 TC4
Non c'est rien	Color Me Barbra	CL 2478/CS 9278 CQ 810/18 K0 0044 TC8 14 K0 0044 TC4
Not Cricket to Picket	Pins and Needles	OL 5810/OS 2210
O Little Town of Bethlehem	A Christmas Album	CL 2757/CS 9557
Once Upon a Summertime	Je m'appelle Barbra	CL 2547/CS 9347 CQ 862/18 K0 0134 TC8 14 K0 0134 TC4
One Kiss	Color Me Barbra	CL 2478/CS 9278 CQ 810/18 K0 0044 TC8 14 K0 0044 TC4
People	People	CL 2215/CS 9015 CQ 686/18 K0 0020 TC8 14 K0 0020 TC4
Quiet Night	My Name Is Barbra, Two . . .	CL 2409/CS 9209 H2C 4/18 K0 0102 TC8 14 K0 0102 TC4
Right As the Rain	The Second Barbra Streisand Album	CL 2054/CS 8854 CQ 607
Sam, You Made the Pants Too Long (Medley)	Color Me Barbra	CL 2478/CS 9278 CQ 810/18 K0 0044 TC8 14 K0 0044 TC4

CL, OL, KOL—Monaural/CS, OS, KOS—Stereo/CQ, H2C—4-Track Stereo Tape
TC8—Continuous Loop 8-Track Stereo Tape Cartridge
TC4—Continuous Loop 4-Track Stereo Tape Cartridge

SONG TITLE	ALBUM TITLE	ALBUM AND TAPE NUMBERS
Second Hand Rose	My Name Is Barbra, Two . . .	CL 2409/CS 9209 H2C 4/18 K0 0102 TC8 14 K0 0102 TC4
Shadow of Your Smile, The	My Name Is Barbra, Two . . .	CL 2409/CS 9209 H2C 4/18 K0 0102 TC8 14 K0 0102 TC4
Sitting on Your Status Quo (and Chorus)	Pins and Needles	OL 5810/OS 2210
Sleepin' Bee, A	The Barbra Streisand Album	CL 2007/CS 8807 CQ 593/18 K0 0166 TC8 14 K0 0166 TC4
Sleep in Heavenly Peace (Silent Night)	A Christmas Album	CL 2757/CS 9557
Small World (Medley)	Color Me Barbra	CL 2478/CS 9278 CQ 810/18 K0 0044 TC8 14 K0 0044 TC4
Someone to Watch Over Me	My Name Is Barbra	CL 2336/CS 9136 CQ 725/H2C 4 18 K0 0168 TC8 14 K0 0168 TC4
Soon It's Gonna Rain	The Barbra Streisand Album	CL 2007/CS 8807 CQ 593/18 K0 0166 TC8 14 K0 0166 TC4
Speak to Me of Love	Je m'appelle Barbra	CL 2547/CS 9347 CQ 862/18 K0 0134 TC8 14 K0 0134 TC4
Spring Can Really Hang You Up the Most	Simply Streisand	CL 2682/CS 9482
Starting Here, Starting Now	Color Me Barbra	CL 2478/CS 9278 CQ 810/18 K0 0044 TC8 14 K0 0044 TC4
Stout-Hearted Men	Simply Streisand	CL 2682/CS 9482
Supper Time	People	CL 2215/CS 9015 CQ 686/18 K0 0020 TC8 14 K0 0020 TC4
Sweet Zoo	My Name Is Barbra	CL 2336/CS 9136 CQ 725/H2C 4 18 K0 0168 TC8 14 K0 0168 TC4
Taking a Chance on Love	Barbra Streisand/The Third Album	CL 2154/CS 8954 CQ 624/18 K0 0206 TC8 14 K0 0206 TC4
Taste of Honey, A	The Barbra Streisand Album	CL 2007/CS 8807 CQ 593/18 K0 0166 TC8 14 K0 0166 TC4
That Face (Medley)	Color Me Barbra	CL 2478/CS 9278 CQ 810/18 K0 0044 TC8 14 K0 0044 TC4
They Didn't Believe Me (Medley)	Color Me Barbra	CL 2478/CS 9278 CQ 810/18 K0 0044 TC8 14 K0 0044 TC4
Were Thine That Special Face (Medley)	Color Me Barbra	CL 2478/CS 9278 CQ 810/18 K0 0044 TC8 14 K0 0044 TC4
What Are They Doing to Us Now? (Ensemble)	I Can Get It for You Wholesale	KOL 5780/KOS 2180

CL, OL, KOL—Monaural/CS, OS, KOS—Stereo/CQ, H2C—4-Track Stereo Tape
TC8—Continuous Loop 8-Track Stereo Tape Cartridge
TC4—Continuous Loop 4-Track Stereo Tape Cartridge

SONG TITLE	ALBUM TITLE	ALBUM AND TAPE NUMBERS
What Good Is Love?	Pins and Needles	OL 5810/OS 2210
What Now My Love	Je m'appelle Barbra	CL 2547/CS 9347 CQ 862/18 K0 0134 TC8 14 K0 0134 TC4
What's New Pussycat? (Medley)	Color Me Barbra	CL 2478/CS 9278 CQ 810/18 K0 0044 TC8 14 K0 0044 TC4
When in Rome	People	CL 2215/CS 9015 CQ 686/18 K0 0020 TC8 14 K0 0020 TC4
When Sunny Gets Blue	Simply Streisand	CL 2682/CS 9482
When the Sun Comes Out	The Second Barbra Streisand Album	CL 2054/CS 8854 CQ 607
Where Am I Going?	Color Me Barbra	CL 2478/CS 9278 CQ 810/18 K0 0044 TC8 14 K0 0044 TC4
Where Is the Wonder	My Name Is Barbra	CL 2336/CS 9136 CQ 725/H2C 4 18 K0 0168 TC8 14 K0 0168 TC4
Where's That Rainbow?	My Name Is Barbra, Two . . .	CL 2409/CS 9209 H2C 4/18 K0 0102 TC8 14 K0 0102 TC4
White Christmas	A Christmas Album	CL 2757/CS 9557
Who's Afraid of the Big Bad Wolf	The Barbra Streisand Album	CL 2007/CS 8807 CQ 593/18 K0 0166 TC8 14 K0 0166 TC4
Who Will Buy?	The Second Barbra Streisand Album	CL 2054/CS 8854 CQ 607
Why Did I Choose You	My Name Is Barbra	CL 2336/CS 9136 CQ 725/H2C 4 18 K0 0168 TC8 14 K0 0168 TC4
Will He Like Me?	People	CL 2215/CS 9015 CQ 686/18 K0 0020 TC8 14 K0 0020 TC4
Willow Weep for Me	Simply Streisand	CL 2682/CS 9482
Yesterdays	Color Me Barbra	CL 2478/CS 9278 CQ 810/18 K0 0044 TC8 14 K0 0044 TC4

On Columbia Records

CL, OL, KOL—Monaural/CS, OS, KOS—Stereo/CQ, H2C—4-Track Stereo Tape
TC8—Continuous Loop 8-Track Stereo Tape Cartridge
TC4—Continuous Loop 4-Track Stereo Tape Cartridge

Songs by Barbra / A complete listing.

Columbia Records put out two singles to promote the album: "Stout-Hearted Men" b/w "Look" (#4-44225) and "Lover Man" b/w "My Funny Valentine" (#4-44331). Collectors should note that "Stout-Hearted Men" is a different take—minus Streisand's Mae West impersonation. "Look" was recorded for *Je m'appelle Barbra* and is rare here too. This is the English recording; the French-language version of "Look" is "Et La Mer," which appears on Barbra's French EP.

Matt on *Simply*

Simply has a lot in common with *The Third Album*—it's Barbra's second "mellow" album, with just a few standout tracks. The album doesn't really ever kick into high gear, even considering the up-tempo tracks (which aren't really that up-tempo).

Still, *Simply Streisand* is a lovely offering, mostly because of Ray Ellis's stunning arrangements.

A trio of songs on *Simply Streisand* are just perfect, two arranged by Ellis.

"The Nearness of You" and "When Sunny Gets Blue" find Barbra floating in a jazzy musical setting. It's no mistake that "The Nearness of You" was the song behind the helicopter shots of New York City in the opening of Barbra's *Happening in Central Park* TV show. The arrangement and vocal are like those birds you see catching the wind in their outspread wings and coasting on air.

"When Sunny Gets Blue," also arranged by Ellis, has a mellow feeling, and Barbra lays back on the relaxed vocal. True story: Barbra rehearsed and thought about including "Sunny" during the *Timeless* concert rehearsals. Wouldn't that have been something to hear live?!

The third song that always knocks me over is "Lover Man"—that arrangement is by David Shire, and it's *hot*. That piano! And the bridge, "I've heard it said that the thrill of romance can be like a heavenly dream," is so electrifying. Then the piano comes back in! It was completely thrilling to hear and watch Barbra sing this arrangement live during her 1994 concert tour too.

Released: October 1967
Produced by: Jack Gold & Ettore Stratta
Arranged and conducted by: Marty Paich & Ray Ellis
Engineering: Rafael O. Valentin, Jack Lattig
Cover photo: Horn/Griner

Catalog Numbers:
CS 9557 (stereo LP)
CL 2757 (mono LP)
16C 00530 (cassette)
18C 00530 (8-track)
CQ 1050 (reel-to-reel)
CK 9557 (CD, 1989 and 1994)
CT 9557 (cassette)
CK 92708 (2004 CD—US "Essential Holiday Classics" version)
518970 2 (2004 CD—UK Christmas Collection)
97722 (2005 CD—US Borders Christmas Collection)
A 712043 (2007 CD—Sony/BMG Custom Marketing Group)
A 712043 (2007 CD—Sony/BMG Custom Marketing Group)
19658888901 (2024 Vinyl)

Side One:

1. Jingle Bells?
2. Have Yourself A Merry Little Christmas
3. The Christmas Song
4. White Christmas
5. My Favorite Things
6. The Best Gift

Side Two:

1. Sleep In Heavenly Peace (Silent Night)
2. Gounod's Ave Maria
3. O Little Town Of Bethlehem
4. I Wonder As I Wander
5. The Lord's Prayer

2024 Vinyl Bonus Track:
Gounod's Ave Maria (English Version)

Barbra recorded four Christmas songs on June 25, 1966, while she was in London performing *Funny Girl* at the Prince of Wales Theatre. With arrangements by Ray Ellis, the songs were recorded at London's Olympia Sound Studios: "The Lord's Prayer," "I Wonder as I Wander," "Silent Night," and "Gounod's Ave Maria." Then, four months later, on October 31, 1966, she remade "Silent Night" with Ray Ellis again arranging and conducting. During the London sessions, Barbra recorded two versions of "Gounod's Ave Maria"—one in English. In 2005, Sony/BMG licensed the English version to a Starbucks's compilation Christmas CD called *Baby, It's Cold Outside*. It had never appeared on a Streisand album before that. In 2024, the English "Ave Maria" was added to the *Christmas Album* rerelease as a bonus track.

With a fall 1967 release date in mind, Streisand recorded the rest of the album while she was in Hollywood making the *Funny Girl* movie. The sessions were on September 9 and 16, 1967—both with Marty Paich arrangements.

Producer Jack Gold said, "[Barbra] didn't want to do ["White Christmas"] because it was too closely associated with Bing Crosby. I remembered that it had a special verse, an introduction that Irving Berlin wrote about being stranded in Beverly Hills on Christmas Eve, with the sunshine and palm trees." (Considine, 1985) Streisand liked the verse and recorded the song for the album.

"I was actually a bit dissatisfied with my original Christmas album, which I made when I was pregnant with Jason," Streisand confessed in 2001. "I was sick and had laryngitis, but we had an orchestra booked in London and I had to sing for three days. I never felt it was good enough, and I always thought I must do another one when I'm not hoarse." (Gundersen, Streisand's Christmas offering, 2001)

Except for "O Little Town of Bethlehem," the second side of *A Christmas Album* is all arranged by Ray Ellis; the first side has all of Paich's arrangements. You could also say that the first side contains secular or popular Christmas songs, whereas side two features only religious-themed carols.

The cover photo is credited to Horn/Griner—a successful graphic design team comprising Steve Horn and Norm Griner, who worked together on design projects for fifteen years into the early 1970s. The photograph was taken at Barbra's rehearsal for her Central Park concert on the evening of June 16, 1967. Several photographers were allowed to capture images of Barbra's rehearsal, so there are many photos from that evening—Streisand wore a fabric band around her hairdo.

Two years after *A Christmas Album* was released, Columbia Records, through its Columbia Special Products subsidiary, exploited its artists' holiday music by releasing *Season's Greetings from Barbra Streisand ... and Friends*. Five Streisand Christmas songs appeared on one side, and the albums were sold for one dollar in grocery stores across America for Maxwell House coffee, a corporate sponsor.

A Christmas Album has been repackaged several different times over the years. The first change came in 2004 when Columbia released the album with a purple, holiday-themed border around the original cover photo. Columbia also assigned this version a new catalog number: CK 92708.

In 2007, Sony/BMG Marketing Group released *A Christmas Album* with a brand-new cover featuring a 1970 photo of Streisand.

The Europe CD (#460536 2) has an altered cover as well. The original photo is cropped so that it is no longer centered, and an extra line has been added in the Streisand typography: "Featuring Jingle Bells?, White Christmas, Sleep in Heavenly Peace, The Lord's Prayer."

There's the 2005 Borders bookstores box set called *The Christmas Collection* (#C2K 97722). It contained two CDs—*A Christmas Album* (1967) and *Christmas Memories* (2001). And in 2013, Sony Legacy combined some (but not all) tracks from both her Christmas albums and packaged it as *The Classic Christmas Album*, with new artwork. Then there is the 2024 rerelease from Legacy Recordings. This album has sold very well over the years, with the last official tally coming in 1999 at five million units.

The 2024 remaster of *A Christmas Album* was completed by Paul Blakemore from new 24-bit files created by Jochem van Der Saag. It was released to stores on vinyl with the bonus track (the English version of "Gounod's Ave Maria"), but not on CD. Fans will find the bonus track on streaming services, though.

Matt on *Christmas*

"Jingle Bells?" divides people. You either love it or you hate it. I love it. The song mixes several time signatures with an arrangement that sounds like something Leonard Bernstein wrote for *West Side Story*. Streisand enunciates "Fanny Bright" to make sure we know she's not singing about "Fanny Brice," her *Funny Girl* character. Then she gives us a hilarious Brooklynese "*Upsot?*" after singing "and then we got upsot"—which was James Lord Pierpont's attempt to make a rhyming joke.

Some singers skip the nonsensical word altogether and sing "upset" instead. It's a thrilling musical ride, and every holiday season I look forward to watching YouTube videos of houses decorated with Christmas lights that are programmed to this song!

"The Best Gift" is a quiet song with a happy surprise at the end. I always add it to Christmas playlists because I think it's one of Streisand's best musical gifts. Barbra wrote in her book: "I was thinking that my baby would be born around Christmas, and that gave me an idea. I talked to Lan O'Kun (who had written those funny lyrics to 'The Minute Waltz'), and he composed a song for me, 'The Best Gift,' which of course was about a child."

"I Wonder as I Wander" and "My Favorite Things" both have a melancholy to them that I appreciate. I like that Barbra gave us a *Sound of Music* song sung as an introspective ballad complete with a minor-key ending. By singing an alternate melody halfway through the song, Barbra elevates "My Favorite Things" from a happy-go-lucky, positive song to a thoughtful inner monologue.

If I had to choose between the two liturgical songs, I'd take "Gounod's Ave Maria" because "The Lord's Prayer" is just too much, what with the orchestra at full throttle and the choir singing behind her. It's a dramatic way to close the album, but it's also a tad overwrought.

A Christmas Album is probably the album most Streisand fans have in their collections. It's taken out every holiday season while cookies are being baked, trees are going up, or presents are being opened.

Released: August 1968
CDs released: 1990 and 2002
Produced by: Jack Gold
Arranged and conducted by: Walter Scharf
Sound supervised by: Warren Vincent
Liner notes: Jack Brodsky

Catalog Numbers:
BOS 3220 (gatefold LP)
SQ 30992 (quadraphonic LP)
OQ 1032 (reel-to-reel)
CK 3220 (CD 1990, remastered CD 1994)
JST 3220 (cassette)
18 12 0034 (8-track)
CK 85151 (CD remastered 2002)
CK 5063582 UK CD Remastered 2002, with bonus track "I'd Rather Be Blue Over You" (single version)

Side One:

1. Overture
2. I'm The Greatest Star
3. If A Girl Isn't Pretty
4. Roller Skate Rag
5. I'd Rather Be Blue Over You (Than Happy With Somebody Else)
6. His Love Makes Me Beautiful

Side Two:

1. People
2. You Are Woman, I Am Man
3. Don't Rain On My Parade
4. Sadie, Sadie
5. The Swan
6. Funny Girl
7. My Man
8. Finale

The original Broadway cast album of *Funny Girl* was released by Capitol Records, but when it came time for the *Funny Girl* movie, Columbia Records retained the rights to release the soundtrack album. Jule Styne and Bob Merrill contributed three new songs for the movie: "The Swan," "Roller Skate Rag," and "Funny Girl."

Period songs not written by Styne and Merrill were added to the film too: "I'd Rather Be Blue Over You," "Second Hand Rose," and "My Man." The real Fanny Brice sang all those songs in her career, although she recorded "I'd Rather Be Blue" much later than the time period the movie covers.

Film composer Walter Scharf was hired as the film's musical supervisor. Scharf received Oscar nominations for his musical work on *Hans Christian Andersen* (1952) and *Willy Wonka & the Chocolate Factory* (1971). For *Funny Girl*'s soundtrack, Scharf explained, "It was a challenge to adapt the music from the Broadway *Funny Girl* and it intrigued me. I wanted to keep the period mood of Fanny Brice's time alive and yet contemporize the music at the same time." (Davis, 1968)

Jule Styne told a Streisand biographer, "I was upset with the orchestrations for the entire movie. They were going for pop arrangements. 'My Man,' which wasn't in the show, and didn't belong in the movie, was like a Las Vegas arrangement. They dropped eight songs from the Broadway show and we were asked to write some new ones . . . But of all my musicals they screwed up, *Funny Girl* came out the best." (Considine, 1985)

Columbia Records went all out to promote the *Funny Girl* soundtrack album. Columbia art director John Berg put together a top-notch package—the gatefold album that opened to Jack Brodsky's liner notes on one side and a photo collage from the movie on the other. Famed movie illustrator Bob Peak created the film's key art. And the vinyl LP was inserted into a picture sleeve that showed all of Barbra's albums to date with Columbia Records.

The *Funny Girl* quadraphonic LP contains different vocal takes from Streisand. And the remastered CD has some changes too. The "Overture" on the CD does not include "Second Hand Rose"—the quad does. The CD includes all of Streisand's spoken dialogue on "I'm the Greatest Star," but there is no dialogue included on the quad. The quad also omits the introductory music on "Don't Rain on My Parade"; it starts cold with Barbra singing "Don't!"

For "Sadie, Sadie," the quad editors left in Omar Sharif's spoken words: "and for Sadie, Sadie, married lady . . ." And finally, on the quad, Barbra's line "Prince!" is included on the track "The Swan." It is not on the CD.

Matt on *Funny Girl* (Movie)

"I'm the Greatest Star" is superior to the Broadway recording simply because Streisand sings the movie version at breakneck speed and it's very funny. The orchestra explodes as she brings down the house at the climax of the song. "Star" never ceases to thrill me.

"People" is notable because of the reprise. There's no other recording of the reprise in Streisand's discography, although she did perform it on stage too. At 3:18 on the track, the orchestra plays in Streisand. Somehow, she imbues the short reprise with such pathos and longing. In the movie, of course, this is the part where the camera swoops in on Fanny holding onto the streetlamp. All of that emotion comes through on the recording as well.

The new ballad, "Funny Girl," went overlooked for years. What a simple, heartbreaking song! We all have to thank Idina Menzel and the TV show *Glee* for its revival, because it might have gone missing if Menzel didn't sing it on the show, then incorporate it in her live concerts with "Don't Rain on My Parade." Of course, Streisand herself resurrected the song in 2006 on tour, and it was charming. I can see her singing it right now with her black sweater shrugged around her creamy shoulders.

Sorry, where was I? Over all these years and in all *Funny Girl*'s iterations (vinyl, CD, digital), I have been bothered by a few things. The track entitled "Finale" is actually the music that played under the title sequence of the movie, following the overture. Columbia should rename that track "Main Title." Therefore, sequentially, it really should not be placed as the last track on the album.

What's missing from the *Funny Girl* movie? Well, there is an orchestra track at the end of the movie, heard after "My Man" as the cast credits roll. This short instrumental has never been included on any of the *Funny Girl* albums—it's a beautiful orchestration of the title song. There is also a two-minute-long intermission orchestral piece that was never included on the soundtrack album. You can hear this on the Blu-ray.

There is also a jarring edit in the overture heard on the soundtrack album for all these years. At about 3:04 into the song, the music jumps from "You Are Woman" to "Don't Rain on My Parade," with "Second Hand Rose" completely edited out. You can hear this playful part of the overture on the Blu-ray of the movie. Curiously, "Second Hand Rose" is not edited from the quadraphonic and masterworks LPs. They're the only version of the soundtrack album (including the CDs of recent years!) that contain the complete "Overture," without the cut.

Barbra's version of "Second Hand Rose," sung on stage for Mr. Ziegfeld, has never appeared on the soundtrack either. Granted, Streisand recorded a studio version of the song for the album *My Name Is Barbra, Two . . .* but it would be nice to have the movie version.

Finally, Barbra's "Nicky Arnstein (Nicky Arnstein)" vocals have never been commercially available either.

SIGNATURE STREISAND

"DON'T RAIN ON MY PARADE"

"Don't Rain on My Parade" is Barbra Streisand's theme song. There's so much ambition and dogged determination in "Parade" that it fits Barbra like a tailored shirt (although the film costume dismayed Streisand: "for that number, Irene [Sharaff] put me in my least favorite color . . . orange").

The movie version is the one played around the world and what comes to mind when people mention Barbra Streisand. The arrangement, with its driving-forward motion, is extraordinary! Barbra's interpretation is so well-known that other singers often mimic her phrasing when performing the song. Barbra singing this song has been etched into all our psyches!

"If someone takes a spill, *it's me and not you!*"

In the 1970s, Peter Matz rearranged the song for Barbra to sing in her Las Vegas club acts. He gave her more of a jazz arrangement, with a playful piano and more leeway for Streisand to sing some different notes.

Barbra waited until the concerts of New Year's Eve 1993 and the tour of 1994 to sing "Don't Rain on My Parade" again. This time, it capped a medley of songs and was given another new arrangement, by Marvin Hamlisch. It's hard to ignore this live version; it's quite good. Hamlisch gives the song a classical tempo, inspired by the music of Bartok or Stravinsky.

Streisand and her codirector, Richard Jay-Alexander, surprised fans in 2006 when, as a finale of her concert tour, they chose the never-before-performed-live "Reprise" version of "Don't Rain on My Parade" from the original Broadway show. "Just give 'em hell, girl, cry a little later/Well, girl, that's life in the theater!"

There's a bonus track on the CDs sold at Target stores of "Don't Rain on My Parade," also from the 2006 concert. William Ross orchestrated this one, and it's an interesting interpretation of the classic tune, borrowing more from the Broadway score than the movie arrangement. Ross introduces some cool string harmonies before the bridge of the song that I like a lot.

Yes, it's true that over the years Streisand has begun singing "one shot, one *rim* shot and bam!" The original lyric is "gun shot." She has never said why she decided to do this. As Linda Richman, the Streisand fanatic portrayed by Mike Myers on *Saturday Night Live*, once said: "You're Barbra Joan Streisand. Ya got enough on your hands!"

Note: One of my biggest pet peeves is when vocalists fail to sing a Streisand signature song with their own voice and interpretation. It's amusing to do a search on YouTube for all the covers of "Don't Rain on My Parade"—it's a hard song to sing and can mow over incapable singers, and often does. But you've all got to look at Lillias White's amazingly original version of "Parade" taped at the 2002 Actors Fund Benefit performance of *Funny Girl*. She sings it strong and unapologetically herself, with some of the most amazing phrasing and alternate notes I've ever heard. Brava! Give yourself the gift of Miss White.

Released: September 1968
Produced by: Jack Gold
Sound supervised by: Warren Vincent
Engineering: Edward T. Graham, Stan Weiss, Phil Macy, Arthur Kendy
Cover photo: *N.Y. Times*

Catalog Numbers:
PC 9710 (LP, 1968)
PCT 9710 (cassette)
CQ 1048 (reel-to-reel)
18 10 0528 (8-track)
CK 9710 (CD remastered 1994)

Side One:

1. I Can See It
2. Love Is Like A Newborn Child
3. Folk Monologue/Value
4. Cry Me A River
5. People

Side Two:

1. He Touched Me
2. Marty The Martian
3. Natural Sounds
4. Second Hand Rose
5. Sleep In Heavenly Peace (Silent Night)
6. Happy Days Are Here Again

Webster's New World Dictionary defines: happen (hap' on) vi 1: to take place; occur; befall. 2: to be or occur by chance...3: to have the luck or occasion..." This, indeed, describes the extraordinary concert that took place on June 17th, 1967, in Central Park—a happening led by the one and only Barbra Streisand!

Never before had such a grand-scale plan been attempted under the stress conditions of uncertainty. There was to be an evening concert in the 93-acre Sheep Meadow area of Central Park—Barbra's Concert—taped by CBS for a color television special and a sound track made for this new album.

Four basic factors, all risky, were involved: the weather, proper lighting over the vast area for television purposes, an audio system for quality sound, and the audience!

Barbra, who was in Hollywood filming "Funny Girl," boarded a plane for New York City Friday night, June 16th, and arrived at the Central Park location at 2 A.M., Saturday—immediately launching into rehearsal for the concert that night! Brief rest periods were taken in two 90-foot trailers set up on the site.

By 6 A.M. (the morning of the concert), crowds of ardent Streisand fans began arriving...the young, middle-aged, elderly, all races and creeds, hippies, the right wing, left wing, Democrats and Republicans ...Barbra's PEOPLE.

At concert time, Sheep Meadow was jammed with 135,000 fans in front of the stage (not to mention an additional 12,000 in a roped-off area behind the platform). So crowded was this 67th Street area of Central Park, that the album cover picture had to be shot from the window of an apartment building at 87th Street and Central Park West!

And there it was...THE HAPPENING...and the largest crowd ever to have assembled for any public performance of a single entertainer in the world. For 2½ hours Barbra belonged to them—and they belonged to Barbra (all 135,000 of them!).

The evening was perfect. The moon payed silvery homage to her and even the stars in the sky took second place to the star on stage. The cool humming winds became part of the orchestration, and Barbra enjoyed this new instrument called Nature—just as her spellbound audience did, while they watched and listened in a state of mass hypnosis.

It was a mutual love affair between 135,000 people and the one girl on the stage. It was 2½ hours of electric intimacy, laced with 33 songs and talk. Barbra kidded and 135,000 people laughed! Barbra sang Second Hand Rose *and 135,000 people sang right along with her!*

Happy-faced people sat everywhere with baskets of food and drink, prepared for THE HAPPENING. And boy—did it happen! The evening went off without a hitch, except for one—one made by Barbra herself. As she was about to make an entrance back on the stage, she asked a park official what he thought the attendance was. He answered "128,000"—and that is what Barbra repeats on this record.

The Streisand admirers who attended THE HAPPENING took home warm memories of an exciting evening. But they left an awful lot behind! It took the N.Y. Sanitation Department 4 days to collect the 5 tons of flotsam and jetsam strewn about. Among the remains, more exotic items included empty vintage champagne bottles, a Scrabble set, a Russian-English dictionary, a half-eaten Hebrew National Salami, assorted empty wine bottles representing 8 foreign countries, a Sterling silver champagne bucket, an upper plate, a jar of quail eggs, an 8-day alarm clock and a black, pleated mini-skirt!

Obviously, Barbra made them forget more than just their worries and cares! But then, she always makes it happen—for BARBRA STREISAND IS A HAPPENING...wherever she goes!

Produced by Jack Gold/Sound Supervised by Warren Vincent
Engineering: Edward T. Graham, Stan Weiss, Phil Macy, Arthur Kendy Cover photo: N.Y. Times/ Manufactured by Columbia Records/CBS, Inc./51 W. 52 Street, New York, N.Y./® "Columbia," Marcas Reg. Printed in U.S.A.

A Happening in Central Park was Barbra Streisand's first live album—not counting the *Bon Soir* (unreleased at this time) and even the recording of Barbra at San Francisco's hungry i nightclub in 1963 (a fine recording, relegated to bootleg status). She performed the concert before thousands of fans, cameras, and audio recording trucks on Saturday, June 17, 1967. Central Park was wedged into the *Funny Girl* movie's filming schedule. "I could only fly in for the weekend, because I was already in the midst of rehearsals for *Funny Girl* in Los Angeles," Streisand wrote. She added: "Ray [Stark] gave me one extra half day off so I could get there in time to have a dress rehearsal on Friday night."

The concert, sponsored by Rheingold Beer and free to the public, was held in the Sheep Meadow section of New York City's Central Park. CBS aired a television special of the concert on September 15, 1968, and Columbia Records released the album of the concert to coincide with the airing of the TV show.

Even though the 1967 concert ran over two hours in length, the 1968 CBS video amounted to about fifty minutes of airtime, and Columbia's album included around thirty-five minutes of the material.

Barbra's set list for the Central Park concert drew from the concerts she was giving in 1966 and, later, at the Hollywood Bowl in 1967. For Central Park, though, Barbra did perform two new songs that she never recorded for any other album.

Oscar Brown Jr. recorded four albums for Columbia Records, and "Love Is Like a Newborn Child" appeared on his 1962 album, *Between Heaven and Hell* (and was arranged by Quincy Jones). The song originated in a 1961 Broadway-bound musical, *Kicks & Co.*, written by Brown about a college campus in the South during segregation. It starred Burgess Meredith (*Rocky*) as a Satan-like character and featured Nichelle Nichols—before she portrayed Uhura on *Star Trek*.

One of the most beautiful songs Barbra sang at this concert was "Natural Sounds" by Lan O'Kun from the musical *The Juggler*—which was unproduced. The musical concerned a street performer who has only his talents as a juggler to offer to a statue of the Virgin Mary as a Christmas present. This medieval religious miracle story by French writer Anatole France (1892) tells that the statue came to life.

O'Kun wrote other songs for Streisand in the 1960s and 1970s: "The Minute Waltz," "The Best Gift," and "Piano Practicing."

Lan O'Kun later wrote the script for a 1982 nonmusical telemovie titled *The Juggler of Notre Dame*, which—coincidentally—starred Melinda Dillon as the Virgin Mary sculptor's transient sister who is redeemed at the end of the movie. Dillon, of course, played Tom Wingo's sister in Barbra Streisand's film *The Prince of Tides*.

A Happening in Central Park's live sound was not the best quality. That is why the 1994 remastered CD is a revelation, with a much more robust sound. The only downside to this is now we can hear the very rowdy audience in the background.

On "Natural Sounds," what sounds like a shouting match between audience members can be heard in the background. "Sit down!" they yelled. Then, about halfway through the song, we hear a small round of applause. It sounds as if someone was standing in the sight line of a group of fans, who yelled about it. When the person finally sat down, this elicited thankful applause from the blocked people.

The tracks on the *Central Park* album do not appear in the order in which they were performed. In cutting a two-hour concert down to a thirty-five-minute album, the producers resequenced and edited some of the songs. For instance, "The Hills Are Alive"/ "Mississippi Mud" in front of "Marty the Martian" was sung ahead of "I Can See It." On the final album, the editors cut from a portion of the overture to "I Can See It" as Barbra's opening number. That evening Barbra began the Central Park show by singing "Any Place I Hang My Hat Is Home."

Streisand has said that one day team Streisand will release the complete Central Park concert, and I happen to know that work has been completed on it.

Matt on *Park*

Despite how lovely Barbra sounds on the recording, this concert was also partly responsible for exacerbating Barbra's well-known stage fright. In 1983, Barbra told Gene Shalit that her stage fright "started in 1967 during the Arab-Israeli War when I was doing my big concert in Central Park. There were 135,000 people there. My movie [*Funny Girl*] was going to be banned in Egypt. The government had said that [because Omar Sharif] was an Arab and I was a Jew, they weren't going to play any of my movies. So I was afraid that somebody might take a shot at me during the concert. So I started walking around the stage fast. And I forgot my words, which is an actor's nightmare. And that frightened me—that absolute lack of control." (*The Today Show*, 1983)

It's been claimed and repeated in Streisand biographies that some of the tracks on this album were not actually recorded at Central Park, that they've been substituted from Barbra's July 9, 1967, concert at the Hollywood Bowl.

In truth, the only track that was replaced on the album was Barbra's monologue preceding the track "Value."

The monologue Barbra gave that evening in Central Park was long and interrupted by some business with her tea, which you can see if you watch the Central Park DVD. For brevity on the album, Columbia Records substituted the Hollywood Bowl monologue, which was short, to the point, and took up less time. Otherwise, the vocals you hear on the DVD and the album were all recorded live in New York on June 17, 1967, and match perfectly.

Marty Erlichman even released a statement in 1986 after these allegations appeared in a Streisand biography: "Every note she sang in Central Park is on this album, including the wrong lyric at the beginning of 'Natural Sounds.' One can also hear the orchestra out of tune, especially on 'People,' because of the hot, humid air. If CBS, in the interest of brevity, substituted a few of her monologues from a second concert—what's the big deal?" (Considine, 1985)

One day, I hope, we'll be able to hear and/or watch the complete concert. I really look forward to getting my blanket out and spreading it under the stars and listening to the complete concert.

LIVE CONCERT 1967	ALBUM 1968	TV SHOW 1968
Overture	I Can See It	The Nearness of You
Any Place I Hang My Hat	Love is Like a Newborn Child	Down With Love
The Nearness of You	Folk Monologue/Value	Love is Like a Newborn Child
My Honey's Lovin' Arms	Cry Me A River	Cry Me A River
I'll Tell the Man in the Street	People	Folk Monologue/Value
Cry Me A River	He Touched Me	I Can See It
Folk Monologue/Value	Marty the Martian	COMMERCIAL BREAK
I Can See It	Natural Sounds	Love is a Bore
More Than You Know	Second Hand Rose	He Touched Me
All the Things You Are	Silent Night	The Schloon Song
Down With Love	Happy Days Are Here Again	I'm All Smiles
Love is Like a Newborn Child		Marty the Martian
I Wish You Love		Natural Sounds
What Now My Love?		Second Hand Rose
Free Again		People
When the Sun Comes Out		Silent Night
INTERMISSION		Happy Days Are Here Again
Entr'acte		
Where Am I Going?		
He Touched Me		
The Schloon Song		
Stout-Hearted Men		
I'm All Smiles		
Marty the Martian		
Love is a Bore		
Always Chasing Rainbows		
Natural Sounds		
Second Hand Rose		
People		
Silent Night		
Happy Days Are Here Again		

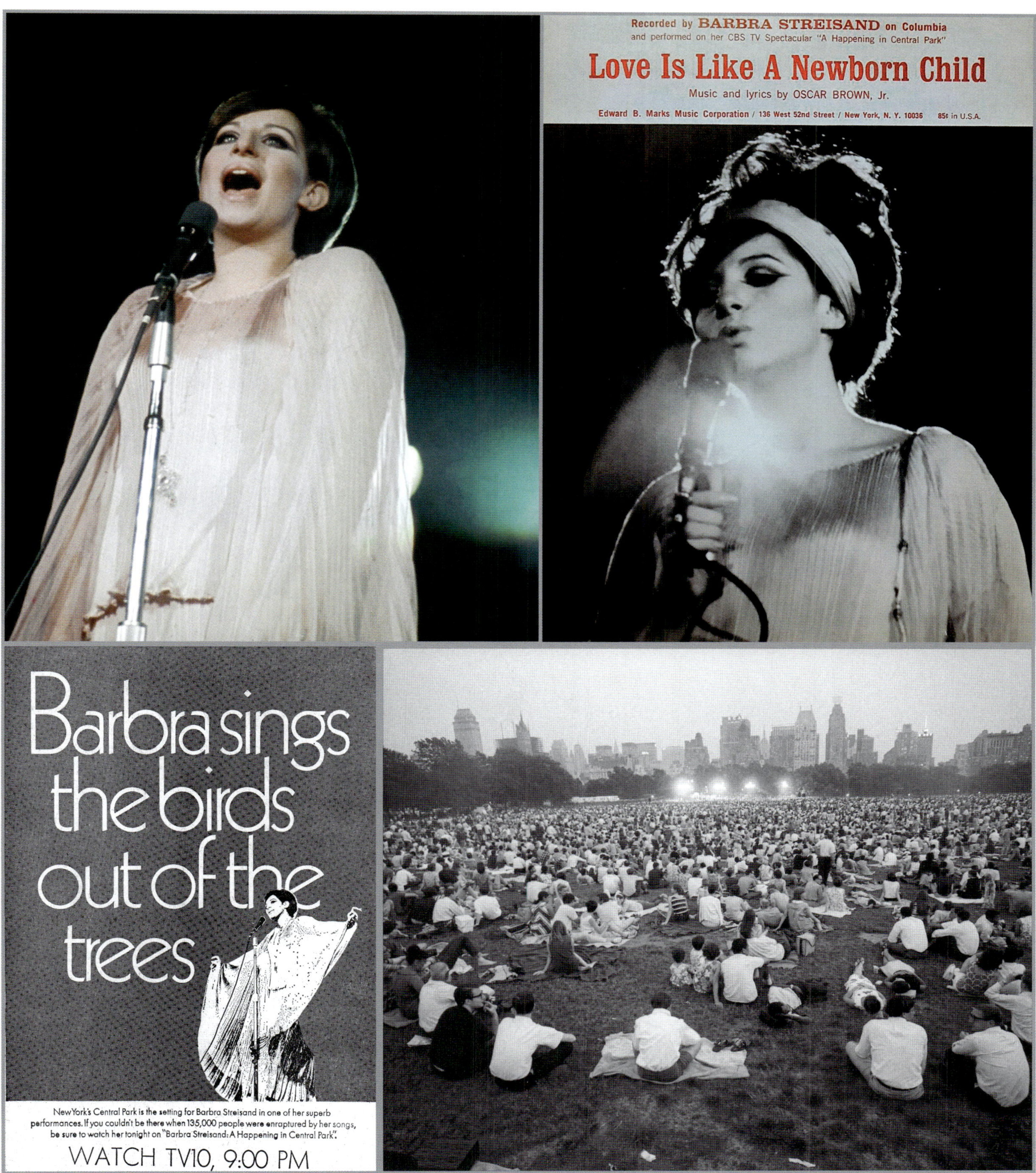
Recorded by BARBRA STREISAND on Columbia
and performed on her CBS TV Spectacular "A Happening in Central Park"
Love Is Like A Newborn Child
Music and lyrics by OSCAR BROWN, Jr.
Edward B. Marks Music Corporation / 136 West 52nd Street / New York, N. Y. 10036 85¢ in U.S.A.
Barbra sings the birds out of the trees
New York's Central Park is the setting for Barbra Streisand in one of her superb performances. If you couldn't be there when 135,000 people were enraptured by her songs, be sure to watch her tonight on "Barbra Streisand: A Happening in Central Park".
WATCH TV10, 9:00 PM

Released: July 1969
Produced by: Wally Gold
Editing engineer: Don Meehan
Photos: Richard Avedon
Liner notes: Barbra Streisand
CD restored by: John Arrias at B&J Studio using the C.A.P. System
CD remastered by: Bernie Grundman

CS 9816 (LP)
HC 1166 (reel-to-reel)
16 10 0658 (cassette)
18 10 0658 (8-track)
PC 9816 (LP, reissue)
CK 47014 (CD remastered 1993)

Side One:

1. What About Today?
2. Ask Yourself Why
3. Honey Pie
4. Punky's Dilemma
5. Until It's Time For You To Go
6. That's A Fine Kind O' Freedom

Side Two:

1. Little Tin Soldier
2. With A Little Help From My Friends
3. Alfie
4. The Morning After
5. Goodnight

Clive Davis became president of Columbia Records in 1967, taking over for the venerable Goddard Lieberson, the man who had signed Barbra Streisand to the record label. Clive Davis brought new energy and youthfulness, signing a great array of rock and pop stars, including, Laura Nyro, Bruce Springsteen, Janice Joplin and Billy Joel.

It was Bob Dylan (another Columbia artist) who summed up this decade best with his song "The Times They Are a-Changin'"—1968 and 1969 marked the civil rights protests in the United States, students were protesting the Vietnam War, and Martin Luther King and Robert F. Kennedy was assassinated. Therefore, it was no surprise that Clive Davis asked Streisand to update her repertoire—especially when Barbra's last album of standards, *Simply Streisand*, failed to crack the top ten albums chart.

Streisand, in January 1968, ventured into new territory when she recorded three pop songs. The session was produced by Jimmy "The Wiz" Wisner, and the songs sound like the Northern Soul hits of the era. On the up-tempo song "Our Corner of the Night," Wisner even double-tracked Streisand's vocal, giving the ditty a bigger sound. Columbia released the single of "Our Corner of the Night" b/w "He Could Show Me" (#4-44474) in February 1968, but it did not sell well. Neither song has ever appeared on a Streisand album, and many of us fans would love to have them on a CD one day.

"Frank Mills" from *Hair* was the third song Barbra recorded during that session. *Hair: The American Tribal Love-Rock Musical* was a counterculture hit on Broadway with a rock score, and many artists were rushing to record songs from it. However, Barbra's "Frank Mills" didn't hit record stores (seven-inch only) until 1969, when the momentum had already passed and *What About Today?* had already been released—although "Frank Mills" did not appear on that album. It too remains unreleased in any digital format.

What About Today? has attained a bad reputation over the years, almost always described as the album in which Streisand failed to capture the new sound sweeping the nation. It is known as the catalyst for *Stoney End*, which *did* succeed in transitioning Streisand to a younger audience.

What probably created this judgment about the album was that *What About Today?* unfortunately presented Streisand as a bit of a poser. After all, the back cover printed a dedication by Streisand to "the young people who push against indifference, shout down mediocrity, demand a better future, and who write and sing the songs of today." The cover image by Avedon sent mixed messages too. "I looked more like Colette than a fellow rebel out on the streets, storming the ramparts," Streisand wrote.

"I admire today's youth," Streisand told columnist Florabel Muir, "though I don't feel a part of it." (Muir, 1969) And yet the arrangements of these songs were created by Peter Matz, Don Costa, and Michel Legrand—not necessarily the most modern collaborators. Barbra's producer here was Wally Gold, who cowrote the Elvis Presley hit "It's Now or Never" and Lesley Gore's "It's My Party." In 2016, Barbra reflected on the album saying, "Even though the songs were contemporary, the production didn't have a particularly modern sound, and the album didn't really catch on. But there's some goodies on it!" (SiriusXM, 2014, 2016)

Matt on *Today?*

So let's not concentrate on how this album missed the mark of being hip. Instead, let's judge it on its own merits. *What About Today?* is a fine Streisand album, consistent with her other 1960s LPs up to that point; it combined big, Broadway-style numbers, quirky comedy songs, and a few masterful, timeless tracks.

The first track, "What About Today?" and "The Morning After" were tunes by Richard Maltby and David Shire. Streisand had already recorded several of their songs, including "Autumn," "No More Songs for Me," and "Starting Here, Starting Now." In 2020, David Shire explained the inspiration for "The Morning After" was the 1968 Detroit riots. "In 1968, I watched in disbelief as flames enveloped a large part of Detroit, and 'The Morning After' was my songwriter's response." (Rosky, 2020)

Both songs certainly show off Streisand's dramatic flair, which Don Costa knew how to arrange for. "The Morning After" was released as a single (#4-44532) ahead of the album with a heavy-handed ad campaign that had Columbia claiming it was "a new single with a message."

It's also unfortunate that "The Morning After" has the same title as the theme song from the 1972 film *The Poseidon Adventure*. Maureen McGovern had a big hit with that song, and several websites now report that Barbra Streisand covered it. These inaccuracies drive me nuts! Just so everyone knows: McGovern sang, "There's got to be a morning after," whereas Streisand sang, "The morning after is too late."

"What About Today?," the album's first song, does not have an important message, but, boy, does Streisand sing the hell out of it. Costa gives her a driving piano and a beat that really propels the song.

Following the explosive opening track, the gentle "Ask Yourself Why" is next. The music was written by Michel Legrand for a 1969 Italian-French psychological-thriller film, *La Piscine* (*The Swimming Pool*), directed by Jacques Deray. "Ask Yourself Why" was the first complete song with lyrics written by Alan and Marilyn Bergman that Streisand recorded in her career. Peter Matz delivers a dynamic arrangement of this song, enabling Streisand to do her thing at the climax; he then resolves it as simply as it began.

Streisand covered three songs by the Beatles (Lennon/McCartney) on *What About Today?*—"Honey Pie," "With a Little Help from My Friends," and "Goodnight."

"Honey Pie" is this album's "Sam, You Made the Pants Too Long" or "Second Hand Rose." Streisand adopts a playful attitude, laughing hysterically during the song as she says, "I like it like that, I like this kind of music!" After her laugh breakdown, Streisand blows a razzie when she sings about the wind that blew the boat across the sea. It's quite a different interpretation from what the

Beatles recorded on their *White Album*. However, you must admire Streisand's bravery to bring an irreverent and vaudevillian humor to the song. "Honey Pie" was written by Paul McCartney as an homage to the English dance-hall songs of his father's generation, so Streisand leans into the nostalgia on this tune. It is a comic ditty and a palate cleanser after two very serious songs.

Following is the unique, almost-art-song "Punky's Dilemma." Paul Simon of Simon & Garfunkel wrote it for Mike Nichols's film *The Graduate*, but it was unused and instead ended up on their album *Bookends*. Peter Matz doesn't overdo his arrangement, and Streisand provides an understated vocal.

Streisand's rendition of Paul Simon's whimsical and clever lyrics to "Punky's Dilemma" reminds me of the story she told about an acting class exercise. "Once I was a chocolate chip," Streisand explained. "It was an exercise in giving life to inanimate objects. I was stuck into a sticky batter, put into an oven where I swelled and started to melt and burn. I was taken out of the oven where the air congealed my outer layer, leaving my insides mushy. My head—meaning my point—started to droop when somebody ate me." (Streisand, Who Am I Anyway?, 1970)

"Punky's Dilemma" is one of my favorites on the album. Yes, I'm a Citizens for Boysenberry Jam fan! Can you believe that Barbra also used to sing "Punky's Dilemma" in her act at the International Hotel in Las Vegas?

One last point to be made about this song: Streisand altered some of the lyrics. Simon wrote: "If I become a first lieutenant, would you put my photo on your piano?" Streisand struck the Vietnam Army draft reference and sang it as "a famous lady" instead of "first lieutenant." This necessitated another lyric change for Streisand. Simon's version has the photo inscribed "To Maryjane, Best wishes, Martin." Streisand sings: "From Maryjane, Best wishes to Martin."

Buffy Sainte-Marie, the Native American singer-songwriter and folk artist, wrote "Until It's Time for You to Go," which perfectly marries a modern song with Streisand's beautiful ballad singing style. It's the second Legrand arrangement on the album that is understated. The rest are a bit overblown.

"With a Little Help from My Friends" is not for everyone's taste. Legrand's take on the song is weird, beginning with a jazzy riff interrupted by a discordant bang on the piano. When Streisand warbles "and I'll try not to sing out of key," Legrand has the pianist bang out the correct key. Five times. "Thank you," Streisand purrs. (It's an obvious, unsubtle joke, no?)

Legrand then has Streisand switch tempo to a waltz as she sings, "What do I do when my love is away?" Following that, "Do you need anybody?" is sung as a big Broadway section. How many tempos does this song have? Streisand fades out "With a Little Help from My Friends" in soft jazz fashion, sounding like the end of Legrand's first number in the musical film *Les demoiselles de Rochefort* (*The Young Girls of Rochefort*). And just in case it wasn't weird enough, Streisand ends the song by vocalizing the word "help" as if she was circling down the drain in a shower. Is Legrand's arrangement of the song brilliant? Abstract? Creative? Weird? It's all the above and then some.

Michel Legrand's "Alfie" arrangement is more palatable. Barbra loves it, too—"the kind of gorgeous ballad I used to sing when I was just starting out." It just gets off to a bad start—that flourishing orchestral introduction is difficult to hear over and over when one listens to this track. The rest of the song is beautifully orchestrated with pretty strings and horn lines. I love that Streisand and Legrand chose to resolve the song with three "Alfies." Maybe I'm prejudiced, but when I hear other singers cover "Alfie," they sometimes choose odd endings that don't sound right to me. Like singing "Alfie" only twice at the end. When Barbra sings "Alfie" three times, it's an acting choice that resolves so much better for me. The first "Alfie" is questioning, the second "Alfie" sounds tender, and the third "Alfie" feels positively conclusive. That being said, I will completely contradict myself when considering Cynthia Erivo's transcendent version of "Alfie" that she sang for Dionne Warwick at her Kennedy Center Honors in 2023. My God!

"Alfie," of course, was the theme song from the 1966 Michael Caine British film of the same name. Streisand waited a few years to record it, though. Burt Bacharach joked with Streisand in 1971 that "there were sixty-four singers who recorded it before you, Barbra."

"They asked me to sing 'Alfie,'" Barbra explained earlier, "and I didn't sing it. I loved it, but they made the mistake of giving me the record of a girl singing it in London." (Twentieth Century-Fox, 1969) Singer Cilla Black recorded the Bacharach/David tune, and it was released as a single on March 25, 1966, in the UK, but the film's producers wanted an American recording artist to cover the song. "I told them to release that one; I thought she was terrific," Streisand continued. "I would feel bad about it if I recorded it in the United States. You know, it was just on my conscience. I just felt so bad about it, like I was taking something away from her, so I didn't do it." (Twentieth Century-Fox, 1969)

As far as Streisand's singing of "Alfie," I prefer her live performance from the *Timeless* concert in 1999, which was recorded by Columbia Records as a CD release. Her vocal and the arrangement for that concert are more . . . timeless.

"That's a Fine Kind o' Freedom"—with lyrics by Broadway's Martin Charnin (*Annie*)—was composed by Harold Arlen, and it took Barbra about three years to record it for an album. She first sang it live in 1965 at the benefit *Broadway Answers Selma*. This is a bold Peter Matz arrangement too. *Dee-dum! That's a fine kind of freedom!*

Barbra had greater success with Jimmy Webb's song "Didn't We" than "Little Tin Soldier," which appears on this album. Webb's allegorical lyrics about toy versus real soldiers are heavy-handed, although Matz gives us another tasteful arrangement on this song.

Finally, the third Beatles song from the *White Album*, "Goodnight," sounds as if it's been lifted from *Peter Pan* or even *Mary Poppins* as performed by Barbra Streisand. Matz scores it as a dreamy orchestral lullaby, and at the end, Streisand bids the listeners: "Everybody everywhere . . . goodnight."

What About Today? is a great Streisand album that, despite being on the cusp of musical and societal changes, ranks high as a classic 1960s Streisand musical offering. Most of the tracks are Streisand classics, and only three were recorded but left off the album: "Lost in Wonderland" and "One Day" surfaced on *Release Me* and *Release Me 2*, respectively. A song titled "Tomorrow I Will Bring You a Rose" remains unreleased. But we can always hope for *Release Me 3*?

LP released: October 1969
CD released: November 1994
Music conducted by: Lennie Hayton and Lionel Newman
Music and lyrics by: Jerry Herman
Recorded: July, August, November 1968; February - July 1969 at 20th Century Fox Recording Stage
Original sound engineer: Murray Spivack
1994 remixed album producer: Nick Redman

Catalog Numbers:
DTCS 5103 (gatefold LP, 1969, 20th Century Fox Records)
55103 (cassette)
ST-102 (LP, Casablanca label release, 1980s)
810 368-2 (CD remastered—Philips 1994)
P10368 (cassette—Philips 1994)

Side One:

1. Just Leave Everything To Me
2. It Takes A Woman
3. It Takes A Woman (Reprise)
4. Put On Your Sunday Clothes
5. Ribbons Down My Back
6. Dancing
7. Before The Parade Passes By

Side Two:

1. Elegance
2. Love Is Only Love
3. Hello, Dolly!
4. It Only Takes A Moment
5. So Long Dearie
6. Finale

Note: Marianne McAndrew's ("Irene Molloy") vocals were dubbed by Melissa Stafford (solo vocals) and Gilda Maiken (ensemble vocals).

The *Hello, Dolly!* soundtrack album was released by 20th Century Fox Records in 1969. When Barbra Streisand was signed to star in the picture, a deal was worked out with her record label to allow Streisand's *Dolly* vocals to appear on the 20th Century Fox Records label. The *Hello, Dolly!* soundtrack is one of only three Streisand albums not released by Columbia Records (the others: *Funny Girl Original Broadway Cast* and *Funny Lady*).

Jerry Herman contributed two new songs for the movie version of *Hello, Dolly!* that were not originally in the Broadway play. The new ballad for the film, "Love Is Only Love," is the same music as "Gotta Be a Dream," which Herman wrote for a 1961 musical called *Madame Aphrodite* (which ran for thirteen performances). The song was then rewritten as "Love Is Only Love" for Herman's 1966 hit musical, *Mame*—but it was cut from the show. Herman then interpolated the song into the *Hello, Dolly!* movie for Streisand. The second song, "Just Leave Everything to Me," was composed for Barbra's specific cadences and opens the film.

Hello, Dolly! has had three incarnations as a soundtrack album. First it was released by 20th Century Fox Records as a "deluxe album" in 1969. The gatefold album unfolded and included liner notes and excerpts of Jerry Herman's lyrics.

In the early 1980s, PolyGram bought 20th Century Fox Records, and all assets were consolidated into the company's Casablanca label. Probably around 1982, Casablanca released the soundtrack again, this time without the gatefold artwork.

For many years, *Hello, Dolly!* was the only Streisand album not available on CD. In 1994, Philips (parent company of PolyGram) released *Dolly* on CD for the first time for the film's twenty-fifth anniversary. (PolyGram has, to date, been absorbed by Universal Music Group.) In 1994, PolyGram owned the rights to the original album, and Fox owned and archived the actual music elements that went into creating the soundtrack album.

Dolly CD producer Nick Redman worked closely with music score remixer Brian Risner and digital mastering technician Dan Hersch (at DigiPrep in Hollywood) on the original multitrack elements. Redman insisted that the CD be created from a remix of the original multitrack tapes instead of simply digitizing the original analog soundtrack album.

Redman and his team used the eight-track analog masters when working with *Dolly*'s soundtrack. "We were able to work with elements that were one generation away from the original source, and we had the latitude and freedom to alter the balance of the music slightly where we felt it fit." (Konder, 1995)

Fox considered releasing a deluxe soundtrack for *Dolly*'s fiftieth anniversary in 2019, but movie insiders told me the original master tapes were too damaged to be used, unfortunately. It was also unlucky timing that in March 2019, Fox's film division was acquired by Disney, causing many films and projects in development at Fox to be paused.

The soundtrack is incomplete and could have benefited from another modern pass before the original sound elements were lost forever. Missing from all versions of the albums are:

- the main credits music
- "Call on Dolly"
- Irene and Cornelius's verse of "Dancing"
- intermission music
- the new verse for "Elegance" ("snobs that slobs throw roses at/we look down our noses at . . . ")
- outro music

Matt on *Hello Dolly*

The joy of the *Hello, Dolly!* soundtrack album is listening to Barbra sing those Jerry Herman songs beautifully. All arguments that "she was too young for the role" disappear. You just enjoy the music and her singing. Barbra is in exquisite voice, particularly on "It Takes a Woman (Reprise)" and "Love Is Only Love." She kills "So Long Dearie" with her fast-paced delivery and comedy.

"Love Is Only Love" is my favorite, though. Barbra sings it so effortlessly with her buoyant voice. Jerry Herman's lyric is so interesting here too. When I was younger, I was annoyed by the sentiment in the song—what do you mean, *love* is only love? The violins are all a *bluff*? How cynical! But now that I'm a fifty-something-aged person, the lyrics hit me deeper. "Love Is Only Love," in fact, has a lot in common with "Isn't This Better" from *Funny Lady*. Both are songs for an older and wiser person who realizes "passion is fine, but passion burns fast." Or, as Jerry Herman wrote, "If you're really wise, the silence of his eyes will tell you love is only love, and it's wonderful enough."

Or as Mary J. Blige sang: "No more drama!"

Finally, this may be heretical to write in a book about Barbra Streisand's music, but is it bad that one of my favorite songs on this album is "Ribbons Down My Back," which was vocalized by Melissa Stafford? Oh, the pure pleasure of that voice on the last phrase, "that he might notice me."

I wonder if Barbra has ever considered recording "Ribbons" or even "It Only Takes a Moment" from this score? Both were not her songs in the movie, but she would sound wonderful singing them.

DECADE 60 ENCORE

Barbra Streisand's recording career in the 1960s began with Broadway cast albums and ended with major motion picture soundtracks. In between those landmark albums, she shared her unique interpretations of song standards and Broadway's most idiosyncratic tunes. In addition to becoming a bona fide movie star, Streisand conquered the medium of television and released albums to support those specials. Streisand's appeal seemed to be her beautiful uniqueness. Her line in *Funny Girl* manifested itself true: "I'm a bagel on a plate full of onion rolls."

Once Barbra signed with Columbia Records, she proceeded to make her own kind of music. She was clear from the start that she'd follow her own muse: "There are so many tunes which have been sung before by great people that I don't feel I have to interpret them. They've been sung already, you know?" (Syndicated, 1963)

She explained: "When I got my first club job, I had to put an act together. I hated mushy love songs. And every other singer always seemed to be doing the same hit numbers from the same Broadway shows. I knew a guy who had a big collection of old seventy-eight r.p.m. records from the 1930s and '40s. I was looking for songs that were actable, songs that had a kind of story in them. People told me I needed chic songs because the club was sophisticated. I couldn't care less. So, I picked the silliest song imaginable: 'Who's Afraid of the Big Bad Wolf?'" (Lobsenz, 1963)

With Barbra's freedom to choose her own material protected by the contracts Marty Erlichman negotiated for her, her output in the sixties was prolific. She put out an album (sometimes two!) each year, all the while completing media appearances, getting married, and having a child too.

In fact, 1963 alone was chock-full of major milestones. Just look at what happened to Barbra in a mere twelve months: Her first two albums with Columbia were released; she appeared on *The Tonight Show*, *The Ed Sullivan Show*, *The Dinah Shore Show*, and *The Judy Garland Show*; she sang at the hungry i, the Cocoanut Grove, Basin Street East, and the Riviera in Las Vegas with Liberace; she performed for President Kennedy; and she was cast as Fanny Brice in *Funny Girl*.

Barbra wrote: "Even I had to admit that 1963 had been an extraordinary year. I had been making $125 a week, and now I was being offered incredible sums to sing for a week . . . $8,000, $10,000, $15,000. It was all like play money to me. I couldn't even comprehend it."

The sixties marched along as Barbra recorded the Great American Songbook while the British Invasion arrived (the Beatles, the Rolling Stones), Motown grooved (the Supremes, Marvin Gaye), rock rocked out (Janis Joplin), and new sounds arrived in the form of the Beach Boys, the Doors, and Simon & Garfunkel.

While hardly anyone expected Barbra Streisand to cover "Piece of My Heart" by Joplin, Columbia Records pressed her to update her sound, as we saw with the album *What About Today?* The music trend must have been perplexing to Barbra, who was raised listening to the *Your Hit Parade* on the radio, with songs by Perry Como, Nat King Cole, Dinah Shore, and (her favorite!) Joni James.

America was changing, though: the equal rights movement was gaining steam, and racial strife and widespread opposition to the Vietnam War were tearing at the fabric of the country.

"Look," Barbra stated, "I'm labeled, pigeonholed. I play for middle-class audiences in Vegas. I made those definitely establishment [movies] . . . But I ask you, twenty-eight—is that old? Is twenty-eight all that old?" (Lewis G. , 1971)

THE 1970S

Released: July 1970
Produced by: Wally Gold
Original recording engineer: Don Meehan
Music by: Burton Lane
Lyrics by: Alan Jay Lerner
Music arranged and conducted by: Nelson Riddle
CD restored by: John Arrias at B&J Studio
CD remastered by: Bernie Grundman

Catalog Numbers:
AS 30086 (Columbia LP)
S 30086 (Columbia Masterworks LP)
SA 30086 (8-track)
SR 30086 (reel-to-reel)
A-20716 (CBS 1989 CD)
CK 57377 (1993 remastered CD)

Side One:

1. Hurry! It's Lovely Up Here
2. Main Title: On A Clear Day
3. Love With All The Trimmings
4. Melinda
5. Go To Sleep

Side Two:

1. He Isn't You
2. What Did I Have That I Don't Have?
3. Come Back To Me
4. On A Clear Day (You Can See Forever)
5. On A Clear Day (You Can See Forever) (Reprise)

The original soundtrack recording of *On a Clear Day You Can See Forever* was released by Columbia Records to coincide with Paramount's release of the film starring Barbra Streisand as a reincarnated student named Daisy Gamble. *Clear Day* was Streisand's third big movie musical, and Columbia gave the album a handsome release—it was gatefold in design, with black-and-white photos inside and a summary of the story.

The soundtrack album is classic Streisand—beautiful vocals, with arrangements by Nelson Riddle—the only time she worked with him. In all my research, I have never found an interview or quote from Riddle about his work with Streisand, which is curious. Riddle's collaborations with Frank Sinatra are legendary, and he had a late-career resurgence when he arranged and conducted Linda Ronstadt's albums of American standards.

The only complaint about *On a Clear Day* is that Yves Montand's vocals are not as exciting and nice to listen to as Barbra's tracks. So, basically, that's every track in which Streisand *doesn't* sing. This is especially true on "Come Back to Me," in which Montand is required to wrap his thick French accent around the intricate rhymes written by Alan Jay Lerner. It was a silly idea to cast him in this movie, which is too bad. "I could tell [Yves Montand] was uncomfortable in the part, and that made me feel bad for him. Here was a man who was virile and strong when he was singing in French, wearing his trademark brown shirt and pants. He could fill concert halls. But when he stepped onto an American sound stage, he had to struggle to act in English. It was as if he wasn't the same person, and that made acting with him a bit strange," Streisand wrote.

On a Clear Day was released in the compact disc format around 1989. The sound was probably taken from the original LP master, because it featured a lot of reverb on Streisand's vocals, just like the original album. Also, the "click" of Streisand's heels in "What Did I Have That I Don't Have?" was very pronounced on the 1989 disc; the remastered CD diminishes the sound of the heels, although it's still audible. *Clear Day* was then restored and remastered on CD in October 1993 as part of Columbia Records's *11 Essential Barbra Streisand Releases*.

SIGNATURE STREISAND

"ON A CLEAR DAY YOU CAN SEE FOREVER"

No one sings "On a Clear Day You Can See Forever" like Barbra Streisand, which sounds obvious but isn't. If you sample the versions of the song on Spotify, you'll notice that it is mostly covered by male singers, and they're generally singing jazz versions. Even Sarah Vaughan and Carmen McRae swing in their versions. Streisand's arrangement starts small and builds to a thundering climax, with the last note held for what seems like "forever more." Her voice blooms on those last notes like Daisy's overstimulated flowers.

Streisand has sung "On a Clear Day You Can See Forever" at almost all her live concert engagements since the 1970s even though she left it out of her repertoire in the 2006-2007 tours as well as the recent "Barbra: The Music . . . The Mem'ries . . . The Magic" tour. It was very exciting during her 2012 concerts when, halfway through the tour, Barbra began singing "Clear Day" as her opening number. Gently descending the stairs, Barbra sang, "You can see forever and ever and ever . . . " as she approached the edge of the stage and her adoring audience. Thrilling!

Whenever I've heard Barbra sing "On a Clear Day" in concert, I am humbled. It's an honor to hear her sing such an iconic and dynamic song—she gives me goosebumps. Not only that . . . the song has such a positive message about becoming who you truly are. Barbra's interpretation of that includes spine-tingling, belting notes!

Stoney End

Released: February 1971
Produced by: Richard Perry
Engineers: Glen Kolotkin, Rafael O. Valentin, Sy Mitchell, and Pete Weiss
Mix down: Sy Mitchell, Glen Kolotkin, and Bob Breault
Design and photography by: Tom Wilkes and Barry Feinstein for Camouflage Productions

Catalog Numbers:
KC 30378 (LP)
PCT 30378 (cassette)
CR 30378 (reel-to-reel)
CA 30378 (8-track)
CK 30378 (CD)
CQ 30378 (quadraphonic LP)
PC 30378 (LP reissue)
CK 725022 (2008, CD, SBME SPECIAL MKTS.)

Side One:

1. I Don't Know Where I Stand
2. Hands Off The Man (Flim Flam Man)
3. If You Could Read My Mind
4. Just A Little Lovin' (Early In The Morning)
5. Let Me Go
6. Stoney End

Side Two:

1. No Easy Way Down
2. Time And Love
3. Maybe
4. Free The People
5. I'll Be Home

In the mid-1970s, Richard Perry was a renowned record producer who crafted number-one singles for Harry Nilsson, Carly Simon, and Ringo Starr.

"I realized when I heard the *What About Today?* album that she hadn't [contemporized her sound]. But I felt very strongly that I could do it with her," Perry explained. "I told Clive Davis, who was the president of Columbia Records at the time, that I would very much like to have the opportunity to take a shot with Barbra. So, Clive told me to get some material together, which I did. He thought it was great, so he set up the meeting. Barbra had been planning on doing another album at the time called *The Singer*, and Clive asked her to put it aside to consider working with this new, young producer, i.e., *moi*. In any event, we met, and we hit it off immediately. Everybody was saying, 'Well, how are you going to get along with her?' I said, 'Two Jews from Brooklyn, you can't go far wrong.'

"She loved the material I played for her," Perry recollected. "I brought her everything from Joni Mitchell, Randy Newman, just a real assortment of contemporary songs at its best." (Perry, 2005)

Barbra recorded *Stoney End* during several studio dates in 1970, all sessions produced by Perry. Studio engineer Bill Schnee confessed, "Richard had quite a reputation in the 1970s, but it wasn't all good. Was he fastidious? Yes. A perfectionist? Definitely. Overbearing sometimes? Maybe. Over budget? Always. But talented? Without question." (Schnee, 2021)

The first session, on July 29, 1970, was the longest session in the history of the Los Angeles musicians' union. "It started at seven o'clock," Perry recounted. "Barbra showed up at eight, and usually when you're working with string players in a big orchestra, they work from seven to ten—on the rare occasion they'll do an hour overtime, seven to eleven—and then they're out the door. Well, the session ended at five thirty in the morning with the full orchestra still there, and nobody said boo; no one complained for a minute. We did half of the album in one night." (Perry, 2005)

Barbra wrote: "I thought, Okay, let me try it. I was open to suggestions . . . as long as he didn't try to turn me into something I was not. Just because something was popular didn't mean it was good for me!"

An interesting note: "For the first time I was working with a producer my own age," she wrote. "We were both twenty-eight and both born in Brooklyn. We became fast friends."

The single of "Stoney End" was released in September 1970—in advance of the album. "We had a bet over whether 'Stoney End' would be a hit," Barbra explained. "He said yes, I said no. The bet was settled when we were driving on Sunset Boulevard, and a local DJ announced on the radio that the record had just hit #1 in Los Angeles. What a great way to lose!" (Streisand, *Just for the Record* liner notes, 1991)

"It's kind of ironic that 'Stoney End' became the title of the album, because that song was not an easy fit for me." Barbra wrote. "I had to put my head into a different space and I had no idea what it was about. The lyrics were baffling. What did 'going down the stoney end' even mean?" Laura Nyro wrote the song when she was a teenager, and Popmatters.com succinctly summarized it: "The song tells the story of a woman who has spent the night with a man whose sexual passion she mistook for love. He's left her, and now she feels guilty. She yearns for the comfort of her mother and to be able to start over. The 'Stoney End' may refer to the Biblical punishment for sex out of wedlock, maybe a return to the mines of her mother, or perhaps a death from drugs that she now uses to end her pain and fury. Or it may just be a metaphor for the rocky road she will now have to travel as an unwed mother herself." (Horowitz, 2017)

Streisand and Perry spent the rest of 1970 in New York recording the album. "Barbra was a consummate pro," Perry said. "She would come in with the song prepared, no matter how far apart it might be from her normal repertoire. I was tremendously impressed by that. There's a reason why she's Barbra Streisand." (Perry, 2005)

The final session for the *Stoney End* album was done in Las Vegas while Barbra was in town performing at the Riviera and Hilton hotels. Barbra sang some of the new songs in her Vegas show—"Let Me Go," "No Easy Way Down," and "I Don't Know Where I Stand" were sung live, and Barbra even closed some of her shows with "Stoney End."

The cover photo on *Stoney End* was shot just outside Las Vegas in the Mojave Desert, looking toward Sunrise Mountain. The album cover design was by Tom Wilkes, and Barry Feinstein photographed Streisand in the desert. Wilkes said: "Someone—probably Barbra—suggested we have antique furniture placed on the truck. So we rented a red velvet couch and some chairs. That afternoon Barbra arrived in a limo. I remember it was winter and very cold. She put up with a lot of different shootings—in the cab of the truck, on back of the truck, and on the road. She was a real trouper. She kept jumping up and down, and putting her hands under her arms, because it was cold, real cold. She never complained; there was no star stuff. Afterwards she invited us all back to her house. She had this rented house in Vegas, and we hung out there for two or three hours. She fed us and gave us drinks and made sure we were comfortable. Later, Barry and I picked the shot for the cover, and both Barbra and Richard Perry agreed on it." (Considine, 1985)

Songwriter Randy Newman, who played the piano during the recording of his songs for the album, also wrote a song called "Lonely at the Top" for Frank Sinatra. He suggested that Streisand record it. "Listen all you fools out there/Go on and love me—I don't care/Oh, it's lonely at the top" were the lyrics. But Streisand declined to record it, telling Newman, "People will think that I mean it."

Other songs recorded but not released for this album include "He's a Runner" by Nyro, "Because" by Lennon/McCartney, and "Your Love's Return" by Gordon Lightfoot.

The *Stoney End* LP was released to stores in February 1971. The album climbed to number ten on the *Billboard* pop charts, with Columbia Records running ads and publicizing the LP as "a new album by a young singer." In fact, *Stoney End* earned a gold certificate from the RIAA only two months after it was released. Streisand's album occupied the music album charts with other big 1971 hits like *Jesus Christ Superstar*, *Close to You* by the Carpenters, and albums by Cat Stevens, 5th Dimension, James Taylor, and Emerson, Lake & Palmer.

The quadraphonic version of *Stoney End* was remixed by Sy Mitchell and had five tracks with different mixes and sometimes alternate vocal takes:

- "Time and Love" is a slightly different tempo, with alternate vocals.
- Barbra's laugh is not included at the beginning of "Maybe."
- There are alternate vocals at the end of "Stoney End."
- "No Easy Way Down" sounds like a different take altogether.
- "Free the People" is a different mix.

For fans, *Stoney End* was an important album in Streisand's discography. It redefined Streisand as an effective pop/rock singer, even though the music critics were split on how successful she was in the transition.

Matt on *Stoney End*

Stoney End certainly feels like a 1970s pop album. Streisand and Perry achieved what they set out to do—make Barbra sound contemporary. I think *Barbra Joan Streisand*, released a mere six months later, had a better recipe as far as its mix of pop and standards.

Stoney End contains three songs by Laura Nyro, whose music was described by *Life* magazine in 1970 as "songs that blend gospel, rock 'n' roll, jazz and blues . . . lyrics that are knowing, evocative, elusive, personal." (Paley, 1970) The songs Streisand chose to record definitely fall into the "good time, gospel, rhythm-and-blues" category that Nyro wrote in.

Streisand's "Time and Love," for instance, sounds remarkably like Nyro's recording, including the background singers. By the way, Clydie King and Venetta Fields—the Oreos from *A Star Is Born*—both appear on *Stoney End* songs as backup singers.

Another Nyro tune, "Flim Flam Man," doesn't stray far from the original arrangement either, including the jaunty piano, horns, and backup singers.

When you add Streisand's cover of "Stoney End," the Nyro trilogy of songs is up-tempo and gospel-esque on this album. I'm not sure gospel is Barbra's most successful genre to sing in, but then "Stoney End" was a big hit for Barbra, and fans were elated to hear her sing it in concert thirty to forty years later!

Barbra seems more at home with "If You Could Read My Mind" and "I Don't Know Where I Stand"—introspective ballads by Gordon Lightfoot and Joni Mitchell respectively. "I Don't Know Where I Stand" is ethereal and, as Mitchell's lyrics say, "all muted and misty, so drowsy now . . . " The song is a stunning opener for the album, and bewitching. I'm surprised Streisand never sang it live in later years.

Listen, Randy Newman's songs have never really thrilled me, but Barbra is successful with "I'll Be Home" and "Let Me Go." Even the Newman outtakes—"I Think It's Going To Rain Today" and "Living Without You," included on *Release Me* and *Release Me 2* respectively—fit well into Streisand's vocal wheelhouse. Randy even played the piano on these tracks.

Barbra's arranger on *Stoney End*, Gene Page, gave Barbra's music a new sound that placed her firmly in the 1970s, without backsliding too much toward the standards and theater songs Streisand sang previously. Page arranged eight of the eleven songs on the album, so his presence is almost complete. He was in his thirties at the time and had a long list of credits, arranging numerous records at the Motown label, strings for Barry White, Diana Ross, the Righteous Brothers, and more.

For me, "No Easy Way Down" and "Free the People" are too gospel and are not my favorites to listen to. Still, it's exciting to hear Barbra play in that sandbox, even if she's a bit tentative. On a bootleg recording of Barbra's 1970 show at the Riviera Hotel, she sounds downright definitive singing "No Easy Way Down," with her band and backup singers really rocking it out supporting her.

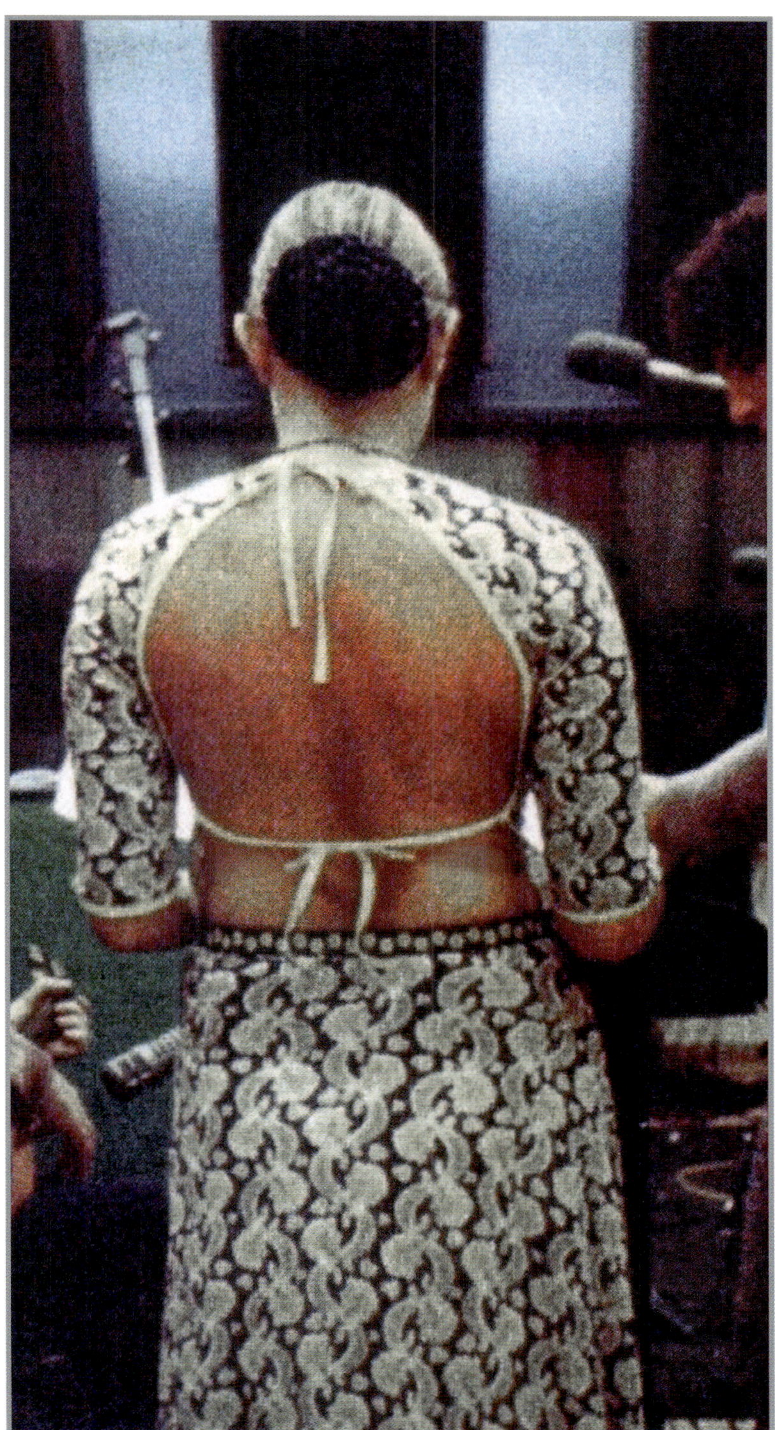

Released: August 1971
Produced by: Richard Perry
Album design: Virginia Team
Photography: Ed Thrasher
Engineering: Sy Mitchell
Remix engineers: Bill Schnee, Sy Mitchell
Recordists: Bill Schnee, George Beauregard, Willie "The Kid" Greer, John Fiore, Jack Andrews
CD digitally remastered by: Joe Gastwirt at Digital Magnetics Studio

Catalog Numbers:
KC 30792 (LP)
PC 30792 (LP, reissue)
CA 30792 (8-track)
CR 30792 (reel-to-reel)
CQ 30792 (quadraphonic LP, 1972)
CK 30792 (CD remastered 1994)

Side One:

1. Beautiful
2. Love
3. Where You Lead
4. I Never Meant To Hurt You
5. One Less Bell To Answer/A House Is Not A Home

Side Two:

1. Space Captain
2. Since I Fell For You
3. Mother
4. The Summer Knows
5. I Mean To Shine
6. You've Got A Friend

My go-to Streisand album of 1970s pop songs is this one, not *Stoney End*. With Richard Perry producing again, *Barbra Joan Streisand* is the album where he hit his stride with her; they seem to be more sympatico on this one, combining standards with contemporary songs.

Gene Page was back only to arrange two songs; a handful of arrangers contributed to the album, including Richard (Dick) Hazard. Hazard was a television composer, orchestrator, conductor, and songwriter who wrote the charts for "I Never Meant to Hurt You" and "The Summer Knows." Years later, he would compose the music (with Ira Newborn) for Barbra's film *All Night Long*.

Since Richard Perry had produced the all-girl rock group Fanny, they worked on *BJS*, arranging and playing on two songs: "Where You Lead" and "Space Captain." One of Fanny's members, Jean Millington, recalled: "We were badass; we just needed to learn how to record. Which we did as fast as we could and in short order, as Richard Perry basically taught us and—he was tremendously skilled, learning constantly, and was as voracious as we were. We were all into it. It was hard work, but fun. And, actually, he was an excellent teacher." (France, 2014)

The group, known for its tight harmonies (all the members sang on its records), comprised sisters June Millington and Jean Millington on guitar and bass guitar, Nickey Barclay on keyboards, and Alice de Buhr on drums.

David Bowie was a huge fan of Fanny and spoke to *Rolling Stone* in 1999 about the group. "They were extraordinary: They wrote everything, they played like motherfuckers, they were just colossal and wonderful, and nobody's ever mentioned them. They're as important as anybody else who's ever been, ever; it just wasn't their time." (Danton, 2018)

Richard Perry used them as studio musicians on Barbra's *Stoney End* album, but for *BJS* he got them involved with arranging and playing for Barbra.

"We met at the [Whisky a Go Go]," June Millington remembered. "[Barbra] didn't put on any airs. She came [to the studio], saying she was nervous because she'd never sung live with a band before, and I believed her. In fact, I sat across from her, knee to knee, and went over the vocal with her. If it were an act, it worked well, 'cause we were by then all ready to go and she nailed it from take one. (I think they took take five but it doesn't matter, she nailed it from the jump)." (Farber, 2018)

Nick DeCaro, a musician, arranger, producer, and songwriter, had a keen ear and arranged the first two songs on the album.

Kenny Welch and his wife Mitzie were a music composer/lyricist duo who wrote, composed, and arranged for Carol Burnett and others. Kenny created the arrangement of "One Less Bell to Answer/A House Is Not a Home" for Barbra when she appeared on Burt Bacharach's television special in March 1971. They were also responsible for Streisand's unique version of "Happy Days Are Here Again."

Richard Perry and Barbra recorded the *BJS* songs quickly, in three sessions: April 20, April 21, and May 4, 1971—all at Columbia Recording Studios in Hollywood, California.

Drummer Jim Keltner played those sessions and loved working with Barbra. "Back then, she was this major, major force, you know?" he stated. "Unbelievable voice. And that was in the days when the artist would record live with you. It was a tremendous thing to hear a voice like that in your headphones." (Zulaica, 2012)

"I Mean to Shine" was written by Donald Fagen and Walter Becker—they later became the group Steely Dan. Kenny Vance, a singer and songwriter in the band Jay & the Americans, reminisced about Fagen and Becker. "In 1970, I got a call from record producer Richard Perry, a friend who was making an album with Barbra Streisand; he was looking for new material," Vance wrote. "Richard placed one of their songs on the album. We met Barbra Streisand. In rehearsal, Donald played the piano and we taught her the song . . . On the recording, Donald played the organ. It was the first mainstream recording of a song written by Becker and Fagen." (Vance, 2017) Streisand actually recorded "I Mean to Shine" during her *Stoney End* sessions in September 1970, but it was used on *BJS* instead.

One of the songs recorded for *BJS* remains unreleased, and I'm desperate to hear it! Barbra sang "Think About Your Troubles" by Harry Nilsson, heard in the animated fable *The Point!*, which aired on ABC. As a child, I was so impressed with the cartoon, which was about a roundheaded boy living with pointy-headed people. "Think About Your Troubles" has a brilliant, stream-of-consciousness lyric and a catchy Nilsson melody that recalls his underrated score for the movie *Popeye*. Hopefully we'll get to hear this song on a future *Release Me* . . . meanwhile, check out Nilsson's recording on YouTube and imagine Streisand's rendition.

BJS was another contemporary music hit for Barbra—earning gold certification (500,000 sold) just four months after its release.

Like *Stoney End*, *BJS* was remixed by Columbia as a quadraphonic album, and six tracks sound different and sometimes have alternate vocals:

- "Beautiful" sounds different due to its alternate mix on the quad.
- "Where You Lead"—an alternate take.
- "Space Captain"—an alternate take with different tempo and vocals.
- "Mother" has alternate vocals.
- "I Mean to Shine" is an alternate take.
- The ocean sounds in "The Summer Knows" have been removed for the quad mix.

Photographer Ed Thrasher shot the cover and inside photos of Streisand, and the session was quite informal, with Thrasher capturing Barbra as she worked in the studio.

A design element is missing from the CD which involves the front and back covers of the LP. Streisand's first name is spelled professionally on the front cover—"Barbra" without the extra 'a.' On the back cover, accompanying a smiling photo of her, the name is spelled "Barbara." *Barbra Joan Streisand* sold over five hundred thousand units, earning its Gold status with the RIAA. "That Gold was gratifying," Barbra wrote: "And I had proved something to myself . . . I could change with the times."

Matt on *BJS*

If you bought the LP in the 1970s, you received a twenty-two-by-thirty-three-inch foldout poster of Streisand wearing a tie-dye T-shirt and a newsboy hat. Some fans still have it hanging on their wall! On this album, Streisand recorded three songs by Carole King that appeared on her iconic 1971 album, *Tapestry*. Also, this time Streisand's arrangers departed from the original recordings, making the songs sound more Streisand than King. The group Head arranged Streisand's version of "You've Got a Friend," and it's beautifully Streisand-esque. Fanny arranged "Where You Lead," and Nick DeCaro was responsible for "Beautiful" (which is in an interesting but lower key than usual for Streisand).

Coming back to Laura Nyro, Streisand strikes gold with "I Never Meant to Hurt You," which is so sensitive and touching.

Streisand manages to include two standards with "One Less Bell" and "The Summer Knows," by her friends the Bergmans. They don't feel out of place, though. Somehow they integrate very well into this contemporary album. Bette Midler used to achieve that balance on her early albums too, mixing old chestnuts like "Am I Blue" and "Skylark" with contemporary tunes like "Superstar" or "Daytime Hustler."

Barbra also sings two John Lennon songs, both from his 1970 album *John Lennon/ Plastic Ono Band.*

Lennon, who had moved on from the Beatles and in with Yoko Ono, has a loyal following, and I've discovered that most Lennon enthusiasts strongly dislike Streisand's rendition of his songs, especially "Mother." The usual complaint is that Lennon shrieked at the end of the song because he'd been participating in primal scream therapy, which sounds exactly like what it is. According to those critics, Barbra didn't "get down" enough with her vocals.

John Kruth, however, in his book about Lennon and Ono, was complimentary, writing that "she didn't try to out scream John on the song's coda. Instead, Streisand's voice soared, sounding like she meant every word of this bitter farewell." (Kruth, 2021)

You must assume Barbra was attracted to the song for some personal reason, and she sings the hell out of it. I also enjoy Gene Page and Richard Perry's new arrangement, featuring Perry playing the pipe organ. Lennon begins his version with the very heavy and depressing sound of a funeral bell ringing; on Streisand's recording, it's a funeral organ as it would be played in a church.

"Love," which is the other John Lennon song, is beautifully sung, spun like a delicate spider's web. Streisand even multitracks her own backup vocals. Bill Schnee was running the tape machine April 21, 1971, when she recorded "Love." He wrote, "I had never heard a singer like Barbra—a singer with so much control—and I'm not sure I have since then either. . . . I realized how doing vocals in the studio was like having a front row seat at a private concert from an artist, giving you an up-close-and-personal touch with them." (Schnee, 2021)

Has anyone else ever considered "Space Captain" as the funky companion song to "Marty the Martian"?

"Since I Fell for You" is expertly supported by Gene Page's classic orchestration and has Barbra's soulful singing. "What can I do? I'm still, I'm still in love with you, oh I . . . " One of the best notes she's ever hit on record. So effortless and, yes, primal. Take that, John Lennon!

Released: October 1972
Recorded live: April 15, 1972
Produced by: Richard Perry
Conducted by: David Shire
Vocal director: Eddie Kendricks
Background singers: The Eddie Kendrix Singers [Venetta Fields, Marti McCall, Geraldine Jones, Clydie King]
Joe Guercio—medley design of "Sweet Inspiration/ Where You Lead" and "Sing /Make Your Own Kind of Music."
Photography: Steve Schapiro
Illustration: Robert Redding
Liner notes: Mort Goode

Catalog Numbers:
KC 31760 (1972 gatefold LP)
PC 31760 (LP reissue, without poster)
CR 31760 (reel-to-reel)
CQ-31760 (quadraphonic LP)
PCT 31760 (cassette)
CM 31760 (MiniDisc, 1994)
CK 31760 (1987 CD; 1994 remastered CD)

Side One:

1. Sing/Make Your Own Kind Of Music
2. Starting Here, Starting Now
3. Don't Rain On My Parade
4. Monologue
5. On A Clear Day (You Can See Forever)
6. Sweet Inspiration/Where You Lead

Side Two:

1. Didn't We
2. My Man
3. Stoney End
4. Sing/Happy Days Are Here Again
5. People

This concert was a political fundraiser for Democratic presidential candidate George McGovern. He was running against the Republican incumbent, Richard Nixon, with a platform that appealed to many young Americans: withdrawal from the Vietnam War, a reduction in defense spending, and ratification of the Equal Rights Amendment.

Streisand's show at the Forum was essentially a record of the Las Vegas act that Barbra performed at the Hilton Hotel in early 1972. At the Forum, she cut three songs from her Vegas show and took an audience poll about one of the songs she would sing. Not sung at the Forum: "Value," "My Buddy"/"How About Me," and "One Less Bell to Answer/"A House Is Not a Home" (yes—she used to sing that live in Vegas with a prerecording of her own voice). Even Barbra's Vegas stage was shipped over to the Forum for the one-night-only concert.

Actor and director Warren Beatty produced the entire concert for McGovern, drafting Carole King, Quincy Jones, and James Taylor to perform (separately).

"I wasn't doing live performances then, but Warren is very persuasive and impressive, as a matter of fact," Streisand recalled in 2008 at Beatty's American Film Institute salute. "He masterminded everything from the invitations to getting famous people to be ushers."

Columbia Records decided to record the show to be released as a live album, so the label parked a mobile recording truck outside the Forum. Knowing the concert would be immortalized as a record, Streisand rehearsed the band from around 2:00 p.m. to 6:00 p.m.

Closing the show, Streisand appeared onstage around 11:00 p.m. wearing a black satin pantsuit with a red tank top underneath. The recording is outstanding, and in the days before punch-ins and digital overdubs, it's impressive that Streisand is pitch-perfect throughout the entire show.

For many years, *Live Concert at the Forum* was my favorite album as a young fan of Miss Streisand, receiving many, many plays on my stereo system. I was a teenager, and Barbra's song selection appealed to me, as did her very funny asides and monologues, including the one about smoking pot.

Did I know she was pretending to smoke a joint? Did I care? Or did she really smoke it? In recent years, Barbra has said she didn't smoke much marijuana. But she told *Rolling Stone* that she got nervous during her Las Vegas hotel shows. Barbra said, "It occurred to me to do this funny little routine—actually telling the audience about my hang-up. Then at the end, I'd take out a joint and light it. First, just faking it. Then I started lighting live joints, passing them around to the band—you know. It was great—it relieved all my tensions. Hmm . . . I wonder if I should tell that story." (Lewis G. , 1971) Have you ever wondered why, after the first verse of "Starting Here," the audience applauds in the middle of the song? Streisand fans who saw these shows tell me that Barbra did a "bit" here—she removed her black choker, which elicited the applause.

Live Concert at the Forum is one of the Streisand albums in her discography that sounds different, depending on which version you play. The original LP has a particular mix in which the backup singers' vocals are more pronounced and the running time is shorter due to the limitations of vinyl. Then there's the quadraphonic version, which contains a short extra comment during Barbra's "facing fears" monologue. Barbra, as she handles her teacup, laughs and says, "Forgot to take it out . . . " I imagine she is kibitzing with the teabag in the cup. Then you get to John Arrias's compact disc remix of the album in 1995. Arrias confirmed that the concert "was completely remixed from scratch." Arrias explained to *ICE* magazine [*International CD Exchange*] that "I went back to the original multi-track master and remixed every track. And some of the versions are extended now; on 'Sweet Inspiration,' for instance, they faded it out early [on the LP and original CD]; I kept it going an extra minute or so." (Streisand Catalog Overhauled, 1995)

Unfortunately, Arrias did not include a short piano intro that preceded "My Man." We're talking about a few seconds of intro piano. But it is gone on the remaster.

Fans who bought the original LP received a large foldout poster of Robert Redding's cover art.

The standout song on this live concert album is "Didn't We," which Streisand had recorded at that time in her career but never released. The studio version of "Didn't We" came out forty years later on her *Release Me* album. Until then, though, this live version was the only one we had, and she certainly sings it passionately. It must be noted that *Forum* contains three really excellent 1970s medleys created for Barbra's Vegas hotel gigs. Don Hannah—one of the Vegas strip's busiest arrangers—created them all. Hannah arranged "Sing" from *Sesame Street* with the pop hit "Make Your Own Kind of Music"; next, he blended the contemporary "Sweet Inspiration" with Carole King's "Where You Lead"; and, finally, he created a musical through line to Barbra's concert by marrying her first song, "Sing," with one of her most famous chestnuts, "Happy Days," to end the concert.

Matt on *Forum*

Even though this book concentrates on Barbra's music and albums, I must mention a lament I hear often from Barbra fans: when will they finally release the home video of this concert? The short answer is *never*! Barbra's concert at the Forum was not filmed or videotaped. Only its audio was recorded.

Back in the 1970s, they simply did not film everything like they do nowadays. Only a few minutes of newsreel footage exists from this concert. Back in 1972, the national news cameramen were not charged with the task of filming the entire show. There were after shots of the crowd and George McGovern onstage with all the stars—the main reason for the event. And that's what exists: a few seconds of Barbra singing "People" and then footage of McGovern walking onstage with King, Taylor, Jones, and Streisand.

Capturing the Central Park concert on videotape was a complicated video magic trick that Barbra and crew pulled off—no retakes, and completely live, battling the elements. But with *Forum*, she was sharing billing with other stars and certainly did not want to take over the proceedings of the concert by staging camera angles or doing retakes. It wasn't until 1986 with *One Voice* that Barbra performed a concert for a live and television audience simultaneously.

Released: November 1973
Produced by: Martin Erlichman
Arranged by: Ken and Mitzie Welch
Musical director: Jack Parnell
Cover photo by: Baron Wolman
Inside cover design: Paul Perlow
Liner notes: Mort Goode

Catalog Numbers:
*KC 32655 (LP)**
*PC 32655 (LP)**
PCT 32655 (cassette)
1R1 6138 (reel-to-reel)
CA 32655 (8-track)
CK 32655 (CD)

** KC vs. PC: these were Columbia Records' catalog numbering delineations. KC was a higher-priced album, while PC was priced lower.*

Side One:

1. Piano Practicing
2. I Got Rhythm
3. Johnny One Note/One Note Samba
4. Glad To Be Unhappy
5. People
6. Second Hand Rose
7. Don't Rain On My Parade

Side Two:

1. Don't Ever Leave Me
2. Monologue (Dialogue)
3. By Myself
4. Come Back To Me
5. I Never Has Seen Snow
6. Lied: Auf Dem Wasser Zu Singen
7. The World Is A Concerto/ Make Your Own Kind Of Music
8. The Sweetest Sound

At this point in her career, Barbra was busy making movies. She starred in *The Owl and the Pussycat* in 1970; *What's Up, Doc?* in 1972; *Up the Sandbox* and *The Way We Were* followed in 1972 and 1973; and next on the docket was the comedy *For Pete's Sake*, coming out in 1974. "She won't be able to do a movie musical until 1975 because of previous commitments," Erlichman explained, "so she agreed that the quickest way to end the speculation would be on television." (Lewis, 1973)

The idea for her fifth television special for CBS-TV began as an album concept that never coalesced: Streisand wanted to record an international album, "The idea was to showcase all these fabulous musicians with their instruments from around the world. And since I've always said how bored I get singing the same songs the same way, I wanted to really shake it up here," she explained.

Mort Goode's liner notes (which appear on both the LP and the CD) are excellently written and explain to the listener what was conceptualized for television. Remember, this special aired once in 1973 but wasn't released on home video until 2005. Many fans did not see the television special for decades and could only listen to this album. They needed descriptive guidance.

The first song is "Piano Practicing," by Lan O'Kun, who was also responsible for "The Minute Waltz" (*Color Me Barbra*) and "The Best Gift" (*A Christmas Album*). A patter song (which Barbra did so well), "Piano Practicing" was the *second* song in the TV special, which highlights the main problem with this album—several songs from the show were not included on the album.

Where is the medley "Sing"/"Make Your Own Kind of Music"? It's true that both "Sing" and the "Sweet Inspiration" medley already appeared on Barbra's *Live at the Forum* album, released only one year earlier. And it was probably argued that Barbra's live version of "Sing" was gentler on the listener's ears than the *Musical Instruments* version, which was orchestrated with tuba and synthesizer. But none of the songs sung by Barbra's guest star, Ray Charles, are here. It's doubtful the producers even struck a soundtrack deal with Charles, as he was employed by another record label altogether. Barbra even recorded a solo version of their duet, "Crying Time," a year later for the *Butterfly* album. The duet with Ray Charles was included on Barbra's big box set, *Just for the Record*—it's the live version from the TV show.

The soundtrack album contains different takes of the songs from the special too, which makes it unique. Streisand often sang live on set while filming the show, the boom microphone dangling above her head just out of camera range, so the songs on videotape are sometimes a little less polished than what she recorded for the album—"Piano Practicing," for instance, sounds effortless on vinyl, while on video Barbra is working hard to wrap her tongue around those lyrics.

The opposite is true for "I Never Has Seen Snow," which must be the best track on this entire album—and which Barbra sings even better live on the show. "Snow" is another song from Harold Arlen's musical *House of Flowers*, which Barbra had an affinity for. The song has stuck in my head for years; with that idealized Haitian dialect written by Truman Capote, "I Never Has Seen Snow" is a quirky song that doesn't seem to follow a common songwriting pattern. Even the great songwriter Ira Gershwin agreed when he said that Arlen's songs are "peculiarly constructed, so that I never know what to expect." (Zinsser, 2001)

Once, a local journalist interviewed me about my Barbra Archives website and asked what song I would love to hear Streisand sing live. My answer was "I Never Has Seen Snow," and I took great care to explain how it was a lesser known "deep cut," and that it was written for a very specific island dwelling character. When the interview came out, the journalist wrote that the song was "I Never *Have* Seen Snow," which is grammatically correct, but also the wrong title. Foiled again, spell-check!

Since it's a favorite song of mine, I've heard it sung by several different artists over the years, and the arrangements can be hit or miss for me. Liza Minnelli's live version from 1987 has that honky-tonk piano sound, which tries to give the feel of "country" but just doesn't sound authentic. Ken and Mitzi Welch's sterling and magisterial orchestral arrangement for Streisand's "Snow" is just perfect. They exaggerate the weird tempo changes that Arlen wrote and allow Streisand to give us some of her vocal Streisand-isms too, including that long-held note on "like . . . my love is" at the end of the song. "Like" is held for so long, it's a wonder Barbra didn't pass out.

Speaking of passing out, *Musical Instruments* contains one of the longest notes that Barbra has sung on record. It occurs in the "I Got Rhythm" medley on side one. She ends the phrase "Who could ask for anything more?" by holding the note on "more" (at full belt!) for 22.88 seconds. The only other Streisand note that rivals this is on *The Concert*'s Disney medley. On the final phrase, "Oh, please make my dreams come true," she holds the note on "true" (*not* at full belt) for 20.30 seconds. There was some press for the special that said Barbra did fall to the stage after singing that note on "I Got Rhythm" . . . but one wonders about hyperbole. For those keeping track, the last note of *Yentl* ("A Piece of Sky") was held for 19.78 seconds ... even though it seems like it's longer.

Another iconic vocal on this album is Barbra's performance of the Rodgers and Hart standard "Glad to Be Unhappy." First, what an interesting and smart lyric for Barbra to interpret. "It's a pleasure to be sad," she sings happily. Again, the beautiful arrangement supports Streisand's vocals, although the casual listener who has not seen the show may wonder why the Japanese instruments were utilized in the mix. On-screen, of course, Barbra in Wonderland is singing with a man (producer/choreographer Joe Layton) in Kabuki makeup who is plucking the strings of the koto.

Barbra Streisand . . . and Other Musical Instruments was released on compact disc (digitally remastered by Joe Gastwirt) in 1989. It's unfortunate that this album wasn't a big seller for Streisand and Columbia Records; it didn't even attain gold status with the RIAA (i.e., selling at least half a million units), and it never rose into the top-fifty albums either. It's a shame Columbia or Legacy hasn't revisited the album after all these digital music years. It would be fun to have "Sing"/"Make Your Own Kind of Music" finally included. But the truth is that anyone who bought the DVDs in 2005 can pop that video disc in their machine any time they want and hear that song (and the rest of them) while watching the TV special.

Matt on *Instruments*

When I first became a fan of Barbra Streisand, I began collecting all of her records. Unfortunately, no one could get them for me wholesale—nor could I afford to buy them retail. So I regularly visited used-record stores in Atlanta and rifled through the LP bins labeled S for Miss Streisand's albums. I had no master list of her albums (yet), so I was sometimes completely surprised with what I found.

Musical Instruments was one of those surprises. I had no idea it was a TV show until I read the liner notes. The track list was promising, and for probably less than one dollar I bought that album and brought it home to be additionally surprised.

Musical Instruments as an album is not a wholly pleasant listening experience, which may account for its lack of popularity. Without the swanky videotape visuals from the show to accompany the music, the album is aurally *busy*. Tracks like "By Myself" and "Come Back to Me" are challenging to listen to. Not to mention Barbra's multitracked vocals competing with all that noise.

Thankfully, Barbra chose the simple song "The Sweetest Sounds" to close the album. And she definitely sings the sweetest sounds.

STREISAND COLLABORATORS

MARVIN HAMLISCH

Though Marvin Hamlisch left us too soon when he died in 2012 at age sixty-eight, his genius is preserved on recordings and film. It all began when Hamlisch, a child prodigy, studied at the prestigious Juilliard School at age seven! His life intersected with Barbra Streisand in 1964 when he was hired as the rehearsal pianist on *Funny Girl* in New York. A year later, he had his first big hit with the song "Sunshine, Lollipops and Rainbows," cowritten with Howard Liebling and recorded by Lesley Gore.

Hamlisch went on to become a successful composer of film music, writing scores for movies like *The Swimmer*, *The Sting*, *The Spy Who Loved Me*, and *Sophie's Choice*. His score for the Broadway hit *A Chorus Line* is a beloved classic too. Like Barbra, Hamlisch is an EGOT, having won Emmy, Grammy, Oscar, and Tony awards.

Barbra and Marvin worked together on 1973's *The Way We Were*, and that song has become part of her repertoire ever since. Hamlisch won the Oscar and the Grammy for his score to that film, as well as the Oscar for Best Original Song and the Grammy for Song of the Year.

But it was Barbra's 1994 concert tour that allowed the two friends to work and play together. "When this whole thing came about, and I was asked to even think over this whole situation—conducting for Barbra and working for her—to me that was a privilege," Hamlisch stated. "We are talking about a great voice. By working with her I realized if she did not have this great voice, she still is a very great lady. What I loved about working with her and doing this is that it gave me a chance to not only get to know her and her to get to know me but make a really good friend. My job was to make her as comfortable as possible so that she would start to enjoy that process." (King, Her Music Man: Marvin Hamlisch, 1994)

Hamlisch won the Emmy for his music direction on the television versions of *The Concert* and *Timeless*. About Hamlisch, Barbra wrote: "I had known Marvin for almost fifty years. He was there at the piano for *Funny Girl*, and he was there for my concert tours, and he even played at my wedding. Success never spoiled Marvin. . . . it just made him more of what he was . . . gifted, adorable, funny, generous, kind, thoughtful."

Why did Marvin Hamlisch love Barbra as a performer? "Well, first of all she has got this voice. You just go, 'Oh, my God.' She, being a very literate, a very smart person, understands what she is singing. Therefore, she understands what the hell she is saying as she is singing these songs. She really gets into lyrics and understands lyrics. She can hold notes and make them soar and make them really quiet." (King, 1994)

After Hamlisch died, Barbra participated in a private concert tribute at the Peter Jay Sharp Theater at New York's Juilliard School for the Arts in September 2012. A few months later, she sang "The Way We Were" at the 2013 Academy Awards show to honor her friend. That evening, Barbra said: "Marvin Hamlisch was a composer of extraordinary depth and versatility. He was also a very kind and generous friend who could always make me laugh. Over the years, we shared many adventures together. Marvin left us way too soon, but I'll always have those wonderful, wonderful memories." Hamlisch's other compositions with Streisand include the music and theme song for *The Mirror Has Two Faces*, and he wrote the songs "Leading with Your Heart," "Niagara," "Ordinary Miracles," and "Any Moment Now."

Released: January 1974
Produced by: Tommy LiPuma, Marty Paich, and Wally Gold
Cover photo: Steve Schapiro
Back cover photo: David Bailey
1994 CD: restored by John Arrias at B&J
Remastered by Bernie Grundman
2002 CD: remastered by Stephen Marcussen
Digitally edited by Stewart Whitmore for Marcussen Mastering, Hollywood

Catalog Numbers:
PC 32801 (1974 LP)
PCQ 32801 (quadraphonic album)
PCA 32801 (8-track)
1R1 6153 (reel-to-reel)
HC 42801 (half-speed mastered 1981 Audiophile LP)
CK 32801 (1989 CD + 1994 remastered CD)
CK 85153 (2002 remastered CD)
CK 5063592 (CD, 2002 UK version with bonus track "The Way We Were" (soundtrack version)
CK 724745 (2008, SBME SPECIAL MKTS.)
N/A—mastered for iTunes (2015 digital download)

Side One:
1. Being At War With Each Other
2. Something So Right
3. The Best Thing You've Ever Done
4. The Way We Were
5. All In Love Is Fair

Side Two:
1. What Are You Doing The Rest Of Your Life?
2. Summer Me, Winter Me
3. Pieces Of Dreams
4. I've Never Been A Woman Before
5. Medley: My Buddy/How About Me?

The Way We Were, which we can refer to as the studio album (to differentiate it from the soundtrack album from the movie), was basically cobbled together from unreleased recordings and the record label's desire to place the song "The Way We Were" onto an album as soon as possible to capitalize on the momentum from Barbra's hit movie with Robert Redford.

Despite its disparate origins, *The Way We Were* is one of Streisand's strongest albums of the 1970s! "I was concentrating on movies and other things at that point in my life," Streisand said, "and the label wanted the record right away." So they turned to unreleased recordings. (SiriusXM, 2014, 2016)

Half of the tracks on this album were initially recorded for *The Singer*—a contemporary album that Barbra was working on but ultimately abandoned. Wally Gold produced those tracks in 1969 and 1970, and Peter Matz and Claus Ogerman contributed the arrangements.

Streisand recorded three new songs in the studio with producer Tommy LiPuma (arrangements by Nick DeCaro) on December 14, 1973, at United Recorders in Los Angeles. Those songs were "All in Love Is Fair," "Something So Right," and "Being at War with Each Other." (A fourth song recorded at that session, "Make the Man Love Me," by Barry Mann and Cynthia Weil, remains unreleased.)

The Way We Were was yet another Streisand album released in the quadraphonic format, and there are two tracks on that remix that differ from the LP and CD: "Being at War with Each Other" has alternate vocals and an orchestra remix, and "The Way We Were" contains a short, alternate vocal by Streisand at the end of the song.

Columbia released the movie soundtrack and the studio album in January 1974, but Barbra's studio album fared better, rising to number one on the Top 200 Albums chart in March and staying in the top ten for four more weeks. "The Way We Were" was Barbra's first number one single, and the album was her second number one album.

Streisand was an album artist, meaning she always sold in the long-play genre better than she did with singles, or 45s. It's remarkable that in 1974, after she had been recording for twelve years, "The Way We Were" was her *first* number one song!

The Way We Were featured a striking cover photo by Steve Schapiro and a duotone back-cover photo by David Bailey. Bailey concentrated his lens on Streisand's long fingernails. An alternate shot from the session reveals that Streisand is smoking in the photo. She says she never really inhaled.

Steve Schapiro did a sitting with Streisand at her home and photographed her wearing different outfits and hairstyles, both inside and out. "She was in all black and knew exactly where she was going to put her fingers so that you saw the red nail polish," Schapiro recalled. "We shot it all outdoors under natural light in the afternoon, so it would glow." (Considine, 1985)

The Way We Were album cover was altered by the record company nearly a year after it was released. Columbia Records exec Bruce Lundvall revealed, "[Ray] Stark wasn't getting a cut of the second LP, so he threatened to sue," he said. The Rastar Productions lawsuit centered on the use of the title of the film on Columbia's studio album, which Rastar felt confused record buyers and diminished the sales of the movie's soundtrack album. "We had to drop the title of the movie from the album cover," Lundvall said. (Considine, 1985)

Columbia responded by reissuing the studio album with the art deco title letters removed, but also with a big sticker that said, "Including the hit singles THE WAY WE WERE and ALL IN LOVE IS FAIR." Years later, when the remastered CD was released, the red title, *The Way We Were*, was restored to the cover art.

Matt on *The Way We Were*

The Way We Were is an interesting mingling of pop-radio tunes and elegant ballads. "Being at War with Each Other" has been one of my favorites for years, and it was so gratifying to hear Barbra sing it live during her 2016 tour.

The trio of the Bergmans/ Michel Legrand songs—"What Are You Doing the Rest of Your Life?," "Summer Me, Winter Me," and "Pieces of Dreams"—are the heart of the album. This foursome made beautiful music together.

"I've Never Been a Woman Before" was by Ron Miller—fans will remember his song "If I Could," from *Higher Ground*, 1997, and the drag queen classic "I've Never Been to Me." "I've Never Been a Woman Before" was the eleven o'clock number from the musical *Cherry*, based on William Inge's *Bus Stop*. *Cherry* didn't open on Broadway until 1972, and it lasted only three performances. Barbra used to sing this song in her Las Vegas act, arranged by Claus Ogerman, her music director.

Martin Charnin wrote "The Best Thing You've Ever Done." Charnin is most known for his lyrics to the musical *Annie*. "The Best Thing" was written for director Herbert Ross and Barbra's movie *The Owl and the Pussycat*. "He asked me if I'd be interested in writing a song for Barbra to sing in the film when the characters separate. I told him I'd like to see the rough cut of the film first, but that I was interested. I wrote the song, sent it to Barbra's people, and that was it. Later, when the film was released, all the music was done by Blood, Sweat & Tears, so I thought my song was just dropped. Barbra, though, liked the song and it ended up on one of her albums three years later." (Kimbrell, 1989)

Barbra also recorded a more stripped-down version of "The Best Thing" with only a trio accompanying her (it's unreleased as of this printing). A third version of "Best Thing" was released as a seven-inch single in 1970 (#4-45147). It has a different, expanded ending.

SIGNATURE STREISAND

"THE WAY WE WERE"

When the Sydney Pollack-directed movie *The Way We Were* was previewed in San Francisco in July 1973, audiences reacted very favorably to the theme song, which was written by Marvin Hamlisch and sung by Streisand, who played the main character, Katie Morosky.

Although Hamlisch had composed scores for *The Swimmer* and Woody Allen's *Bananas*, in 1973 he was still new to film scores and theme songs. Hamlisch said it was producer Ray Stark who "called me up and told me he needed a song that was roughly a cross between Michel Legrand and Carole King." (Budge, 1974) Stark's deal was that he would hire Hamlisch to score the movie . . . if the song worked.

Hamlisch wrote in his memoir, "I put in weeks and weeks of struggle to find the right theme."

He explained that "on the surface it was a pretty difficult assignment. I thought about the script, and I was quite depressed because the perfect combination didn't come to me right away. I went to bed one night, still depressed, but I woke up at 2 a.m. and I had the song. It was there. I wrote it down and when I got up the next morning, I made some minor changes and had the finished product." (Marvin Hamlisch, 1992)

Hamlisch wrote the song in a major key. He felt a song composed in a minor key would be the obvious, "sad" choice for a tearjerker movie. "By doing this," he said, "I tried to give a sense of hope to this tragic story."

Hamlisch was also customizing a song for the formidable Streisand. "I wanted to give her the notes that let her soar," he wrote. "I was determined not to write something drippingly sentimental."

Hamlisch had an emotional, not intellectual response to the "right" melody. "When I feel the emotional tug, when I react the way I hope the audience will, then I know I've got it." (Hamlisch, 1992)

Ray Stark hired Marilyn and Alan Bergman to write the lyrics to Hamlisch's melody. Marilyn Bergman elaborated on working with Hamlisch on "The Way We Were." "Well, first of all it's a wonderful title," she said. "The main title of the movie had to function as a passageway back in time.

We were underscoring the flashback, in a way." (Bergman, 2013)

"[Barbra] made two suggestions," Marilyn Bergman recalled. "One was the change of a note in the first phrase of the tune. And the other was a change of a word, a very important suggestion. We had the lyric beginning with 'daydreams light the corners of your mind,' and she suggested that the first word of the song be 'mem'ries.'" (Bergman, 2013)

Now it was time to record the song. "Barbra and I met to discuss exactly what the song would sound like when it was orchestrated," Hamlisch remembered. He prepared three arrangements for the date, worried that Streisand might want changes. Hamlisch wrote that they recorded his arrangement B, which was "written with less romance and more introspection." (Hamlisch, 1992)

For the movie, Streisand sang "The Way We Were" twice—during the opening credits and flashback, and again over the end credits.

Columbia Pictures serviced a promotional seven-inch record of "The Way We Were" to movie theaters to help publicize the film. It was an orchestral arrangement with no humming.

Meanwhile, work began on a pop single version of the song.

"The song as performed by Barbra in the movie did not work for a pop record," explained Marty Paich, who arranged and produced the hit single. "'The Way We Were' in the movie was very laid back. It worked fine with the picture, with the visuals, but for radio, for the ears only, it kind of put you to sleep. So, they called me in, and Marvin and I went over to see Barbra, to her house on Carolwood, in Beverly Hills. They played the song for me and asked if I'd do something with it, to make it more commercial. So, I took it home and worked on an arrangement. I rewrote it with a much hipper rhythm section." (Considine, 1985)

Streisand, Paich, and Hamlisch recorded the single on September 12, 1973, at RCA Recording Studios in Los Angeles.

Carol Kaye, who played bass on many studio recordings, recalled the session: "The huge orchestra finally assembled from our break, and we did thirty-three straight takes of 'The Way We Were' with Barbra singing every one, with Marvin Hamlisch conducting, and the songwriting team (Marilyn and Alan Bergman) in the booth . . . Take after take, we kept going, each take as intensive as the last one, until I looked at Paul Humphrey the drummer like, 'When is this going to end?' . . . After a few arpeggios, especially in the bridge, it felt like 'the' take, I looked up and caught Ms. Streisand's fast gaze from her little sound booth as she was holding a long note (through the glass window), our eyes locked like, 'Wheeeee. This is it,' and finished the take. Paul looked at me and we both smiled, having played on a lot of hits together. We knew this was the take, too." (Marinucci, n.d.)

Marty Paich confirmed that it took about four hours to record and four hours to mix, and that Streisand stayed over "to repair a few lines" by doing audio punch-ins.

"The Way We Were" was awarded twice at the Grammy Awards. Hamlisch and the Bergmans won for Song of the Year as well as Album of Best Original Score Written for a Motion Picture or a Television Special.

Streisand has incorporated "The Way We Were" into many of her concerts, starting in 1975 when she sang it at the

Kennedy Center for the premiere of her movie *Funny Lady*. In 1980, Barbra sang the alternate version of the song for the Bergmans at an American Civil Liberties Union Foundation of Southern California fundraiser. She called this version "The Way We Weren't." After finishing that version, written to a different melody with a different lyric, she asked the audience, "Isn't that pretty?" before reprising the familiar, number one hit version. The song became her second-act opener during *The Concert* tour in 1994.

Sex and the City reinvigorated the energy around the movie and song in 1999 for the Season 2 episode "Ex and the City." Sarah Jessica Parker's iconic character, Carrie Bradshaw, compared herself to Streisand's character, Katie: "The world is made up of two types of women. The simple girls and the Katie girls. I'm a Katie girl." She broke up with Mr. Big in front of the Plaza Hotel—the exact location of the finale of *The Way We Were* with Streisand and Redford. Carrie tells him, "Your girl is lovely, Hubble." He responds, "I don't get it." She caps it off with, "And you never did." Carrie walks away.

It was touching, ten years later, when Parker, sitting in the front row of Streisand's exclusive small club performance at the Village Vanguard, wiped the tears from her eyes when Barbra sang "The Way We Were."

Barbra's 2012-2013 tours featured a very melancholy version of "The Way We Were," which was paired with another Hamlisch composition, "Through the Eyes of Love," a love theme from the movie *Ice Castles*. This was Barbra's touching dedication to Marvin Hamlisch. I don't know how Barbra performed this song without crying—the audience certainly did. "If you believe in the spirit living on," she told the audience, "then maybe he's hearing me now." On the recording of her New York shows, an audience member answers her: "Yes he is!"

You can't ignore Barbra's duet of this song with Lionel Richie on the 2014 album *Partners*. It's very good.

Released: October 1974
Produced by: Jon Peters
Arranged by: Tom Scott, Lee Holdridge, and John Bahler
Art direction and design: Jon Peters
Cover photo: Carl Furuta
Inside photos: Steve Schapiro
Back cover painting: Bill Shirley

Catalog Numbers:
PC 33005 (LP)
1R1 6275 (reel-to-reel)
PCA 33005 (8-track)
PCT 33005 (cassette)
PCQ 33005 (quadraphonic LP, 1974)
CK 33005 (CD)

Side One:

1. Love In The Afternoon
2. Guava Jelly
3. Grandma's Hands
4. I Won't Last A Day Without You
5. Jubilation

Side Two:

1. Simple Man
2. Life On Mars
3. Since I Don't Have You
4. Crying Time
5. Let The Good Times Roll

Butterfly marked a change in Barbra Streisand's career when the man she was dating—Jon Peters—began taking a bigger role in her recording and movie projects. Peters produced *Butterfly* despite having no experience whatsoever in record producing. The gossip columns and entertainment writers had an opinion that they didn't shy away from printing.

Jon Peters, age twenty-nine, was a hairdresser who owned and ran three hair salons in Los Angeles with his uncle Adolf Pagano and business partner Paul Cantor. His $100,000 a week income and a client list that included Jacqueline Bisset and Anne Bancroft made him a successful man. Peters first met Barbra in August 1973 when she requested that he style a short wig that she wore in *For Pete's Sake*. Jon, separated from wife Lesley Ann Warren (and soon divorced from her), began dating Streisand and they were spotted together often in public in 1974.

Then, in June of 1974, newspapers reported that "Jon Peters will produce the new Barbra Streisand album scheduled for a September release. The album, which will include several songs of the '50s, will also feature a cover designed by Peters." (Streisand Album Set, 1974) Streisand wrote about Jon's producing *Butterfly*: "I already knew I could produce a record. So I thought, Let him do it. It will give him some stature, and I can always rescue him, if necessary . . . because Jon knew nothing about producing records."

Unfortunately, the first selection of songs Jon and Barbra chose did not materialize into usable tracks: "You Light Up My Life" by Carole King; an R & B song called "Type Thang," written by Isaac Hayes for the movie *Shaft's Big Score*; "On Broadway" by the songwriting team of Jerry Leiber and Mike Stoller (which was a big hit for George Benson); and "Everything Must Change" by Benard Ighner. Fans know now that "You Light Up My Life" ended up being redone, with new musical elements added by Jochem van der Saag for *Release Me 2* in 2021. The same is true for Ighner's "Everything Must Change"—she recorded it anew on the 1997 album *Higher Ground*.

The album recording sessions took place in March and July 1974. At this point, Columbia Records's president Bruce Lundvall asked Charles Koppelman (head of A & R) to interfere. Enter Gary Klein.

"I was a staff producer for CBS," Klein told *Billboard*, "and Charles Koppelman of The Entertainment Company asked me to talk to Barbra and Jon Peters about *Butterfly* ... Both Charles and I didn't think it was up to Barbra's standards, and he wanted me to go out to California, sit down with them and tell them why.

"It was very difficult to meet her for the first time to criticize an album that her boyfriend—who is sitting right there—had produced. But I went over the album cut by cut, and I was very specific about what I thought was wrong with it, and they knew that I knew what I was talking about, so I gained their respect." (Spada, 1983)

Veteran recording engineer Al Schmitt was brought in to remix the recordings. Schmitt quit after three days—and he spoke to *Los Angeles Times* about it late June 1974. "They've recorded seven or eight songs for this new LP," Schmitt explained. "Columbia played them, and they were unhappy with what they heard. Barbra always gives me goosebumps: She has that incredible sound. This album has a flat, one-dimensional sound. It needs to be opened up. It needs climaxes."

But Schmitt's biggest complaint was Peters. "Essentially Peters wants all the money, and I'd be doing all the work." (Haber, 1974)Reportedly, music contractor Kathy Kasper also did some last-minute work on the album by bringing in several new songs and rescoring some of the tracks that were deemed unusable. (Brenner, 1975)

Koppelman then spoke to Joyce Haber in her follow-up column to explain his position. "Schmitt went in to listen to the album. He came out and said it wasn't right. He told Jon he wanted to coproduce with him. Obviously, he was upset because he was going to be on the gravy train. He told Peters, 'I've been in the business 25 years, and you've been in it 25 minutes.'" (Haber, Streisand 'Happiest She's Ever Been', 1974)

Barbra called up Joyce Haber too. "Is Schmitt trying to imply that I've given up my career for Jon Peters?" Barbra asked. "This is possibly the best singing I've ever done. It's the most open, the most free, the most happy."

Barbra explained further to Haber: "From a sound point of view, Columbia may have wanted more amplification. You can have 100 mixers on one song. Schmitt did three cuts. I didn't like them. I wanted this soft, then rising."

Streisand returned to the recording studio in July—this time with Tom Scott providing arrangements for seven songs. He accomplished this task in four days. "She did more songs in less time than she's ever done," Scott said. Streisand herself said Scott was "terrific to work with. Rhythm is normally very difficult to lay down, but with Tom it was definite, clear and unified." (Studio Star, 1975) Why title it *Butterfly*? "During our courtship," Barbra explained, "[Jon] came on the set one day with a beautiful diamond-and-sapphire butterfly, just really my taste, and that's hard to do. And then a week later he gave me this hundred-year-old Indian butterfly and it was just something ...." (Kaye, 1975)

Columbia released *Butterfly* in October 1974. The reviews were mixed; most mentioned Jon Peters's influence or questioned why he was pictured in so many of the photographs that appeared on the album's foldout.

Columnist Shirley Eder reported that the album cost around $158,000 to complete. "Tony Bennett told me he brings his albums in for about $5,000 each," Eder wrote. (Eder, 1974)

Jon Peters designed the *Butterfly* album cover, using a fly on a stick of butter. "I just threw it out," he said, "I said butter and a fly—Butterfly. She said, 'Great!' And that was it. The front cover was done." (Hopkins, 1974)

Carl Furuta was the photographer hired to create the cover image of the *Butterfly* album. "It had to be a dead fly," he recalled, "so we had to go to a garbage can and put a bag over a fly and let him suffocate to death. Then you had to spread out his wings and his feet with tweezers. We went through a lot of flies. And maybe the butter melted under the lights. But to me it was just another job." (People Etc., 1986)

The cover is certainly the most "artistic" of them all. But it was still a downer, what with a fly and a stick of butter. Columbia sneakily affixed a sticker on the back of the album—with William Shirley's funky but gorgeous painting of Streisand. The sticker announced the album's title and all of its tracks on top of the face of Streisand; record buyers were sure to buy the album, right? *Butterfly* has the most alternate tracks of any of Streisand's quadraphonic albums:

- Barbra's beautiful background vocals are much more present in the quad remix of "Love in the Afternoon." Also, the awkward vocal edit at 2:35 on the CD is not present on the quad version.
- "Guava Jelly"—alternate vocals.
- "Jubilation"—alternate vocals.
- Barbra's background vocals on "Simple Man" have been remixed and are placed more forward in the mix than on the CD.
- "Life on Mars" is a completely different take. I like this version much better—the effects on Streisand's vocal are not present on the quad remix.
- "Since I Don't Have You"—alternate vocals.
- "Let the Good Times Roll" is a different mix.

Matt on *Butterfly*

I'd say five out of the ten tracks on *Butterfly* are excellent and timeless. That's not to say that the other five are horrible. In fact, the five less successful tracks get an A-plus for effort.

My top five tracks are "Love in the Afternoon," "I Won't Last a Day Without You," "Simple Man," "Since I Don't Have You," and "Let the Good Times Roll."

The others don't catch my attention because Barbra is singing genre songs that are outside her wheelhouse. "Guava Jelly" could never be considered a definitive performance of the song for many reasons … But Barbra doesn't suck. It's fun to hear her sing reggae! But reggae artists and fans would be judgmental of this track, for sure. The same for "Grandma's Hands" and "Jubilation"—it's a similar complaint I had with *Stoney End*. These 1970s "white gospel" songs just don't sound authentic to me, although they are very enjoyable.

David Bowie was critical of Barbra's cut of "Life on Mars." He told *Playboy* magazine Streisand's version of his song was "bloody awful. Sorry, Barb, but it was atrocious." (Crowe, 1976) I'm sorry that the Thin White Duke wasn't impressed by Streisand's take on "Mars." I don't think it's horrible, though. It is an extremely cinematic tune that Barbra was attracted to.

Listen, when I first heard Barbra sing "Life on Mars" I didn't know anything about Bowie's work other than "Let's Dance" from 1983. In fact, even as a young man I admired the lyrics and meaning of "Mars" as sung by Streisand. "Sailors fighting in the dance hall, oh man, look at those cavemen go … it's the freakiest show." I got it. My only complaint about Streisand's version are her rhymes in the second verse. "Brow" and "cow" is a stretch. But, hell, Bowie wrote it that way!

The most egregious rhyme is "the workers have struck for fame" with "Lenin's unsane again." That couplet is rough. Streisand rhyming "fame" with "again" (pronounced agān) sounds stagey and not very hip. However, I will prove how hip I am by revealing that most Bowie critics argue over whether he was taking the piss out of John Lennon or the Russian revolutionary Vladimir Lenin.

Still, "Life on Mars" is a song I listen to often and enjoy. Bowie was brilliant, and I can see why Barbra liked his lyric and the message of the song.

By the way … I like "Crying Time." But I like Barbra's duet with Ray Charles better, which is not on this album. The takeaway from the album *Butterfly* . . . Let the good times roll!

Released: March 1975
Produced by: Rick Chertoff
Soundtrack album coordination: Peter Matz
Arranged and conducted by: Peter Matz
Original songs by: John Kander and Fred Ebb
Original recording engineers: Jerry Block, Alex Casanegras, Kevin Cleary, Richard Mantel, John Neal, Mike Stone at The Record Plant, Los Angeles, and Sunset Highland Recording Studios, Los Angeles.
Art direction: Bob Heimall
Design: Richard Mantel
Cover illustration: Vincent Petragnani
Photography: Steve Schapiro

Catalog Numbers:
Arista AL 9004 (gatefold LP)
Arista AQ 9004 (gatefold quadraphonic LP)
7301-9004 N (8-track tape quadraphonic)
1R1 6358 (reel-to-reel)
ACB6-8347 (cassette)
Bay Cities 3006 (1990 CD)
Arista Masters 19006-2 (1998 CD)
Sony Legacy 2009 CD (same Arista catalog #)

Side One:
1. How Lucky Can You Get?
2. So Long, Honey Lamb
3. I Found A Million Dollar Baby (In A Five And Ten Cent Store)
4. Isn't This Better?
5. Me And My Shadow
6. If I Love Again
7. I Got A Code In My Doze
8. (It's Gonna Be A) Great Day

Side Two:
1. Blind Date
2. Am I Blue?
3. It's Only A Paper Moon/I Like Him
4. It's Only A Paper Moon/I Like Her
5. More Than You Know
6. Clap Hands, Here Comes Charley
7. Let's Hear It For Me

The *Funny Lady* soundtrack was released by Arista Records, which was created by Clive Davis, former head of Columbia Records, who partnered with Columbia Pictures to found the new record label in 1974. Their big "get" was Streisand's movie soundtrack.

"After many discussions between me and [Streisand's] devoted manager, Marty Erlichman, he and Barbra agreed to let Arista have the album," wrote Clive Davis in his 2013 memoir. (Davis, 2013) The original *Funny Lady* album contained fifteen tracks, including the James Caan vocal of "Me and My Shadow," even though that song and scene were cut from the final film. Also included on the soundtrack was the complete track of "So Long Honey Lamb," which lasted only a few seconds in the movie.

As usual, there are mixes and takes on Arista's quadraphonic release that do not appear on the LP or CD:

- How Lucky Can You Get?—The second half of the song is a different take, with alternate Streisand vocals; the orchestra plays a different ending too.
- If I Love Again—Features a more intimate Streisand vocal and different piano ending.
- Blind Date—Same vocals; extra orchestra "vamp" after the Rosalie entrance, which is not on the regular LP.
- Clap Hands, Here Comes Charley—Completely different take by Ben Vereen.
- Let's Hear It for Me—Completely different take! Alternate Streisand vocals.

Arista promoted "How Lucky Can You Get?" as the single from the *Funny Lady* soundtrack. A 45 rpm single of the song was released, which contained different Streisand vocals and a different musical arrangement from the album version.

Later, an Arista compilation album titled *Soundtrack Memories* (ARISTA/2005) featured yet another version of "How Lucky Can You Get?" On this one, the first half of the song is sung in a lower key by male backup singers who add a few more "doo-ahh's" than on other versions. Plus, Streisand sings different vocals.

The *Funny Lady* soundtrack first appeared on CD in 1990 on the Bay Cities label with new liner notes by Merrick S. Talcove. The tracks on the CD were placed in the same order as on the original vinyl album.

Eight years later, back on the Arista label, *Funny Lady* was released again on CD. This time, the reissue producer, Didier C. Deutsch, dug into the Arista master tapes and remastered the tracks in twenty-bit digital technology. He put the tracks in the order in which they appear in the film. Unfortunately, Deutsch edited track ten, "How Lucky Can You Get?," by adding a Victrola sound effect at the beginning of the song. Yes, it mimicked the scene in the movie in which Fanny plays this record and sings along. But . . . it was never recorded that way. Yuck!

However, Deutsch makes up for that by including a bonus track of the single mix of "How Lucky Can You Get?" (This was in the stores as single #AS 0123.)

Another addition to the Arista *Funny Lady* soundtrack CD was the dramatic introduction before "Let's Hear It for Me," sung by Streisand in the film as she leaves Nicky Arnstein for good. ("Well, I'll be damned. No, I won't be damned. 'Cause I have been damned. But I won't be damned anymore.") This introduction did not appear on previous *Funny Lady* soundtracks.

The most interesting change on the 1998 *Funny Lady* CD is "(It's Gonna Be A) Great Day." It's an *entirely* different version of "Great Day," complete with the minor chords that Streisand sings as the song opens, as well as the complex middle section with clapping hands. The original soundtrack album and the 1990 Bay Cities CD contained "Great Day" as a 5:16 track, which Streisand fans refer to as the sky-high version because Streisand belts out a long note when she sings the lyrics "angels in the sky, high."

There was no explanation why Arista and Deutsch decided to substitute a different version of "Great Day" on the 1998 disc. For collectors, it presents a problem, because there are now two versions of the song out there, and not many people bought the older, Bay Cities CD with the "sky-high" version. The only explanation for the existence of two distinctly different versions of this song is the rumor that Marvin Hamlisch was hired to rework Peter Matz's arrangement of "Great Day" during production of the movie. My best guess is this: the 1998 Arista CD is the original Peter Matz arrangement, never released. The 1990 Bay Cities CD and the LP version, which sounds just like the movie, is the Hamlisch redo.

Matt on *Funny Lady*

Funny Lady marks the last great collaboration between Peter Matz and Streisand until *The Broadway Album* in 1985. His arrangements for this movie are first-class, and Streisand's vocals are fantastic, with her singing at the top of her game.

On the 2002 Columbia Pictures DVD of *Funny Lady*, we can hear a mysterious instrumental cue on the "Special Features" option. The background music is a forty-second instrumental version of "If I Love Again." It's also possible to hear a twenty-nine-second instrumental cue from the aquacade number by clicking on the "Song Highlights" option. Were these part of the unused *Funny Lady* overture or intermission music?

Another missing track is Streisand's ballad version of "Let's Hear It for Me," sung as the finale of the film. Let's hope this is found in the vault and released someday.

In the movie, Billy Rose's show, "Crazy Quilt," contained several songs that have never appeared on a *Funny Lady* recording: "Beautiful Face Have a Heart," "If You Want the Rainbow, You Must Have the Rain," and "Fifty Million Frenchmen Can't Be Wrong." Granted, these songs are sung by a chorus and are probably not that interesting to a general audience. *What's wrong with wanting more*?

Finally, there are two other songs from the *Funny Lady* score that could have been included in a deluxe CD release if the audio sources are not corrupted: "Am I Blue"—Barbra speaks a comedic monologue in the middle, which is hilarious. At the end, she sings a quote of "Love for Sale" by Cole Porter, and I can only assume it was cut because of rights and royalties. Then there is "All My Life on a Stage"—Although the Arista CD restored the "Well, I'll be damned" verse, there was a whole section that was deleted. "All My Life on a Stage" has approximately three minutes more of this song before it cuts to Fanny in the car singing "Let's Hear It for Me." This entire sequence was filmed and one day, let's hppe we see the music and imagine combined.

STREISAND COLLABORATORS

JON PETERS

Love Jon Peters or hate him, you cannot ignore that he affected Barbra Streisand's career in many positive ways, especially as the world of music and movies was evolving. While we will probably never know about their combustive but loving personal life, we can look at the career milestones Streisand achieved with Peters from around 1973 to 1984.

Almost from their first meeting, Jon without an "h" and Barbra without an "a" sparked fire. At twenty-eight years old, he owned hairdressing salons in Beverly Hills, Encino, and Woodland Hills. Because Peters had celebrity clients, Streisand asked him to design a short hairdo for her film *For Pete's Sake*. "When I arrived at her house for the appointment," he relayed, "she kept me waiting an hour and a half. I was ready to leave. Then she came down and told me she wanted me to do a wig. I never do wigs. What an insult." (Cox, 1974)

Peters made the wig, then began dating Streisand. With no recording experience whatsoever, he produced her album *Butterfly*. Next, he became a film producer, the driving force behind *A Star Is Born*. The Hollywood press (and everyone else in that town) disliked his bald ambition, always referring to him as "hairdresser turned producer." They felt he lacked humility, jumping ahead in line, riding on Streisand's coattails.

"My boyfriend's a hairdresser," Barbra stated defiantly at the time. "People say, 'How can he possibly produce?' Just like they said, 'She's a singer, how can she act, or play the guitar or write songs?' Well—we'll see." (Orange, 1976)

But then *A Star Is Born* earned millions at the box office and at record stores, and Peters was mollified. "I can tell you that Barbra went along with me on instinct, not on total belief," he said. "But look, she's no fool. I didn't walk into her life, make love to her and have her say, 'Ohhh, please produce my movie.' Also, let's face it, once that movie got rolling, it was her brilliance, her energies, her talents that made it come together." (Beck, A Producer Is Born: Jon Peters, 1977)

About Jon Peters, Barbra wrote in her book: "I realize now why I was drawn to him. . . . He was the tough guy . . . the one who would protect me."

It's unquestionable: Jon Peters ignited the rocket that blasted Streisand into superstardom in the 1970s. He complained that Barbra was too young to play Ray Stark's mother-in-law in *Funny Lady*; Peters developed and produced *A Star Is Born* and *The Main Event*, two contemporary, timely, and successful movies for Streisand. It was Peters who prodded Barbra to record hugely popular duets and albums with Donna Summer and Barry Gibb. Peters also pressed Streisand to perform live during their time together, although it never panned out. Barbra made *Yentl* instead.

Then they split up. In the 1980s and 1990s, Jon Peters teamed with business partner Peter Guber, and together they produced huge Hollywood blockbuster movies like *Flashdance*, *The Witches of Eastwick*, and *Batman*. Streisand became a successful movie director, sang in concert, and eventually found happiness and marriage with James Brolin.

"She was probably the love of my life," Peters admitted in 2017. "She was the most captivating, interesting, creative person I have ever met. I owe her. I will always owe her for giving me the life that I've had." (Siegel, 2017)

Released: October 1975
Arranged and conducted by: Rupert Holmes
Produced by: Jeffrey Lesser and Rupert Holmes for Widescreen Productions
Engineered and mixed by: Jeffrey Lesser
Recorded live at Record Plant, RCA, and Capitol Recording Studios in Hollywood
Recording and associate engineers: Baker Bigsby, Mickey Crawford, Hugh Davies, Grover Helsely, Gary Kelgren, Deni King, Gary Ladisky, Ron Nevison, Larry Quinn, and Kent Tunks
Photography: Steve Schapiro
Black and white photography: Sam Emerson
Design: Nancy Donald

Catalog Numbers:
PC 33815 (LP)
PCQ 33815 (quadraphonic LP)
PCA 33815 (8-track)
PCT 33815 (cassette)
1R1 6436 (reel-to-reel)
CK 33815 (CD)

Side One:

1. Lazy Afternoon
2. My Father's Song
3. By The Way
4. Shake Me, Wake Me (When It's Over)
5. I Never Had It So Good

Side Two:

1. Letters That Cross In The Mail
2. You And I
3. Moanin' Low
4. A Child Is Born
5. Widescreen

"I heard an album called *Widescreen* by a young singer-songwriter named Rupert Holmes," Barbra explained. "I was really impressed with his cinematic approach to writing and producing. So I asked if he'd like to try making an album with me!" (SiriusXM, 2014, 2016)

Before generations of fans sang in karaoke bars about piña coladas and getting caught in the rain, Rupert Holmes had a 1974 album on Epic Records called *Widescreen*. (He didn't have his "Piña Colada Song" hit until 1979.)

He recalled that an Epic executive sent Streisand two songs he thought she'd like, "Widescreen" and "Letters That Cross in the Mail." Rupert said, "The next day I got a call from Barbra. She told me to send her two lead sheets. I thought it was somebody playing a joke, so I made her hum 'People.' She hit a note you can't believe. The next day she called again, saying I'd better go out there. I did. I rushed to California." (Campbell, 1978)

Streisand wrote that "I was going on instinct. We just hit it off, and it didn't bother me that he was basically unknown and had never done anything on this scale before. I knew it was a risk, but I like risks." At her house, Barbra played his album and sang along to the songs. This began a dialogue between the two artists about when and what they would record.

After that first meeting, Holmes wrote "My Father's Song" with Streisand in mind. "She talked a little bit with me in our early meeting about growing up and not really knowing her father. I don't remember all the details. But I remember coming away from it and just sitting down and writing this song and trying to put in it everything that a daughter might want to hear her father say to her." (Howe, Rupert Holmes Interview, 2003) "How did he know?" Streisand expressed. "I was deeply touched."

Holmes ended up staying at Barbra's guest house at her Carolwood estate, where he wrote charts for songs and worked with Streisand when she had free moments—Barbra had wrapped the movie *Funny Lady* and was in preproduction for *A Star Is Born*.

Streisand and Holmes, with his producing partner, Jeffrey Lesser, recorded the *Lazy Afternoon* album in three recording sessions—April 11, June 12, and June 26, 1975.

The title track sets the mood of the album. "Lazy Afternoon" is a theater song from a musical called *The Golden Apple*, with lyrics by John La Touche and music by Jerome Moross. Director Francis Ford Coppola suggested it to Streisand over dinner one night. Streisand said, "When I heard [the song], I was just amazed by the beauty of it. And I somehow felt that the arrangement should convey that sense of the silence of hearing grass grow. Something slow and hypnotic." (SiriusXM, 2014, 2016)

Streisand first met David Foster during the *Lazy Afternoon* sessions—this was while he was still playing piano at recording sessions, years before he became a famous record producer. Foster was credited as a featured soloist on the electric piano. Guitarist Danny "Kootch" Kortchmar (producer of Billy Joel's *River of Dreams* album) recalled that Foster "was very officious, had a winning attitude, didn't do drugs like everyone else in L.A., and he could just play his ass off. He could do any style—he could play funk like nobody's business." (Hurwitz, 2013)

Barbra remembered, "I heard him play a figure on the piano on that session and I said, 'Who's playing that?' That's how I met David." (Avrich, 2019)

Foster, of course, went on to produce Celine Dion, Whitney Houston, Michael Bublé, and others. For Streisand, he produced several songs as well as her *Back to Broadway* album. More on that later.

Columbia released two singles from the album: "My Father's Song"/"By the Way" (# 3-10198) and "Shake Me, Wake Me (When It's Over)"/"Widescreen" (# 3-10272). As the era of disco music approached, Columbia also put out a twelve-inch, 4:55 minute remix of "Shake Me, Wake Me" on a white "demonstration" label. It sounds mostly the same as the album track, except for some moog synthesizer music breaks between the stanzas.

"By the Way" was the second song released that Barbra Streisand had a hand in writing. She must be fond of it because it's shown up on a couple of compilation albums, and Barbra has also sung it live in concert, most recently during her 2016 shows.

Rupert Holmes collaborated with Streisand on the song, with Streisand singing a melody she heard in her head to Holmes and both writing the lyrics. Holmes had noted that Barbra used the phrase "by the way" often when speaking. "I thought to myself, How many ways can we find to use that phrase in a song each time with a different meaning?" (SiriusXM, 2014, 2016)

Streisand looks positively languorous in the Steve Schapiro cover

photo, captured in Streisand's living room at her Malibu ranch in "The Barn." She wrote: "I wrapped a scarf around my head because I didn't want to fool with my hair, put on a pink vintage-looking top and skirt and pink lipstick, and lounged on the mattress that served as the main seating area in the barn. I was barefoot and relaxed. It was kind of a bohemian look, to create a romantic, lazy atmosphere. I think Steve and I were done in about twenty minutes, which is what can happen when you have a good photographer whom you trust."

Streisand and Jon Peters had designed a sofa-less sitting area, and she is sitting on a mattress on the floor, enclosed by an L-shaped cabinet. "It was thrown with all kinds of pillows, antique embroideries, 1940s fabrics, and furs—before they became politically incorrect," she explained. (Bethany, 1994)

Afternoon holds the distinction of being the first Streisand album for which she wrote the liner notes. "I was so eager to share something about each song," she revealed. They are fun to read, especially when she builds in a recurring joke: "Isn't it amazing how well food and music go together?"

Just a handful of songs recorded with Rupert Holmes remain unreleased from the *Lazy Afternoon* sessions. Holmes wrote a song called "Everything" for this album, and they recorded it, but it remains unreleased. It is not the same-titled song from *A Star Is Born*—the unreleased "Everything" has a different melody and lyric.

Streisand also recorded "Better" by Ed Kleban (who wrote the lyrics to Marvin Hamlisch's music for 1975's *A Chorus Line*). This song too remains unreleased. This was Streisand's third attempt at "Better." She recorded it in a 1973 session produced by Richard Perry; then again in September 1973 with an arrangement by Marty Paich, conducted by Hamlisch; and a third time with Holmes.

Also unreleased is a version of "A Child Is Born" recorded with an orchestra, not just a piano track, as it appears on the final album—wouldn't you love to hear this version?

The great pianist Glenn Gould loved Dave Grusin's "A Child Is Born." He stated in an interview: "There are two descending scales, in different modes, in that song and to hear Streisand inflect them—well, it's just unbelievable, it's spellbinding. It's very hard to find words to say why something moves one as much as that moves me." (Mach, 1980)

The *Lazy Afternoon* quad has no discernable differences as far as arrangements and vocals go, making this probably the only Streisand album in that format that doesn't differ! Streisand wrote that *Lazy Afternoon* "was kind of an odd and dreamy album, and I still remember it fondly."

Matt on *Afternoon*

The title track is one of the most memorable on the album, with its dreamy arrangement. When Barbra sang it live at her 1994 concert in the DC area, my mouth dropped to the floor. I thought, Could that possibly be the musical introduction for "Lazy Afternoon"?! Barbra had excavated this beautiful gem of a song from 1975, and it was perfect. She sang it on her tour that year.

"You and I" is also a favorite of mine from *Lazy Afternoon*. Given Barbra's renditions of "You and I" and "All In Love Is Fair," it's a shame she didn't record more Stevie Wonder tunes.

Despite Rupert Holmes crafting a very pop album for Barbra, the track "Moanin' Low" is a hugely appealing throwback song, performed and orchestrated, as Streisand wrote in her album liner notes, "in the Cotton Club style: a smoky nightclub with flame-blue spotlight, tiers of Manhattan glasses stacked high against pale pink mirrors."

Streisand even included a couple of stylistic vocal homages to Billie Holiday—listen to Barbra sing "my sweet man is *gonna* go" mimicking Holiday's iconic note slide.

Released: February 1976
Produced by: Claus Ogerman
Arranged and conducted by: Claus Ogerman (with the Columbia Symphony Orchestra)
Original recording engineers: Mickey Crofford, Lee Hirschberg, Eddie Brackett, Frank Laico
Audio supervision: Fred Plaut
Photography: Francesco Scavullo
Liner notes/texts and translations edited by: Homer Dennison
2013 remaster:
A & R: Cathleen Murphy
Reissue producer: David Foil
Reissue art direction: Roxanne Slimak
Product development: Jennifer Liebeskind

Catalog Numbers:
M 33452 (LP)
MK 33452 (US CD)
MT 33452 (cassette)
SK 33452 (Europe CD)
SM 33452 (MiniDisc, 1994)
88691922552 (2013 remaster)

Side One:

1. Beau Soir
2. Brezairola ("Berceuse" From *Songs Of The Auvergne*)
3. Verschwiegene Liebe
4. Pavane (Vocalise)
5. Après Un Rêve

Side Two:

1. In Trutina (From *Carmina Burana*)
2. Lascia Ch'io Pianga (From *Rinaldo*)
3. Mondnacht
4. Dank Sei Dir, Herr
5. I Loved You

2013 Remastered CD bonus tracks:
"An Sylvia", D.891
"Auf dem Wasser zu singen", D.774

Classical Barbra was released February 1976, only nine months before the rock-pop soundtrack to her big blockbuster movie *A Star Is Born*, and the irony is not lost. The tracks were all recorded in 1973, three years before the album was released. Streisand was stretching—musically and cinematically. It just happened to be in different directions. *Classical* reached into the past, and *Star* placed her firmly in the present.

"I love classical music, and classical lieder, especially the songs of Schubert and Schumann," said Streisand. "I keep thinking I'd like to do an album of lieder myself and call it *Follow the Lieder*. It's a great title. I've discovered that if you can get a good title, the album just follows naturally along," she added. (Wilson B., 1972)

In her memoir, Streisand revealed she listened to opera star Maria Callas when she was younger. "I bought an album of her singing Puccini arias and it's the one record I kept playing over and over through the years." Streisand wrote that "Senza Mamma" from the opera *Suor Angelica* inspired *Classical Barbra*.

Barbra's 1960s record producer Wally Gold (*What About Today?*) introduced her to Claus Ogerman, a prolific arranger and orchestrator, who had created arrangements for albums by Frank Sinatra and Antônio Carlos Jobim, and others at the Verve label. Ogerman was extremely versatile, able to compose and arrange in the style of jazz, Brazilian music, the standards, and classical. He first worked with Streisand in April 1970 when he created beautiful charts for "Didn't We" and the Legrand/Bergman song "Pieces of Dreams." He also conducted the orchestra for Barbra during her engagement at the Riviera Hotel in November and December 1970.

Classical Barbra came to fruition in April and May 1973 when Streisand recorded several classical art songs at Western Recorders, TTG Studios, and RCA Recording Studios in Hollywood. Ogerman acted as producer, arranger, conductor, pianist, and vocal coach on these sessions. "Claus was incredibly gifted," she wrote, "a multitalent who could compose a concerto, conduct a symphony orchestra, and arrange a number 1 single. He crossed effortlessly between genres . . . jazz, pop, rhythm and blues, classical ... He was born in Germany, so he knew the full repertoire of German lieder."

Streisand recalled her work on the album: "Musically, I've felt compelled to try everything. The most difficult singing project was my classical album, because classical singing is such a disciplined art form. As in rock, the rhythms are very specific. But even though I'm not satisfied with it, I'm still happy I made it." (Holden, 1985)

The only original song on *Classical Barbra* is "I Loved You," composed by Ogerman with lyrics from a poem by Alexander Pushkin.

"Singing lieder is such a disciplined art form, and the rhythms are very specific, which is not my natural style," Barbra explained. "I like to be free to phrase however I want. I also felt the album should have a level of vocal purity, which I wasn't sure I had achieved. I wanted to write "This is a work in progress" on the back, but Columbia asked me not to, so I didn't." Barbra then wrote, "The biggest thrill was something that I never expected . . . being nominated for a Grammy for Best Classical Vocal Soloist Performance. That was a huge surprise."

Matt on *Classical*

There are lots of criticisms one could have about Streisand tackling these songs, but I am not equipped to make those arguments. I'm not knowledgeable about lieder and don't have an opinion about how well (or not well) Streisand succeeded in tackling this project. I know that soprano coloratura is not a form of singing that I enjoy, so the fact that Streisand sings in her natural range on *Classical Barbra* and doesn't use an "opera voice" appeals to me. She made fun of a German opera diva on her TV special *The Belle of 14th Street*, in 1967. As Madame Schmausen-Schmidt, Barbra sang "Liebestraum," a Franz Liszt piano composition, with all the opera vocalist's affectations: runs, trills, and wide melodic leaps. (Ouch! My ears! I don't like that vocal style, which is why I don't listen to Maria Callas or Reneé Fleming. I can take Broadway singers like Kristin Chenoweth and Barbara Cook in only small doses too.)

Classical Barbra is a warm and calming recording that avoids operatic trappings. I can play it in the background for a dinner party, or I can listen to it before bedtime, and it is beautiful and soothing.

"Pavane," for me, is the most special track on this album. Streisand doesn't need words; her vocalization is beautiful enough. The melody and arrangement are melancholy and evoke a restless journey.

Released: November 1976
Produced by: Barbra Streisand and Phil Ramone
Recording engineers: Phil Ramone, Tom Vicari, Dan Wallin
All songs recorded live at: Sun Devil Stadium; Grady Gammage Auditorium; The Handlebar (Wally Heider Recording); A&M Recording Studios
Remix engineer: Phil Ramone
Orchestrations by: Roger Kellaway, Jim Pankow, Kenny Ascher, Ian Freebairn-Smith, Tom Scott, Pat Williams
Front cover photo: Francesco Scavullo
Back cover photo: Steve Schapiro

Catalog Numbers:
JS 34403 (LP)
JSA 34403 (8-Trace Tape)
JST 34403 (cassette)
CK 57375 (1994 CD)
CK 86119 (2002 CD)
CK 5063602 (2002 UK version with bonus track "Evergreen" [Spanish Version])

Side One:

1. Watch Closely Now †
2. Queen Bee *
3. Everything *
4. Lost Inside Of You (with Kris Kristofferson) *†
5. Hellacious Acres †
6. Love Theme From A Star Is Born (Evergreen) *

Side Two:

1. The Woman In The Moon *
2. I Believe In Love *
3. Crippled Crow †
4. Finale: With One More Look At You/Watch Closely Now *
5. Reprise: Love Theme From A Star Is Born (Evergreen) *

* Streisand vocals
† Kristofferson vocals

A Star Is Born, for many Barbra Streisand fans, was the gateway drug for becoming a lifelong fan of hers. The album, of course, was the super-selling soundtrack to her big-hit film, released in 1976.

A Star Is Born was also Barbra's third number one album (after *People* and *The Way We Were*), with monumental sales. The album was certified platinum (over one million records sold) by the RIAA merely two months after it was released to stores. Streisand was the darling of Top 40 pop radio, with her number one song "Evergreen" selling millions too. To date, the album has sold over four million copies and is considered the first "mega-soundtrack album," predating the blockbuster albums from *Grease* and *Saturday Night Fever*. Barbra won her second Academy Award as a writer of "Evergreen."

Jon Peters designed a savvy publicity campaign for the movie that included Francesco Scavullo's iconic photography on the film's posters, album, and advertising: "Evergreen," on the radio; a paperback novelization of the film; and the soundtrack album, which was released by Columbia Records nearly a month before the movie hit theaters. According to *Variety*, "the campaign had Columbia concentrate its $400,000 budget over a two-week period with Warners-controlled ads that also plugged the paperback and film." (Fishbein, 1977)

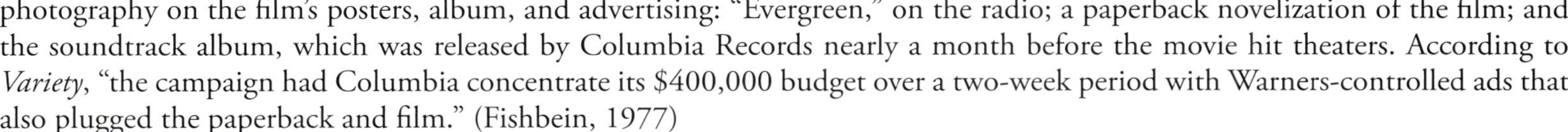

The soundtrack featured the film's stars, Streisand and Kris Kristofferson, singing the tunes of a variety of amazing songwriters: Rupert Holmes, Paul Williams, Kenny Ascher, Kenny Loggins, the Bergmans, and Donna Weiss. Peters deemed that Barbra's big single from the album be clumsily (but cannily) titled not just "Evergreen" but "Love Theme from A Star is Born (Evergreen)." Streisand wrote the melody for the song, and Paul Williams provided the lyrics. "She sat down and played on a guitar the melody for 'Evergreen' that she'd written," Williams told writer Carl Wiser. "It was just such a beautiful melody. I said, 'There's your love song. There's the big love song.' I asked her for the melody. She put it on tape for me, and I took it home. I actually wrote that as the last thing, which I think bothered her. But all the Kris Kristofferson stuff was the first thing up on the shoot schedule. So I wrote the songs for Kris first." (Wiser, 2007)

The soundtrack was a hot seller despite Columbia's $8.98 list price—criticized at the time because it set a new high for the price of a single LP. The slickness of the album's tracks (most of which were recorded live at the venues where the movie filmed) was because Streisand, backup singers, and musicians rehearsed for a month on a Warner Bros. soundstage to run the songs down, set keys, and create the arrangements.

After the album was released, Streisand went back into the studio with producer Gary Klein on February 24, 1977, to record new studio versions of songs from *A Star Is Born* with arrangements by Nick DeCaro: "With One More Look at You" and a solo version of "Lost Inside of You." Barbra didn't use them, though. ("Lost Inside" found a home on the *Memories* album; "One More Look" ended up on *Release Me*.)

Matt on *Star*

One thing that's bugged me all these years is the missing stanza from the song "Queen Bee." It can be seen on screen (with a lot of dialogue playing over the singing) but, for some reason, was not included on the album.

It was gratifying that she finally sang "Everything" during her concert tour in 2016 and 2017, because it was always a favorite of mine from this album. The audiences were appreciative too. I also think "I Believe in Love" is a successful Streisand track and underplayed. It's always exciting to hear Streisand negotiate lyrics at a fast pace, and that song soars.

Now for some honest confessions: I skip the Kris Kristofferson songs. When I hear the opening guitar strums on "Crippled Crow," my hand reaches for the forward button. And "Hellacious Acres" sounds to me like the title states. I can handle these songs in the context of watching the movie, but

I don't want to hear them at home.

Even though *A Star Is Born* is beloved by so many Streisand fans, I'll also state an unpopular opinion. For various reasons (mostly overprotective parents), I never saw the movie until the 1980s. I was not allowed to see R-rated films, and *Star* was deemed too adult for me. So, when I finally saw it, watching it with a slightly younger friend, something happened when Barbra made her first appearance singing "Queen Bee." My friend—who loved Bowie, the Beatles, Pat Benatar, and Fleetwood Mac—heard just a few bars of "Queen Bee" and immediately recoiled. "Oh noooo," he expressed in displeasure.

Why was Streisand singing "Vegas rock"?

Even Rupert Holmes, who wrote "Queen Bee," agreed with this complaint. Recently he confessed: "I thought, why do you have to be a rock and roller? That was what I thought was weird. The script was pushing her towards being a hard-edged rock and roller, and I thought, but you've already proven you're a huge, international star singing the kinds of songs you sing. So I thought, can't you just be a pop star?" (Holmes, 2021)

For me, only "Evergreen" and "Everything" ring true from Streisand in *Star*. She stretches credibility on "The Woman in the Moon," "Queen Bee," and even parts of "I Believe in Love." I cry when she sings "With One More Look at You," but I shut down when she switches to rocker mode on "Watch Closely Now." I've heard other artists cover "I Believe in Love," and I believe it could have been performed with a better, more pop arrangement. "Woman in the Moon" showcases Streisand's incredible voice, but the lyrics and attitude are too obvious and a little dated for me.

I don't like to compare artists; it's like saying a begonia is better than a daffodil. All flowers are beautiful! But let's look at Bradley Cooper's *A Star Is Born* for a quick moment. Gaga's last song, "I'll Never Love Again," works better than "With One More Look/Watch Closely Now" does. As you probably know, she plays Ally, the 2018 version of Barbra's character, Esther. Ally's song works better because it sounds like a song her character would sing, even as it incorporates songwriting by Bradley Cooper's character. It's a big emotional payoff at the end of the movie. "Watch Closely Now" is just too far out there for Esther Hoffman. Yes, thematically, Esther Hoffman has taken on the mantle of John Norman, but there's still the "Vegas rock" problem that is difficult for me to overcome.

One last point about Barbra's *Star*: the movie and soundtrack exist for me as a time capsule; they are not timeless. Judy Garland's 1954 version achieves that classic status. The 1976 *Star Is Born* definitively and strongly reflects the year it was made—which, frankly, is why it was such a big success.

All that being said, it is undeniable that *A Star is Born* made Barbra Streisand a big, big movie star and an enormous, worldwide recording star. With Jon Peters steering the boat, Barbra rode that popularity wave for the rest of the 1970s and through the next millenium.

SIGNATURE STREISAND

"EVERGREEN"

"Love Theme from A Star Is Born (Evergreen)" was not Barbra's first musical composition, but it happens to be her more popular one and has the distinction of being her second number one single. Because it's such a beautiful song, she and lyricist Paul Williams were awarded Grammy, Oscar, and Golden Globe awards for it. She recorded, in fact, three alternate versions of the song for international audiences: a French-language version ("De Rève En Rèverie," with French lyrics by Eddy Marnay), an Italian adaptation ("Sempreverde," with lyrics by Luigi Albertelli), and a Spanish release ("Tema De Amor De Nace Una Estrell," with lyrics by Julio Cèsar).

In the movie *A Star Is Born*, Barbra's character describes the arrangement she wants for the song as having a "rolling piano," which continues throughout the recording. The unmistakable classical-like strumming of the guitar that begins the record makes the song instantly recognizable to fans.

Star producer Phil Ramone remarked that hearing "Evergreen" for the first time was a memory he'd never forget. "Barbra was learning to play guitar so her movement would look real in the film, and she'd improvised a pretty melody while practicing one night," he wrote. "The next day she came in and played it for us and it was superb—almost classical in its simplicity. She also played the song for Leon Russell, who also affirmed its beauty. Barbra was very proud of 'Evergreen.' She was reticent about contributing to the film something she'd written, but it was by far the finest song in the picture." (Ramone, 2007)

Paul Williams recalled that "the only thing that the finished song had that was different from the way it is now is the first two lines were switched," he said. "I wrote 'Love, fresh as the morning air/Love, soft as an easy chair.' That 'easy' doesn't sing good. (If you switch the lines), it works better." (Paulson, 2015) The truth is that Williams wrote different lyrics to the bridge of the song on an earlier version that Streisand rehearsed: *Spirits high, we will satisfy our thirst/With much to discover/In loving each other/Two love lights that shine as one . . .*

Barbra has performed "Evergreen" live since 1986; she sang it at President Clinton's Inaugural Gala in 1993, wearing a pinstripe "peekaboo power suit," as the *New York Times* christened the outfit. In her sports arena concerts, she sang "Evergreen" with Il Divo and trumpeter Chris Botti; she dueted the song with Babyface on her 2014 album, *Partners*. The most unusual official recording of "Evergreen" was included on *Just for the Record*, where we hear Streisand's demo recording, with her picking out the tune on guitar.

"Evergreen" succeeds because Streisand sings such beautiful, legato lines in her warm and vibrant tone. Whenever she sings it, there's an ease and effortlessness to her vocal. My favorite version of "Evergreen" is the one she performed during *One Voice* in 1986. She takes some real singing risks during the concert, giving us unexpected notes and reimagining her vocals. I'm thinking of "ti-i-ime won't change the meaning of," near the end of the live version. I'm told the note she sings on "time" is a D sharp 5, which is so damn exciting. "Evergreen" never fails to please because it "blooms" when the guitar, classical piano, and strings all swell to a climax. Then Streisand sings the last word of the song, always holding that note as long as she can, illustrating with her voice that love never sheds its foliage, but is always persistent and "evergreeeeeeeeeeen."

A dictionary definition of the word "evergreen" sums up how I feel about this song: "something that is *enduringly fresh*." In 2023, "Evergreen" received a new mix for Barbra's compilation album, *Evergreens*. Walter Afanasieff produced it and Jochem van der Saag co-produced and mixed it.

Released: June 1977
Produced by: Gary Klein for The Entertainment Company
All songs engineered by: Armin Steiner (except "Answer Me": Tommy Vicari)
Assistant engineers: Don Henderson, Linda Tyler, Mitch Tannenbum
Album re-mixed by: Armin Steiner
Musical contractor and coordinator: Frank DeCaro
Mastering: The Mastering Lab
Album recorded at: Sound Labs Inc., Capitol Recording Studios, United Western Recorders
Photos: Steve Schapiro
Art direction: Seiniger and Associates

Catalog Numbers:
JC 34830 (LP)
PCT 34830 (cassette)
JCA 34830 (8-track)
1R1 6673 (reel-to-reel)
CK 34830 (CD)

Side One:
1. Superman
2. Don't Believe What You Read
3. Baby Me Baby
4. I Found You Love
5. Answer Me

Side Two:
1. My Heart Belongs To Me
2. Cabin Fever
3. Love Comes From Unexpected Places
4. New York State Of Mind
5. Lullaby For Myself

Ron Oberman—vice president of A & R at Columbia Records—wrote an internal memo in June 1977: "With *A Star is Born* on the way to the four-million-unit level, Barbra Streisand's following has never been larger. A number one single, number one album, and one of the year's biggest grossing films have combined to catapult Barbra beyond her already accepted superstar status. Now, with perfect timing, comes the new Barbra Streisand album, *Streisand Superman*."

Barbra Streisand's career began a new chapter in 1977 when Jon Peters took over the management role that Marty Erlichman had held for two decades. To fulfill her next album for Columbia Records, Streisand and Peters turned to The Entertainment Company.

Comprising producers Gary Klein and Charles Koppelman, The Entertainment Company promoted song catalogs, acquired major songs, and produced a series of hits in which superstar recording artists were paired. For Streisand, their idea was to keep her at the top of the pop charts. Klein put together a ten-song album using arrangers Nick DeCaro, Jack Nitzsche, and Charlie Calello. The album was built around Richie Snyder's song "Superman."

"I like the idea that a woman could be thought of as Superman," Streisand told Sirius XM. She was also ahead of the times—Warner Bros.'s big film *Superman: The Movie*, starring Christopher Reeve, would not hit theaters until December 1978.

Barbra recorded *Superman* in Los Angeles, mostly in April 1977. The album included two songs that were written for *A Star Is Born*—"Answer Me" by Streisand, Paul Williams, and Kenny Ascher and "Lullaby for Myself" by Rupert Holmes. There were a few songs left on the cutting room floor:

- "Here in the City" (Janis Ian)—Recorded March 23, 1977, at Sound Labs, Hollywood.
- "I Love Making Love to You" (Germinaro/Sands/Weisman)—Recorded April 12-13, 1977, at United Western Recorders, Los Angeles
- "Music Man" (Paul Anka)—Recorded April 20, 1977, at Capitol Records, Los Angeles.

Columbia Records acted quickly and released the single "My Heart Belongs to Me" on May 13, 1977, ahead of the album. Columbia and Barbra also put together a publicity film for "My Heart Belongs to Me" that was shown at Columbia's 1977 convention to industry insiders. This was, technically, Barbra's first music video, although the format as we know it today didn't really arrive and thrive until MTV launched in 1981.

The *Superman* album, slickly packaged with sexy photos of Barbra wearing a Superman T-shirt and short shorts, hit stores a month later. Her album look was inspired by a short scene in *A Star Is Born* in which Streisand wears the outfit at her character's home in Sonoita, Arizona. "That cover was a departure for me," she wrote. "Actually the whole outfit was, because it was way more revealing than anything I would normally wear . . . it was me, Barbra, claiming my own strength and sexuality, or at least not being afraid of it anymore. And that was a big step for me, because I've always had such doubts about my looks."

Barbra helped write the song "Don't Believe What You Read" as a response to a horrible *Los Angeles Magazine* column about her with the subtitle "A Pigeon Is Born." The magazine claimed that Barbra and Jon kept an indoor aviary and that the birds flew around the house. "[They] were intimating that they were crapping on people's heads," Barbra exclaimed in a KHJ Radio interview.

Barbra could have simply ignored the column. However, "one night I invited Neil Sedaka and his wife to come over and play some music," Streisand explained, "and she told me later that she was afraid to come because she had read I had birds flying around on the loose. Another friend's barber . . . also asked if this was really true."

Despite the bird story, *Superman* sold over two million units and peaked on the *Billboard* chart at number three.

Matt on *Superman*

What I love most about Barbra's albums in the '70s is that she was on point with her themes, which always matched her covers! *Superman* was no exception, down to the packaging and artwork. For the sexy cover and inside photos, Steve Schapiro shot Streisand against seamless paper in her Holmby Hills home.

For the second time in her career (*Lazy Afternoon* was the first), Barbra contributed liner notes to the album. The *Superman* LP insert contained Barbra's thoughts on each of the songs, and she wittily wrapped up the notes by referencing the superhero: "Thanks for reading. Now I've got to go into the nearest telephone booth and change clothes."

As for the songs, I must admit that when Barbra ventures down the rock and roll path on "Cabin Fever" and "Don't Believe What You Read," I'm not one-hundred-percent on board, despite her passionate vocals. I cranked up "Cabin Fever" recently, and I will admit it is fun. I'm just not sure it holds up in the pantheon of Streisand recordings.

The opening song, "Superman," is a far-out choice, but I concede it works well in the context of the album's theme. The arrangement allows Barbra to soar like a bird . . . like a plane . . . like Superman! I can't imagine she'd have recorded this song if it hadn't been the concept of the album, though.

"I Found You Love" is atypical for Streisand too, but I love it. It manages to be bouncy and fun. And I love a good "doo, doo, doo" chorus. Did you know Cher and her boyfriend Gregg Allman sang a duet version of this song on their 1977 album, *Allman and Woman: Two the Hard Way*?

As for this 1977 solo version of "New York State of Mind" . . . I like it better than the duet with Billy Joel that Streisand recorded on *Partners* in 2014. The '77 version has an easier feel to it, and Barbra's groove is pleasing. And who doesn't like a saxophone solo?

"My Heart Belongs to Me" was the big single and became the best known song from the album. Gary Klein told me, "Alan Gordon was a brilliant songwriter. Period. He understood what pop songs were all about, and this was one of his best. I loved the arrangement and the dynamic range of the melody. Barbra nailed it." (Howe, Interview with Gary Klein, 2011)

There are three unique yet tricky tunes on *Superman* that I'm most drawn to, maybe because they stick out as being so different and are not typical pop songs.

"Answer Me" deserves a second and third listen; it's a sensitive song with an intricate construction. It's placed perfectly on the album because it's basically an art song masquerading as a pop song. Nick DeCaro creatively echoes the opening stanza at the end of the song with his beautiful string orchestration. Barbra was quizzical herself about the song in her book. "I don't know how to describe it. I guess you could call it an atonal tone poem." Barbra points out that "Answer Me" uses a similar approach as "By the Way" when it uses the title in a different way at the end. After asking to "answer me" throughout the song, she ends, hoping "should someone ask who's touched your heart Perhaps you'll answer—me." Clever!

Another gentle song is "Love Comes from Unexpected Places." Again, it's a complicated melody, but Streisand is at the top of her singing powers and negotiates the intervals perfectly.

"Lullaby for Myself" modulates all over the place, with its stream-of-consciousness lyrics and striding tempo.

Columbia Records seemed to have a fun time promoting the album in '77. It ran several print ads riffing on the comic book hero theme. In one featuring Streisand's posterior, they wrote the headline "Clark Kent, eat your heart out."

When the album got a platinum certification, Columbia ran an ad with a telephone booth, stating, "Faster than a speeding bullet!!!" which referenced a phrase used often in the music biz, "with a bullet," and *Billboard*'s practice of putting a bullet sign in front of fast rising songs on its music charts.

Mostly, *Superman* is one of the quintessential mid-1970s pop albums and brings back fond memories of that magical summer of 1977. Can you imagine two million households across America playing the album after seeing *Star Wars* at the movies, hearing that Elvis Presley died, watching *Roots* on TV, and electing Jimmy Carter as president?

SIGNATURE STREISAND

"YOU DON'T BRING ME FLOWERS"

Even though Barbra's solo version of "You Don't Bring Me Flowers" originated on *Songbird*, it was the duet with Neil Diamond, released as Columbia single #3-10840, that made this song a classic. Columbia also included the song on *Barbra Streisand's Greatest Hits: Volume 2*.

Marilyn Bergman told A.S.C.A.P. that Diamond was at a dinner party with Norman Lear, "He asked if Norman had any great television series coming up, because he'd like to write the theme song. And Norman said, 'Yes, I've got a show that we're getting ready to do a pilot on called *All That Glitters*, and I don't have a main title for it.' Neil offered to write it, and Norman asked that he write it with us. So we wrote this 45-second (because that's all the time we had for a theme) song called 'You Don't Bring Me Flowers.'" (ASCAP, 1996)

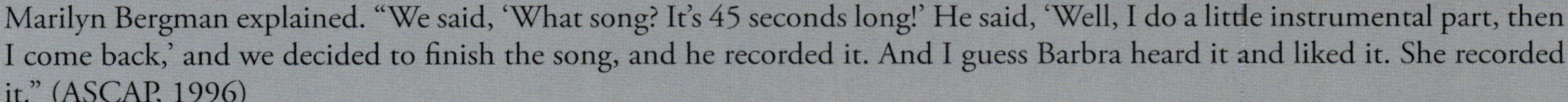

"About six or eight months later we ran into Neil, and he said that he was doing the song on the road and that everybody liked it," Marilyn Bergman explained. "We said, 'What song? It's 45 seconds long!' He said, 'Well, I do a little instrumental part, then I come back,' and we decided to finish the song, and he recorded it. And I guess Barbra heard it and liked it. She recorded it." (ASCAP, 1996)

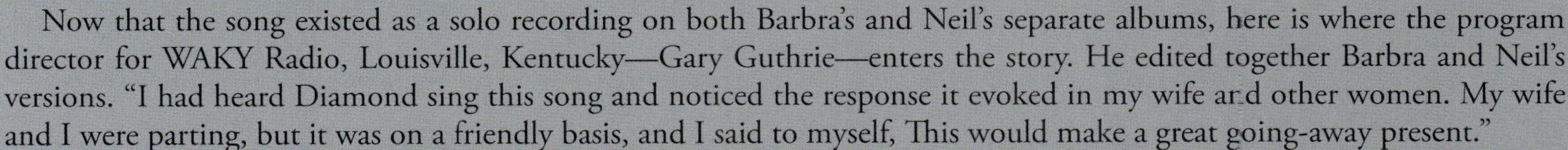

Now that the song existed as a solo recording on both Barbra's and Neil's separate albums, here is where the program director for WAKY Radio, Louisville, Kentucky—Gary Guthrie—enters the story. He edited together Barbra and Neil's versions. "I had heard Diamond sing this song and noticed the response it evoked in my wife and other women. My wife and I were parting, but it was on a friendly basis, and I said to myself, This would make a great going-away present."

Once Guthrie played his homemade duet on the air, there was an overwhelming response from listeners. "These guys would call me up and say, 'Hey, look here, buddy. I've spent the last four hours going to shopping malls all over this county to get this record for my wife and they tell me it doesn't exist—that you have the only copy.'" (Dorsey, 1978)

Guthrie sent a copy to Columbia Records, and president Bruce Lundvall pounced. "When Lundvall heard it, he flipped out and called Neil and his manager and played it for them on the phone," said Guthrie.

Neil Diamond managed to get to Streisand and Jon Peters, which led to Streisand and Diamond recording a real, face-to-face version of the duet in the studio in late September 1978.

On the *Billboard* Hot 100 chart, "Flowers" was number one for two weeks, and it spent a total of seventeen weeks on the chart, ultimately selling more than two million copies in stores.

"Flowers" was also nominated for two Grammy Awards: Record of the Year and Best Pop Vocal Performance—Duo, Group, or Chorus. It didn't win either.

Diamond and Streisand surprised the 1980 Grammy audience when they appeared unannounced on the televised show and sang the duet to screaming adulation. The live performance is truly an iconic duet, replayed for years as a special Grammy moment.

Since that 1980 appearance, Streisand has sung "Flowers" with Diamond on stage only twice: again in 1980, at an American Civil Liberties Union concert for the Bergmans, and in 2004 at a John Kerry fundraiser. She has sung the solo version of the song during several concert tours.

Released: May 1978
Produced by: Gary Klein for The Entertainment Company
Executive producer: Charles Koppelman
Miss Streisand's hair styled by: Carrie White
Front cover photograph: Steve Schapiro
Back cover photographs: Barbra Streisand and Jon Peters
Design: Seiniger/Morrison & Associates

Catalog Numbers:
JC 35375 (LP)
JCT 35375 (cassette)
1R1 6789 (reel-to-reel)
JCA 35375 (8-track)
CK 35375 (CD)

Side One:

1. Tomorrow
2. A Man I Loved
3. I Don't Break Easily
4. Love Breakdown
5. You Don't Bring Me Flowers

Side Two:

1. Honey Can I Put On Your Clothes?
2. One More Night
3. Stay Away
4. Deep In The Night
5. Songbird

Before Barbra Streisand began work on her next studio album for Columbia Records, there was the matter of her contract with the label, which was up for renewal at the end of 1977. She had just delivered two red-hot albums for Columbia (*A Star Is Born* and *Superman*), so Jon Peters had some negotiating power.

Reportedly, the renewed contract with Columbia contained these concessions for Streisand: five albums delivered in the next five years; a greatest-hits album; a budget of $250,000 per album; and a guaranteed payment of $1.5 million to Streisand for each album, plus about a 20 percent royalty on the albums' retail prices (Streisand received almost $1.50 for every album she sold!). (Considine, 1985)

With *Songbird*, Barbra worked with Gary Klein and The Entertainment Company again. She began recording tracks for the album in November 1977 while she was in New York with Peters, who was producing the film *The Eyes of Laura Mars*. This was the first time since 1971 that she'd recorded in New York City.

"We'll do about 12 or 13 sides," Gary Klein told the *LA Times*. "We're not sure which ones we'll finally use. This should be a fairly typical Streisand album. There won't be any radical changes in her style or in the kind of material she sings." (Hunt, Pop News, 1978) Though Streisand recorded most of this album in New York, she booked six more sessions in Los Angeles on February 6-8, 13, 15-16, 1978.

The biggest mystical synchronicity about this album, however, is that author Pat Conroy told Streisand years later that "I was playing your album *Songbird* while I was writing this book." Which book? *The Prince of Tides*. More on that later.

For a while, "Tomorrow" was the working title of the album, since Barbra was so impressed with the song, which was the big hit from Charles Strouse and Martin Charnin's Broadway musical *Annie*, starring Andrea McArdle. Streisand, in fact, went backstage to meet McArdle after one of the shows—and to ask her permission to record the song. "Of course, I didn't think anything of it when Barbra Streisand came backstage during the original production to ask me if she could record ['Tomorrow']," she recalled, "but then ten years later, I thought, 'That's really pretty cool.'" (Wong, 2013)

"A Man I Loved" was written by Nicki Oosterveen and George Michalski, and it was Jon Peters who discovered the writing duo. After hearing their songs, Peters sent a limousine to pick them up and signed them to a management deal with CBS Records. Then Oosterveen and Michalski spent an afternoon at Streisand's Malibu home playing their songs for her. Streisand chose "A Man I Loved." When she recorded it, Oosterveen and Michalski provided backing vocals. (Larry Shultz, 2013)

"Deep in the Night" was another Broadway song, from a 1971-72 musical called *Inner City*, which was based on Eve Merriam's book *The Inner City Mother Goose*, about the tough life in New York City. Linda Hopkins sang it in the show and won the Tony Award for it.

Elkie Brooks, with her husky voice, recorded "Honey, Can I Put on Your Clothes?" on her 1977 album, *Two Days Away*. The great songwriting team of Leiber and Stoller noted that Streisand asked them to change the original lyric from "'cause they feel so good/And they smell like you" to "And they feel like you."

Barbra was nominated for this solo version of "You Don't Bring Me Flowers" at the Grammys for Best Pop Vocal Performance, Female.

There are three songs still unreleased from the *Songbird* sessions:

- "Til I Get It Right" (Larry Henley, Red Lane)—Recorded November 13, 1977, at Media Sound, New York
- "Nightmoves" (Michael Franks, Michael Small)—Recorded November 13, 1977, at Media Sound, New York
- "Lookin' Out for Number One" (Carole King)—Recorded February 1978, at Sound Labs, Los Angeles

The cover of the album was another home run for Team Barbra. Her 1970s go-to photographer, Steve Schapiro, shot the cover, as well as the inside sleeve photos. That's Sadie posing with Barbra. Jon Peters told the *LA Times* that he didn't style Streisand's hair anymore. Instead, the former hairdresser sent Streisand to Carrie White, a celebrated celebrity hairstylist famous for creating Nurse Ratched's hairstyle in *One Flew Over the Cuckoo's Nest*. "I gave her more red and more highlights," she confided, adding that she also tamed Streisand's frizz into a "controlled perm." (Staff, 1978)

Although not as popular as *A Star Is Born* or *Superman*, *Songbird* charted impressively, peaking at number twelve, and selling over a million units.

Matt on *Songbird*

Maybe Barbra couldn't find a bird to pose with on the cover, but *Songbird* as an album makes up for that—it's extraordinary!

Songbird in fact mirrors her collaborations with Richard Perry at the beginning of the decade (*Stony End* and *Barbra Joan Streisand*), as it took her and The Entertainment Company two albums to find a mutual groove. Next to *Superman*, *Songbird* feels effortless, and the selection of songs is married well to her talent. After all, Gary Klein wasn't trying to reinvent the wheel with her; he just wanted to sell a lot of records.

Gene Page, who was responsible for so many of the top-notch arrangements on Barbra's Richard Perry albums, reunited with Streisand to orchestrate "Tomorrow," the first track. With that happy strumming of the guitar, it's joyous, fresh, and airy, which distances Barbra's version miles away from Andrea McArdle's Broadway recording. When it came time to sing it live on the 1978 television special *The Stars Salute Israel at 30*, she completely changed the normal arrangement—she begins a cappella as Zubin Mehta and the Los Angeles Philharmonic orchestra pick up the tempo; Streisand finishes it with powerful, long-held, belting notes. Check it out on YouTube.

The lyrics to "A Man I Loved" are so interesting, but also confuse me. When I reexamined them recently, I thought it was a song about God because it begins describing an almost-all-powerful man who lives "in the clouds above." After the opening confidence ("Maybe someday, he will happen to you"), the lyric backpedals. "The dream is over, but I don't wanna hear," she sings. At the bridge, the lyric reveals the singer is "lonely" and "the dream is over." Then, resolutely, Nikki Oosterveen's lyrics repeat several times: "I don't wanna hear." The track dissolves into a dreamy soundscape and fades out. Is the song about a dead lover? Is Streisand singing about her deceased father? I really don't know.

Roberts and Gordon are back as songwriters, and "I Don't Break Easily" and "Love Breakdown" are both delicious.

Please revisit the two "night" songs the next time you decide to listen to the *Songbird* album. Both "One More Night" and "Deep in the Night" are fantastic, big, belting songs that are very satisfactory.

Finally, the title tune, "Songbird," by David Wolfert and Steve Nelson, is a beautiful melody and the promoted single from the album. For me, the song walks a fine line between autobiography and self-pity. It reminds me of the lyrics to "I Write the Songs," in which music itself is personified. As "Songbird" is written, the singer knows she touches the listeners with her voice, but insists that it's a lonely gig, wondering who sings songs for her. It's an interesting point of view and maybe a revelation of the price a singer like Streisand pays to give us all the feelings we get through her music. "Who sings for Songbird?"

Released: October 1979
Produced by: Gary Klein for The Entertainment Company
Executive producer: Charles Koppelman
Recorded and mixed by: John Arrias
Photography: Mario Casilli
Visual coordination: Tony Lane, A.D.
Inner sleeve color-tinting: Ginger Canzoneri

Catalog Numbers:
FC 36258 (LP)
FCA 36258 (8-track)
FCT 36258 (cassette)
CK 36258 (CD)

Side One:

1. Wet
2. Come Rain Or Come Shine
3. Splish Splash
4. On Rainy Afternoons
5. After The Rain

Side Two:

1. No More Tears (Enough Is Enough) (with Donna Summer)
2. Niagara
3. I Ain't Gonna Cry Tonight
4. Kiss Me In The Rain

After Barbra wrapped filming *The Main Event* for Warner Bros., she began work on a new studio album for Columbia Records with Gary Klein of The Entertainment Company (her third album with Klein producing). At this point in her career, Streisand had been producing an album each year since 1974, and her last three albums (*A Star Is Born*, *Superman*, and *Songbird*) were her biggest-selling ones to date.

"Many times," explained Barbra, "the title of an album comes to me before the actual songs. I love the ocean, the rain, lakes, waterfalls, ponds, and Jacuzzis! I thought it would be a nice idea to have wet and water as a unifying theme for a group of songs." (SiriusXM, 2014, 2016)

Playboy photographer Mario Casilli took provocative and sexy photos of Barbra in the hot tub on her forty-acre estate on Ramirez Canyon Road. *Wet*, therefore, became a concept album for Streisand—even down to the first and last word that Barbra sang on the album: "wet."

The title track, with lyrics cowritten by Barbra, was recorded on July 23, 1979, at Capitol Studios with a fifty-five-piece orchestra. John Arrias was the sound engineer on that session. He told author Karen Swenson, "Barbra walked in as we were rehearsing the orchestra—this is one moment she can't remember—dressed in purple, and she went straight into the vocal booth where I had everything set up for her. Right away, we had a headphone problem. . . . It turned out it was because I gave her a mono mix and she likes to hear it in stereo; she likes to hear the 'openness' in her headphones. Mono sounds much smaller. So I worked out a technical way of giving her stereo and she said, 'Oh, there it is. Wonderful.' And from that day to today she has never raised her voice to me, never said a harsh word, she's always been super kind." (Swenson, 1986)

"On Rainy Afternoons," a song with lyrics by the Bergmans and music by Lalo Schifrin, was originally composed for a 1976 war adventure film starring Michael Caine and Robert Duvall, *The Eagle Has Landed*—for that film, the musical composition was known as "The Eagle Has Landed Love Theme," or "Eagles in Love." In his autobiography, Schifrin told how Streisand contacted him because she loved the melody, but he explained it had no lyrics. So Streisand had the Bergmans write what became "On Rainy Afternoons" for the *Wet* album. Then Barbra asked Schifrin to write the arrangement. When he met Streisand to set the song in her key, Schifrin confessed, "I started to change the harmonies in Monkish fashion. Barbra interrupted my playing and said, 'What happened, are you getting tired of your own composition? Don't tamper with success.'" Schifrin showed up at Capitol Records a week later for a midnight recording session. "One arranger after another was taking turns conducting the orchestra. At 12:00 midnight it was time for me to get to the podium. She is so great that we completed the recording in one take." (Schifrin, 2008)

Barbra recorded five songs that were not used on the album. Three songs were not "wet" enough for the album's theme: "Understand Your Man," by Alan Gordon (he also wrote "My Heart Belongs to Me" and "I Found You Love"); "Something's Missing (In My Life)" by Paul Jabara and Jay Asher, which was also recorded by Jabara himself, Donna Summer, and Karen Carpenter as a solo artist; and another Alan Gordon song, "I Am Alone Tonight."

Barbra and Gary Klein also recorded a solo version of "Rainbow Connection" from *The Muppet Movie* that remained unreleased for years until it was remixed as a duet with Kermit the Frog for Barbra's 2021 album, *Release Me 2*.

As it did with "No More Tears," Columbia Records released "Kiss Me in the Rain/I Ain't Gonna Cry Tonight" (# 1-11179) as a single in December 1979.

Unfortunately, *Wet* was not nominated for any Grammy Awards; instead, "You Don't Bring Me Flowers," Barbra's successful duet with Neil Diamond, attracted the Grammys' attention.

Matt on *Wet*

Barbra's concept album isn't as serious and formal as Beyoncé's *I Am . . . Sasha Fierce,* Frank Sinatra's *Watertown*, or even The Who's *Tommy*. Barbra's *Wet* is light and fun . . . and as sexy as a bubbling Jacuzzi!

The opening song, "Wet," is a beautiful poem-like art song that Streisand excels at. David Wolfert (who wrote "Songbird") and Sue Sheridan are credited alongside Streisand for writing the song. Lee Holdridge provides a beautiful orchestral arrangement that does not try to be a number one single. Holdridge said about being an orchestrator, "The composer is one thing, and the orchestrator is like a painter in a strange way, because you now paint colors into the composition." (Academy, 2021)

It's no wonder Richard Jay-Alexander and Barbra resurrected "Come Rain or Come Shine" for Barbra's 2006 concert tour. The version on *Wet* is so contemporary and succeeds mostly due to guitar virtuoso Larry Carlton serenading Streisand. He has a long list of studio and album credits, and his playing really makes the song vital and full of personality.

"Splish Splash" is a breath of fresh (but funky) air! Guess who arranged it . . . David Foster (see *Back to Broadway*). I like "Splish Splash" because Barbra sounds like she's having a blast. Had the album's theme not been "wet," it's doubtful Barbra would have ever sung this song. There is an elemental joy hearing Barbra get down while singing *"slippin' slidin' slidin' glidin' movin' groovin' rollin' strollin', sure do love to splish and splash with you!"*

Just when you think it couldn't get any freakier, Barbra closes out the song with some ad-libs: "Oh, Billy, don't be silly. Stop that! Oh, you're crazy. It's gettin' hot!"

What is going on in that hot tub??

Three songs on *Wet* are lush, tender, and sophisticated. "On Rainy Afternoons" evokes such afternoons and makes me want to snuggle up in a soft blanket with my cat and some chamomile tea.

Could "After the Rain" possibly be more gently sensuous? Barbra's voice really blooms on the second stanza as the orchestra swells around her.

And "Niagara," in addition to its beautiful melody, is a great acting song for Barbra in which she recognizes her partner has changed but still recalls the bliss they once had together at Niagara Falls. Marvin Hamlisch wrote the tune, and the lyrics are by Carole Bayer Sager and Bruce Roberts. Bayer Sager tells a funny story in her memoir about writing this song. Hamlisch, whom she was dating at the time, innocently ate a brownie from her refrigerator that happened to be baked with *special* ingredients. Bruce Roberts and Bayer Sager then finished the song with a stoned Marvin Hamlisch. Later, they drove to Barbra's Ramirez Canyon home to present the song. When she heard the title, Bayer Sager wrote, Barbra "turned and seriously asked, 'Is that wet enough?' 'It's very wet, Barbra,'" Bayer Sager replied. "'It's Niagara Falls. What's wetter?'" (Sager, 2017)

SIGNATURE STREISAND

"NO MORE TEARS (ENOUGH IS ENOUGH)"

On August 14, 1979, Barbra and Donna Summer began recording the duet "(No More Tears) Enough Is Enough" in Santa Monica. Paul Jabara wrote the song with his partner Bruce Roberts. The disco duet was Barbra's fourth number one single on the *Billboard* Hot 100 list. Casablanca (Summer's label) also released a twelve-inch disco remix of the song.

"It was Paul Jabara who came up with the idea of doing the duet," Donna Summer wrote in her memoir. "Paul had won the Oscar for 'Last Dance,' and Charles Koppelman, Barbra's producer from Columbia, knew a good song when he heard it." (Donna Summer, 2008)

"Paul was the kind of writer who couldn't be deterred," Streisand laughed, "so he brought back this wonderful intro, a play on the children's nursery rhyme 'It's raining, it's pouring, the old man is snoring,' which he made into 'My love life is boring me to tears.' He kind of shoehorned the tears and pouring rain to fit the wet concept. And it became the big hit from the album." (SiriusXM, 2014, 2016)

Jabara brought the song, along with Donna Summer, to Streisand's home. He discovered that Barbra's son, Jason, was a big fan of Donna Summer.

Jabara continued: "The minute Donna and I arrived at Barbra's, I said, 'This is the duet I've been trying to get you two to do.' They both got excited. Barbra kept asking, 'What part do I sing?' I knew if I could just get them together, they'd do it." (Streisand & Summer team up for a duet of disco and egos, 1979)

"The next day," Summer wrote, "Paul began to look for a place for us to record the song. We wound up trying four different studios. In one the sound wasn't right for Paul, in another it wasn't right for me, in still another Barbra didn't like it, and the fourth seemed wrong to all three of us. Once we finally found a studio we all agreed on, it was smooth sailing." (Donna Summer, 2008)

"Barbra was not as comfortable in the genre of disco or dance music," said Bruce Roberts, "so I first went in and sang Barbra's part as a guide vocal. It was finished overnight." (Pener, 2012)

"Enough Is Enough" was recorded over two weeks in Los Angeles at a reported cost of $100,000.

Jabara was ecstatic. "There was Streisand," he said, "hands flaring, and Donna, throwing her head back—and they're both belting, sparking each other. It was a songwriter's dream. Forget 'Enough Is Enough,' I want 'More and More.'" (Streisand & Summer team up for a duet of disco and egos, 1979)

Jabara stated that the master tracks of this song were recorded in person, face-to-face. But engineer John Arrias confirmed that the singers did some overdubbing separately. "They never could quite feed off each other," he said, "so they decided, 'Okay, let's try it individually.' Donna singing to Barbra's scratch part and Barbra singing to Donna's." (Swenson, 1986) Streisand commented in her book about the reason that she wanted to do this song. It was due to a very important person in her life, her son, "They played the song, and Jason loved it . . . so that was a great reason to do it . . . and he loved Donna. So did I. She was a doll, and I said yes."

DECADE 70 ENCORE

Barbra Streisand's creative output during the 1970s is outsized, making my head spin. I am grateful when I get maybe three things done. Streisand, for a decade, managed to act, sing, and give concerts, all while raising a son and entering into a new relationship with Jon Peters.

In the 1970s, Streisand was busy making movies, and yet she managed to release an album (sometimes two!) every year from 1970 to 1979. Not only that, but Barbra was experimenting in those years, singing rock and pop and classical songs.

Barbra's star ascended during the sixties, but the seventies saw her reach superstar status, becoming more well-known than ever. With Jon Peters encouraging her to be youthful and relevant to her younger fans, Barbra became much more mainstream, a part of pop culture. She was no longer Dolly or Fanny Brice—characters from the turn of the century. Now she was Esther Hoffman, a curly-haired woman of the seventies in *A Star Is Born!* She was Hillary Kramer, a self-made business woman in *The Main Event* . . . with red curly hair.

In retrospect, Barbra's musical collaborations were of the era too. She sang with the queen of disco, Donna Summer; she dueted about lost love with fellow Brooklyn boy and unlikely movie star Neil Diamond (see *The Jazz Singer*); and although she shared only a couple of duets with Kris Kristofferson, he was a sexy man who paired well with Barbra—their chemistry was palatable.

When Barbra received the Grammy Legend Award in 1992, she was apologetic, thanking her fans: "You were there when I attempted to change with the times, and you were there when I came back home," referring to her big hit, *The Broadway Album*. Then, in her 1994 concert, Barbra comedically sang, "I've been through funk and it stunk."

But musical audiences of the seventies didn't agree, as her record sales prove. When I interact with Barbra Streisand fans at her concerts, so many have told me they began following her career after seeing *A Star Is Born*. That film inspired a whole new legion of fans and holds a dear place in their hearts. For them, when you mention Barbra Streisand, an image of Barbra with her perm, wearing suspenders and jeans, comes to mind. For others, pre-perm Barbra is the vision they see in their mind's eye from the 1970s—her long, straight hair and casual clothes.

Since this is a book about her music, let's not forget that Barbra sounded damn good during this part of her career. The voice is singularly irreproachable. You may not like the arrangements or the vibe of the 1970s, but you must admire her tone, her notes, her stamina, and—frankly—her nerve. With very few exceptions, Barbra made just about everything she sang practically flawless.

In future decades, Barbra seemed less interested in cranking out Top 40 hits and followed a more spiritual path of growth and adaptation. There was also a disco backlash, evidenced in July 1979 at the Disco Demolition Night in Chicago when a Chicago radio disc jockey burned a crate of disco albums to the delight of a stadium full of rock music fans.

Barbra Streisand had one big popular album in her, though . . . and she needed a Bee Gee to help her achieve it.

INTERMISSION:

GREATEST HITS/ MOVIE SCORES/ FEATURING

GREATEST HITS ALBUMS

Greatest-hits albums used to be a reliable cash cow for record companies. By mining an artist's music catalog, the labels could easily (and inexpensively) release several albums containing previously released hits that millions would buy. Elton John has over twenty compilation albums featuring his big hits. And even though iconic acts like the Supremes or the Beatles no longer perform together, their music has been released in anthologies and in "definitive collections" for decades.

Columbia released two Streisand greatest hits albums in the 1970s—*Barbra Streisand's Greatest Hits* in 1970, then followed that with *Volume 2* in 1978.

The 1970 *Hits* album comprised Barbra's recordings from the 1960s. Of note is the track "Sam, You Made the Pants Too Long," because it was previously available only as a seven-inch single (#4-43612). It's possible some Streisand fans did not own this single, and this was its first time appearing on an LP.

Track three, "Why Did I Choose You?," is 2:48 minutes on both the LP and CD (and Spotify) of *Barbra Streisand's Greatest Hits*. The complete, 3:44 minute track can be found on Spotify, and on Columbia's remastered CD, *My Name Is Barbra*.

Streisand included the 1967 live version of "Happy Days Are Here Again," sung in New York's Central Park, on her 1970 *Hits* album. Since Barbra was not happy with the arrangement of "Happy Days" as it appeared on her first album, she changed it for live performances and used one of those recordings on *Barbra Streisand's Greatest Hits* instead of the studio version from 1963.

Eight years later, there was a whole new repertoire of contemporary pop songs included on *Barbra Streisand's Greatest Hits Volume 2*. The album had two selling points. One, it contained Barbra's huge hit duet with Neil Diamond, "You Don't Bring Me Flowers." Its second selling point was Barbra's rocking "Love Theme from Eyes of Laura Mars," also known as "Prisoner." The song was written by Karen Lawrence and drummer John Desautels, part of a group called 1994. Lawrence used to be a member of another group, called L.A. Jets, and The Entertainment Company handled their musical publishing chores. Streisand, of course, worked with The Entertainment Company's Gary Klein on several of her albums.

Klein's associate Charles Koppelman played the song for Streisand and producer Jon Peters, and they liked it as a theme song for the movie. Lawrence met Streisand in Phoenix, where she was filming the big outdoor concert for *A Star Is Born*. "I thought Barbra would be able to do a great job on the song—she can sing full blast, flat out, but she's sensitive too. Now that she's really doing it, it's just a mind blower. They even kept the little piano intro I wrote, which is very flattering." (Sutherland, 1978)

Streisand's vocal on "Prisoner" is very good and authentic. She really "gets down" on the track and sings the hell out of it. She wasn't always successful tackling rock songs, but this one works very well.

One more quirk about *Volume 2* is the inclusion of "The Way We Were." For some reason, Columbia began including the *album* version of this song on all future compilation albums. The *single* version sounds practically the same but has an alternate Streisand vocal on the line "smiles we gave to one another" at approximately 1:20 into the song. That single (Columbia #4-45944) went to number one on the *Billboard* charts and was Barbra's first number one hit, so it's curious that it has never appeared in Streisand's catalogue since that 1973 vinyl and radio hit.

In the 1980s, Columbia Records double- and triple-dipped on Streisand compilation albums. *Memories* (known as *Love Songs* in the UK) was released in 1981, mostly because Barbra was busy working on her movie *Yentl* and did not have time to record a new album for the label. She did have time to record two new songs, though—"Memory" from the musical *Cats* and "Comin' In and Out of Your Life," a pop song by Bobby Whiteside.

Robert Hilburn's review in the *Los Angeles Times* was spot-on: "If you read the small print on the back of Barbra Streisand's new 10-song *Memories* album, you'll find this advisory: 'This album contains some previously released material.' A more accurate description would be: 'This album contains a couple of new songs.'"

Memories is notable for the single version of "No More Tears (Enough Is Enough)" and an alternate, solo version of "Lost Inside of You" from *A Star Is Born*. "Lost" is from a 1977 recording session in which Barbra and arranger Nick DeCaro recorded new, studio versions of some of the songs from *A Star Is Born*. "With One More Look At You," which ended up on *Release Me*, was from this session. "Woman in the Moon" and "Everything," also with new arrangements, remain unreleased.

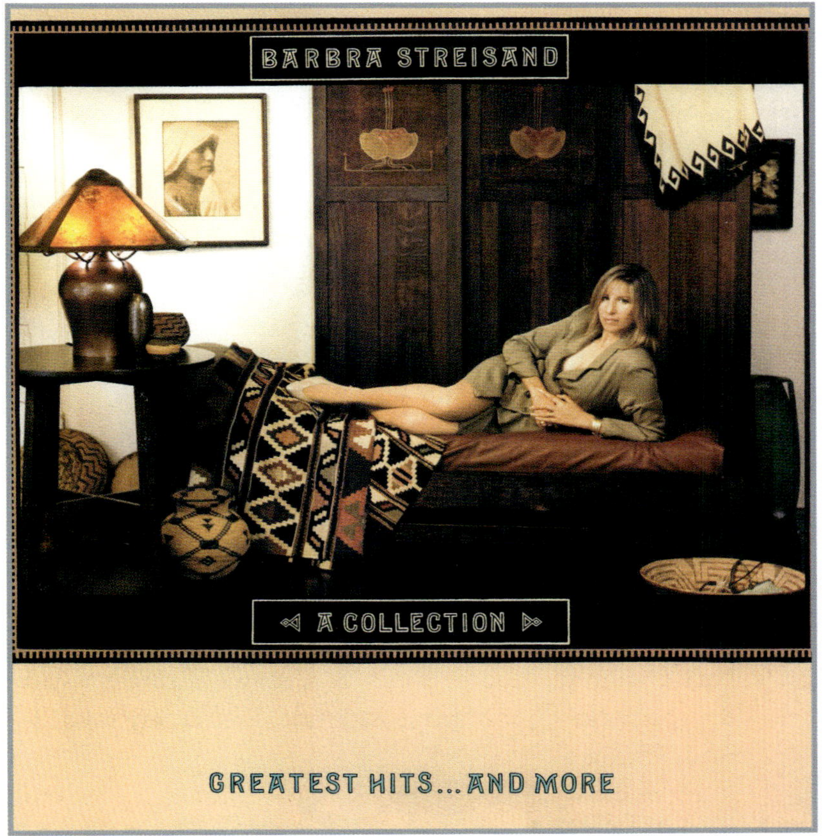

A mere eight years later, Columbia revisited Streisand's catalog again, this time for *A Collection: Greatest Hits and More*. This one repeated the formula from 1981: Streisand recorded two new songs; the rest were previously released tracks. The first new song was "We're Not Makin' Love Anymore," written by Michael Bolton and Diane Warren. The track was produced by Narada Michael Walden. The other brand new song, "Someone That I Used to Love," was written by Michael Masser and Gerry Goffin and produced by Masser. A third song, "Halfway Through the Night" by Masser and Cynthia Weil, was recorded but has never been released.

I like "We're Not Makin' Love" even though it's not Barbra's usual musical style. But she manages to sing it well and authentically, giving us some Streisand vocal runs. This music video use to be in heavy rotation on VH1.

"Someone That I Used to Love," however, is a bit hysterical. I can see why Streisand was attracted to the lyric of that song; it's about how we have to live in the present after a breakup, all the while trying to compartmentalize our ex-lover and our feelings about them. However, the synthesized strings and entire production of the song get out of hand at the climax.

Both "Memory" and "Comin' In and Out of Your Life" had already appeared on the 1981 collection. The rest were from Barbra's huge hit albums *Guilty* and *The Broadway Album*. Surprisingly, "By the Way" was included, a "deep cut" from the album *Lazy Afternoon*.

In 2002, Legacy Recordings, a division of Sony BMG, established *The Essential* series—compilation albums from its artists' back catalogs (*The Essential Johnny Cash*, *The Essential Neil Diamond*, etc.). With *The Essential Barbra Streisand*, Sony collected Streisand's hits onto two CDs and enticed buyers to purchase the collection once again by including two new tracks. "You'll Never Walk Alone" by Rodgers and Hammerstein had already appeared on Barbra's 1997 album, *Higher Ground*. But in October 2001, Streisand recorded the song again, with a new arrangement by William Ross—this was the studio version of the song she sang live on her post-September 11 appearance on the Emmy Awards. She also recorded the *Snow White and the Seven Dwarfs* Disney song "Someday My Prince Will Come" in March 2001. Only "I've Dreamed of You" on Disc Two was altered for *The Essential Barbra Streisand*—it has an extended introduction and runs 4:53, compared with its 4:46 running time on Barbra's 1999 album, *A Love Like Ours*.

Then, in 2008, SonyBMG did something weird. It repackaged many of the *Essential* albums with the newly monikered branding *Essential 3.0*. *The Essential Barbra Streisand 3.0* included a third CD, all packaged in an eco-friendly cardboard case, which eliminated the wasteful plastic CD jewel box. There are nine tracks, all recycled too. Two of them are live songs ("Evergreen" from the 1994 concert and "Unusual Way") that fade the audience's applause out.

The 2002's *Duets* album was a "greatest hits" of sorts; it was a comprehensive, career-spanning collection of Barbra's duets with other singers, all previously released tracks. Columbia surprised no one by including *two* newly recorded duets: "All I Know of Love" with Josh Groban and "I Won't Be the One to Let Go," with Barry Manilow, who also wrote the song.

Sony BMG Special Markets released a series of CDs in November 2007 called *Super Hits*—all priced inexpensively and featuring well-known songs by artists like Kenny Chesney, the Jackson 5, and Judas Priest. The CDs were marketed to the record buyer shopping at drugstores or Walmart. The Barbra Streisand *Super Hits* CD had ten tracks, all previously released.

Barbra Streisand: The Collection was a 2004 box set from Columbia that contained three albums in one box: *Funny Girl* soundtrack, *The Way We Were* (studio album), and *A Star Is Born* soundtrack. Columbia literally took the CDs you could buy off the rack and put them in this box.

Barbra Streisand: The Ultimate Collection was released by Sony/Legacy in the UK in 2010 (US fans ordered it online as an import CD). The standard edition came in cardboard packaging. The deluxe edition came handsomely packaged in a collector's box with five collectible photographs. All songs were previously released. Legacy repackaged the CD in 2012 with a different cover and a longer title: *Barbra Streisand: A Woman in Love, the Greatest Hits*. The new version retained all the same tracks, but (for some reason) all were resequenced.

In October 2013, Legacy Recordings released new CDs titled the *Classic Christmas Album* series. The CDs collected holiday songs from label artists like Alabama, Johnny Cash, Neil Diamond, George Jones & Tammy Wynette, Gladys Knight & the Pips, Martina McBride, Barbra Streisand, and Andy Williams.

Streisand's *Classic Christmas Album* contained previously released material culled from her 1967 *A Christmas Album* and her 2001 album of holiday material, *Christmas Memories*.

The End of Hits?

The 2023 collection of Barbra's hand-selected cuts, *Evergreens*, was a "hits" album of sorts (although they deliberately avoided including any tunes from other hits albums). In any case, Columbia had not released any sort of collection of previously-released songs since 2010.

Blame it on the internet?

In 2020, the RIAA reported that streaming (digital downloads and subscriptions to services like Spotify) made up 85 percent of all music revenue in the United States. (Heater, 2020)

What that tells us is that these days, "greatest hits" albums sell fewer units because people stream their own playlists of hit songs.

It's also true that Barbra's long-term fans have already bought these "hits" albums several times over.

"Hits" Catalog Numbers

Barbra Streisand's Greatest Hits—KCS 9968 (LP); CM 9968 (MiniDisc); CK 9968 (CD)
Greatest Hits Volume II—FC 35679 (LP); MD 86079 (Europe MiniDisc); CK 35679 (CD)
Memories—TC 37678 (LP); CBS 10031 (UK *Love Songs*); CK 37678 (CD); CD 10031 (UK *Love Songs* CD)
A Collection: Greatest Hits and More—OC 45369 (LP); CK 45369 (CD); CM 45369 (MiniDisc)
The Essential Barbra Streisand—C2K 86123 (CD)
The Essential Barbra Streisand 3.0—886973457023
Duets—CK 86126 (CD); CM 86126 (MiniDisc)
Barbra Streisand: The Collection—024639 (3 CDs)
Super Hits—A 721560
Barbra: The Ultimate Collection—88697 790432
Barbra Streisand: A Woman in Love, the Greatest Hits—88691992562
The Classic Christmas Album—88843 01308 2

MOVIE SCORES

In Barbra Streisand's discography, there are six titles I classify as "Soundtrack Score Albums"—they fit into Streisand's body of work because they supported movies in which she starred, but the albums contain mostly the scores for her films, supplemented by a Streisand song . . . or two.

The first one, which doesn't technically fit into this category, is 1971's *The Owl and the Pussycat* (#AS 30401). Released by Columbia, the album is subtitled "Comedy Highlights and Music from the Soundtrack." The vinyl LP features actual dialogue from the film, plus rock songs from the movie performed by Blood, Sweat & Tears.

The album has never appeared on CD, and modern fans may wonder why this album even exists. Well, back in the 1970s, there was no home video market, nor could you rent or stream movies. There was no easy way to see a movie again after it played in your local movie theater. But listening to a soundtrack album with dialogue and music was a way to relive the movie in your own living room. In 2014, Blood, Sweat & Tears released an album titled *Rare, Rarer & Rarest* that contained only the group's music for *The Owl and the Pussycat*—with no Barbra Streisand/George Segal dialogue.

Columbia released the original soundtrack recording of *The Way We Were* in 1974. This is an album of Marvin Hamlisch's score for the blockbuster movie, including a couple of period songs. Barbra Streisand opens and closes the album with the Hamlisch/Bergman song "The Way We Were." The first track is the beautifully orchestrated (i.e., not pop) version of the song that plays under the movie's opening credits. And the last track—a rare one—is a reprise of the song, but the version that accompanies the movie's closing credits, again with Barbra singing passionately. Columbia released the original soundtrack recording of *The Way We Were* in 1974 (LP #PC 32830). A remastered compact disc of this soundtrack was released by Columbia in October 1993 (#CK 57381).

Even though *Eyes of Laura Mars* is not a Barbra Streisand movie, it's important to mention the out-of-print soundtrack album, on which Streisand sings the theme song, "Prisoner," twice. The first track is the same mix as the single and the *Greatest Hits Volume 2* version. However, the last track is worth noting. Instead of opening with the usual piano intro, the song has been eerily scored with moody strings, which continue throughout the track. There are no new vocals on that track, however. Check it out—Columbia (#35487).

The soundtrack album to Barbra Streisand's 1979 comedy film with Ryan O'Neal, *The Main Event*, is subtitled "Music from the Original Motion Picture Soundtrack." In truth, the album contains only nine tracks, three of which are the same title song sung by Barbra Streisand—Columbia LP (#JS 36115) and CD (#CK 57376).

"Barbra had hired Marilyn and Alan Bergman to write a *Way We Were* type of ballad for the movie," songwriter Bob Esty explained, "but Jon Peters thought it should be an up-tempo tune, since the movie's a comedy. So he talked [Streisand] into reconsidering, because he wanted her to do a contemporary thing, a dance tune." (Grein, 1979) Soundtrack album producer Gary Le Mel justified to some degree the lackluster album package. "We didn't want to cheat the public," he said. "We wanted to give them what they heard on the radio. We had made a twelve-inch disco version of the song, but it was only for discos and disco radio . . . so we put them both on the album." (Ruber, 1979)

So on one album, Streisand fans get an almost twelve-minute disco version of "The Main Event," plus the 4:55 "short version" of the song, and then the 4:16 "ballad version." The ballad version, which is lovely, has strings conducted by Esty, and Bruce Roberts accompanying Barbra on piano. It's an overlooked track, with Barbra delivering a passionate vocal. I often wonder why, on later greatest hits packages, Columbia never used the ballad. It would be familiar to fans, but sound fresh and new.

The Main Event peaked on *Billboard* at number twenty and was certified gold (five hundred thousand units) by the RIAA. It was restored, remastered, and released for the first time on CD in October 1993. The single hit number three on *Billboard's* Hot 100 chart.

The *Nuts* original score CD is more of an EP than an album, with a total run time of only thirteen-plus minutes. It contains music by Barbra Streisand—her first motion picture score. She wrote that "For some time, I had dreamed of scoring a movie. When I produced *Nuts*, the dream became a reality—after all, who else would hire me . . . or fire me?!"

Barbra explained, "As a courtroom drama, *Nuts* required very little music, so I decided to give it a shot." (Streisand, *Just for the Record* liner notes, 1991)

When *Nuts* was released in 1987 on vinyl (#4C 40876), CD (#CXK 40876), and cassette (#4CT 40876), Columbia reportedly pressed only twelve thousand CDs. That makes the soundtrack very rare, and when it shows up on eBay, I've noted, it sells for seventy-five dollars and up. As of 2025, though, *Nuts* is available for streaming online. By the way, the *Nuts* track "The Bar" became the song "Here We Are At Last," on the album *Emotion*. The main theme of the film was turned into the song "Two People," with lyrics by the Bergmans, and is contained on *Till I Loved You*.

The original motion picture soundtrack for *The Prince of Tides* (#CK 48627) features mostly tracks composed by James Newton Howard from the movie's score. Released in November 1991, this CD carries the curious disclaimer "Ms. Streisand's vocal performances were recorded exclusively for this Compact Disc release. They do not appear in the film *The Prince of Tides*."

Streisand sings two songs on this soundtrack album. "For All We Know" underscored the romantic scene in which Nick Nolte's character dances with Streisand's at the Rainbow Room. Barbra's son, Jason Gould, had given her Billie Holiday's album *Lady in Satin*, and Streisand connected with Holiday's cover of "For All We Know." "It was so beautiful, and the lyric was so perfect—as if it were written especially for the film," Barbra wrote in the CD notes.

Johnny Mandel started working with Streisand on "For All We Know" in late spring 1991. "I played some synthesizer parts for her and she sang," he said. "I worked out what chords I needed, then went home and wrote the arrangement." (Stewart, 1991)

Mandel then took about a week to score the chart for the song before returning to the studio to record it. "The recording, done in June in Capitol Records's Studio A, didn't take long," Mandel said. "Barbra came in, and we did eight or nine great takes, each one of which could have been a release." Kirk Whalum, the jazz saxophonist from Memphis, soloed on this track. "[Streisand] heard my version of 'For All We Know' and wanted me to be a part of the movie *The Prince of Tides*," Whalum recalled. "In the studio, she sang it and I played the solo. Everybody was sort of holding their breath, because she can be a perfectionist. She looks over at me and says, 'What do you think?' Yeah, I'm a boy from Memphis sitting there in Hollywood and Barbra Streisand is asking me what I think. A moment that will live in infamy." (Edgar, 1991)

The second song, "Places That Belong to You," was considered as an end credit theme and a big single to promote the movie. But Streisand had other considerations. "It's [Tom Wingo's] story," she said. "That's why I didn't sing the song at the end of the movie. I would have been paid a lot of money to sing the song, as much as I got paid to produce. But I felt it wasn't right. It was his story and what right would I have to come in and sing this song? My character is a secondary character." (Carr, 1991) Despite this decision, Barbra wrote in her liner notes for the CD that "it was such a beautiful melody that we asked Alan and Marilyn Bergman to write a lyric to it so I could include it on this soundtrack recording. If Lowenstein did sing, I think this is what she would say."

The last Barbra Streisand movie to receive a soundtrack album release was *The Mirror Has Two Faces* (#CK 67887) in 1996. There were twenty-four tracks on this CD—Barbra's lucky number. Two of those tracks were Streisand vocals; singer-songwriter Richard Marx has one song—"The Power Inside," which was the background song for the scene in the film in which Streisand's character, Rose, transforms her appearance at the gym and the makeup counter. The rest of the album comprises Marvin Hamlisch's score, which is still fun to listen to, with Barbra's love theme interpolated throughout. Hamlisch also incorporates a couple of standards: "Try a Little Tenderness," with David Sanborn on saxophone, and "Ruby." Of course, there's the highly dramatic "Nessun dorma" at the end, performed by Luciano Pavarotti and conducted by Zubin Mehta. Those who have seen Barbra's movie know that this song is set up earlier in the film, when Rose explains that "when we fall in love, we hear Puccini in our heads." Apparently, Streisand heard Pavarotti singing *Turandot*. The soundtrack sold quite well, achieving platinum status and peaking at number sixteen on the *Billboard* chart. "I Finally Found Someone" was Barbra's big hit duet with singer/songwriter Bryan Adams. An alternate title song, "All of My Life," written by Hamlisch, Streisand, and the Bergmans, was included as a bonus track. You can still hear Streisand's love theme on this one, and the Bergmans' lyrics are exquisite, as always. The elusive, unreleased "It Doesn't Get Better Than This" is a third version of the title song.

FEATURING BARBRA STREISAND

The first album in Barbra Streisand's discography that isn't really part of her discography and isn't really a "Streisand album" is *Harold Sings Arlen (with Friend)*, from March 1966. The artist was Harold Arlen (the great American composer of standards and show tunes), and Streisand was the friend. Peter Matz was the arranger-conductor.

Producer Thomas Z. Shepard wrote on his website, "Arlen and I spent a lot of time choosing the songs. Picking twelve gems out of a barrelful of hits was an excruciating task. We had chosen ten and had two slots left, so we decided that it would be a creative stroke to bring in an additional singer."

It wasn't such a crazy "ask"—"Harold and Barbra Streisand had a mutual admiration," wrote Shepard. "Therefore, it wasn't hard for me to convince her manager that she ought to participate." Arlen even wrote in the album's liner notes: "Barbra's version of 'House of Flowers' is the most moving, exciting rendition imaginable—and I'm delighted. As for Barbra joining me on this album—I'm gratulant and grateful and an indebted idolater."

Barbra said, "His album gave me a chance to sing with the man who, in my opinion, is the greatest composer of American music next to George Gershwin. His melodies hit you in the gut . . . soulful, almost painful, moving." (Harold Arlen Centennial Celebration, 2005)

Streisand had fun in the recording booth with Arlen too. "She came to the recording studio, in mink coat and jeans, straight from performing a matinee of *Funny Girl*, and participated lovingly with Harold in a duet of 'Ding Dong the Witch Is Dead' before doing an exquisite solo in 'The House of Flowers,'" recalled Shepard.

Arlen's singing on the album is pleasant enough. Matz's arrangements are good despite Columbia session singers providing backing vocals, which ages the album. The album (LP #AOS 2920 and CD #CK 52722) is out of print, though Barbra's two songs appear on *Just for the Record*. "Ding Dong!" also appears on Barbra's 2002 CD, *Duets*. One last note on *Harold Sings Arlen*: he sings his song "That's a Fine Kind of Freedom" here for the first time, although Matz would reimagine it for Streisand on her 1968 album, *What About Today?*

Twenty-three years later, Barbra Streisand made her next guest appearance on another singer's album, one far removed from Harold Arlen. She is credited as a background vocalist (along with five other female singers) in 1989 on Don Johnson's song "What If It Takes All Night?" The sexy *Miami Vice* television star was dating Streisand at that time, and even recorded a duet with her (more on that later). "What If It Takes All Night?" was on Johnson's solo album for Epic Records, *Let It Roll*. This entire paragraph is superfluous, because the truth is you cannot hear Streisand's voice on the track. This information, however, will help you win Streisand trivia one night. You're welcome.

One notable collaboration, though, is Streisand's duet of "I've Got A Crush on You" with Frank Sinatra in 1993. Sinatra's *Duets* album consisted of his duets with popular singers from various genres. Producer Phil Ramone wrote that he was "confident that pairing Sinatra with a variety of legendary artists will make for an attention-grabbing record." (Ramone, 2007) The album was a big commercial success, selling over three million copies in the US.

Ramone relied on a fiber optics system called EDNet to record tracks in real time from different locations. In many cases,

Sinatra and his duet partners recorded separately.

Jay Landers was asked by Charles Koppelman if Barbra would be open to singing with Sinatra. "I listened to all the possible songs (some had already been spoken for by other artists) and was delighted that 'I've Got A Crush On You' was still available," Landers recalled, having already worked on a solo demo of the song for *Back to Broadway* with Barbra. "Phil Ramone and I put together a demo with a female demo singer so Barbra could imagine how the duet would go. She made some significant improvements to the vocal arrangement, which we then recut, incorporating her ideas." The song modulated between Sinatra's key (F) and Streisand's (E flat). "Then," Jay continued, "by a stroke of luck, I was at a recording studio when I bumped into none other than David Foster."

Ramone recalled, "We did a whole new intro for her before Sinatra comes in. David Foster and I had fun with that, and a lot of laughs." (McClintick, 1993)

Barbra recorded her vocals to "I've Got A Crush on You" on August 17, 1993, at Todd-AO in Hollywood. Sinatra arranged for a large bouquet of flowers to greet her; Barbra wrote a thank you note to Sinatra and included a note that he had written to her after seeing her on Broadway in *Funny Girl*.

Jay explained, "In the studio, David did all the heavy lifting, meaning he produced the orchestra and Barbra's sterling vocal and even found a brilliant way to make Frank 'answer' Barbra on one of the lines. If I may be so bold, it's by far the best track on that album!"

Sinatra recorded his response to Streisand's "You make me blush, Francis," while he was performing in Chicago, singing into a Digital Audio Tape machine, "I have got a crush, my Barbra on you…"

"I've Got A Crush on You" was nominated for a Grammy for Best Instrumental Arrangement Accompanying Vocals.

Thirteen years later, Barbra appeared as a guest vocalist on a similar album concept—this time Tony Bennett's *Duets*. The two icons sang the Charlie Chaplin song "Smile."

Bennett recalled: "We did that song at her home out in Malibu on a beautiful day. We recorded it in one or two takes in her living room, which happens to have a spectacular view of the ocean. Barbra didn't really understand why I chose that particular song, so I explained that even though the song was written many, many years ago by Charlie Chaplin for the movie *Modern Times*, one of the great movies that he made, it still has a particular relevance today because of 9/11 . . . I said, 'Barbra, this is the kind of thing you believe in!' I got through to her, and she sung it beautifully—she smacked it right out of the ballpark." (Touzeau, 2009)

In 2011, Barbra's 1985 vocals from her recording of "Somewhere" were repurposed to create a duet with 11-year-old Jackie Evancho on her premiere album, *Dream With Me*.

In 2012, Streisand's original vocals recorded in 2001 for *Christmas Memories* were repurposed for the Olivia Newton-John and John Travolta album *This Christmas*. All three sang together on the track "I'll Be Home for Christmas," which was produced by veteran keyboardist/arranger/orchestrator Randy Waldman—who had played and conducted for Streisand for decades.

The amazing Grammy Award-winning singer and actress Mary J. Blige recorded "When You Wish Upon a Star" with Streisand for her 2013 holiday album, *A Mary Christmas*. Blige told covermg.com: "Barbra was one of my idols growing up, but the sad thing was, we didn't work together again in the studio on our song, because our schedules just don't permit these things. The production [David Foster] used their magic to put our vocals together and it still came out great."

THE 1980S

Released: September 1980
Produced by: Barry Gibb, Albhy Galuten, and Karl Richardson for Barry Gibb Productions and Karlbhy Productions
Recorded at: Criteria Studios, Middle Ear, Inc., Miami; Sound Lab Studios, Inc, Hollywood; Mediasound Studios, New York
Engineered and mixed by: Karl Richardson and Don Gehman
Mastered by: Bob Carbone at A&M Records

Catalog Numbers:
FC 36750 (LP)
FCA 36750 (8-track)
FCT 36750 (cassette)
HC 46750 (half speed mastered LP)
CK 36750 (CD)
MD 36750 (MiniDisc, 1992)
CN 85155 (2005 DualDisc remaster—2-sided disc)
5205475 (2005 UK version of DualDisc w/ 1 CD + 1 DVD)

Side One:

1. Guilty (with Barry Gibb)
2. Woman In Love
3. Run Wild
4. Promises
5. The Love Inside

Side Two:

1. What Kind Of Fool (with Barry Gibb)
2. Life Story
3. Never Give Up
4. Make It Like A Memory

DualDiscs were a new technology introduced from 2004-2007. They were a double-sided hybrid disc which contained CD content on one side and DVD content on the other.
2005 *Guilty* DVD: All nine songs in PCM Stereo; video interview w/ Barbra and Barry; music videos: Guilty (live w/Barry Gibb), What Kind Of Fool (live w/Barry Gibb), Stranger In A Strange Land (excerpt/preview); *Guilty* photo gallery

The three brothers who called themselves the Bee Gees had a unique sound: tight R & B harmonies and falsetto vocals. Barry, Robin, and Maurice Gibb were born in England and grew up in Australia. After a string of hits in the 1960s, the brothers broke up, but then rejoined in 1970. Promoted by their manager and impresario, Robert Stigwood, the Bee Gees ventured into R & B-flavored disco tunes in the midseventies and hit the big time when they recorded an extremely popular soundtrack album for the 1977 hit movie *Saturday Night Fever*, starring John Travolta. They had huge hits with "Stayin' Alive," "Night Fever," and "How Deep Is Your Love." In the United States, the album sold sixteen million units!

"The Bee Gees were the biggest group in the world," Barbra Streisand recalled. "They had a distinct sound . . . some great songs with lyrics that were—shall we say—nonlinear. They kind of sounded like the Chipmunks. It was a very unique but pleasant sound." (SiriusXM, 2014, 2016)

How in the world did a Bee Gee and Barbra Streisand come together? During the success of *Saturday Night Fever*, a reporter asked the Gibb brothers which artist they would most like to produce. When they said Barbra Streisand, Charles Koppelman got on the phone to Streisand. She ended up attending a Bee Gees concert at LA's Dodger Stadium in July 1979. When Barbra was spotted taking her seat in the left field stands, the audience roared.

Barry Gibb stated, "Obviously they were interested in getting one or two songs, but basically what they wanted in the beginning was just a clear production job. They sent us a bunch of songs they'd planned for her to do. But they just weren't right for the vision we had of how she should sound; we wanted to get her more into the mainstream and sell more records than she ever had before." (Matre, 1981)

Koppelman asked for five songs, and within two months (October 1979) Barry and Robin Gibb had written and recorded demos of Barry singing the songs "Woman in Love," "Run Wild," "Promises," "Life Story," and an unused song titled "Secrets."

"When I first heard Barry's demos, I was blown away," Koppelman exclaimed. "I said to myself, *Holy mackerel. I sure hope Barbra will make me forget I ever heard Barry singing these songs*. Well, that concern lasted about two minutes, until the first time Barbra opened her mouth to sing." (Grammy Record Nominee, 1981) At this point in the career of the brothers Gibb, the group had decided to transition into being producers and songwriters, with Robin Gibb working on an album with soul singer Jimmy Ruffin, and Maurice Gibb taking some time off to deal with health issues. Barry went to work on the Barbra Streisand album.

Barbra wrote that "I instantly responded to the melodies and the feel of the songs, but I was less certain about the lyrics. They were kind of abstract, with lots of intriguing, impressionistic images that were open to interpretation. (In other words, I didn't know what they meant.)" Ultimately, "I decided to trust him, to just put myself in his hands and go with the flow," she stated.

Barry Gibb confessed: "We all had heard stories about how tough she is, and she is this enormous star. That's got to intimidate anyone. I didn't want to do it at first, but my wife told me to do it or she'd divorce me! I even called Neil Diamond to ask what it was like to work with her. He had nothing but glowing reports, so I felt a little less scared." (Spada, 1983)

The last song submitted for the album project was "Guilty," in late 1979. It's the only song on the album written by all the Bee Gees. Streisand stated, "I actually said I feel like there should be another kind of—not up-tempo, but a rhythmic [song]. It had a breezy, almost jazzlike quality that I just loved." (SiriusXM, 2014, 2016)

Gibb worked with a team comprising Albhy Galuten and Karl Richardson, and he recorded instrumental tracks at the Bee Gees' studio, Middle Ear, in Miami Beach. Orchestral parts were added at Criteria Studio in Miami.

Richardson explained: "We cut the first versions of the tracks at Criteria to take them to Los Angeles so we could capture Barbra singing there, because I believe she was filming a movie at the time. Recording was sort of like a hobby for her at that moment, and we could only get her for so many hours of so many days, originally. So, the decision was to cut the music in Miami, then produce her vocals, then come back to [Miami] do the mix." (Walters, 2020)

In all, Gibb estimated that the album took six months of work, with about two weeks of work from Streisand. Although Barbra was used to recording with a live orchestra, for *Guilty* she sang to Gibb's prerecorded tracks. During the breaks, she would work on the script for *Yentl*.

One fun fact: Bernard Lupe, credited as the drummer on "Woman in Love," "What Kind of Fool," and "Life Story," is not a real person—in the days before digital editing and sampling, engineer Albhy Galuten invented a tape loop that was lifted from two bars of the song "Night Fever." Because the *Guilty* session drummer's father died in the middle of a recording session and Gibb was unable to replace him, the tape loop of his rhythmic drumming was necessary to complete the song. Galuten reused the loop on the *Guilty* album's tracks.

Ultimately, *Guilty* was a worldwide phenomenon for Streisand and became her biggest-selling album to date—over five million units worldwide. The single "Woman in Love" reached number one in five countries, while the "Guilty" single was number one in the Netherlands, Belgium, Austria, Australia, New Zealand, and the UK. In the US, the album went to number one on the *Billboard* charts.

At the Grammys, *Guilty* was nominated for Album of the Year; "Woman in Love" for Record of the Year; and Barbra for Best Pop Female Vocal Performance on "Woman in Love." Barbra and Barry won the Grammy for Best Pop Vocal Performance, Duo or Group, for the song "Guilty." Upon presenting an award at the 1981 Grammy show, Barbra hilariously quipped to Barry Gibb, "I feel like I'm cheating on Neil Diamond."

Streisand remarked, "I've always looked back on the *Guilty* album as one of the easiest, most pleasant recording experiences I've ever had. Barry just made the process a delight. Maybe because he's an artist himself, he understands what it takes to be a producer for another singer." (SiriusXM, 2014, 2016) Barry Gibb said *Guilty* was an album "I'm very proud of. I wanted to produce her best-selling album, and I accomplished that." (Spada, 1983)

Matt on *Guilty*

Guilty, despite coming out as the decade changed and disco waned, sounds surprisingly fresh, even with some telltale musical sounds that age some (but not all) of its tracks. "Never Give Up" and "Promises" are the two that come to mind as sounding "too disco."

Among the others: I always rush to play "Run Wild," one of my favorites on the disc. It has a slow but sexy build to it, and it's blissful to hear Streisand's vocal after the instrumental break: "Ru-u-u-un wi-i-ild . . . "

"The Love Inside" becomes almost meditative and spiritual with Streisand's meticulous singing and Barry Gibb's lovely chords. When Barbra and the backup singers come together at the end, it almost sounds like she's surrounded by angels on a beautiful cloud.

"Life Story" is probably the precursor to "Come Tomorrow" (*Guilty Pleasures*), with a 1950s doo-wop feel. But it's also sexy, because it has a "bad girl" vibe to it, with an obstinate, rebellious lyric.

The Oscar for Best Dramatic Song goes to "Make It Like a Memory," the album's closing track. The number starts simply but dramatically with a piano intro; the drums eventually kick in, and Streisand gives us a light-rock vocal. Gibb's lyric writing here is so good, especially the couplets "So forever do or die" and "kiss hello nor wave goodbye." After the guitar solo, Barbra gives us a fantastic vocal, hitting the most amazing high notes. Then Gibb and Galuten boldly end the song with two minutes of orchestra. Wow! Now that's the way to finish an album.

It goes without saying that the two duets with Barry Gibb are forever-classics! "Guilty" is just as infectious as when I first heard it on the radio, and "What Kind of Fool" is still an emotional and bittersweet ballad that tugs at my heartstrings: "You let the stranger in. Who's sorry now?"

When Barbra and Barry joined voices to sing these two songs live during the *One Voice* concert in 1986, it felt nostalgic even though the *Guilty* album was only six years old at that point. That just goes to show how quickly the music business changes. Thank goodness we have those moments on videotape, with the two of them singing brilliant live vocals—Gibb sounds particularly awesome.

The fantastic collaboration of Streisand and Gibb was so agreeable that the duo reunited twenty-five years later to record a follow-up album called *Guilty Pleasures*.

SIGNATURE STREISAND

"WOMAN IN LOVE"

Barry Gibb recalled that Streisand "felt that ['Woman in Love'] was a little bit liberationist, that it might be a little too strong for a pop song." (Spada, 1983) Nonetheless, "Woman in Love" was released as the first single from the *Guilty* album, and it debuted at number forty-nine on *Billboard*'s Hot 100 chart in early September 1980.

"I thought the lyric wasn't something that I would say," Streisand confessed. (SiriusXM, 2014, 2016) But she went along with Barry Gibb's plan to release the song ahead of the album.

"Woman in Love" became Streisand's fifth number one single in the US, staying at that position for three weeks. The single enjoyed similar success around the world, peaking at number one in Australia, the UK, Canada, and more countries. "Woman in Love" also has the distinction of being Barbra's *last* number one single in the US.

The song has a great, catchy, melody that people love to sing along with. Yes, the lyrics don't make a lot of sense, but who cares? "It's a right I defend" sounds a bit defensive, and the song even begins cosmically: "Life is a moment in space . . . " With Barry Gibb's multilayered backup vocals, "Woman in Love" has a relentless but striving beat with Streisand soaring on her riffs, holding those long notes over Gibb's solid chorus.

Streisand eventually included "Woman in Love" in some of her last concerts, knowing how much the audience loved to hear her sing it.

"GUILTY"

The second single from the *Guilty* album was the song "Guilty," and it peaked on the *Billboard* charts at number three. Over the years, though, it's become one of Streisand's best-loved hits. It has an infectious Latin-inspired rhythm, and Streisand's voice is so silvery on this track. The chorus hooks us from the start—"and we got nothing to be guil-tee of . . . " When Barry Gibb comes in, the song takes off, with Streisand dancing vocally around his dynamic voice. "Guilty" is relentless and uncompromising! That's why we love it so much. The Gibb brothers did not bother to write a bridge for this song; instead, Barbra and Barry sing "we got nothing to be guil-tee of" over and over and over, giving us vocal performances that are "in the pocket," as they say in the music business (meaning that they're right in the groove of the song, singing the rhythm perfectly together).

The song's producer, Albhy Galuten, explained how the song was changed during the production of the album. "Barry was not going to do any duets," he said. "They talked him into it. So, for his verses, we had to change the key and had worked out modulations to go from one key to another, from verse to chorus, and then overdub the instruments, fit them in, and fly that stuff around to literally create the verses for Barry that were in another key." (Walters, 2020)

"Guilty" (the single) won a Grammy Award for Best Pop Vocal by Duo or Group, which must have pleased Gibb and Streisand. Six years after recording the album, Gibb joined Streisand onstage at her Malibu home for the concert *One Voice* and sang "Guilty" and "What Kind of Fool" live with Barbra. The "Guilty" performance is outstanding, with Streisand faking surprise when Gibb strides out on stage. They proceed to bop and groove for four minutes as they duet on the song, obviously enjoying each other. "I love singing with you, Barry, I love your voice," Streisand tells him onstage.

Released: November 8, 1983
Produced by: Barbra Streisand and Alan and Marilyn Bergman
Associate producer: Michel Legrand
Postproduction supervised by: Phil Ramone
Soundtrack arranged and conducted by: Michel Legrand
Music by: Michel Legrand
Lyrics by: Alan and Marilyn Bergman
Album photographs by: David James
Recorded at: Olympic Studios, London
Engineered by: Keith Grant
Assistant engineers: Nigel Brooke-Harte, Steve Schmitt, Larry Fergusson, and Clif Jones

Catalog Numbers:
JS 39152 (LP)
JST 39152 (cassette)
JSA 39152 (8-track)
CK 39152 (CD)

Side One:
1. Where Is It Written?
2. Papa, Can You Hear Me?
3. This Is One Of Those Moments
4. No Wonder
5. The Way He Makes Me Feel
6. No Wonder (Part Two)

Side Two:
1. Tomorrow Night
2. Will Someone Ever Look At Me That Way?
3. No Matter What Happens
4. No Wonder (Reprise)
5. A Piece Of Sky
6. The Way He Makes Me Feel (Studio Version)
7. No Matter What Happens (Studio Version)

Yentl was Barbra Streisand's movie passion project, which she directed, starred in, wrote, and produced. The movie concerns Yentl, who, in 1904, lives in a shtetl and longs to study the Talmud like men do. After her father's death, Yentl disguises herself as a man in order to follow her passion for study.

Streisand's friends Marilyn and Alan Bergman wrote the lyrics, and the brilliant Michel Legrand composed and conducted the music. The film's musical conceit was that only the character of Yentl would sing—her songs expressed her inner thoughts. Streisand explained, "Once Yentl leaves her village, she lives a secret life that cannot be shared with anyone, and we all believed that the best way to capture that inner voice was in musical narrative. There was really no better way to reveal Yentl's unique perspective." (MGM/UA Entertainment, 1983)

Phil Ramone was put in charge of supervising postproduction on the film's music, soundtrack, and singles. Ramone had worked with Streisand for years in the studio, going back to his sound design for her concert in Central Park.

Ramone described the technically difficult job of putting together the *Yentl* soundtrack, which straddled the worlds of digital and analog. Streisand wanted to utilize the new Sony twenty-four-track digital recorder. However, she had already recorded the score on tape (aka analog). Streisand requested that Legrand's *Yentl* score be rerecorded on digital tape, with Legrand conducting to Barbra's already recorded analog vocals, effectively replacing the analog-recorded music with digitally recorded music.

"Engineering-wise I'd never seen anything like it," Jim Boyer (audio remixer) explained in Ramone's book. "We were distilling both analog and digital media to a single analog master—for film and record." He continued: "I was blown away by Barbra's memory; we had dozens of tapes, and she could remember specific words and phrases that she wanted from each in the final take. It was awesome—scary, really. When we matched the vocals to the printed music score, the unfolded vocal take sheet was the size of the console. This was before automation—if you didn't write it down, it didn't get remembered. It was the beginning of the digital age, and Barbra, Phil, and Columbia Records wanted to be in on it." (Phil Ramone, 2007)

The *Yentl* soundtrack was remixed at Lion Share Studios in Hollywood. Streisand spent the evenings working on the album mix, following a full day of mixing the film soundtrack in Culver City, California. "Once the picture had finally been put together and Columbia Records heard it, the perennial question of 'Where's the single?' [came up]," Phil Ramone stated.

In April 1983, seven months before the film and soundtrack were released, Streisand recorded three songs from *Yentl* with pop arrangements by Dave Grusin (*The Fabulous Baker Boys*, *Tootsie*)—"The Way He Makes Me Feel," "No Matter What Happens," and "Papa, Can You Hear Me?"

Ramone told me, in an interview I conducted with him in 2005: "You know, making a pop record for radio is very difficult, because, *Do you compromise? Do you not? Can you not just add stupid rhythm to something that'll work?* You don't. And so the phrasings and the readings of the so-called singles had a different meaning. Dave Grusin and I did those together.

"Barbra's wonderful about this kind of stuff. At first, she wanted to reject [the singles] because they didn't fit into the period of the picture. There are not too many percussion instruments running around [at the turn of the century]. How do you popularize it? How do you turn it around without cheapening or changing the intent of the picture? So that was part of the big challenge.

"Mixing it for the movie is one set of circumstances. The other is making pop records. When you buy the album are [the fans] going to be upset? It's a tough shoe to wear, because if you give them a record that goes to the top ten, let's say, when you go

buy the [album] it has nothing to do with what you did for the single version. So there's an interesting way in which we treated the music, and I think we succeeded." (Howe, Phil Ramone Interview, 2005) Ultimately, two of the studio-version songs were added to the *Yentl* soundtrack album—"The Way He Makes Me Feel" and "No Matter What Happens." Columbia Records released a lushly packaged LP of the *Yentl* soundtrack, which was Grammy nominated in 1984 for Best Album of Original Score Written for a Motion Picture or Television Special. Prince's *Purple Rain* soundtrack won that year.

Matt on *Yentl*

Yentl was the project that first hooked me on Barbra Streisand and her amazing career. The truth is that I had the soundtrack album weeks before I even saw the movie. I lived in Atlanta, and the Tara theater didn't start showing the movie until December 9.

But getting the soundtrack album was a fluke. First, I bought an Olivia Newton-John album for my sister's birthday and had to return it to the record store twice because both copies were warped and unplayable. So I took a chance and exchanged ONJ for *Yentl* and ended up playing the soundtrack more than my sister did! When I finally saw the movie in the theater, I was blown away and deeply moved. I used to sit and read the lyrics from the album insert as Barbra sang. When I graduated from high school, I wrote *Yentl* lyrics in my friends' yearbooks. I get a little teary-eyed remembering that Barbra Streisand, through her movie and songs, gave me such an important message as a young person: nothing's impossible.

In 2012, I let out a squeal during Barbra's *Back to Brooklyn* dress rehearsal. Suddenly . . . finally . . . she was right in front of me singing "The Way He Makes Me Feel" live. For whatever reasons, Barbra and Richard Jay-Alexander had ignored the song in Barbra's concert repertoire until then. What a pleasure to hear Barbra sing it for the audience!

"A Piece of Sky" is the exclamation point at the end of *Yentl*'s sentence. I recently went down a YouTube rabbit hole when I searched for "A Piece of Sky" reaction videos. There's a whole genre of "reaction" channels in which YouTube creators play a song they've never heard, then react on camera in real time. The "Piece of Sky" videos are so pleasing! Many of these creators have never heard of Barbra Streisand outside of *Meet the Fockers*. Some have heard only a few songs sung by her. So when they cue up "A Piece of Sky," they are confused at first (what? why? where?), until they hear Barbra's voice. By the time they get to "What's wrong with wanting more/If you can fly then soar," the listeners are awestruck. And as Barbra sings the long, belted final note, they are all astonished.

I was similarly astonished back in 1983 when I first heard "A Piece of Sky" outside of the context of the movie. For me, that last note that Barbra held was a preternatural feat. I'd never heard such a thing.

Then, when I finally got to a theater to see the movie, when I put a moving image with the song, I saw Barbra holding tight to the side of the boat as she sang, "Papa, watch me fly"—as if she were actually taking off in flight. Barbra's amazing, expressive voice took off and flew across the ocean, through the theater screen, and into my heart.

SIGNATURE STREISAND

"PAPA, CAN YOU HEAR ME?"

"Papa, Can You Hear Me?" is forever associated with Barbra Streisand mostly because it touches a very primal part of our hearts: the desire of a child for a parent's love, especially when that parent has died.

The song has been covered and referenced in pop culture ever since. The amazing Nina Simone recorded a version, and Lea Michele sang it on an episode of *Glee* (what Streisand song didn't she cover on that show?). Donna Summer performed "Papa" on the 1984 Academy Awards show, where it was nominated for an Oscar.

Perhaps the hippest appearance of "Papa" occurred in the movie *Deadpool 2* with Ryan Reynolds. His character is obsessively fixated on how the songs "Papa" and "Do You Want to Build a Snowman" (from *Frozen*) are so similar.

When Columbia released the single version of "Papa" (#38-04357), it substituted a brief string instrumental introduction for the chanted vocal prayer that we hear on the *Yentl* album track. This change, of course, merely shortened the single's duration, which was considered best for radio play. By the way, "Papa" did not chart on the *Billboard* Hot 100. It entered *Billboard*'s Adult Contemporary chart at number thirty-seven and stayed there for several weeks, never climbing any higher. This is not surprising, considering the hit songs charting at the same time: "Karma Chameleon" by Culture Club, "Say, Say, Say" by Paul McCartney and Michael Jackson, and "I Guess That's Why They Call It the Blues" by Elton John.

Barbra has sung the song several times in her live concerts to the delight of fans. Perhaps its most interesting use was in the *Timeless* shows, where it was paired in a medley with "You'll Never Know."

The best staging of "Papa" has to be during Barbra's 2016 concert tour. She allows her movie version of *Yentl* to begin the song on a large screen at the back of the stage. Then Streisand sings the song live, culminating in a dramatic lightning storm and an interpolation of the end of "A Piece of Sky."

Released: October 1984
Executive producer: Charles Koppelman for The Entertainment Music Company in association with Barwood Productions
Recorded at: The Record Plant Hollywood; Evergreen Studios Burbank; Studio 55 Los Angeles
Production coordinator for Barbra Streisand: Kim Skalecki
Production coordinator for The Entertainment Music Company: Linda Gerrity
Mastered by: Stephen Marcussen at Precision Lacquer Hollywood
Mastering supervised by: John Arrias
Front cover photography: Greg Gorman
Back cover photography: Steve Schapiro

Catalog Numbers:
OC 39480 (1984 LP)
OCA 39480 (8-track)
OCT 39480 (cassette)
CK 39480 (CD)

Side One:

1. Emotion
2. Make No Mistake, He's Mine (with Kim Carnes)
3. Time Machine
4. Best I Could
5. Left In The Dark

Side Two:

1. Heart Don't Change My Mind
2. When I Dream
3. You're A Step In The Right Direction
4. Clear Sailing
5. Here We Are At Last

Emotion is an album I am so in love with that I forgive all the synthesizers and 1980s sounds. In fact, I celebrate *Emotion* because it unabashedly embraces the 1980s! From its album design (turquoise and pink!) to its production, *Emotion* is definitely a trip down memory lane . . . in leg warmers.

Barbra was busy for three years producing, writing, directing, and starring in *Yentl*, and it was time to return to the studio for a new album for Columbia Records. "I barely remember it," she confessed in her memoir. So Streisand and her team began collecting songs for the album. One song considered was "Over and Over (Am I Strong Enough)" by Roger Edelman. Also considered was "Why Let It Go?" (used instead on 1988's *Till I Loved You* album). Meetings were held with Styx's Dennis DeYoung to record his song "First Time" and a new song he was to write for Streisand. Another song, "Dreams on Hold" (writer unknown), was also an early choice never recorded.

Ironically, the title track, "Emotion," was the last song to be recorded. Richard Perry (*Stoney End* and *Barbra Joan Streisand* albums) was brought in to produce it. He tried to replicate Peter Bliss's original demo tape for Barbra's version of the song. Bliss told *The Barbra Streisand Music Guide*, "Only three days into our recording sessions during the last week of June, Barbra arrived to sing. The track I did in the studio for Barbra was three keys higher than the demo, and I sang the guide vocal for her. She had a little difficulty finding the phrasing of the song in her first four run-throughs. She took me aside in the control room and asked me to be honest with her regarding her performance. Barbra commented on how great she thought my voice was (something I wish I had on tape) and listened carefully to my instructions. Finally, she thanked me for the song itself and my honesty, then proceeded to sing it better than ever. Because it felt right to Barbra and me, I didn't mind Barbra changing my line 'Sometimes I need to turn the beat around' to 'Sometimes I need to turn it all around.'" (Bliss, 1996)

"Make No Mistake, He's Mine," a duet with Kim Carnes, was recorded on June 21, 1984, at Bill Schnee Studios. Carnes told *Rolling Stone* that "Barbra Streisand had already cut two songs of mine, 'Love Comes from Unexpected Places' and 'Stay Away.' I'd gotten a call from Jon Peters [Streisand's then manager] to write a duet to sing with her. While I was extremely flattered, I said, 'Let me think about it. I'll try my best.' As I hung up the phone, I thought, 'That is so bizarre, and it will never work in a million years because our voices are so different. I can't pull this off.'" (Betts, 2015)

But Carnes persisted at the piano and admitted "an hour later the song was written. It's a love triangle, and these two girls are singing back and forth to each other about being in love with the same dude. It just wrote itself. I knew as I sang it that it was the perfect song for Barbra's voice and for my voice. I could sing it the way I sing ballads. She could sing it the way she sings ballads. Nobody had to be another person."

Producer Bill Cuomo and Carnes created a demo the next day; Streisand loved it and invited them to her home to rehearse. "It's just the three of us," Cuomo said. "I'm in her living room playing piano. I got Barbra and Kim singing. You could have hit me with a feather and knocked me off that piano stool! I'm listening to them sing and I'm thinking, '*Oh, man! This is going to be great.*' It was just fantastic. It was like they were whispering in your ear."

Cuomo explained that "Barbra loved the demo and the string/synth parts so much that she wanted the exact feel on the master only with a real orchestra. [Kim] and Barbra sounded amazing together. It was like silk and gravel, in a sense. It worked great." (Wikane, 2017)

Maurice White, from the Grammy-winning group Earth, Wind & Fire, produced three tracks on *Emotion*: "Time Machine," "When I Dream," and "Heart Don't Change My Mind." "I was brought in at the very end of the project," White wrote in his memoir. "Columbia felt it did not have a strong first single. For a project like this, in many cases, the company will give you the songs it wants you to record. That wasn't the case this time. I was kind of shocked that they didn't have it together; this was Barbra's first studio/pop album since *Guilty* in 1980. I had to find the songs and get going in a hurry." (White, 2016)

He recalled driving to Streisand's house to pitch Barbra the idea of "Time Machine"—the song he wrote with Martin Page and Brian Fairweather. "I explained that it was a story about having the ability to look back over your life and understand its changes, the theme being that your life makes sense in the end."

Page recalled that "it was a thrill to go to Streisand's home to do some preproduction. When she entered the room, she immediately gravitated to Brian and me—she loved our irreverent humor, and we got on with her like a house on fire." (Page, 2016)

White enjoyed working with Streisand in the recording studio. "Streisand is a perfectionist, and so am I, and I was happy with our work. . . . Streisand doesn't need any particular producer to do a good record. The bell-like purity of her voice stands alone in pop music." (White, 2016)

White was ultimately frustrated that Columbia never released his tracks as the album's singles. "They could have been hits,"

he told the *LA Times*. "I know it. I talked to Columbia about it, but they didn't have the final say on the selection of singles. The whole thing was very frustrating."

White was upset that Barbra "had gone back into the studio and remixed my songs. This was after I thought they were completely finished. They snuck back and did it and didn't tell me. I wasn't happy with that at all. Obviously, she didn't like the way she sounded. That I can understand. But if you change my work at least have the courtesy to let me know." (Hunt, "Maurice White Still Has the Fire at 44," 1986)

Engineer John Arrias explained that on the song "Heart Don't Change My Mind," "Maurice was in San Francisco working on another project and he couldn't come down to work on it, so we called him. Barbra wanted a certain section of the song to have a short string passage . . . and at the end of the song she wanted her vocal to continue with the orchestra—Maurice had turned her vocal off." (Swenson, 1986)

"Heart Don't Change My Mind" by Diane Warren and Robbie Buchanan was one of the standout ballads on *Emotion*. "Diane actually wrote a lot of the melody," Buchanan told Barbra Archives. "I wrote all the music, and then she started messing with the melody based on that music and then we finished the melody together and she wrote all the lyrics. That's the first song I ever wrote with her, actually." (Howe, Interview with Robbie Buchanan, 2003)

"You're a Step in the Right Direction" featured music by John Mellencamp and lyrics by Barbra Streisand—her first lyrics on an album since cowriting "Wet" in 1979. Monty Byrom (sounding a bit like Mellencamp) performed the background vocals and enacted the spoken bridge on the song. Columbia released three singles from *Emotion*: "Left in the Dark"/"Here We Are at Last" (# 38-04605); "Make No Mistake, He's Mine"/"Clear Sailing" (# 38-04695); and "Emotion"/"Here We Are at Last" (# 38-04707).

The label also put out a twelve-inch remix of "Emotion," created by John "Jellybean" Benitez—a music producer, composer, performer, film producer, executive, and mogul—who had worked with Madonna, Michael Jackson, Whitney Houston, Santana, and Sting. "Emotion"/"Emotion" (Instrumental)" # 44-05167 hit stores and discos in February 1985. Barbra wrote that *Emotion* "was a hodgepodge. I didn't relate to the material. And I told myself, Never again. Life's too short to spend time on something I don't believe in."

Emotion peaked on the *Billboard* charts at number nineteen. Although commonly considered a dud for Streisand, *Emotion* was awarded platinum status by the RIAA, meaning that it sold more than one million copies. That's hardly a dud.

Matt on *Emotion*

"I need the emotion!"

I was seventeen years old when *Emotion* was released. Barbra's first music video of the MTV age, "Left in the Dark," had a big premiere on *Entertainment Tonight*, the syndicated showbiz news show. I still have the VHS tape I recorded it on.

Emotion represents a certain time and place for me. When I listen to it today, it sounds like the '80s . . . lots of synthesizers and that quintessential Los Angeles studio sound from the era.

As an album, *Emotion* is consistent and is a solid collection of tunes. It may suffer from "too many cooks in the kitchen" with its overabundance of producers (nine), whereas *Guilty* had the singular vision of Barry Gibb.

Barbra's up-tempo tracks with Maurice White ("Time Machine" and "When I Dream") sound the most dated, but, boy, are they 1980s good! White gives Streisand a funky soundscape to vocalize in; I don't think we've ever heard her make this kind of music, and it suits her. The ballad White produced, "Heart Don't Change My Mind," is one of my favorite tracks on the album.

"Best I Could" is another decent ballad, even if it rambles a touch. Barbra's last line of the song is heartbreaking: "We both loved the best we-ee could."

"Clear Sailing," from *Guilty* producer Albhy Galuten, is as smooth as a sailboat gliding through the water. I always thought this tune should have received more attention. Barbra's vocal is remarkably subtle.

Meanwhile, "Make No Mistake, He's Mine" is a better and more dynamic duet than "Tell Him" ever was. Kim Carnes and Barbra Streisand together are perfection. The notes and harmonies are to die for!

"Left in the Dark" is an unexpected and unconventional track for Streisand to sing. The Jim Steinman song first appeared on his 1981 album, *Bad for Good*. Streisand sings it better, and that is being kind. The opening monologue is just as it is on his original recording, and as surreal as Streisand's sounds, his is even more over-the-top as well as petulant. Steinman's version of the song goes further off the edge when he closes it with an *outro* monologue! Streisand thankfully left that off her recording. Steinman was noted for his bombastic ballads and his collaboration with Meatloaf (*Bat Out of Hell*) as well as his hits with Bonnie Tyler ("Total Eclipse of the Heart") and Air Supply ("Making Love Out of Nothing at All"). He produced "Left in the Dark" for Barbra and seems to have tamed his arrangement for her. He told *Tower Record Magazine* in 1989 that he was tiring of working with big-name recording stars. "Barbra Streisand was great though," he said. "She didn't want to sing some of the lyrics on my song 'Left In the Dark' because they conflicted with her feminist ideals! Amazing voice." (Robertson, 1989)

Steinman's memory wasn't exactly true, though. I noticed only two small changes in the lyrics when I compared the two artists' versions of the song. "How long did you do it?" in the opening monologue became "How long did it last?" for Streisand. Later in the song, Steinman's original lyric was "so take off your dress," whereas Streisand sang "when I see you undress"—which doesn't sound like a feminist statement but was probably changed because of logic: her lover (at least in the video) was cis male Kris Kristofferson, who didn't wear a dress.

Let's wrap up *Emotion* by listening to "Here We Are at Last," which is an underrated song that she wrote the music for, and one I wish she would have sung live in concert at some point. Barbra used the tune for her movie *Nuts*—it's played by a piano on track two, "The Bar."

"I'd originally written the melody as a theme for *The Main Event*," Streisand stated, "but put it on the shelf after recording an up-tempo song, which was more appropriate for a comedy. Eventually, my friend Richard Baskin put lyrics to it, and the song found a home on my *Emotion* album." (Streisand, *Just for the Record* liner notes, 1991)

STREISAND COLLABORATORS

STEPHEN SONDHEIM

"It's interesting that I hadn't sung any of Stephen's songs before," Streisand told author Craig Zadan. Before *The Broadway Album*, Barbra had recorded a few bars of "Small World" (*Gypsy*) in a *Color Me Barbra* medley, as well as "There Won't Be Trumpets" (*Anyone Can Whistle*). But in 1985, "Trumpets" was an unreleased song recorded back in 1974.

"I like songs that have an emotional arc," Streisand revealed in her memoir, "a beginning, a middle, and an end . . . and Steve is so good at telling a story in song. He's the rare composer who is equally gifted at both words and music. It's a rich talent . . . rich in substance and wit. You can't help but be dazzled by the intricacy of the rhymes, the delicious double-entendres, and the clever plays on words."

She continued: "He understands passion and can capture it in a lyric. His insight into human nature is profound. As an actress, I'm given so much to work with because there are so many layers to each song."

Streisand worked with Sondheim on seven of the twelve tracks on *The Broadway Album*. The two began their collaboration on the telephone in March 1985 and continued through the summer while Streisand recorded the album in Los Angeles. Zadan wrote that "they collaborated as if they were doing a show, not an album." (Zadan, 1986)

"I had been thinking about doing an album of Broadway songs for years," Streisand said. "When I finally got around to it, I called up Steve and said I was interested in doing some of his songs. We hardly knew each other, and I had only recorded one of his songs. It turned into a process that was so exhilarating, there were moments I was screaming with joy over the phone." (Holden, Barbra Streisand: "This Is the Music I Love. It Is My Roots," 1985)

For the medley of "Pretty Women" (from *Sweeney Todd*) and "The Ladies Who Lunch" (from *Company*), Streisand asked Sondheim to contribute a coda. "I wanted to put the two songs together, because I loved the melody of 'Pretty Women' but didn't feel comfortable singing from a male point of view," Streisand told Stephen Holden. "When I listened to 'The Ladies Who Lunch,' I thought it would be interesting to put the songs together to present two opposing views of women—a superficial view versus what their lives might really be like—but I needed a lyrical ending that would pull the two together."

Sondheim was willing to tailor his material. "Barbra Streisand has one of the two or three best voices in the world of singing voices," he explained to Holden. Sondheim even came west and spent a few weeks in the recording studio with Streisand.

"It's all about Barbra," Sondheim said. "If anyone else had recorded the exact same set of songs and sung them very well, it might not have sold. But she's got one of the best voices on the planet. And it's not just her voice, it's her intensity, her passion, her control. Although every moment has been thought out, you don't see all the sweat and decisions that went into the work. It is as though she just stepped out of the shower and began singing at you." (Zadan, 1986)

Sondheim, who had rewritten "Send in the Clowns" for her, stated in *Finishing the Hat* that "Barbra Streisand is a performer who examines the lyrics she sings very carefully, and who questioned the dramatic connection between the two choruses (that is, the moment leading to the stanza that begins with the second iteration of 'Isn't it rich?')."

Sondheim admitted that without the dramatic scene that occurred onstage during the musical—the character Fredrik apologized to the character Desiree, then left the room—"there is indeed an emotional gap" in the song. When Streisand brought this to Sondheim's attention, he agreed that "it seemed a logical request rather than the whim of a diva." (Sondheim, 2011)

Sondheim and Streisand continued to collaborate after *The Broadway Album*. She recorded more of his songs for *Back to Broadway* (1993). He wrote special lyrics for "I'm Still Here," which she performed in *The Concert* in 1994. "I Remember," with a new, holiday-themed introduction, was included on *Christmas Memories* (2001), and "Goodbye for Now," his theme song for the movie *Reds*, made it on *The Movie Album* (2003). Barbra's last album of Broadway tunes, *Encore*, included five Sondheim tunes: "Loving You," "The Best Thing That Ever Has Happened," "Take Me to the World," "Not a Day Goes By," and "Losing My Mind."

Fans of Sondheim were saddened Thanksgiving 2021 when the news broke that he had passed away at the age of ninety-one. On social media, Barbra posted: "Thank the Lord that Sondheim lived to be 91 years old so he had the time to write such wonderful music and GREAT lyrics! May he Rest In Peace." Only three months before, when she was interviewed by Zane Lowe for Apple Music, Barbra mentioned that one idea she had for a future album was *Streisand Sings Sondheim*.

Released: November 4, 1985
Executive producers: Barbra Streisand and Peter Matz
Cover photos: Richard Corman
Inside photos: Mark Sennet
Art direction: Lane/Donald
Songs recorded live at A&M Recording Studios, Hollywood
Assistant engineers: Magic Moreno, Benny Faccone
Mastering by: Stephen Marcussen at Precision Lacquer
Project coordinator: Kim Skalecki

Catalog Numbers:
OC 40092 (LP)
CK 40092 (CD)
OCT 40092 (cassette)
CM 40092 (MiniDisc, 1997)
CK 85159 (CD, 2002)
CK 5063612 (CD, 2002 UK with bonus track I Know Him So Well)

Side One:

1. Putting It Together (*Sunday in the Park with George*) 2. If I Loved You (*Carousel*) 3. Something's Coming (*West Side Story*) 4. Not While I'm Around (*Sweeney Todd*) 5. Being Alive (*Company*) 6. I Have Dreamed/We Kiss In A Shadow/Something Wonderful (*The King and I*)

Side Two:

1. Send In The Clowns (*A Little Night Music*) 2. Pretty Women (*Sweeney Todd*)/The Ladies Who Lunch (*Company*) 3. Can't Help Lovin' That Man (*Showboat*) 4. I Loves You Porgy/Porgy, I's Your Woman Now (*Porgy and Bess*) 5. Somewhere (*West Side Story*)

"Adelaide's Lament" (*Guys and Dolls*) did not appear on the original LP; it was added as a bonus track (appearing before "Send In The Clowns") on the 1986 CD and remained on the album in later releases and formats.

"Anybody could have done the songs on *Emotion* as well as or better than I could have done them," Barbra explained about her last pop album. "It was time to do something I truly believed in."

Streisand told Stephen Holden, "Making *Yentl* wiped me out and left me with no drive for two years. But once I commit to a project, whether it's a record or a movie, I become so involved with every aspect that I become obsessed. . . . This is the music I love, it is where I came from, it is my roots". (Holden, Barbra Streisand: "This Is the Music I Love. It Is My Roots," 1985)

Peter Matz, who worked on Streisand's first few albums, recalled that Barbra mentioned the album to him in late 1984. "We were at her house at Christmas, and she said she was going to go ahead with the project," Matz stated. "I always felt very strongly that she was right to do it and that it was a good idea." (Grein, "Producer Enjoys 'Broadway' LP's Success," 1986)

"It was her idea," Sandy Gallin said. "The first big hit album that she had in many years. It was an absolute labor of love for her and for me." Sandy Gallin was an agent and talent manager (later an interior designer) who boosted the careers of Whoopi Goldberg, Cher, Neil Diamond, and more. (Gallin, 2016) Gallin's original pitch for the project was ambitious and exciting: a double album; a live concert sold as a pay-per-view; a European theatrical release of the concert; syndication of the concert to network TV; and a videocassette for commercial sale.

Eventually, the scope of *Barbra on Broadway* (as it was originally titled) was narrowed to just a double album. Barbra balked at the one-woman show. "Are you kidding?" she exclaimed at the idea. "With the energy that would take I could do another movie." (McKuen, 1986)

Instead, Barbra spent eight months recording seventeen songs. "I've been making lists for this album for a long time," she confessed. "I love the songs we recorded, and left out as many as those that made the final disc." (McKuen, 1986)

Peter Matz explained the process that he and Streisand went through choosing songs for the album: "When I got into it last March or April [1985]," he said, "she had already been going through material. She had a piano player come over, and she'd do some songs. She had already weeded out a lot, and there was a strange, abstract shape to it by the time I got involved." (Taylor, 1986) Matz and Streisand worked together closely in June 1985 on the keys, arrangements, and song choices. Matz played piano, and Streisand sang and offered her opinions.

There was drama brewing between Streisand and her record company over her Broadway passion project, though. Marty Erlichman explained the problem to writer Karen Swenson: "Barbra's contract with Columbia says she has to deliver X number of albums, but they have to be approved albums—meaning most of them have to be contemporary albums. CBS never approved this album; it was not considered to be a pop album. Therefore, she didn't get the advance she was entitled to (she only got half her usual advance) and it wasn't going to count as an approved album contract. Except if it sold 2.5 million copies—at that point it would automatically become an approved album whether they okayed it in advance or not." (Swenson, 1986)

Gallin remembered that "Sony not only didn't want *The Broadway Album*; Walter Yetnikoff [president of the record label] called me up one morning screaming at me at the top of his lungs!" According to Gallin, Yetnikoff yelled, "You and David Geffen walk with her on the beach, convince her to do this Broadway album, which is the stupidest idea I've ever heard. You get her to write me a check for $10 million and get it on my desk this afternoon and she has a release [from her contract]." (Yetnikoff was an admitted alcohol and cocaine abuser at that time, by the way.) Matz stated, "A lot of people were hesitant about the whole concept, how it would fare commercially, and some were unsure about my involvement. Barbra, though, was straight-ahead about the project, as she is with everything she does. She made all the decisions about the material, and always has total control of everything, from the songs to the liner notes." (Berk, 1985)

"I had been with Columbia for twenty-three years," Barbra explained. "I had made twenty-three albums (and ten soundtrack or compilation albums) for them. And now, after five number 1 albums and seven Grammy awards and millions of dollars in record sales, I basically had to sell myself again. It was actually kind of humiliating."

Along the way, Columbia dissuaded Streisand and Matz from producing a double album. Once the two-LP set was abandoned, so was the long medley of songs from *The King and I*, created by Paul Jabara and Bob Esty, the team behind Barbra's hit single "The Main Event." The medley would have featured "I Have Dreamed," "We Kiss in a Shadow," "Something Wonderful," as well as "Shall We Dance" and a few lines from "Hello Young Lovers."

While rehearsing "Shall We Dance," Barbra had misgivings about the "whimsical Latin arrangement" (as Jabara described it). "I don't sing this good," she explained to Jabara and Esty. "When I sing 'If I Loved You,' that's like in my . . . I know what I'm doing." (Hammerstein, Esty Rehearsal Tapes, 1985) The complete medley, running eight minutes, was substantial. I've heard two different mixes of "Shall We Dance/Hello Young Lovers" from Bob Esty, and both begin with Barbra thoughtfully and slowly singing the introduction. But as soon as she intones "Shall we dance?" the electronic drum and synth keyboards kick in. "Shall We Dance/Hello Young Lovers" is a disco track with some sassy backup singers imploring the listener to "come on, make me dance!" Barbra sounds much more playful and authentic on the rehearsal tapes with Esty playing piano. This disco arrangement would have stood out like a sore thumb had it been included.

The album opener, "Putting It Together," was added late in the process. At one point, Streisand wanted the album to begin with "Being Good Isn't Good Enough," but that was filed away until 2012, when it opened *Release Me*. Back in 1985, Streisand called up Stephen Sondheim about making changes to the lyric of "Putting It Together," which appeared in the second act of *Sunday in the Park with George*. "I told him of my conversation with my record company," she said, "where I told them I didn't want to do another pop album at this time, that I wanted to do an album of Broadway songs. And they were very resistant and unhappy, and they said, 'Barbra, you can't do a record like this. It's not commercial. This is like your old records. Nobody's going to buy it.' Every word they said only encouraged me. I wanted to put all their comments into this song. And I thought, *What a great way to open this album*." (Zadan, 1986)

Sondheim wrote: "I suggested that all she needed to do was to change 'I remember lasers are expensive' to 'I remember vinyl is expensive' and the rest of the lyric, being a generalized set of statements about patronage and its effects, would take care of itself." (Sondheim, 2011) Sondheim, however, realized that other parts of the lyric needed changing. "And I said, 'Let me look at the rest of the lyric, if you want to personalize it. I'm sure I can make it more record oriented and less art related, which is what it was in the context of the show." (Sondheim, 2011)

Streisand told Zadan she talked to Sondheim "for hours. I felt I couldn't ignore the truth . . . you don't hide it; you use it. So I told him, 'Here I am, a very successful recording star, and yet I have to fight for everything I believe in. I'm still auditioning after twenty-three years.' I asked him if he could encompass that thought and he wrote, 'Even though you get the recognition/ Everything you do you still audition.' You see what I mean? It took a month to work on one song, which is what I love about singing this kind of material."

When it came time to record the song, the forty-eight-piece orchestra conducted by Matz was joined in the studio by voice actors Sydney Pollack (Barbra's director on *The Way We Were*), David Geffen (a real-life music mogul), and Ken Sylk (an actor and Barbra's friend). "'Putting It Together' was the most complicated song to record," engineer Don Hahn revealed. "The thing that I remember most about it was that Barbra didn't want the orchestra overpowering the electronic effects. She wanted the synthesizer and her voice supported by the orchestra—which is a turnaround in the way most artists would want to do a song like this—and it worked." (Swenson, 1986)

Streisand confessed there was a technical glitch

on this song, though. "What you'll see on the [TV] special is all there was, because the 24-track master tape was 'accidentally' erased. This has never happened to me before, not in 20 years of recording. The sound you'll hear on the song is taken off a 2-track Nagra. Unbelievable." (McKuen, 1986) Sondheim wrote later: "I used to make fun and say 'Putting It Together' is gonna be number one on the hit parade. Next to 'Comedy Tonight' and 'Send in the Clowns,' 'Putting It Together' has been recorded more than anything else. It's the whole Streisand thing." (DVD Commentary, 2010)

Columbia released two singles to promote *The Broadway Album*. The first, out in November 1985, was "Somewhere"/"Not While I'm Around" (# 38-05680). Following that, in February 1986, it released "Send in the Clowns"/"Being Alive" (# 38-05837). "I'll bet when the Columbia executives looked at the lineup of songs, they were relieved to see that David Foster, a smart, hip Grammy-winning producer, was involved with 'Somewhere.' And they decided it should be the first single," Barbra wrote. She also revealed that Leonard Bernstein, the song's composer, wrote to tell her "'Somewhere' is something else!"

Sondheim called "Send in the Clowns" (a song he wrote for *A Little Night Music*) "a tiny little throwaway song for a little voice. I didn't know it was going to be popular. And so, it never had a so-called second chorus." (Zadan, 1986) "I am a singing actress who likes to create little dramas," Streisand told Holden. "And as an actress I didn't understand the last line [of 'Send in the Clowns'], 'Well, maybe next year,' so I asked Steve how he would feel if I ended it with the line 'Don't bother, they're here.' I didn't know how he would react, but he was so cute. He said a lot of people had asked him what the song meant—now they would understand it." (Holden, Barbra Streisand "This Is the Music I Love, This Is My Roots", 1985)

The Broadway Album, despite all the behind-the-scenes drama, became Streisand's sixth number one album on the *Billboard* charts, selling over four million units—exceeding her contract requirements! It also won two Grammy Awards. In 1987, Barbra won Best Pop Female Vocal Performance. David Foster was awarded the Grammy for Best Instrumental Arrangement Accompanying Vocalist for "Somewhere." It is very unfortunate that since 1987, Barbra has *never* won another competitive Grammy as of 2024, despite all her excellent recordings and nominations over the years.

Unreleased (and Unrealized) *Broadway*

Still on the cutting room floor from *The Broadway Album* recording sessions are "Show Me" from *My Fair Lady* and "Unusual Way" from *Nine*. Streisand did perform the song from *Nine* twenty-one years later on her North American concert tour, but the original studio version remains unreleased.

Barbra recorded "Home" from *The Wiz*, but it was dropped from the album. It, along with "Being Good Isn't Good Enough," ended up on *Release Me*—although Barbra recorded new tracks for the drums, bass, and piano against her original vocal.

"I Know Him So Well" was from the musical *Chess*. It was eventually included on the 1991 retrospective box set *Just for the Record*. Barbra, in her liner notes, said the track did not make it onto *The Broadway Album* for two reasons: one, *Chess* hadn't opened on Broadway yet, so it was technically not a Broadway tune. Secondly, Barbra wrote, "I thought it sounded too 'Pop', like it was trying to

be a contemporary hit, and seemed out of context with the rest of the material." "I Know Him So Well" was included as a bonus track on the 2002 reissue of *The Broadway Album* in Europe.

Richard Page (from the group Mr. Mister) provided the male vocal on this track. "She was great," Page said about Streisand. "I spent one afternoon with her, although she lives in my neighborhood, and I see her from time to time. But she's really in control and is all those things that people say about her. She definitely knew what she was doing in the recording studio and was very kind. It was a good experience." (Parker, 2010) I have also heard another version of "I Know Him So Well," in which Barbra duets with herself on the song. It's the same arrangement, but with Barbra singing the Richard Page part—in her own, Streisand way, of course.

Streisand was interested in performing the showstopping "Rose's Turn" from *Gypsy* (another Jule Styne show, with lyrics by Stephen Sondheim). She and Matz consulted Sondheim and tried to make a medley out of it and "Some People." Barbra eventually performed this medley during her 2012 concert tour.

Streisand loved the songs from *Sunday in the Park with George* by Sondheim and considered recording "Finishing the Hat" and "Children and Art."

Barbra also experimented with different orchestrations of some of the songs that did make it onto *The Broadway Album*. She recorded three versions of "Can't Help Loving That Man of Mine." A sexy, jazz version can be heard for a moment on the HBO television special on the making of the album. The hot trumpet gave the song a completely different feel. A second version of the song split the difference between the other two—the first half was performed as a ballad; then, at "Tell me he's lazy" the song launched into a jazz tempo, and Streisand belted it. The third version, using Conrad Salinger's original orchestration from the movie *Showboat*, is what's on the album.

Streisand also recorded two versions of "Not While I'm Around." "The first was too lush and grand," she explained. "The arrangement was too big for the song and overpowered the delicacy of it. The second one, which was what we used, was more fitting to the size of the song . . . The first time I was singing it as a lover to her lover. The second time I sang it, I was more of a mother singing to my son. My character changed." (Zadan, 1986)

Matt on *Broadway*

I have such nostalgic memories of the year this album was released. Despite not originally supporting the project, Columbia went all in promoting *The Broadway Album*—Barbra was interviewed by Barbara Walters; she filmed a "Somewhere" music video that played on MTV; there was an HBO special about the making of the album; and the LP package was so lush and elegant! I could read all the lyrics on the LP sleeve and learn the words to the songs.

The Broadway Album was also released as a compact disc! Nowadays we have immediate digital downloads, so it's hard to imagine a time several decades ago when compact discs were the new technology. But in 1985, most people did not even own a CD player—they still had turntables that played vinyl records.

I bought the CD—it was $14.99 (a fortune!)—and I didn't even own a CD player. I went over to my friend David's house because he had an expensive player, and I desperately wanted to hear the bonus track, "Adelaide's Lament."

One critique I have of "Lament" is that Barbra overuses sound editing—to my ears, some of the coughs and wheezes are inserted where she couldn't have possibly sung them live, and it sounds like it. This track has been obviously tinkered with in the editing room, and I can hear the edits.

The Broadway Album is one of Streisand's best. It sounds timeless and definitive, mostly because of Matz's brilliant orchestrations.

I can be a little critical of synthesizers when writing about Streisand's music because of the distinct sound they make and the era of music they evoke. Synth-pop became the quintessential sound of 1980s pop, characterized by synthesizers and drum machines. Although trendy at the time, it sounds dated today, especially compared with real instruments and musical sounds made by wind, strumming, fiddling and bowing.

The songs "Somewhere" and "Something's Coming" do sound dated on *The Broadway Album*. David Foster is responsible for producing "Somewhere." She wanted "Somewhere" to sound otherworldly, and that's certainly what Foster gave her with his synthesizers. I actually like the 1994 live version better, though. Barbra rattles the rafters of Madison Square Garden with her amazing belt and Marvin Hamlisch's fantastic arrangement.

Here's a true story about "Somewhere": when this album came out, I was a theater geek and computer nerd. My friend Jonathan and I used to get stoned and lay on the floor between our stereo speakers and blast "Somewhere" as loud as we could. It was a truly resplendent listen, what with the cosmos swirling around our heads. "It's still illegal?"

Foster's arrangement of "Somewhere" isn't as egregious as "Something's Coming," however. That track is complete synth—drum machine, electric horns, and sampled snaps. You can get a taste of "Something's Coming" played by real instruments during Barbra's *Timeless* concert recording. It sounds so much better backed by an orchestra, but it's unfortunate that it's a duet with Lauren Frost and features the *Timeless* dialogue.

Yes, *The King and I* medley is played by keyboards and has an electronic sound, but for some reason my ears are not offended by this Esty/Jabara arrangement. After all, the medley begins with the song "I Have Dreamed" . . . the soundscape certainly sounds *dreamy*. Streisand returned to her roots, to the music that she loves. It's the exact type of music that I am most excited to hear her perform.

SIGNATURE STREISAND

"SOMEWHERE"

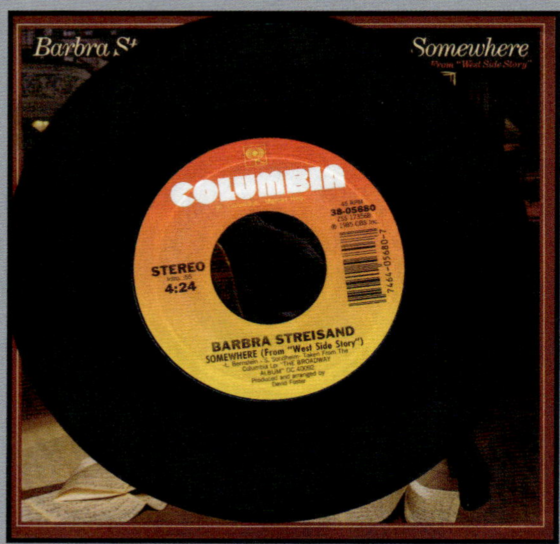

"Somewhere," from the timeless musical *West Side Story*, has music by Leonard Bernstein and lyrics by Stephen Sondheim. Ever since the song was recorded by Barbra for *The Broadway Album*, it has been in her repertoire, and audiences love to hear it. According to my calculations, Barbra has sung "Somewhere" at every major concert since *One Voice* (except for her last tour, in 2019).

In 2006, Barbra introduced the song as "a kind of prayer for tolerance, compassion, and peace" because, she cautioned, "No matter what era, hate accomplishes nothing."

Props must be given to David Foster for the original arrangement, which, according to him, Streisand requested "sound like it was not created on this planet."

Foster said, "I ended up using only synthesizers to get a richly layered background—no orchestra at all—and I worked every day for a month, with seven different programmers, to get it right." (Foster, 2008)

In Barbra's subsequent concert performances of "Somewhere," Foster's synthesizers were superseded by arrangements that used an actual orchestra. Marvin Hamlisch's 1994 arrangement was the first; then, in 2000, Hamlisch and Streisand paired "Somewhere" with "I Believe" and added a reprise of the song's climax; Streisand sang the song with Il Divo in 2006, again with that repeat at the end and some delicious harmony too.

Streisand has recorded the song two other times—in 2011, her original *Broadway Album* vocals were utilized in a duet with ten-year-old Jackie Evancho. Now, this little girl's voice creeps me out. I blame Foster, who produced her album and this track.

The next time Barbra revisited "Somewhere" was in 2014 for her album *Partners*, this time as a duet with the handsome Josh Groban. William Ross created the arrangement, which is strikingly different from previous ones. Josh and Barbra end the song with spine-tingling harmonies because Ross has given them a thoughtful and reflective climax instead of having them belt long notes.

If Streisand ever sings in public again and chooses to include "Somewhere" in her setlist, it would be so lovely to hear the 2014 arrangement live.

One Voice

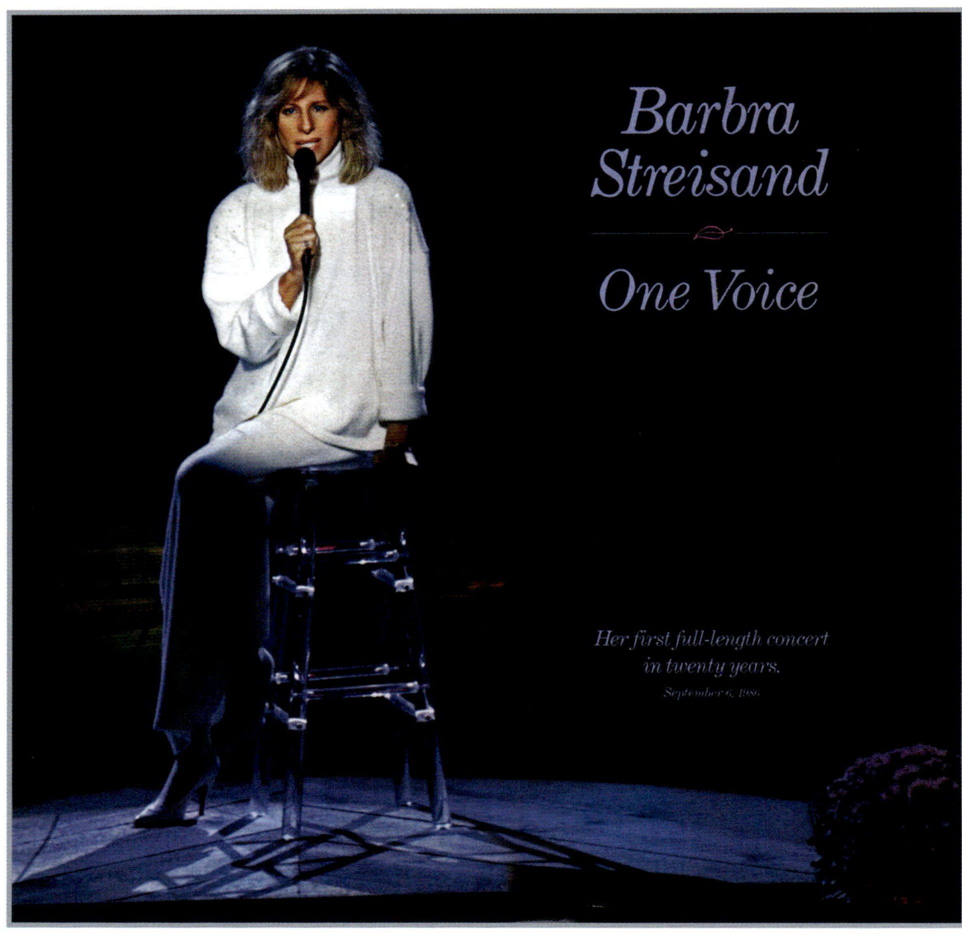

Released: April 20, 1987
Produced by: Richard Baskin
Musical director: Randy Kerber
Recording engineer: Ed Greene
Mastering engineer: Bernie Grundman
Remix engineer and mastering supervision: John Arrias
Recorded live at: Malibu, California, September 6, 1986
Excerpts from the show written by: Marilyn and Alan Bergman and Barbra Streisand
Photography: Richard Corman
Art direction: Tony Lane/Nancy Donald

Catalog Numbers:
OC 40788 (LP)
CK 40788 (CD)
OCT 40788 (cassette)
CM 40788 (MiniDisc, 1993)

Side One:

1. Somewhere
2. Evergreen (Love Theme From A Star Is Born)
3. Something's Coming
4. People
5. Over The Rainbow
6. Guilty (with Barry Gibb)

Side Two:

1. What Kind Of Fool (with Barry Gibb)
2. Papa, Can You Hear Me?
3. The Way We Were
4. It's A New World
5. Happy Days Are Here Again
6. America, The Beautiful

"Send In The Clowns" was added as the fifth track on the CD release of *One Voice*

Barbra and her friend Marilyn Bergman decided that in order to raise a lot of money to support Democrats taking back the Senate, she should return to the concert stage. Although they pondered several venues to produce such a concert, Barbra ultimately decided she'd feel most comfortable in her backyard at her ranch in Ramirez Canyon. "Drinks and dinner were served out on the tennis court, where Marilyn welcomed everyone and the extraordinary congresswoman Barbara Jordan introduced the candidates," Streisand wrote.

As she said that evening at the concert, Barbra was musically accompanied on stage by "eight guys and some big electric bill!"

Barry Gibb even joined Barbra on two songs from *Guilty*. "I was surprised by how much fun I was having," Barbra confessed in her book. "You can't help but move to that music. I think I forgot some word or missed a beat, but I did do some dipping and swaying. That's about as much dancing in public as I've ever done!"

Billed as Barbra's "first full-length concert in twenty years," *One Voice* enjoyed retail synergy as an HBO concert special, an album, and eventually a home video release. Backed by eight musicians, and joined on two songs by Barry Gibb, Barbra sang in front of several hundred guests—friends, movie stars, and politicians. The evening raised $1.5 million for the Hollywood Women's Political Committee, which distributed the money to six Democratic senatorial candidates.

For the album, Columbia Records edited Barbra's patter, leaving us with more music and less talking. To my ears, the CD has always sounded undynamic, like many of the CDs that were released in the 1980s, when the format was still new. Rhino Entertainment put out a DVD of *One Voice* in 2006, with John Arrias credited as "remix engineer and mastering supervision." Now, this audio sounds fantastic, much clearer and better mixed than the CD.

In 1987, the *One Voice* CD was priced from thirteen to sixteen dollars—almost double the cost of an LP or cassette. In my research, I observed that Tower Records and other music stores never advertised that the CD contained the bonus track of "Send in the Clowns." The LP and cassette did not include that song, probably due to length and the limitations of those formats.

One Voice was recognized generously at the Grammy Awards. It was nominated for (but did not win) Best Pop Female Vocal Performance, Best Music Video Performance, Best Instrumental Arrangement Accompanying Vocal Nomination: Randy Kerber—"Over the Rainbow," and Best Performance/Music Video.

Matt on *Voice*

Barbra's vocals for this concert are so on point! She first mentions her desire to record a movie album during this concert and rewarded us with two stellar compositions by Harold Arlen—"It's a New World" (from Garland's *A Star Is Born*) and "Over the Rainbow" from that timeless classic *The Wizard of Oz*.

In case you're wondering why Barbra never recorded a studio version of "Over the Rainbow," I would posit that it's because she nailed the vocal when she sang it live this evening. The recording is perfect. I love Streisand's sentiment on "Rainbow," and I sometimes imagine young Barbra (with bows in her hair) singing this on a Brooklyn stoop.

I said it earlier, but *One Voice* also has my favorite version of "Happy Days"—I cannot resist the pleasure I get when I hear her sing "All together SHOU-UT it now." Goosebumps!

Released: October 25, 1988
Produced by: Quincy Jones, Barbra Streisand, Phil Ramone, Burt Bacharach, Carole Bayer Sager, and Denny Diante
Recorded at: B&J Studio
Photographs by: Randee St. Nicholas

Catalog Numbers:
OC 40880 (LP)
OCT 40880 (cassette)
CK 40880 (CD)

Side One:

1. The Places You Find Love
2. On My Way To You
3. Till I Loved You (with Don Johnson)
4. Love Light
5. All I Ask Of You
6. You And Me For Always

Side Two:

1. Why Let It Go?
2. Two People
3. What Were We Thinking Of?
4. Some Good Things Never Last
5. One More Time Around

Barbra's sensuous pop album was released in the fall of 1988. *Till I Loved You* was a concept album: it followed the stages of a relationship from the beginning ("The Places You Find Love") to the end ("Some Good Things Never Last") and then wrapped up the theme with a positive song about the future ("One More Time Around").

The opening song, "The Places You Find Love," was produced by the inimitable Quincy Jones, and its journey onto this Streisand album is fascinating. Written by Clif Magness and Glen Ballard, the song was destined for Quincy Jones's solo album, but that album got delayed several years when Jones became overly involved scoring Steven Spielberg's *The Color Purple*. "Barbra Streisand was the catalyst for reenergizing that song," said Clif Magness. "Quincy and Glen and I were in the studio with her every day for a month working on it."

Magness revealed that they did twenty-nine takes of Barbra's lead vocal on "The Places You Find Love." "Every take that she sang, she made notes while she was singing. And at the end of the take she would say, 'You know, I think I can do that word a little better,'" he said.

Magness also explained that "Barbra insisted on comping by committee"—which means the final vocal was compiled of the best segments from those twenty-nine takes. "She had a photographic memory," he stated, "or I should say an audiophile memory." (Magness, 2020)

A year later, "Places You Find Love" was included on Jones's 1989 album, *Back on the Block,* sung by Siedah Garrett and Chaka Khan. "He used a lot of elements from [Barbra's] track for his record as well," said Clif Magness. Jones added a funky guitar and incorporated some African chanting during the bridge and climax of the song.

Jones and his songwriters won a 1991 Grammy Award for their arrangement of "Places"—for the version on Jones's album!

Barbra was dating Don Johnson and recorded the duet "Till I Loved You" with him. The song was from *Goya . . . A Life in Song,* a project developed by CBS Records, Freddie Gershon, and Allan Carr for opera star Placido Domingo performing the role of artist Francisco Goya. The duet was officially titled "Till I Loved You (The Love Theme from *Goya*)" and was written by composer/lyricist Maury Yeston (*Grand Hotel*, *Nine*, and *Titanic*). Yeston released his music as an album first, much like Andrew Lloyd Weber had done with *Evita*, with the idea that eventually the show would go to Broadway. It did not.

"That song had been my idea," Barbra said in her book. "I knew Don wanted to broaden his career . . . he had already recorded one album a couple of years earlier, at the height of his fame on *Miami Vice*. A single from it had gotten a lot of airplay, and he was hoping to build on that success. The session in the studio seemed to go well. We were improvising at the end . . . having fun in the moment, and laughing." But Johnson became distant and uncommunicative afterward, according to Barbra. "I couldn't care less if the single ever came out . . . our relationship was more important than any record."

In 2006, Don Johnson talked to TV host Jonathan Ross about recording the duet with Streisand. "It was amazing," Johnson said. "First of all, she's probably the diva of all time, in terms of voices . . . I was under contract to Columbia at the time—her studio. Of course, at the time I was the 'biggy wow-wow' in television and film and with *Miami Vice*. And I'd just put out a record that had made the top five. This is how I met Barbra—Columbia came to me and said, 'Would you like to do a duet with Barbra?' At first I said, 'It's a different kind of music.' Then I went, *What are you, crazy? You've got to do a duet with Barbra Streisand!*" (Ross, 2006)

Streisand and Johnson sang together in the same studio for the recording. "There was studio glass between us so that she could watch me sing—because it was a duet," Johnson said. "It was a little nerve-racking, as I recall. She's a perfectionist; she's impeccable about everything, impeccable about every note. I want to be that way; it's just that I don't have the equipment that she has to do it." (Ross, 2006)

Burt Bacharach produced and wrote three tracks on *Till I Loved You* (with lyricist Carole Bayer Sager, his wife at the time). "[Barbra] has great range," Bacharach stated. "Nobody sounds like her when she's up that high, with that kind of clarity and purity. You can tell right away it's her. You can't say that about many singers." (Zutell, 2000)

Phil Ramone produced the song "All I Ask of You," which was originally a duet in Andrew Lloyd Webber's musical *The Phantom of the Opera.*

"It's an interesting concept—messing with Andrew Lloyd Webber stuff," Ramone said. "It's not easy. Barbra's always approached music from both a lyrical point of view and a sensibility of *Why can't I sing this? Why wouldn't I sing this? Why wouldn't I sing this to him?* You know, it's established for too long that it's a duet. You can take a song and revoice it or change keys. But this song is written as a duet. I don't know, we just took a shot [laughs]. We worked on it so it could be a meaningful song as it is." (Howe, Phil Ramone Interview, 2005) Ramone confirmed that the song's lyricists, Charles Hart and Richard Stilgoe, worked on Barbra's version of "All I Ask of You."

"Some Good Things Never Last" was also recorded by Barry Manilow for his 1989 self-titled album. Mark Radice wrote the song for his girlfriend at the time, George-Ann Greth. Radice told Barbra Archives that EMI publishing, which represented him, "put out a special Valentine CD of what they considered to be their best 'uncovered' love ballads in their catalog. Barbra's producer Phil Ramone heard the song somehow and got it to her and that's how I met Phil."

Streisand recorded "Some Good Things Never Last" twice, Radice revealed. Barbra "didn't like the first version and said, 'Can we just get the guy who wrote the song to come out?' So, they flew me to LA and in three takes and 20 minutes she had the track she wanted. Then Phil [Ramone] built the track around my piano and her vocal, added strings, etc." It's interesting to note that both Manilow and Radice sing the lyric "I guess when reality steps in, it all depends," whereas Streisand sings, "I guess when reality steps in, the dreaming ends." Radice explained that both Streisand and Manilow asked for minor changes in the lyrics. "What am I gonna say, NO?" he asked, rhetorically.

Till I Loved You sold very well, achieving platinum status with the RIAA by December 1988 and peaking at number ten on the *Billboard* 200 album chart.

Matt on *Till I Loved You*

This is another Streisand album that has a very special place in my heart, mostly because it was released at a very specific time in my life—I was in college in Los Angeles. I drove down to the Wherehouse, my local record store, and bought *Till I Loved You* on cassette tape (because then I could play it in my car's cassette player!).

I also had my first heartbreak in college, and I recall driving back to Los Angeles after visiting him one weekend, playing *Till I Loved You* and bawling my eyes out because "some good things never last."

Yes, the album's music is highly synthesized, but somehow it doesn't bother me so much because it did sound contemporary—at the time.

"On My Way to You" was written by Legrand and the Bergmans and is so beautiful and thoughtful, like the beginning of a relationship. That's Randy Waldman playing acoustic piano on the track too. The song has a complex piano introduction that is syncopated and changes rhythms and keys over the first few bars. Scott Ryan and I interviewed the man who played that piano part, Randy Waldman, for our YouTube series, *Matt & Scott Talk Barbra*. When we asked Randy about the song he explained, "It's very pretty. It was written out and I was just playing what was written. It's the same thing a drummer has to do. A drummer is playing different things with both feet and both hands. As a keyboard player—it's a melodic percussion instrument. At first, it would be very awkward and difficult for somebody who hasn't done it, but after doing things like that and really challenging things, after years, you kind of look at it and naturally know what to do." Streisand's breathing on "On My Way to You" is a master class in singing. Listen to her interpret the lyrics yet at the same time take in enough breath to hit those crazy notes that Legrand wrote.

"Two People" is another Streisand-written tune I wish she would have sung live in concert at some point. The Bergmans' lyrics are so touching, and, again, there's Waldman on piano, and *real* strings arranged and conducted by Patrick Williams. This song began as an instrumental theme on Barbra's soundtrack to the movie *Nuts*. The Bergmans know Streisand so well their words reflect Barbra's emotionally rough childhood and the growth she went through regarding relationships.

"Love Light" has one of those unexpected, jaunty melodies by the amazing Burt Bacharach. I find it frustrating that Bacharach and Carole Bayer Sager are not on record anywhere about these songs. Sager makes no mention of them in her recent memoir either, and that's too bad.

DECADE 80 ENCORE

By the end of the eighties, Barbra Streisand had been acting and recording for nearly twenty years, and although she probably had released more albums and movies in the seventies, it was during this next decade that she returned to her roots. That meant not only her Jewish roots with *Yentl*, but also her showbiz roots when she reunited after a ten-year break with manager Marty Erlichman in the aftermath of *The Broadway Album*.

"She and I jumped right into it like there had been no gap," Marty stated. "It's like we were married for sixteen years, and then split; when you get back together you kind of know each other. Age has worked well for both of us in the sense that we can talk more shorthand than we used to." (Grein, 1986)

With respect to recordings, Streisand began the decade with a monster hit, *Guilty*, which gave her three top ten singles played on every pop radio station: "Woman in Love," "Guilty," and "What Kind of Fool." Walter Yetnikoff, president of CBS Records during the eighties, stated: "She's in a class by herself. Her demographic boundaries are endless. The type of talent she has can stretch from ballads to rock." (Spada, 1983)

"I'm hard-pressed to find someone who means more to the business," added Bob Sherwood, VP of marketing at the record label. "Whenever she gives us music, the marketing campaign is real simple. You go anywhere with it. She appeals to the broadest demographic audience. If we just do our job by getting the single on radio and inform the public that it is out, then they will flock to the stores to get it." (Spada, 1983)

Streisand produced nine albums in the decade—three pop albums, the *Yentl* and *Nuts* soundtracks, and *The Broadway Album*. She released her first live album in fifteen years, *One Voice*. And Columbia repackaged previously released songs into two "hits" packages.

Yentl and *The Broadway Album* were indicators of the direction Streisand's recording career would take in the next decade—more movies and more Broadway songs. But there was a boom about to happen in radio, followed by a drought.

THE 1990S

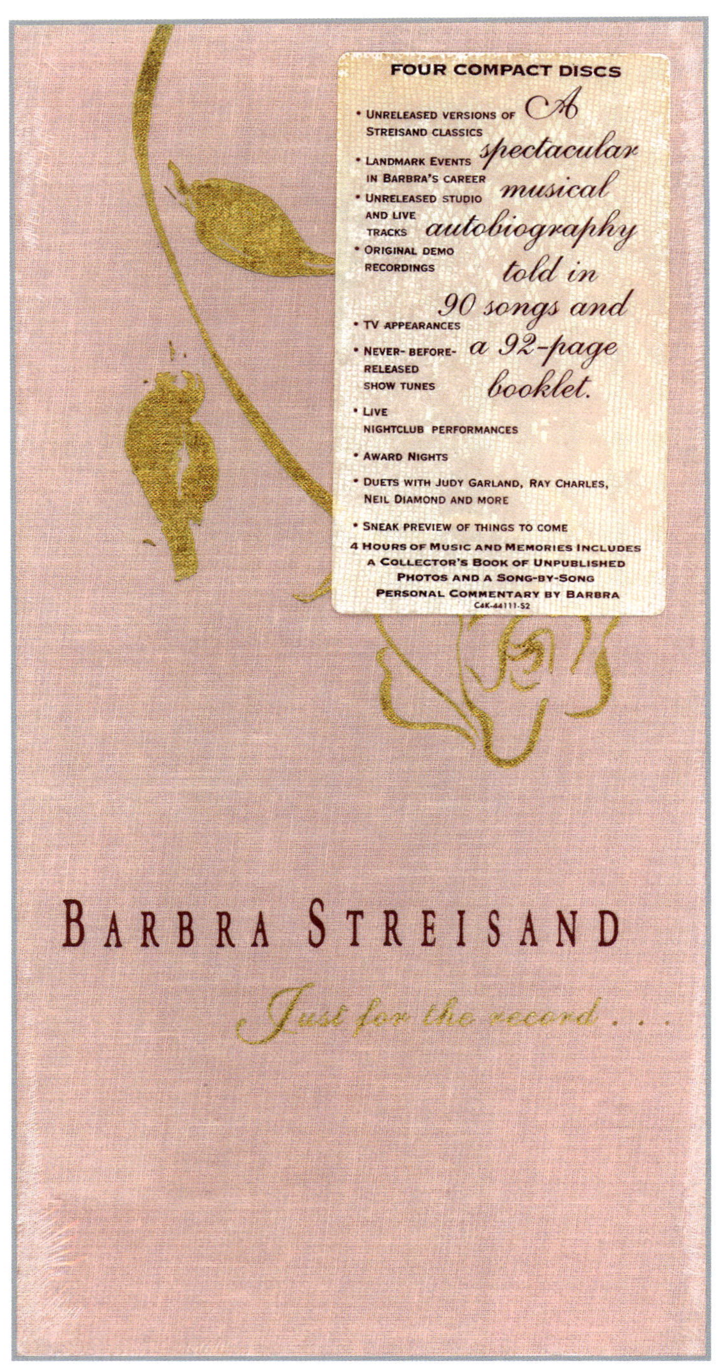

Released: September 24, 1991
Rereleased/repackaged: December 8, 1998
Rereleased/repackaged: July 1, 2003
Produced by: Barbra Streisand and Martin Erlichman
Engineered and coproduced by: John Arrias
Additional engineering: Debbie Johnson, Frank Dookun
Project coordinator: Karen Swenson
A & R for Columbia Records: Jay Landers
Art direction and design: Gabrielle Raumberger
Album notes: Barbra Streisand
For Columbia Records—project manager: Peter Fletcher
Executive art director: Nancy Donald
Associate director of graphic arts: Jeff Beck
Assistant to Miss Streisand: Kim Skalecki
Mastered by: Bernie Grundman
Front and back cover booklet, cassette, CD and still life environmental photos by: Stuart Watson
Awards-page roses photography by: David Skernick

Catalog Numbers:
C4K 44111 (1991—4 CDs)
CT 48645 (1991—4 cassettes)
COL 471640 1 (1991—2 LPs of highlights, released in Greece only)
CXK 68614 (1998—jewelbox configuration)
C4K 89077 (2003—booklet pocket configuration)

Disc 1: The 60's (Part I):

1. You'll Never Know (1955)
2. *Jack Paar Show*: A Sleepin' Bee
3. *P.M. East*: Moon River
4. Miss Marmelstein
5. *Garry Moore Show*: Happy Days Are Here Again
6. Bon Soir: Keepin' Out Of Mischief Now
7. Bon Soir: I Hate Music
8. Bon Soir: Nobody's Heart (Belongs To Me)
9. Bon Soir: Value
10. Bon Soir: Cry Me A River
11. Bon Soir: Who's Afraid Of The Big Bad Wolf?
12. Bon Soir: (I Had Myself A) True Love
13. Bon Soir: Lover, Come Back To Me
14. *Tonight Show*: Spring Can Really Hang You Up The Most
15. My Honey's Lovin' Arms
16. Any Place I Hang My Hat Is Home
17. *Ed Sullivan Show*: When The Sun Comes Out
18. *Judy Garland Show*: Be My Guest/Dialogue with Judy Garland and Ethel Merman
19. *Judy Garland Show*: Medley #1 (with Judy Garland)
20. *Judy Garland Show*: Get Happy/Happy Days (with Judy Garland)

Disc 2: The 60's (Part II):

1. I'm The Greatest Star (live)
2. My Man/Auld Lang Syne (live)
3. People (single)
4. Second Hand Rose (Barbra's mother)/Act II medley from *My Name Is Barbra* *
5. 1965 Emmy Awards
6. He Touched Me
7. You Wanna Bet
8. House Of Flowers
9. Ding-Dong! The Witch Is Dead (with Harold Arlen)
10. (Have I Stayed) Too Long At The Fair/Look At That Face
11. Starting Here, Starting Now
12. *Belle Of 14th Street*: A Good Man Is Hard To Find/Some Of These Days
13. *Belle Of 14th Street*: I'm Always Chasing Rainbows
14. Sleep In Heavenly Peace (Silent Night)
15. Don't Rain On My Parade
16. Funny Girl
17. 1969 Academy Awards
18. Friars Club Tribute - Harold Arlen
19. Friars Club Tribute - Jule Styne
20. Friars Club Tribute - Don Rickles
21. Friars Club Tribute - Richard Rodgers
22. Hello, Dolly! (with Louis Armstrong)
23. On A Clear Day (You Can See Forever)
24. When You Gotta Go/In The Wee Small Hours Of The Morning

*Note: For this compilation, "I've Got Plenty Of Nothing/Brother, Can You Spare A Dime" was edited from the "Act II Medley from *My Name Is Barbra*." The complete medley appears on *My Name Is Barbra, Two*.

Disc 3: The 70's:

1. The Singer
2. I Can Do It
3. Stoney End
4. Close To You (with Burt Bacharach)
5. We've Only Just Begun
6. Since I Fell For You
7. You're The Top (with Ryan O'Neal)
8. What Are You Doing The Rest Of Your Life? (with Michel Legrand) (demo)/album version
9. If I Close My Eyes
10. Between Yesterday And Tomorrow
11. Can You Tell The Moment?
12. The Way We Were (soundtrack version)
13. Cryin' Time (with Ray Charles)
14. God Bless The Child
15. A Quiet Thing/There Won't Be Trumpets
16. Lost Inside Of You (film dialogue/alternate soundtrack version)
17. Evergreen (demo/soundtrack version)
18. 1977 Academy Awards
19. *The Stars Salute Israel At 30* - telephone conversation with Golda Meir; Hatikvah

Disc 4: The 80's:

1. Grammy Awards: You Don't Bring Me Flowers (with Neil Diamond)
2. The Way We Weren't (live)/The Way We Were (single)
3. Guilty (with Barry Gibb)*
4. Papa, Can You Hear Me? (demo)
5. The Moon And I (demo)
6. A Piece Of Sky (demo/soundtrack version)
7. I Know Him So Well
8. If I Loved You
9. Putting It Together
10. Over The Rainbow (live)
11. Theme From *Nuts* (End Credits)
12. Here We Are At Last
13. Warm All Over
14. You'll Never Know (Duet)

* Note: This version of "Guilty" has a different beginning, with Barry Gibb counting down to begin the track. At the end of this song, there is another recording studio comment. Gibb says, "There's a lot of things about that I like." Rare!

Just for the Record was an enormously generous box set of four CDs spanning thirty years of Streisand's extraordinary career; it was packaged elaborately in a long, pink, fabric-covered foldout box—a collection of music and career milestones running over four hours long. "The plan was to pull together all this historical material that people would never get to hear otherwise, and it was one of those projects that just kept growing as I worked on it over the years," Streisand wrote.

The set contained over eighty tracks, most of which were previously unreleased performances. Included were her first recording, at age thirteen; live songs from *Funny Girl* on Broadway; home recordings; a demo of "Evergreen" with Barbra playing guitar; and several awards show acceptance speeches. Barbra first mentioned the collection in 1983 during an interview with Gene Shalit. "I'm working on a retrospective album that's called *Just for the Record*. This record will open with my demo at twelve years old." (*The Today Show*, 1983)

The record closed with the same song it began with—"You'll Never Know." In 1988, Barbra recorded her forty-six-year-old self dueting with her younger self during studio sessions with Rupert Holmes. "Warm All Over" was recorded then too.

The project picked up speed near the end of the 1980s when Marty Erlichman placed ads asking fans to contribute rare material. Tapes, kinescopes, and even an old wire recording were sent. "A lot of the old TV shows, like Johnny Carson and Mike Wallace's *PM East*, were all erased," Erlichman told *Entertainment Weekly*. "So the only way to get them was if fans had them." (News, 1991)

Team Barbra went searching for other archived tapes in Barbra's vaults. "If someone hadn't already taken the title, we'd have called it *Act One*," said Marty Erlichman. "The intention of the set is to give a 'you are there' quality. The project meant a lot to Barbra. When we first sat down to listen to the tapes, it was a very emotional experience for her. It brought back all kinds of memories." (Goldstein, 1991)

Karen Swenson, credited as project coordinator, assembled many of the recordings for *Just for the Record*. Barry Dennen's tapes, made back in 1961 at the Bon Soir and the Lion, were considered. Erlichman tried to work with Dennen to include the tapes on the box set, but eventually he gave up. Swenson told the *LA Times*, "A private collector had one of Barbra's *Tonight Show* appearances that we couldn't find anywhere else. And I found her *Yentl* audition tapes, with her sitting at the piano with Michel Legrand, in her closet—she'd forgotten she even had them."

Swenson and Jay Landers not only uncovered rare tracks, they sometimes had to salvage the original recordings. "We had one tape that was in such poor condition that the oxide was peeling off," Swenson recalled. "But we learned a neat trick—we sent it to an expert at Columbia, who baked it in an oven at 350 degrees, which somehow brought the tape back to life long enough for us to make a new copy." (Goldstein, 1991)

Landers told Barbra News, "*Just for the Record* gave me a chance to look through her archives and revisit many aspects of her artistic accomplishments that were before my time. One day, it would be great to expand the box set with even more of the material we simply couldn't fit onto the four discs." (Hall, BarbraNews Talks to Jay Landers, 2005) Barbra told the press, "You don't know how difficult it is to listen to those things [the archival material]. I picked a lot of the songs. For two and a half years they were trying to master them, engineer them, recut several things together, find the tapes, all that stuff. The last two months I had to write the notes." Streisand elaborated: "I started three years ago, talking into a tape recorder. Then, when it was time to release it . . . at the last minute it was a horror. That's why it took so long. It was supposed to come out at Christmas 1990. But we just got it out a few weeks ago. I didn't want both products out at the same time." (Blank, 1991)

As it turns out, the release of *Just for the Record* coincided with Barbra's big movie *The Prince of Tides* as well as its soundtrack album from Columbia Records. A two-VHS videotape companion to the four-CD set was prepared utilizing rare footage of Streisand's career, but ultimately was not released. Despite its hefty price tag of $79.99, *Just for the Record* ended up going platinum (over one million units) and stayed on the *Billboard* 200 albums chart for sixteen weeks. At the Grammys, the set received a nomination for Traditional Pop Performance ("Warm All Over"). Gabrielle Raumberger's excellent work on the packaging was nominated as well.

Columbia released on June 30, 1992, *Highlights from Just for the Record*, a one-disc, shortened version of the big box set (#CK 52849). *Highlights* probably fulfilled Streisand's contract with Columbia to put out so many records. Essentially, it was an affordable but much shorter version of *Just for the Record*. It came with a full-color-insert booklet that had abbreviated versions of Streisand's original liner notes.

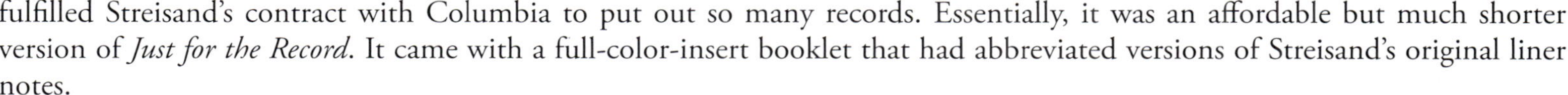

Matt on *JFTR*

I don't remember how I afforded to buy *Just for the Record* in 1991 at its eighty dollar price point. A quick online inflation calculator tells me the price would be $166 in today's dollars.

What I do remember was the unboxing! I was able to carve out a few hours alone with the box set and a bottle of Chianti wine. When I put in disc one, followed by the other three, the box set was telling me the story of Barbra Streisand's career. Even though several reviews and fans complained there was too much talking on the compilation, I was happily overwhelmed with Barbra's career milestones and impressed to no end.

Listening to *JFTR* today, I agree—too much talking. That being said, I can easily skip those spoken-word tracks or even make my own playlist of music-only tracks. So there.

What I recall from thirty years ago and first listening to this set is that the 60's discs blew me away. Such rarities! The Bon Soir tracks slayed me. The live tracks from *Funny Girl*—what?! The tantalizing, teasing tracks from *The Belle of 14th Street* toyed with me because at that point we would still have to wait almost fourteen years for that TV special to come out on DVD. Funny, I was disappointed every time a previously released track played, especially from her first two albums. I wanted more, more, more unreleased songs! And I concur today that the Friar's Club talk tracks, although clearly iconic and historical, probably mean more to Barbra than they do to the average listener.

After relistening to *JFTR*, I decided that the third disc ("The 70's") is my favorite. "The Singer" is special, as is "I Can Do It" and "We've Only Just Begun." Barbra was really a great pop singer on those tracks. Next, there's the Bergmans' "If I Close My Eyes," "Between Yesterday and Tomorrow," and "Can You Tell the Moment." It was such a treat to finally hear those tracks. I often forget to listen to "God Bless the Child," but Barbra sings it well and is supported by a tasteful arrangement by Lee Holdridge. Finally, you've got to laugh at Barbra's telephone conversation with Golda Meir—it illustrates clearly why she didn't want to have guest stars on her early TV shows. Meir cannot be charmed into warming up to Barbra. She's an immovable mountain when Barbra says, "The country needs you, the world needs you." You can hear Meir shrug and dismiss her. "Oh, well, look . . ."

Although fans had traded the *Yentl* demos through the mail during the 1980s, it was fun to have a trio of them included on *JFTR's* last disc. Jay Landers and Barbra topped themselves with more demos on the 40th deluxe *Yentl* CD, though.

JFTR will always be an amazing box set with so many treasures that it felt like Christmas morning with hundreds of presents under the tree! It's unfortunate that box sets seem to have been a fad, gone by the 2000s. Streisand took the format and raised the standard, giving us a truly special collection of her musical legacy.

Released: June 29, 1993
Produced by: David Foster, Andrew Lloyd Webber and Nigel Wright, and Barbra Streisand
Photography (front cover): Firooz Zahedi
Photography (back cover): Michael Halsband
Art direction: Nancy Donald
Design: Cheri Grey
Liner notes: Barbra Streisand
Mixed by: Humberto Gatica for Hum Inc. Productions
A & R: Jay Landers

Catalog Numbers:
CK 44189 (CD)
4738801 (LP, Europe only—back cover below)
CM 44189 (MiniDisc)

Tracks:

1. Some Enchanted Evening (*South Pacific*)
2. Everybody Says Don't (*Anyone Can Whistle*)
3. The Music Of The Night (*The Phantom of the Opera*) (with Michael Crawford)
4. Speak Low (*One Touch of Venus*)
5. As If We Never Said Goodbye (*Sunset Blvd.*)
6. Children Will Listen (*Into the Woods*)
7. I Have A Love/One Hand, One Heart (*West Side Story*) (with Johnny Mathis)
8. I've Never Been In Love Before (*Guys and Dolls*)
9. Luck Be A Lady (*Guys and Dolls*)
10. With One Look (*Sunset Blvd.*)
11. The Man I Love (written for *Lady, Be Good*)
12. Move On (*Sunday In The Park With George*)

Back to Broadway was a milestone in Barbra Streisand's recording career because it followed on the heels of a $60 million contract she signed in December 1992 with Sony Corporation. The contract gave Streisand deals for both film and recording projects. The contract was negotiated by Marty Erlichman and Barbra's attorney Lee Phillips, and in the area of recording it reportedly paid her $5 million for every album, with royalties of 42 percent on the wholesale price of each unit sold. The contract called for her to produce six albums plus two reissues. (Lightman, 1993) (AP, 1992)

Back to Broadway was not only a sequel to her multiplatinum 1985 record, *The Broadway Album*, it was also Barbra's fiftieth album for Columbia Records, and it became her seventh number one album!

Back to Broadway was also the first major Barbra Streisand album that did not go to stores as a vinyl release; in the US, it was sold only as a CD and cassette. Columbia would stick with this CD-only trend until vinyl had a resurgence circa 2009. (Come on, Columbia, let's get those missing albums released on vinyl.)

Unfortunately, I'm not a big fan of *Back to Broadway*. I remember being disappointed when I first listened to it. I couldn't express my reasons at the time, but I can articulate them now. I've just relistened (carefully!) to the album, so my argument follows below.

Back to Broadway feels brassy and bombastic. Streisand's singing on many of the tracks is strident and lacking in her usual care. I blame David Foster. David Foster produced eight of the twelve tracks, and that's why most of the album is problematic for me. Too many of the songs sound like electronic demos. It's confusing because the CD credits orchestras and conductors on several of the offensive tracks, but they still sound like video games (I'm looking at you, "Luck Be a Lady").

I played some tracks from *What Matters Most* (2011) after relistening to *Back to Broadway*, just as a comparison. The orchestra on *What Matters Most* is recorded beautifully and sounds present and vibrant on my headphones and speakers. On *Back to Broadway*, the orchestra is always diminished and sounds flat and tinny.

I found myself wondering: did Barbra actually sing in a studio with musicians on this album? Some of the tracks don't have the organic feel of Barbra being in the same room with an orchestra. And for that—I blame David Foster.

Then there's the matter of the material and the sequencing of the tracks. In my car today, taking another listen from start to finish of *Back to Broadway*, I felt a relaxation and a sigh of relief inside me when "I've Never Been in Love Before" came on. Now, granted, "Never Been in Love Before" is the *eighth* track! Up until that point, the album has a very ALL CAPS attitude and production, as if Foster is trying to impress upon us that BARBRA STREISAND IS SINGING BROADWAY SONGS!

Here's a breakdown of the album: "Some Enchanted Evening" lacks subtlety. As the opening track, it certainly showcases Barbra's voice . . . it's just so darn LOUD. Then "Everybody Says Don't" steamrolls us. It worked far better as part of a medley with "Don't Rain on My Parade" on Barbra's 1994 concert tour. Following that, Barbra and Michael Crawford navigate a highly dramatic operatic duet from *Phantom of the Opera*. Again, Barbra outdid this recording live in 2006 with Il Divo. "Speak Low" sounds like a karaoke track—again I ask: where's the orchestra? It's credited. I don't hear it. Marvin Hamlisch incorporated "Speak Low" into a medley for the 1993 concert, and it comes off much better there, with a sexy piano, strings, a bossa nova beat, and a saxophone. After "Speak Low," the songs from *Sunset Blvd.* and *Into the Woods* are just fine, but I believe they were done better in concert, live. The duet with Johnny Mathis of *West Side Story* songs irks me because it sounds like a demo. Like I said earlier, "I've Never Been in Love Before" is the first time Barbra gives us subtle song acting on this album, and it's lovely. Then, "Luck Be a Lady" stomps on that mood with its synthesizers, sounding like the theme song to *Tron*. The credits state this song was arranged and conducted—WHERE IS THE ORCHESTRA? All I hear are synthesizers. "With One Look" won me back with its tasteful orchestral arrangement, and "The Man I Love" sounds analog—which is a compliment for a song on this album. Finally, "Move On" is a good closer, without a synthesizer to be heard. Barbra Streisand is the only producer listed for "Move On" and "Children Will Listen," which is interesting, because these two Sondheim tracks sound great.

Johnny Mathis, speaking to *Goldmine* magazine, verified my grievances. In explaining the process of recording "I Have a Love"/One Hand, One Heart," Mathis stated: "[David Foster] sat down and did a $20 recording of the background on a synthesizer, and that's what we first rehearsed to for about a month or so. Then we went into the studio over at MGM, and I think it was about a 106-piece orchestra, and we rerecorded it and Barbra didn't like that, so we scrapped that. Then we tried

something else and something else again, and what we did is we went back to David's original $20 little thing he did on the synthesizer and that's what the record ended up as. It sounds great." (Carpenter, 1993) I disagree with Mr. Mathis. It sounds like twenty dollars backing up two million-dollar voices. Mathis loved Streisand, though. He told Todd Sussman in *Cabaret Scenes* that "we are very, very, very big fans of each other! We had vocal ranges from the moon above to the cellar below, and we utilized that in our singing." When working on the *West Side Story* medley, Mathis said, "the important thing about voices is you don't want one voice to overshadow the other because of the vocal ranges that you have. The blending of our voices was sensational. It was so much fun to sing with her because we could sing loud, then soft, and we could sing fast, then slow. We loved what we were doing."

One track that definitely sounds beautifully orchestrated is "Music of the Night," which Barbra sings with her former *Hello, Dolly!* costar, Michael Crawford. Crawford, of course, originated the title role in *Phantom of the Opera*. Andrew Jackman flew to America to work with Barbra on the arrangement, singing Crawford's part with Barbra. "Then we went into the studio," Michael Crawford recalled to BBC Radio 2, "and sang it together. She said the timing isn't right. She wasn't happy with the timing. She said, 'You sing it first.' Normally, if it's your album, you sing first, and the guest follows you. I said, 'It's your album.' She said, 'It's your song.'"

Back to Broadway sounds dated and very un-Broadway-like because of its overreliance on synthesizers and electronic arrangements. As an interesting comparison, there is the 2016 album *Encore: Movie Partners Sing Broadway*. Many of those tracks utilize synths too, but somehow Walter Afanasieff's production doesn't sound overly electronic.

It was only six years earlier that *The Broadway Album* came out, and if you compare *Back to Broadway* with it, the first one sounds like a masterpiece, a definitive work. Peter Matz provided many outstanding orchestral arrangements, and the use of synthesizers is tasteful, with only "Something's Coming" and "Somewhere" sounding completely electronic.

Back to Broadway began with Rupert Holmes at the helm in 1988. Unfortunately, those sessions were abandoned, and Foster and Streisand started over. "We attempted to do [a *Broadway Album* sequel] years ago," Marty Erlichman told *Billboard*, "but we didn't have the excitement of the first album." (Lightman, 1993) Still in the vaults from the Holmes sessions are lovely recordings made with a full orchestra of "On My Own" from *Les Misérables*, "A Funny Thing Happened on My Way to Love" from *I Can Get It for You Wholesale*, "Moonfall" from *The Mystery of Edwin Drood*, and "Make Our Garden Grow" from *Candide*.

For Foster's *Back to Broadway*, he and Barbra worked on "Unusual Way" and "Smoke Gets in Your Eyes," but never recorded them. (I've heard the demo of "Smoke"—it's horrible, with programmed drums, electronic snaps, and a twangy synthesized piano. Streisand sounds completely frustrated doing a sing-through of it.)

Another song that did not end up on the final album is Barbra's breathy, sexy *solo* version of "I've Got A Crush on You." It was rerecorded with a new arrangement as a duet with Frank Sinatra that appeared on his *Duets* album. "I've Got A Crush On You" is a song that Jay Landers suggested for the album and that Foster produced as a demo for Barbra to sing solo. Jay shared, "One of David Foster's greatest gifts as a producer and arranger is that he can sit down at a keyboard—piano, electric piano, or synth piano—play a song one time through, and make it sound almost like a finished record. In the case of 'I've Got A Crush on You,' the demo was never taken further.

Another song intended for the album that never went as far as the demo was "Anything You Can Do, I Can Do Better," from the musical *Annie Get Your Gun*. "David Foster created a demo and we said, 'Well, who could we do this with?'" Jay Landers recalled. "And we chose Madonna and Bette [Midler]. So it was going to be the three of them." According to Jay, the "brilliant" arrangement by Foster featured verses sung by the Queen of Pop and the Divine Miss M in their respective styles of music. The song would end with the three women in the ladies' room, Madonna and Bette gossiping, "'God, she's such a bitch! She's so controlling' and this and that . . . And then we hear another stall open and [Barbra says], 'Ladies! I'm in here!' And that's how

the song was going to end." Alas, this trio was not meant to be. Jay wrangled all the talents together, but "at the eleventh hour, Madonna couldn't do it for some reason or another." (A year after Jay told this story on my Barbra Archives YouTube channel, the story went viral, posted on RollingStone.com and other music and entertainment websites. But no one credited me or my channel, instead linking to a random Madonna Instagram account that posted my video without tagging or crediting me. Oy . . . when will creators on the internet be properly credited?)

The *Sunset Blvd.* songs—Andrew Lloyd Webber's "With One Look" and "As If We Never Said Goodbye"—are another annoyance with *Back to Broadway*. Although Barbra's recordings are marvelous, their existence has provided years of fuel to the rumor that Barbra would play Norma Desmond in the movie version of Sir Andrew's musical. To date, that movie has *never* been made.

Streisand fans seem split down the middle about whether she should have played Norma on-screen. Of course, there's a whole contingency who believe Lloyd Webber's musical has only two or three good songs, and that it never transcended the exceptional original film, with Gloria Swanson.

Barbra herself wasn't keen on the idea. She stated: "Well it [the *Sunset* movie] actually was happening for a while, and I turned it down twice. And it's a hard one, because it was a great movie. I thought she was a little over-the-top, Gloria Swanson. He was very good, William Holden. It would need work for the film, a lot of work." (Streisand, The Way I Am—BBC Radio 2, 2009)

Barbra asked Don Black to amend the *Sunset Blvd.* song "With One Look" for this album. "She wanted me to do a verse to it," Black told Gloria Hunniford on BBC's Radio 2. "So I said, 'Why do you want me to do that?' And she said, 'Well, it's okay if you've seen *Sunset Blvd.* You know it's about a faded film star. But if you haven't, and people are just going to hear it on the radio, we need to set the picture.' So I wrote those lines at the very beginning . . . just a few lines to set it up." *They don't want me anymore. They all say I'm through; well, it's time they knew.*

What's something positive about *Back to Broadway*? "Move On" is a victory, earning my admiration. Importing it from the score of *Sunday in the Park with George* was facilitated by the genius of Stephen Sondheim, and this song works well on the album, out of show context. Sondheim replaced the lyric references to "George"—*Sunday*'s main character, an artist—with "you," "though," and "no," which work perfectly. The track is a combination of "We Do Not Belong Together" from the first act of *Sunday* and "Move On" from the finale.

Foster is a titan in the music business, and there are songs he's produced that I actually enjoy, like Celine Dion's "All by Myself," Whitney Houston's "I Will Always Love You," and even Barbra and Bryan Adams's "I Finally Found Someone." But in general, I don't like his work with Streisand. When I watched the documentary *David Foster: Off the Record*, I really got the impression that he's a competitive man, daring singers to hit impossible notes and go out of their comfort zones. That's all very good, but there's also a lot of ego involved. *Back to Broadway* is the only album he's produced for Barbra, and I feel he shows off on it, which sidelines Barbra's usual artistry and restraint. I don't want to get into his head too much but it almost feels like Foster wanted a huge hit with *Back to Broadway* and ended up overproducing it, wanting every track to be a blockbuster. *Back to Broadway* was Grammy nominated for Best Traditional Pop Vocal Performance, but the votes went to Tony Bennett and his album *Steppin' Out*. This began a frustrating trend that I'll mention later.

With all of the potential *Back to Broadway* had, it's a shame that despite selling so many copies, the album doesn't stand the test of time. Why? Well, I blame David Foster. Thankfully, Foster worked less with Streisand on her following albums, with William Ross and Walter Afanasieff becoming more prevalent collaborators.

Released: September 27, 1994
Produced by: Barbra Streisand and Jay Landers
Arranged and conducted by: Marvin Hamlisch
Mixed by: Dave Reitzas
Mixed at: Record Plant, Los Angeles
Remote recording engineered by: Dave Hewitt with David Reitzas
Concert production conceived and directed by: Barbra Streisand
Cover photo: Kevin Mazur
Photography: Spike Nanarello, Matthew Rolston, Firooz Zahedi
Liner notes: Jay Landers with Dan Pine
Recorded live at: Madison Square Garden, New York, June 20, 23, 26, 28, 30, 1994.
Design: Dylan Tran

Catalog Numbers:
C2K 66109 (CD)
661097-4 (cassette)
CM2 66109—CM 66456 and CM 66457 (MiniDisc 1994)
COL 477599 1 (LP, Spain only)

Disc 1/Act 1:

1. Overture
2. As If We Never Said Goodbye
3. Opening Remarks
4. I'm Still Here/Everybody Says Don't/Don't Rain On My Parade
5. Can't Help Lovin' That Man
6. I'll Know (with Marlon Brando)
7. People
8. Lover Man
9. Therapist Dialogue #1
10. Will He Like Me?
11. Therapist Dialogue #2
12. He Touched Me
13. Evergreen
14. Therapist Dialogue #3
15. The Man That Got Away
16. On A Clear Day (You Can See Forever)

Disc 2/Act 2:

1. Entr'acte
2. The Way We Were
3. You Don't Bring Me Flowers
4. Lazy Afternoon
5. Disney Medley (Once Upon A Dream, When You Wish Upon A Star, Someday My Prince Will Come)
6. Not While I'm Around
7. Ordinary Miracles
8. *Yentl* Medley (Where Is It Written?, Papa, Can You Hear Me?, Will Someone Ever Look At Me That Way?, A Piece Of Sky)
9. Happy Days Are Here Again
10. My Man
11. For All We Know
12. Somewhere

The Concert was Streisand's fourth live album since she began recording with Columbia Records in 1962—and it was a complete recording of her concert spread across two CDs. Her much publicized return to the concert stage awarded her glowing reviews and made her longtime fans happy. At her stop in New York, "anticipation of her six-night engagement at Madison Square Garden galvanized the city. New York was in a state of terminal buzz over its best-loved favorite daughter. Everyone wanted to be at the Garden," wrote Jay Landers and Dan Pine in the album's liner notes.

Streisand constructed the show to "reflect the values, musical influences, personal disappointments and triumphs that shaped her as an artist, as a woman, as a citizen, as a human being," Landers and Pine wrote. For Columbia's record of the shows, "all of the performances are as they happened," Landers explained. "Nothing with Barbra is ever just handed in," Marty Erlichman told the *Los Angeles Times Calendar*. "On these recordings there were 64 musicians, and it takes a lot of mixing and editing to make it really sound live." (Hochman, 1994)

After Marvin Hamlisch's outstanding overture plays, Streisand can be heard making her entrance to tumultuous applause. She sings "As If We Never Said Goodbye" from Lloyd Webber's musical *Sunset Blvd.* but with new lyrics from Don Black, who traveled from London to Los Angeles to update the song for Streisand. Black told Gloria Hunniford in 1994 on BBC Radio 2: "Marilyn and Alan Bergman called me up and said, 'Barbra would like to open with this song. She loves the opening lines . . . but all the images about movies don't make sense. So I did things about the band, the lights, familiar sights, and stuff like that."

Black continued: "It wasn't that easy to work with her. She is, without doubt, the perfectionist of all time. I spent six hours with her like this. Anything from Barbra Streisand is perfect. It was a joy to work with her."

Jay Landers told me that capturing the *Yentl* medley and the stage business with the overhead screens "required a lot of audio work on our engineer David Reitzas's part. We captured all five shows by hiring a famous mobile recording truck that was owned and operated by Dave Hewitt. A few days after the concert, Dave (Reitzas) and I reviewed all five shows and selected what we thought were the best performances. It was a fun exercise because Barbra was truly in the zone for each show. As we listened, it was always a choice between great and greater performances. For example, if she sang a particularly inspired note or brought an extra tear to the eye on some ballad, we'd make note of it."

As for the *Yentl* medley itself, in which Barbra sings live with a film clip of herself, accompanied by Hamlisch's orchestra, Randy Waldman explained in our *Matt & Scott* YouTube interview that "to make it work, it's all about the technical end. In order to stay in sync with the video, we have to hear some reference in our earphones. Normally in the concert, we're not wearing earphones. But when we're playing with the video, we do. And they build a click track to match the video. And we determine how many clicks we hear preparatory to her entrance—it could be four, it could be two, it could be three—we work it out with the engineer to figure out what we need to hear to stay in sync with what's onscreen."

When I asked Jay about how they mix a live album for the CD, he explained, "I encouraged Dave to find that perfect sweet spot where the listener could feel the electricity in the air, as if they'd scored the best seats in the house. In layman's terms, we strove to apply the right amount of echo to each song to convey the enormity of the arena and all the energy from the audience, but also dialed in the clarity so we could hear the rhythm section, orchestra, and especially Barbra's vocals with the kind of dynamics that are sometimes lost inside the cavernous venue."

Columbia promoted the live set by releasing a CD single (#44K 77534) and a 45 (#38-77533) of the Hamlisch/Bergmans' song "Ordinary Miracles." This is now a rare single, because it included a studio version of "Ordinary Miracles" that has never appeared on another Streisand album or compilation, along with a live version from Las Vegas. What makes that a bit frustrating is that Barbra's studio vocal was nominated for a Grammy Award! *The Concert* sold very well despite costing almost twenty-five dollars; it also charted as high as number ten on the *Billboard* 200 chart, going three times multiplatinum (about three million units). The CD set was nominated for Best Traditional Pop Vocal Performance. Tony Bennett won that year . . . again.

The next year, Columbia edited together *The Concert Highlights* (#CK 67100), a one-CD release that accomplished two things: it fulfilled a numerical quotient of Streisand albums, and it provided a less-expensive price point. Most of Streisand's patter was edited out, and the songs were blended seamlessly using the audience applause as a bridge. The *Highlights* CD sold well, spending seven weeks on the chart and achieving gold status—500,000 units.

Fans have emailed me in confusion over the years about the home video versions. Barbra's 1994 New York concerts were recorded for CD, but were not videotaped for television. However, Barbra's 1994 Anaheim show became an Emmy- and Peabody-winning HBO concert special that was released on home video (VHS and laser disc). That show was finally released in 2009 on DVD in a box set. The Anaheim TV special is not to be confused with *The Concert: Live at the MGM Grand*, a DVD that Sony BMG released in 2004. That DVD is a record of Barbra's first shows in Las Vegas on New Year's Eve 1993. If Anaheim was the end of the tour, then the MGM Grand was the beginning. Confused? Now you know what I mean.

Matt on *The Concert*

The package and the recording of this concert are impressive. Let's face it, for twenty-five dollars, fans who couldn't afford the concert tickets were able to hear the complete show, and it's a gorgeous recording. And for those who were there, it's a great souvenir.

I like Barbra's patter on these discs. We get the mention of the Gay Games in "Opening Remarks"; we hear her call out Jule Styne and tell Liza Minnelli "That was for your mom" after singing Judy Garland's iconic song "The Man That Got Away." Barbra's version never fails to entertain me. I love that she takes the first two verses out of tempo, really feeling the words she's singing. Then the tempo kicks in, and Barbra belts it.

I've listened to the "*Yentl* Medley," at nine minutes in length, often as well. I love that Barbra essentially gives us "story time" by relaying the tale of *Yentl* and including four of its songs. I never thought I'd hear "Will Someone Ever Look at Me That Way" sung live. Then Barbra astonishes us by singing "A Piece of Sky" live too. I attended this concert in Landover, Maryland—which was her first stop after London. I had no idea she was going to duet with herself on "A Piece of Sky." I remember thinking: *She's not going to sing that. Is she?* And she did. And we all jumped to our feet screaming our appreciation and joy.

That happened with "Lazy Afternoon" too. Again, in Landover, I had no idea this song was going to happen. When I heard that dreamy introduction, I thought: *She's not possibly going to sing 'Lazy Afternoon' from the seventies. Is she?* And she did. It's another favorite of mine from the New York recording.

I've always thought "For All We Know" was a clever "get off the stage" song for this tour. Sure, it was from her big movie *The Prince of Tides*, but it also served as a song-monologue to the fans. It's a hoot to hear the audience sigh when Barbra sings "we may never meet again."

The most satisfying track for me is the medley after Barbra's opening remarks. Streisand wrote that she thought Sondheim's "I'm Still Here" was perfect for her, but "all the Depression-era references that worked for the character who sang it in *Follies* had nothing to do with me. And this time it wouldn't be simply a matter of changing a few words. It would mean rewriting the whole song." So, "I'm Still Here," was customized for Barbra by Sondheim, who confessed, "When it's a performer I admire and who asks me to rewrite the lyric rather than destabilize it themselves, I occasionally oblige. I'd oblige more often," he wrote, "except that the plethora of mercilessly brief rhymed lines in the lyric makes it a difficult job." (Sondheim, 2011) His best rhymed line is "I kept my nose to spite my face." Funny! The "I'm Still Here" versions on the CD and LA video release are shorter than the Vegas version.

Next, she sings a brief section of Sondheim's "Everybody Says Don't," then shocks and awes us with a crazy-good arrangement of "Don't Rain on My Parade." Marvin Hamlisch was responsible for the orchestration, and it was one of his favorite moments of the tour. "I kind of modernized the arrangement . . . and every time we got to that point, which is very early, having her do it brilliantly used to be one of my fabulous moments." (King, 1994)

This version of "People" is my favorite one! Over the years, Barbra has always surprised us by singing different phrasings of the climax, but this recording stands out for me. She sings "First be a person who needs PE-EO-PLE," and I plotz.

SIGNATURE STREISAND

"I FINALLY FOUND SOMEONE"

Barbra Streisand had historically done very well singing theme songs to movies . . . mostly *her* movies. There's "Evergreen," "The Way We Were," "The Main Event," and "Prisoner." So when it was time to release her romance film *The Mirror Has Two Faces*, it went without saying that it would need a hit theme song. Because rocker Bryan Adams was the king of movie theme songs at the time, it made sense for Barbra to record a duet with him. After all, he'd had huge hits with "I Do It for You" from *Robin Hood: Prince of Thieves*, "All for Love" from *The Three Musketeers*, and "Have You Ever Really Loved a Woman" from *Don Juan De Marco*.

Although Streisand, Hamlisch, and the Bergmans worked on two tunes, ultimately it took a village to come up with the final song: Barbra Streisand, Marvin Hamlisch, R. J. Lange, and Bryan Adams are credited with writing "I Finally Found Someone." David Foster produced and arranged it, and Lange and Adams share arrangement credits with Foster.

The first Hamlisch/Bergmans song, "All of My Life," is included on the soundtrack album, and you can hear the original melody on it. There is another, unreleased, end-title song called "It Doesn't Get Better than This," which featured Barbra's "love theme," but not Bryan Adams.

Barbra explained the process: "I had written a love theme, and the Bergmans started a lyric based on the theme, although we didn't complete how the theme integrated with the bridge. . . . It was very difficult musically, because when you play something orchestrally, you can do all sorts of wonderful keys, but when the voice has to sing it, it changes that pattern. Then, I asked my friend David Foster, who produced a lot of records for me, 'Please, please, please become involved.' He had one week, a five-day period that he could give me time. And he came to Sony one night, and we just played around—asked five of my favorite musicians who were playing on the score to hang around and we kind of had a jam session and made this track. I was humming the words because we only had some of the words. And David recommended singing

the duet with Bryan Adams. So, I sent him this track, and he fell in love with my little theme and wrote this counter melody to this theme and around this theme. And that's how it happened. He's a doll. Talk about a perfectionist!" (TriStar Pictures, 1996)

Columbia released the single as a three-track CD (#38K 78480) that is rare because it also includes the Spanish version of "Evergreen."

"I Finally Found Someone" debuted on *Billboard*'s Hot 100 chart at number twenty-eight and peaked at number seven. The same week it peaked in sales it was only number twenty-six on Hot 100 Airplay, *Billboard*'s radio chart, which meant radio stations weren't really playing it that much. It's unlikely Barbra will have such a successful single anytime soon, so "Someone" may mark Barbra's last big-charting single.

The song was nominated for a Grammy (Best Pop Collaboration with Vocals) and an Oscar (Best Original Song). There was a huge scandal at the Academy Awards show when Celine Dion stepped in at the last minute to sing "I Finally Found Someone" because Natalie Cole, who was originally scheduled to perform it, took ill. When Dion sang a lovely version of Barbra's song, Barbra just happened to be in the bathroom—shocking! "They don't have it printed in the program when the songs are," Barbra explained. "I went what I thought was during an intermission, come back, and the song's over. Now, I was heartbroken. Because I knew that this would be a wonderful moment on television. To have her singing, flash to me next to my love, Jim Brolin, of a song that I wrote called 'I Finally Found Someone.' This is a wonderful moment to capture on tape, right? Why would I miss it? Is the press this cynical? To make up a story that I would have deliberately done this to her?" (*20/20* Barbara Walters interview, 1997)

Barbra integrated "Someone" into her 2007 European concert tour with the Broadway Singers (Peter Lockyer, Sean McDermott, Michael Arden, and Hugh Panaro). Bryan Adams, by the way, performs a lovely solo acoustic version of "Someone" in concert.

"I Finally Found Someone," besides being a big hit for Barbra, has probably been sung or played at millions of weddings. That is, if the bride and groom didn't choose "Evergreen" first.

Released: November 11, 1997
Executive producers: Barbra Streisand and Jay Landers
Album coordinator for Barbra Streisand: Kim Skalecki
Personal assistant to Barbra Streisand: Renata Buser
Album project coordinators: Nancy Roof and Allan Stein
Product manager: Peter Fletcher
Art direction: Nancy Donald
Design: Hooshik
Liner notes: Barbra Streisand
Photos (Front cover, back cover, tray card): Randee St Nicholas
Photo of Celine Dion and Barbra Streisand: Firooz Zahedi
All orchestral recording by: Dave Reitzas (except "Avinu Malkeinu" and "On Holy Ground")

Catalog Numbers:
CK 66181 (CD)
CT 66181 (cassette)
CM 66181 (US) 488532 8 (Europe) (MiniDisc)

Tracks:

1. I Believe/You'll Never Walk Alone
2. Higher Ground
3. At The Same Time
4. Tell Him (with Celine Dion)
5. On Holy Ground
6. If I Could
7. Circle
8. The Water Is Wide/Deep River
9. Leading With Your Heart
10. Lessons To Be Learned
11. Everything Must Change
12. Avinu Malkeinu

Higher Ground was Barbra Streisand's eighth number one album, touted by the record company as "a collection of songs that celebrate love and faith." *Higher Ground* charted at number one on November 29, 1997, with 207,000 units sold, which was significantly more than *Back to Broadway* (121,000 units).

Barbra was inspired to record this album when she heard the song "On Holy Ground" at Virginia Clinton Kelley's funeral in 1994. Streisand was close to President Bill Clinton's mother before her death. "I called her my Southern mom," Streisand recalled about the Arkansas-born woman. "She knew how to soothe with words. Virginia would say, 'Do you know how precious you are?' Every conversation, she'd say, 'I love you.' The way I was brought up, nobody ever used words like 'I love you.'" (Dreifus, 1997)

At the funeral, a nineteen-year-old vocalist named Janice Sjostrand sang the hymn, and Barbra described it as an "electrifying moment." In her liner notes for the album, Barbra wrote, "I love the sound of a gospel choir, with all its earthly passion. . . . The lyric says that whenever we stand in the presence of God, we're on holy ground." Streisand explained that "the music united us, invoking Virginia's essence and elevating our spirits with every note. I knew then that I had to sing that song, and others like it. The idea for this album was born at that moment."

The man who wrote "On Holy Ground" was Geron Davis. "Here's a lady," Davis said about Streisand, "who's sung on Broadway. She has sung duets with every famous person in the country. She's produced, starred in, and directed movies. You think a nineteen-year-old's song is gonna electrify her? That's not what electrified Barbra Streisand. What happened to Barbra Streisand—and I believe she would agree—is that she got into the presence of the King of Kings and the Lord of Lords. She was electrified not by my song, but by the presence of God that she felt in the room." (Christensen, 2007)

Streisand recorded the *Higher Ground* album quickly after diligent preparation. Sessions were completed in two weeks during the months of August and September 1997. "I wanted to go back to the way I recorded in the 1960s," Streisand told the *Los Angeles Times*. "With my first few albums, I made an album in four days. I did three songs at a session. But now they do all this stuff with synthesizers and layers and stuff and then you sing again. So, I just wanted to be spontaneous with an orchestra. My goal was to do three songs that first day and we did it." (Hilburn, 1997)

Former Atlantic Records producer Arif Mardin (see the documentary *The Greatest Ears in Town*) produced four tracks on *Higher Ground*: "I Believe"/"You'll Never Walk Alone," "Higher Ground," "If I Could," and "The Water is Wide"/"Deep River." *Higher Ground* marked the first time Streisand and Arif Mardin worked together. "I'm an arranger-producer," he explained, "so I think of enhancing the song with my arrangement and making it accessible to a certain segment of the record-buying public. I arrange according to style, and the artist involved." (Niles, 2021)

Mardin's musical pedigree was exceptional. At Atlantic Records, he produced Ray Charles and Aretha Franklin. *Dusty* [Springfield] *in Memphis* was by Mardin. Likewise "I Feel for You" by Chaka Khan and Norah Jones's *Come Away with Me*. The impressive list of music icons he had worked with also included Laura Nyro, Roberta Flack and Donny Hathaway ("Where Is the Love?"), Hall & Oates ("She's Gone"), the Bee Gees ("Jive Talkin'"), Judy Collins ("Send in the Clowns"), and Bette Midler ("From a Distance").

Jay Landers recalled, "Barbra had the idea of putting two of her favorite songs together, 'I Believe' and 'You'll Never Walk Alone.' The former was a big hit in 1953 by Frankie Laine and the latter was the tear-inducing epic from the Broadway musical *Carousel*. Arif did a beautiful arrangement of the Steve Dorff song 'Higher Ground,' which I think is one of Barbra's most heartfelt performances. Barbra told me she loved the traditional spiritual song 'Deep River,' which gave me the idea of pairing it with 'The Water Is Wide.' Arif had a wonderful team of musicians and programmers, which enabled him to make 'demos' of his arrangements for Barbra's review. Barbra would then add other elements that satisfied her ear. Whenever we're recording, she always tries to find what she calls 'the rubs'—two notes when played together create a beautifully dissonant sound, or rub. She likes how these rubs can momentarily disrupt the more obvious harmony chords."

The beautiful medley of "The Water Is Wide" and "Deep River" comprises a Scottish folk song ("Water," circa 1900) and an African American spiritual ("Deep," circa 1876). The original composers are unknown. Arif Mardin disclosed that "to save time at the session, [Barbra] asked me if I would do a demo of the arrangement." Streisand asked him for a 'rough draft' of what the orchestra would be playing. "First of all, I wrote the arrangement—the old-fashioned way!" Mardin said, emphasizing writing out the notes by hand. "Then I went to my son Joe's home studio and put together a mock-up of the arrangement. When I flew to LA to talk about the session, I played it. She loved it. 'Please change this one here . . . .' She's the artist, of course, if she says she wants it changed, you change it. It saved so much time and money! In the studio, of course, there were some more changes, but the other way around would have been truly a disaster. Because it was written for a fifty-piece orchestra." (Niles, 2021)

What Barbra had learned after thirty-something years of recording is that studio time is expensive with fifty session musicians commanding high salaries and overtime. Any last-minute alterations meant they all had to be paid to stay and work through key changes or an amended arrangement. Of course, before those changes could be recorded, they must be rehearsed. And let's not forget that Streisand herself—like any member of the orchestra—needed appropriate studio time to finesse her vocals. By providing a demo, Mardin cut those possible alterations and time-taking changes by half or more.

Ann Hampton Callaway, a gifted cabaret performer and songwriter, contributed "At the Same Time" to the album. She told Barbra News: "When I exchanged my first words with Barbra about some lyric rewrites for her, I was too cool for words, trying to remain as dignified as possible," Callaway said. "We had a very interesting conversation about what she was looking for in the rewriting of the bridge of my song. It was important to her that the words be 'simple but profound' and understandable to the listener upon first hearing. She was warm and expressive about the message she wanted to convey.

"[Barbra] has a certain clout and star wattage that is dazzling beyond almost anyone," Callaway continued. "The powerful impact she's had on me and anyone I know as a singer, as an interpreter of great American songs . . . she's a force of nature. When she does a song, she owns it." (Hall, 2005)

"Higher Ground," the album's title song, was written by Steve Dorff, George Green, and Kent Agee. Dorff wrote in his memoir that Green was contacted by Sony Music's Tommy Mottola to write a meaningful song for the label's new artist Mariah Carey. Green faxed Dorff his lyrics. "From the first line of the song, I was completely hooked," Dorff wrote, "and by the time I had read it all the way through, I was starting to hear what the tune would eventually be." (Dorff, 2017) Mottola turned down "Higher Ground" for Carey but suggested that the song would be perfect for Streisand. A few years later Jay Landers recognized how well the song would fit into her album of inspirational songs. "When I first heard this song, I was told the writers had conceived the lyrics in a religious context," Streisand wrote in the CD booklet. "I thought it was a love song . . . but then again, aren't all religions about love?"

"If I Could," by Ronald Miller, Kenny Hirsch, and Martha Sharron, has been covered by many artists, including Celine Dion, Linda Eder, Ray Charles, and Nancy Wilson. The song obviously struck a chord with Streisand, who dedicated it to her son, Jason, on *Higher Ground*. Streisand also recorded Miller's song "I've Never Been a Woman Before."

Walter Afanasieff, who became so prevalent in Barbra's later recording career, stepped forward for this album, producing four tracks. Previously, he'd produced the single release of "Ordinary Miracles" and "Sweet Forgiveness" (a song he cowrote, which ended up on *Release Me 2*).

Since Barbra was very close with Virginia Clinton Kelley, she asked her friends to write a song using the title of Kelley's autobiography, "Leading with My Heart." Barbra wanted the Bergmans and Marvin Hamlisch to create a song that would capture Virginia's spirit. A slight title change happened, with the song becoming "Leading With *Your* Heart." After hearing the song, Barbra made a few suggestions. She explained, "That line, about being caught by surprise, was added. The original lyric doesn't say that. The original line was something about a rose, very pretty alliteration, but it didn't relate to what I knew inside of me. You have to have that turning point [in your life] to take you from being afraid to a place where you can feel this love . . . and it's usually another person who does it." (Hilburn, 1997)

"Lessons to Be Learned" was a song by Marsha Malamute, Allan Rich, and Dorothy Sea Gazeley. Jay Landers recalled, "My good friend Allan Rich is a wonderful songwriter. When he played me his demo of 'Lessons to Be Learned,' I knew in one listen it was a good song for Barbra. Barbra is the eternal student, and I instinctively felt the philosophy of the lyric—there are no mistakes, just lessons to be learned—would appeal to her. I also loved the melody. As I recall, Allan played me the demo in 1992 or 1993 when Barbra was prepping and recording *Back To Broadway*. I promised Allan that I'd save it for her next album. So it wasn't until 1997 when she was recording *Higher Ground* that I finally had the opportunity to present it to her. As I'd hoped, she responded to it as immediately as I had five years before. Allan and his cowriters were very generous to allow me to hold onto the song for that long . . . but I think they'd all say it was worth the wait!"

Streisand had first attempted to record "Everything Must Change" by Bernard Ighner in the summer of 1974 for her album *Butterfly*, but she never completed it. The song must have stuck with her, though, since Streisand returned to it twenty-three years later for *Higher Ground* and has also sung it live in concert.

To market the album, Columbia sent out promotional CDs to radio stations of "Tell Him," "If I Could," and "Higher Ground." *Higher Ground* received two Grammy nominations, but no awards. "Tell Him" was nominated for Best Pop Collaboration with Vocals. Also, Jeremy Lubbock was nominated for his instrumental arrangement of "I Believe."

The Celine Dion Duet

Barbra Streisand and Celine Dion are superstars. In 1997, Dion was ascendent, and Barbra was still creatively engaged and beloved by fans. The song they sang together may not have been high art, but it was popular. And—admit it!—it's sing-alongable! "Tell Him" paired Streisand and the twenty-nine-year-old Dion on a dynamic ballad written for them by David Foster; his then wife, Linda Thompson; and Walter Afanasieff. The song was produced by Foster and Afanasieff.

After Dion sang Barbra's Oscar-nominated song "I Finally Found Someone" on the 1997 Academy Awards broadcast, Streisand sent her flowers with a congratulatory note that ended with "Next time let's do one together." Well, that's all Dion's ambitious manager-husband, René Angélil, had to hear! "He quickly contacted Marty Erlichman, Barbra's agent, and asked David Foster to write a song for us." (Dion, 2001)

Dion, meanwhile, told Foster that Streisand was her idol. "She's the most extraordinary singer in the world, and actress. I adore her. And I always wanted to sing with her one day." (Cliporama, 1997) So the two powerful singers came together to record the duet—on different coasts. "Barbra sang her part in Los Angeles," Dion wrote, "and a few days later in New York, I added my voice to hers. One evening, after the arrangers and technicians had mixed the song, we listened to it together, Barbra at the Record Plant in Los Angeles, and I at the Hit Factory in New York."After they listened, Streisand called Dion in the studio and they discussed the duet and traded compliments. Celine began to cry. "For Celine, you've always been a role model and an idol," Angélil told Streisand. "I know," Barbra replied. "I felt the same thing the first time I sang with Judy Garland." (Dion, 2001)

"Tell Him" was beamed to radio stations via satellite, then slated for stores November 4, 1997, a few weeks before the album dropped. In the US, however, the single (on CD, cassette, and vinyl) was canceled without any explanation. Over at *Billboard* magazine, Theda Sandiford-Waller discussed it in her column,

revealing that the single had already been manufactured before it was canceled! "I'd have to blame the reversal on the lukewarm reception 'Tell Him' has received at mainstream Top 40 radio." (Sandiford-Waller, 1997) The single did hit stores throughout Europe and in Australia, Canada, and other countries (#665305-2). US fans had to purchase it at stores like Tower Records that stocked imports. To qualify the song for the fortieth Grammy Awards, Sony Music did release a seven-inch vinyl single containing only "Tell Him" in late September/early October in the US (#36 78737). The two women appeared together in the same studio for the "Tell Him" music video and promotional video footage featuring their discussion. The video was directed by Scott Lochmus, by the way, who directed Barbra's *Village Vanguard* and *Back to Brooklyn* concert TV specials.

Jay Landers said, "It was a thrilling session, produced by David Foster and Walter Afanasieff. Both David and Walter had already produced great solo records for Celine and Barbra, so they were both on the same page in terms of knowing how to guide them in the studio. Columbia and Epic Records are sister labels—both owned by Sony. In that era, there was a lot of competitive friction and rivalry between Columbia (Barbra's label) and Epic (Celine's label). In a way that always struck me as counterproductive, the executives at each label tried to 'protect' their stars, or perhaps I should say 'overprotect' them. Meaning if Epic had a Celine album set for imminent release, they wouldn't fully support her having a hit with Barbra on Columbia. I don't think that interlabel hostility exists today with the same ferocity, but it was quite prevalent then."

Matt on *Higher Ground*

Somebody has to say it, so I will. Rosie O'Donnell was single-handedly responsible for *Higher Ground*'s outstanding sales and number one status. Three million album sales!

On her hit daily syndicated talk show, Rosie promoted the album for weeks. The ultimate climax to her tease was when Streisand herself was a guest on November 21, 1997, making Rosie's dreams come true. O'Donnell revealed: "Streisand's voice filled the house on Rhonda Lane [in Commack, Long Island, where O'Donnell grew up], and it filled me as well, and became a substance that was soothing, a sound I could return to when the going got bad, when my mother died." (O'Donnell, 2007)

O'Donnell had everyone crying at the get-go of the program when she introduced Streisand: "For every boy and girl out there watching, dreams do come true: please welcome Barbra Streisand."

Streisand, wearing an off-the-shoulder black sweater and slacks, walked through the curtain and hugged O'Donnell.

"She held my hand, she wiped my (tearstained) face and said, 'Are you OK?'" said Rosie to *USA Today*. "She was everything I ever dreamed she'd be and more, so warm and kind to me, all at once like a friend, a sister, a mother . . . I said to myself, I have to get a grip . . . I don't want it to be about me crying because she's here." (Williams, 1997)

As Streisand sat in the chair across from her, O'Donnell told her idol, "You were a constant source of light in an often dark childhood. You inspired me and gave me the courage to dream a life better than the one I knew. I am profoundly grateful to you in so many ways."

My eyes fill with tears remembering it (check it out on YouTube). Rosie really represented all of us in that moment, and her statement to Streisand was heartfelt.

The television algorithms agreed. Barbra's appearance earned Rosie's show its highest ratings ever since it began airing in 1996. It was the most watched talk show for that day, and the highest-rated episode of daytime programming across-the-board for the 1997-98 season at the time, according to Warner Bros., the show's distributor.

The data in that WB press release did not take into account all the album plugging O'Donnell had done before Barbra guested—Rosie played snippets of "Tell Him," discussed Barbra's upcoming appearance with guests, and shared her Barbra Streisand collectibles.

Love it or hate it, photographer Randee St Nicholas's sepia-toned image of Streisand on the cover is striking, and the lace that Streisand wraps around herself is very photogenic. St Nicholas has some outtakes from this session on her website, and several of them are even better than the final album cover choice.

As for songs, "On Holy Ground" is my go-to choice from this album lately. It's a straight-up gospel song, complete with an expressive choir that kicks the song into the next gear about halfway through and allows Barbra to ad-lib her vocals. Running over six minutes in length, "On Holy Ground" is a slow build with an enormous payoff. It works only if you start at the beginning and stay on the ride to the end. Barbra was fifty-five years old when she recorded this song (my age as I write this), and the last note is strong and passionate. It's sobering to compare my age with hers at certain of her career highlights. For instance, Barbra was fifty-seven years old when she performed the *Timeless* concert . . . what?!?

"Everything Must Change," with Jeremy Lubbock's beautiful arrangement, is certainly a Streisand classic.

The modulation on "If I Could" is worth mentioning too. What a pleasure to hear Barbra navigate that exciting key change halfway through the song by singing the word "way" three times in escalating tones!

It's a special thrill to hear Barbra sing "Avinu Malkeinu." The song asks God to have compassion on us and our children and to help bring an end to war and famine and cause all hate and oppression to vanish from the earth. It's a timeless and important recording . . . elemental and beautiful.

Four years after *Higher Ground* was released, after the attacks of September 11, Barbra asked William Ross to create a new, more dynamic arrangement of "You'll Never Walk Alone," which she sang on the Emmy Awards. That year, the awards aired much later than usual because the fall of the World Trade Towers had shocked the nation. As you may recall, many Americans were afraid to ride the subway or attend large gatherings because the threat of terrorism was made real. The host of the 2001 Emmys was Ellen DeGeneres, who managed to walk a perfect tightrope between comedy and compassion. After Streisand's performance, backed by a choir whose vocals were arranged by Bob Esty, she explained to *Extra's* Leeza Gibbons, "I came to give a message in song and be part of the patriotism that is overwhelming the country in a positive way."

STREISAND COLLABORATORS

JAY LANDERS

Jay Landers has been Streisand's A & R man since the Nineties. I asked Jay to explain for those who may not know what the heck an A & R person is.

He said, "I think A & R was a term born in the late 1940s, when recording artists were signed to a label, and the Artist & Repertoire person would literally tell them what songs they were going to sing. Over the years, the term morphed into a catchall description of a label executive trying to find the right material, and someone who is a talent scout. In the sixties and seventies, when more artists wrote their own songs—the scout part of the job became more important. Artists who didn't write their own songs were often underserved by the label."

As for his A & R work with Barbra, Jay said, "She generally likes to settle on a concept—Broadway songs, movie songs, inspirational songs, love songs, and duets, to name a few. Then I try to find the best combination of new and old material to fulfill her vision. When I listen to old records or new demos, my criteria is a combination of factors, none more important than the other. Do the words and music lend themselves to Barbra's natural phrasing style? Will she find the melody challenging and appealing? Do the words sound like the truth coming from her mouth? In many cases Barbra has compiled lists of her own songs that she's always loved but never got around to recording. Depending upon how she envisions the arrangement, I'll suggest the right producer, engineer, and arranger to help her realize the sounds she's hearing in her head. When I play a song to Barbra—old or new—I usually have an idea how I'd like to hear it arranged, so that's often the starting point. Bottom line, though, it's Barbra who either rejects or accepts, or is at least willing to try various ideas, but the end product is hers alone. By the end of this process, Barbra is like 'Lola' in *Damn Yankees—whatever she wants, she gets!*"

Jay Landers has held A & R positions at Columbia Records, EMI Records Group, and Walt Disney Records, and he is currently at Universal Music Group, but also works independently. He first became Barbra's A & R man for *Just for the Record.*

Since he has been most involved in her recording career since 1981, I asked him what a typical recording session with Barbra is like. "Before Barbra sets foot in the studio, she's already been so involved in building the arrangement that she's fully gotten the song under her skin. She's loath to over rehearse, but she does privately listen to and sing along to the demos in her car. She doesn't want to plot out every single note, because she's always surprising us by throwing in a surprising chord substitution or expanding on the written melody. Those moments are surprising to her too. Whatever her process is, by the time she sets foot in the studio, she's remarkably prepared. There's zero laziness in her approach. When she's recording with an orchestra, she's really in her element. She's not only inspired by the aliveness of the moment, she also knows how to feather or emphasize her vocal with an amazing combination of 'acting' and dynamic control. You know the expression that someone with highly attuned ears can hear a pin drop? Well Barbra has that to the extreme. If she hears one instrument play an unpleasing note, even if the conductor and sixty-plus piece orchestra misses it, she will start to investigate the problem until she finds the answer. Although everyone is keenly aware that we're working in a high-pressure environment, Barbra herself is usually the most calm, cool, and collected person in the room!" The team of Streisand and Landers has flourished for decades, with his scope of work expanding to include music supervisor for Barbra's live concert performances. And Jay couldn't be nicer—he usually pops out into the audience before a concert begins, saying hello to associates and fans alike.

Released: September 21, 1999
Executive producers: Barbra Streisand and Jay Landers
Art direction: Nancy Donald
Design: Gabrielle Raumberger and Clifford Singontiko
Front cover photography: Alberto Tolot
Mastered by: Vlado Meller at Sony Music Studios, Santa Monica
Mastering supervision: David Reitzas
Project coordinator: Shari Sutcliffe

Catalog Numbers:
CK 69601 (CD)
CT 69601 (cassette)
CK 63981 (limited quantity CD with bonus CD [#CSK 43719] of "Let's Start Right Now"—only at On Cue and Sam Goody stores.)
494934 8 (MiniDisc, Europe)

Tracks:

1. I've Dreamed Of You
2. Isn't It A Pity?
3. The Island
4. Love Like Ours
5. If You Ever Leave Me (with Vince Gill)
6. We Must Be Loving Right
7. If I Never Met You
8. It Must Be You
9. Just One Lifetime
10. If I Didn't Love You
11. Wait
12. The Music That Makes Me Dance

Bonus track: Let's Start Right Now

When Barbra was participating in an America Online chat in 1998, she revealed that she was working on a new album that would probably be called *Barbra . . . in Love*. Four months later, Barbra completed principal recording sessions for the new album, and by July 1999 mixing and mastering of the album were finished. Barbra titled it *A Love Like Ours*, after the fourth track, "Love Like Ours," composed back in 1986 by Dave Grusin, with lyrics by Alan and Marilyn Bergman.

Arif Mardin, back as Barbra's producer, said: "We worked very fast, contrary to what people keep asking me. Barbra is such a fabulous talent. We were at Sony Studios with a sixty-piece orchestra. She sings live, of course. She belongs to the tradition where, for example, if she feels emotional and wants to slow down a beat, the conductor will watch for her cues and slow down the orchestra. It's all organic." (Beck, Streisand's new album echoes her wedding, 1999)

On this album, Barbra was inspired to sing about love because she was in love . . . with James Brolin, whom she married in July 1998. Streisand arranged for her buddy Marvin Hamlisch to organize the music for the ceremony, which took place at her Malibu home. "I've never seen a more accommodating, brilliant musician. Only Marvin could do this on such short notice," Streisand exclaimed. (Streisand, A Wedding Planned with a Director's Eye, 1999)

Wedding guests were treated to uilleann pipe music during prewedding cocktails; strolling violinists as they entered her home to witness the vows; and Barbra herself singing to her groom in the dinner tent. Two of the songs on the album, in fact, were sung at her wedding. First, there's the instrumental song by the New Age group Secret Garden called "Heartstrings," a favorite melody of the couple. Ann Hampton Callaway was asked to write lyrics, and before she knew it, Barbra was singing "I've Dreamed of You" to Jim Brolin, accompanied by the original demo. "I've Dreamed of You" was the album's first single too (#38K 79211). Released July 1999, it peaked at number twenty-four on the *Billboard* 100 chart.

Melissa Manchester rewrote "Just One Lifetime" for Barbra. She told Todd Sussman in *Cabaret Scenes*: "It turned out that Barbra really loved the choruses but couldn't quite follow the verses. So I went back to my collaborator, Tom Snow, and asked him if he would consider revisiting it, to deconstruct and reconstruct the song, and he agreed. We really thought about where Barbra was in her life and how spiritual she had become, and that she had finally met her destiny in James [Brolin] ... Arif Mardin did such a masterful job of orchestration. It was really a high point in my career, because I grew up loving her. She was a maverick and singularly brilliant. So it was really touching."

Even the album cover reflected Barbra's romance. *A Love Like Ours* is the only Streisand album to feature another person on the cover—and he just happens to be her husband. Of course, I'm not counting Barry Gibb or Kris Kristofferson in that statement. The photo of the couple standing on the beach at sunset, captured by Alberto Tolot, is very romantic. It is also an homage to the cover of *People* in which Barbra is pictured standing alone on the beach. "As you can see, I'm no longer alone on the cover," Streisand wrote in her liner notes. "I stand side by side with my husband, embracing the sunset. I guess Fanny was right—'People who need people are the luckiest people in the world.'"

The only radio-ready song on the album was the duet with country artist Vince Gill on "If You Ever Leave Me," which ended up being the second single from the album (#CSK-42713), although it really didn't chart well, coming in around sixty-fourth on *Billboard*'s Hot Country Singles chart.

Richard Marx wrote the song and coproduced it with David Foster in Los Angeles. Vince Gill recorded his vocals first, then finally met Streisand in person at another session. Gill recalled that when Streisand heard his vocal playback, she said, "You're pretty damn good," but asked why he pronounced the word "my" as "muh." Gill, born in Oklahoma, replied, "Well, that's the way muh mama and muh daddy taught me." (Orr, 1999)

Barbra and the six-foot, three-inch Gill filmed a music video of the song at Sony Picture Studios, which was directed by Jim Shea and beautifully lensed by cinematographer Andrzej Bartkowiak.

A Love Like Ours was not nominated for any awards at the forty-second Grammys. The winners that year included "Smooth" by Rob Thomas and Santana; "Believe" by Cher; and, in Streisand's usual category, *Bennett Sings Ellington* by . . . you guessed it—Tony Bennett.

Fans of eBay shopping should keep a lookout for the European discs, which contained the songs "Just Because" and "Let's Start Right Now." Both were recorded during the album sessions but did not make it onto the final disc. The Australia EP CD (#667914-2) includes both. So does the UK EP CD (#668124-2).

"Just Because" was written by Mervyn Warren and Jeremy Lubbock, and "Let's Start Right Now" by Cristovão Bastos, Abel Silva, and Roxanne Seeman. "Let's Start Right Now" originated from a Brazilian song ("Raios De Luz"), and its English lyric is by Seeman.

Matt on *Like Ours*

This is an album that has grown on me since it was first released. Back in the day, I gravitated toward *Higher Ground*, not *A Love Like Ours*. Revisiting it, however, I prefer this one. It's very sensual, with lots of passion. Even the CD booklet's color palette is pleasing to the eyes.

Pleasing to the ears, though, is just about every single track on the album. The title track sounds like something Barbra would sing in an intimate nightclub. Even "We Must Be Loving Right," which was a country hit for George Strait, fits in exceptionally well here, almost like a jazz song despite its steel guitars.

There are three "If" songs on this album! My favorite is Dean Pitchford and Tom Snow's "If I Never Met You." It's such a touching song, especially the sentiment in the lyrics, which, Pitchford confessed, were written with his husband, Michael, in mind.

"If You Ever Leave Me" is fun! I enjoy singing along with this one in the car, and despite the criticism that the lyrics are a little silly, I think the whole thing is a joy.

"If I Didn't Love You," the third "If" song on A *Love Like Ours*, is by Bruce Roberts and Junior Miles. Junior Miles is the songwriting pseudonym for Edgar Bronfman, Jr., by the way. Bronfman, in addition to his songwriting skills, is part of the family whose fortune came from the Seagram Company.

To close out the album, Streisand chose to revisit "The Music That Makes Me Dance," her "eleven o'clock number" from the Broadway version of *Funny Girl*. William Ross provides his usual strong work on the arrangement for the new version, and Kenny G serenades Streisand with his sexy saxophone. I like it when Barbra rerecords classic songs, and this one is very successful with its jazz club vibe. Streisand's final notes, a declaration of love that's accompanied by the orchestra referencing the tune of "People," ends the album on a strong yet nostalgic note.

DECADE 90 ENCORE

In the United States, the radio industry went through major changes in the 1990s and especially the 2000s. In the nineties, there was big money in radio because stations were drawing huge ratings, which also meant reaping millions in ad revenue.

Let's face it: Barbra's first big album of the nineties, *Back to Broadway*, had no radio hits. In fact, Columbia released singles to promote the album only in the UK, where showtunes still had a fighting chance on the public airways.

With pop-oriented albums *Higher Ground* and *A Love Like Ours*, Barbra managed to get radio airplay with "Tell Him" and "If You Ever Leave Me." Of course, "I Finally Found Someone" was a huge hit for her. Jay Landers explained, "Barbra has never considered herself a singles artist. With rare exception, she's not trying to grasp that particular commercial brass ring. A perfect illustration of this is when she released *The Broadway Album* in 1985. The biggest hits that year were pop confections by Madonna and Wham! In that sense, Barbra has always been in an exclusive lane of her own design."

After the 1996 Telecommunications Act, the radio industry was upended, because the new law allowed a single company to own any number of stations in a single market. By 1999, three companies monopolized radio: Clear Channel, Cumulus Broadcasting, and Citadel Broadcasting.

"Consolidation killed local radio, it dumbed down content, stripped news departments, and eliminated the diversity that once made it such an enjoyable medium," said Stephen Soboroff, owner of an independent radio station. "Big Radio has made it worse." (Ryan L. L., 2004)

Radio as I knew it growing up was dead by the 2000s. Many of the stations that were bought up in the nineties found themselves in debt ten years later. "Cost-cutting compromised the quality of programming, and a tendency to put more advertising on the air, alienating listeners with what's known as advertising 'clutter.'" (Sutel, 2005)

All this talk about radio! It's important because I believe the change in radio altered the course of Streisand's recordings when the 2000s came around. She was no longer chasing radio hits—not that that was ever extremely important to her. The truth is that after the radio business restructured, Barbra's music was being played only on nostalgia channels like Hits of the 70s.

Also, Streisand was mostly focused on directing movies in the 1990s. It took her years to develop, film, and edit *The Prince of Tides* and *The Mirror Has Two Faces*. Her musical output, therefore, dwindled; she released just three studio albums over the course of the decade. Granted, they were all enormous hits, selling millions of units.

Meanwhile, Columbia concentrated on releasing her back catalog. "After we released *Just for the Record*, I was approached by Columbia Records to prepare Barbra's first three albums for CD release," John Arrias recalled. "It went so well that they just kept sending me more recordings that had never been released on CD. The condition of some of the tapes was so bad that it soon became an archival project. I am proud to say that Barbra's entire catalog is now digitally preserved and in the vaults." (Howe, Streisand Remastered, 2012)

Columbia began rolling out eleven remastered CDs in 1993. Between 1994 and 1998, the label issued twenty-four other remastered CDs, adding up to thirty-five Streisand albums in the compact disc format. The packaging had a white sticker affixed to the jewel box that read: "Digitally Restored From The Original Master Tapes/Digitally Remastered."

Also of note were the two Streisand film soundtracks released on CD for the first time during the nineties: *Hello, Dolly!* from Philips in 1994 and *Funny Lady*, which was remastered and released by Arista in 1998.

THE 2000S

Released: September 19, 2000
Produced by: Barbra Streisand
Executive producer: Jay Landers
Mixed by: David Reitzas
Front cover photography: Firooz Zahedi
Liner notes: Jay Landers
Recorded by: David Reitzas
Mastered by: Stephen Marcussen
Digitally edited by: Stewart Whitmore for Marcussen Mastering, Hollywood
Coordinator: Shari Sutcliffe
Album package art direction and design: Gabrielle Raumberger
Album package design: Jennifer Miller, Matthew Neth

Catalog Numbers:
C2K 63778 (2-CDs)
497435 8 (MiniDisc, Europe)
C2K 61635 (Barnes & Noble version with bonus disc)

Disc 1/Act 1:

1. Opening/You'll Never Know (Lauren Frost, Alec Ledd, and Randee Heller)
2. Something's Coming (with Lauren Frost)
3. The Way We Were
4. Shirley MacLaine Y1K
5. Cry Me A River
6. Lover, Come Back To Me
7. A Sleepin' Bee
8. Miss Marmelstein
9. I'm The Greatest Star/Second Hand Rose/ Don't Rain On My Parade
10. Something Wonderful/Being Alive
11. As Time Goes By/Speak Low
12. Alfie
13. Evergreen
14. Dialogue (Father, Part #1)
15. Papa, Can You Hear Me?/You'll Never Know (with Lauren Frost)
16. A Piece of Sky (with Lauren Frost)

Disc 2/Act 2:

1. Entr'acte
2. Putting It Together
3. On A Clear Day (You Can See Forever)
4. Send In The Clowns
5. Duets (with Judy Garland, Barry Gibb, Bryan Adams, Celine Dion, and Neil Diamond)
6. Sing (with Jason Gould)/I've Got A Crush On You (with Frank Sinatra)
7. Technology (Dialogue)
8. The Clicker Blues
9. Simple Pleasures
10. The Main Event/Fight
11. Dialogue (Father, Part #2)
12. I've Dreamed Of You
13. At The Same Time
14. Auld Lang Syne
15. Dialogue (Barbra and Brother Time)
16. People
17. New Year's Eve/Auld Lang Syne
18. Everytime You Hear Auld Lang Syne
19. Happy Days Are Here Again
20. Don't Like Goodbyes
21. I Believe/Somewhere (with Lauren Frost)

On April 28, 1999, Marty Erlichman and the MGM Grand Hotel put out a press release announcing Barbra's Millennium Concert, to be performed on December 31 at the 13,000-seat MGM Grand Garden in Las Vegas. Marvin Hamlisch would return to conduct, just as he had when Barbra performed at the MGM Grand on New Year's Eve 1993 and New Year's Day 1994. The concerts, titled *Timeless*, were a big success and were recorded by Columbia Records on December 31, 1999, and January 1, 2000. Streisand's go-to studio technician, David Reitzas, recorded the shows—it was a mind-blowing technical task with over one hundred inputs from the orchestra, from which he produced a digital multitrack. Columbia released a double CD of *Timeless* on September 19, 2000, running advertisements on US cable TV channels for the album that included mail order info.

A *Timeless* TV special of the New Year's Eve and New Year's Day performances was also released as a DVD, but not until 2001—nearly one year after the concerts were filmed. At the time, fans were perplexed by the video's delay. Erlichman explained to the *Chicago Tribune* that he "couldn't give anybody a release date for [the TV special]. Barbra didn't make up her mind to do additional concerts until February; then she was going to give her final shows in Australia. She then changed her mind and decided to do a couple more for her fans in the United States." (Bobbin, 2001)

The television special captured Barbra's New Year's Eve and New Year's Day performances at the MGM Grand Hotel. "Barbra wasn't sure at that time if she was ever going to do any more concerts beyond those, so we just wanted something in the memory bank," Marty Erlichman said.

That being said, it is an interesting exercise to compare the Columbia Records CDs with the Columbia Music Video DVD. There are noticeable differences, even though these recordings were supposedly made at the same time. We can assume the final audio mix was made up of the two live shows, dress rehearsals, and TV retakes. This should not be surprising or scandalous, because everyone knows that recording artists create whole tracks from compilations of their best vocal takes. For me, hearing Barbra's alternate version of anything is always a joy. So discerning listeners who care to compare the *Timeless* concert's two mediums will hear some differences. The audio editors probably made certain editorial choices for the CDs because those are aural experiences, not supported by camera angles or visual information. For instance, some of the song introductions are faster takes that involve less kibitzing from Streisand on stage. On "Lover, Come Back to Me," Barbra sings different opening notes and even says "Hello" to someone she spots in the audience. And after singing "I remember every little thing you used to do," she follows with "Oh my oh my" on the CD, whereas on the TV special she sings an elongated "Oh-oh-oh-oh."

"Sleepin' Bee" and "Miss Marmelstein" have a few different lines and notes. The CD "Marmelstein" even uses different office voices from those on the DVD (sometimes a male voice, whereas the video uses a female one). Another weird choice is on "Second Hand Rose." On the video, in the wide shot, while she sings "even our piano in the parlor," Barbra drops her microphone for a second to deal with her boa. On the CD, "piano" is lost in that second; on the DVD, "piano" is dubbed in so no sound is lost. On "Don't Rain on My Parade," the section with "Hey, Mister Ziegfeld, here I am" also differs between versions, as does "your turn at bat, sir"—on the video, Streisand loses the tempo a bit, which doesn't happen on the CD.

Barbra's "Main Event/Fight" buddy Bob Esty was hired to arrange the choir for this concert, which was a new sound for some of these Streisand classics. Esty performed the same function for Barbra again, arranging the choir vocals on "You'll Never Walk

Alone" (2001 Emmy Awards) and "Ave Maria" on *Christmas Memories*. For *Timeless*, you can hear the choir backing Streisand on "Clear Day," "At the Same Time," "People," and "Somewhere." The truth is that the *Timeless* concert production used different choirs at different venues. For instance, the Loyola Marymount University Choir (my college alma mater!) sang at Barbra's Los Angeles concerts. In New York, the University of Pennsylvania Choir and Manhattan Central Baptist Church Choir are credited. On the *Timeless* CD, however, the credit goes to Bob Esty and the Sydney Philharmonia Choir and Sydney Children's Choir.

On the CD version of "As Time Goes By," Streisand sings "I still say I love you" in a baby voice. And her spoken introductions to "Alfie," "Evergreen," and the first part of "Dialogue (Father, Part #1)" are from different performances altogether on the CD from those on the CMV video. "I've Got A Crush on You" (duet with Frank Sinatra) has some different notes between the two versions. "Simple Pleasures," a track on the CD, doesn't even appear on the video—it was cut from the video release. "The Main Event" sounds mostly the same, although some of Barbra's asides were edited from the CD ("It's a rock concert!" when she spots the flashlights in the audience has been excised). *Timeless—Live in Concert* was nominated for a Best Traditional Pop Vocal Album Grammy in 2001 but lost to Joni Mitchell's *Both Sides Now*, even though Tony Bennett was nominated. What the heck, Grammys? No Tony Bennett win this year??

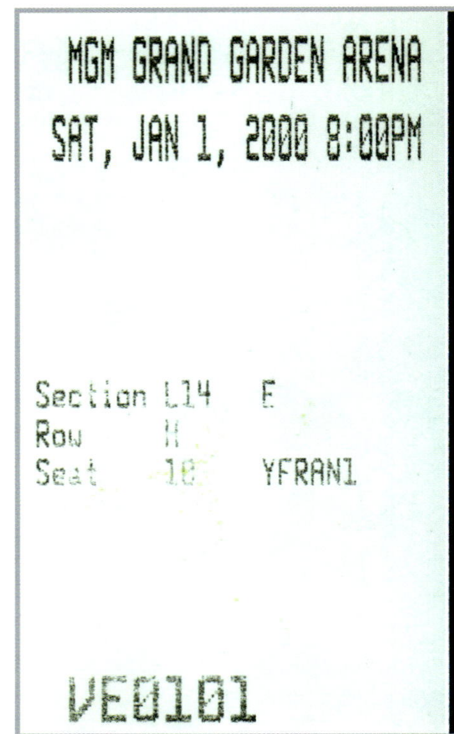

Matt on *Timeless*

To my ears, Streisand's live singing voice during the *Timeless* period is so clear and direct. She has a steely timbre on *Timeless*. She sings her signature songs in a straightforward manner with little improvisation or riffing, still effortlessly hitting those last belting notes on songs like "Somewhere" and "On a Clear Day."

Perhaps the best parts of Barbra's *Timeless* song selection are the early 1960s songs that she revisited. This was her first live recording (pre-*Bon Soir,* released in 2022) of "A Sleepin' Bee," for instance, and isn't it beautifully sung? "Cry Me a River" sounds like her early performances of the song, but in *Timeless* it has that soulful piano and lapses into a sexy film noir arrangement at the end.

I've already mentioned that I prefer this live version of "Alfie" to Barbra's 1969 studio cut.

Finally, the track "Simple Pleasures" is delightful. The Marvin Hamlisch melody is sweet, and the Bergmans' lyrics might start to approach saccharine territory, but isn't the idea they're conveying an important one? I'm very glad the reader has decided to "curl up with a book in a cozy corner/happy getting lost in its pages."

STREISAND COLLABORATORS

LAUREN FROST

These days the little girl who played "mini-Barbra" in the *Timeless* concerts is a grown-up actor, stylist, and vintage clothes curator in Los Angeles.

Back in 1999, when Team Streisand was casting a girl to play young Barbra for her Millennium concerts, Lauren was in the dark about who and what she was auditioning for. "It was a top-secret project," she told me in 2024. She sang the classic "Someone to Watch Over Me" as her audition song. "The audition process was such that I had to audition several times, but I was ready to start high school so I had to go back to Illinois and in those days, you know for the callbacks, we were getting bits and pieces of information … at one point they asked me to learn 'You'll Never Know' – thankfully my dad is a musician so he had a keyboard and we plucked it out and I learned it. I remember specifically they sent us a piece of sheet music and they had whited out Streisand's name. My dad was holding it up to light, trying to figure out 'Is it her?'"

Ultimately, Lauren was flown to L.A. to sing for Barbra and Marvin Hamlisch at Grandma's House on Barbra's property and she was cast. Lauren found herself taking the stage first on opening night as teen Barbra. When "Something's Coming" started, the audience at the MGM Grand roared with approval. She left the stage, accompanied by two security guards, recalling that the audience "went crazy and I was riding the wave of that rush."

Lauren said they rehearsed the magic trick for Barbra's entrance a lot. "He had that big cloak," she recalled of Savion Glover, who played Brother Time, "and it was filled with mirrors. The trick involved hydraulics. I had a little elevator that I came out of."

Lauren's mom took a leave of absence from her work so that she could accompany her and her dad to the Australian leg of the *Timeless* concerts. "We played football stadiums there. It was raining at one of the shows and it was an outdoor venue. Barbra showed up on stage wearing all black. One of the grips had an Australian outback hat – they put it on her. I don't know how … They found a matching outfit for me."

What did Lauren learn working with Barbra? "Watching her in rehearsals and how she treats everyone around her was so beneficial to me. She's such a professional; she's very collaborative. She trusts her people; she's extremely loyal to who she works with. It was really apparent that she valued every person – their talents and the part that they played. I think I've taken that with me going forward."

Lauren, who afterward starred in the Disney Channel's teen hit *Even Stevens*, summed it up: "She's an icon. She didn't have to stop and ask people 'How's your day? How's your kids?' It's a great lesson in loyalty and humility."

Released: October 30, 2001
Executive producers: Barbra Streisand and Jay Landers
Mixed by David Reitzas at Grandma's House
Project coordinators: Marsha Burns and Shari Sutcliffe
Product manager: Peter Fletcher
Album project coordinator: Allan Stein
Art direction: Gabrielle Raumberger
Design: Chad M. Goodson
Photography (Ms. Streisand): Firooz Zahedi
Photography (still life): Ian Logan
Prop stylist: Lisa Crockatt
Assistants to Barbra Streisand: Renata Buser and Kim Skalecki

Catalog Numbers:
CK 85920 (CD)
CM 85920 (MiniDisc)
CK 86203 (Target version)
CSK 54832 (Target special bonus disc—"God Bless America")
19658892841 (2024 red vinyl Barnes & Noble)

Tracks:

1. I'll Be Home For Christmas
2. A Christmas Love Song
3. What Are You Doing New Year's Eve?
4. I Remember
5. Snowbound
6. It Must Have Been The Mistletoe
7. Christmas Lullaby
8. Christmas Mem'ries
9. Grown-Up Christmas List
10. Ave Maria
11. Closer
12. One God

In 2001, Target stores sold an exclusive version of *Christmas Memories* that contained an extra CD with the song, "God Bless America," taken from Barbra's live performance at Voices for Change in 1992. The CD is no longer available for sale. In 2025, Columbia made "God Bless America" a digital single, available on streamers like Spotify and Apple Music.

Christmas Memories was Barbra Streisand's first full-length studio album since 1999's platinum-selling *A Love Like Ours* and her first new recording since *Timeless—Live in Concert*. It was also Streisand's second collection of holiday songs and first since *A Christmas Album* in 1967.

Christmas Memories was recorded between July 19, 2001 and September 7, 2001, and mixed—except for "It Must Have Been the Mistletoe" and "Grown-Up Christmas List"—by David Reitzas at Grandma's House in Malibu. Most of *Christmas Memories* was recorded live, in the studio, with a ninety-piece orchestra.

Christmas Memories had the bad fortune to hit stores one month after the September 11 terrorist attacks. Before that happened, though, the tone of the album was up for discussion. Jay Landers said, "I really wanted Barbra to record a new Christmas album. I just thought it was time. However, I came to learn that she'd already sung most of the Christmas songs that appealed to her in her classic 1967 release. So the A & R-ing of *Christmas Memories* was a two-fold task—finding songs that Barbra could connect with and not making it so esoteric that the general audience, who basically listens to Christmas music playing in the background at shopping malls, could still relate to. I gave Barbra a lovely compilation CD called *Christmas Belles*. The first two songs she decided upon were 'Snowbound' as recorded by Sarah Vaughn and the standard 'What Are You Doing New Year's Eve?' as recorded by Lena Horne, both from that compilation CD."

Streisand echoed Landers's sentiment. "I'm so glad I didn't give in and sing 'Let It Snow,' 'Winter Wonderland,' and all those other up-tempo ditties," she said. "I was almost talked into it, but I'm glad I didn't. I don't know what Christmas is going to be like this year, but I think this album will fit with what a lot of people are thinking." (Gundersen, Streisand's Christmas Offering, 2001)

It's heartbreaking to know that Dean Pitchford's song on the album, "Closer," which is dedicated to Streisand's friend Stephan Weiss, actually became "my sister's epitaph," Pitchford explained. She died in the World Trade Center attacks. "For the first time in my life, no words come to me. The last words I wrote were for *Closer*," he said (Gundersen, Streisand's Christmas Offering, 2001)

Television advertisements for the album ran on various national networks and local stations, and print ads appeared in major magazines like *People*, *Vanity Fair*, and *InStyle*. The Home Shopping Network sold the Barbra Streisand Christmas Gift Set in limited quantities during the 2001 holiday season, which included both Streisand Christmas CDs (1967 and 2001) and a red glass ornament with Barbra's photo. The album sold very well, peaking at number fifteen on the *Billboard* 200 and number three on *Billboard*'s Top Holiday Albums chart. *Christmas Memories* was nominated for Best Traditional Pop Vocal Album. Surprising no one, the winner was *Playin' with My Friends—Bennett Sings the Blues*. What is the Grammy voters' preoccupation with Mr. Bennett? He is a wonderful singer and an icon, but possibly the most overdecorated singer by the Grammy Awards.

Matt on *Christmas*

What I like about *Christmas Memories*, which, I'm very aware, is the reason some people *don't* like it, is that it's the un-Christmas album. Streisand has handpicked holidayesque songs that wouldn't be everyone's first choices. Now, five of the twelve tracks do have the word "Christmas" in their title, so there's no mistaking their appropriateness. But then there's "What Are You Doing on New Year's Eve?" and "Snowbound," both of which evoke the holiday season. "One God," "Closer," and "I Remember" are tangentially related to the holiday, but still fit beautifully with the album's quiet, thoughtful vibe.

"Christmas Lullaby" by Ann Hampton Callaway became a new Christmas classic for me after I heard Streisand sing it. It's so gentle, especially the line "for someone lovely as snow falling."

"It Must Have Been the Mistletoe" is the most fun track on the collection—I do love to sing along with this one.

"I Remember" is so moody and sad. Stephen Sondheim wrote a brand new verse for

Streisand to sing. The song first appeared in a television musical titled *Evening Primrose*, which originally aired in 1966 and starred Anthony Perkins (*Psycho*) as a poet who escapes the world by hiding in a New York department store. Sondheim's new opening verse perfectly set up the rest of the song as happening at Christmas. "I Remember" is easily one of Streisand's best song-acting recordings; her subtle vocals are on point.

I find "Snowbound" to be very sexy and a smart fit for the album's Christmas theme. I also think it's a sign of things to come on *The Movie Album*. Based on the original Don Costa arrangement and updated by Eddie Karam, it is the most cinematic orchestration on the album and one of my favorites.

I must be careful where I listen to "Closer," because it always elicits tears from me. With its lyrics comparing loss to the ocean's tides, the minute hand on a clock, and an ember in a fire, who cannot be affected by this song? Isn't it true that most of us take a quiet moment on important occasions or holidays to honor a loved one who is no longer with us? "Every thought of you will bring us closer," Streisand sings quietly. It's a beautiful and moving sentiment.

Jay Landers confessed to me, "The only truly popular song on the album is 'I'll Be Home for Christmas.' The album was a million seller, so it was successful, but in hindsight, I wished I'd worked harder to find Barbra a few more popular standards to balance the playlist."

Columbia rewarded patient fans in 2024 with this albums's first and only release on vinyl. Let's hope this is just the beginning of Barbra's catalog getting vinyl releases from the nineties.

STREISAND COLLABORATORS

RICHARD JAY-ALEXANDER

"I listen to Barbra's recordings all the time," Richard told me. "There's always something to learn." His connection to Barbra goes way back. "I was at college listening to *Barbra Joan* and *What About Today?* while I was playing Carole King's *Tapestry*." Richard's career began on Broadway in the 1970s as an actor; he then transitioned to working with some of the world's greatest performers on stages across the world: Bette Midler, Bernadette Peters, Johnny Mathis, and Barbra Streisand. It was Lisa Sharkey at Harper Collins Publishing who dubbed him the Diva Whisperer in the midst of their very first meeting.

Of his concert work with Barbra, Richard says, "We have a true collaboration; we are codirectors. But you're worthless as a collaborator unless you know her catalog. I know every recording of every Barbra song, of every television special, and am an encyclopedia of her career, loaded with highlights and accomplishments. You have to understand the career to be of any creative use. I don't have to study … but LISTEN? Always!"

Richard explained that tackling Streisand favorites like "People" over the years in concert is challenging. "No, we don't have to sing it, but I don't want to be around when they throw tomatoes. So how do you do 'People'? How do you do 'The Way We Were'? There is ALWAYS a new and fresh way to approach her legendary tunes."

As far as his contributions to newer Streisand albums, Richard explains that "Jay Landers is instrumental in song delivery, especially from new writers." But Richard passed Desmond Child's song "Lady Liberty" to Jay for consideration by Barbra after hearing it. Another song Barbra took as a suggestion was "You're Gonna Hear from Me" from *Inside Daisy Clover* for *The Movie Album*, which was the first time Richard joined Jay Landers in writing the liner notes.

"In these later years," Richard says about albums like *Partners* and *Encore*, "all the phone calls, all the reaching out is Jay and Barbra at the forefront, then having Marty make the big calls so he can wheel and deal … and, of course, the record company is always at the ready. But Barbra is there for every moment of the planning and even calls fellow artists herself. I mean, who doesn't want to sing with Barbra Streisand?" Richard stressed that because he is a director, he advocates for songs he can stage. For instance, he still has a huge list of songs he would love to tackle with the star should she ever do concerts again and already has ideas for how to open the next show. "Of course, you fantasize all the time, thinking, *If we ever do this again, I would love to stage Barbra singing 'C'est Si Bon.'*"

Richard told me a great story about her 2007 concert at the Waldbuhne in Berlin. Barbra and Jim's wedding anniversary was the next day, which was a day off for them in their touring schedule. He said,"During the Q&A [segment], I stuffed a card in there that said, 'Give Bill [Ross] the mic,' and he spoke to Barbra and the audience, explaining that tomorrow would be their anniversary, and because we wouldn't be together, offered up the entire orchestra playing 'The Four Horseman of the Apocalypse'—this was a song from *The Movie Album* that Barbra loved, and although the recording had special lyrics by Marilyn and Alan Bergman, this was purely orchestral. She was clearly moved. Right after that, Jim & the Broadway Boys (Hugh Panaro, Michael Arden, Peter Lockyer, and Sean McDermott) came out with cake. She was caught totally off guard. We hijacked the show from her, and she was blindsided and loving every minute of it. The next song was 'You Don't Bring Me Flowers,' and she could barely get through it. Those are moments you never forget."

Released: October 14, 2003
SACD released: December 9, 2003
Executive producers: Barbra Streisand and Jay Landers
Recorded and mixed by: David Reitzas
Recorded at: Sony Pictures Studios (Culver City, California); Grandma's House (Malibu); The Hop (Studio City)
Album notes: Jay Landers and Richard Jay-Alexander
Album project coordinator: Allan Stein
Photography (front cover): Terry O'Neill
Additional photos: Annie Liebowitz
Art direction: Nancy Donald, Mary Maurer, Hooshik Bayliss
5.1 multichannel version and 2-channel stereo versions: mixed and mastered by David Reitzas
SACD authored by Woody Pornpitaksuk at Sony Music Studios, New York

Catalog Numbers:
CK 89018 (CD only—jewel case)
CK 90742 (CD/DVD—Digipak)
CH 90748 (SACD—jewel case)

Tracks:

1. Smile (*Modern Times*)
2. Moon River (*Breakfast At Tiffany's*)
3. I'm In The Mood For Love (*Every Night At Eight*)
4. Wild Is The Wind (*Wild Is The Wind*)
5. Emily (*The Americanization Of Emily*)
6. More In Love With You (*The Four Horsemen Of The Apocalypse*)
7. How Do You Keep The Music Playing? (*Best Friends*)
8. But Beautiful (*Road to Rio*)
9. Calling You (*Bagdad Cafe*)
10. The Second Time Around (*High Time*)
11. Goodbye For Now (*Reds*)
12. You're Gonna Hear From Me (*Inside Daisy Clover*)

Barbra Streisand's career was running at an unhurried pace in 2003 when *The Movie Album* was released. Columbia Records announced it as her sixtieth album, and Barbra had performed her "final concerts" in Los Angeles and New York three years before. She hadn't made a movie since *The Mirror Has Two Faces* in 1996. And her last studio album was *Christmas Memories* in 2001. Following that album, Barbra released two music collections—*Essential* and *Duets*—in 2002. She was still happily married to James Brolin, having tied the knot in 1998. "I'm enjoying having my own space," Barbra said. "I can say, 'No, I have a life, a husband. I need private time.'" (Gundersen, 2001)

For her newest album, Barbra returned to an idea she had as early as 1986—to sing songs from movies, which she had mentioned onstage during the *One Voice* concert. Streisand has recorded movie music since the beginning of her career. "Who's Afraid of the Big Bad Wolf" was from Disney's *The Three Little Pigs*, and "I've Got No Strings" was featured in *Pinocchio*. There's also "The Shadow of Your Smile," "Ding-Dong! The Witch Is Dead," "The Boy Next Door," and "Alfie"—all from movies.

Recording sessions for *The Movie Album* commenced in spring 2003 at Sony Pictures Studios in a scoring stage that hosted a seventy-five-piece orchestra. Streisand sang live with the orchestra, and the sessions continued into July, followed by additional recording and mixing primarily at Grandma's House (Barbra's home studio) in August.

Streisand had collected song ideas for this album for years. She mentioned in interviews that she had considered a medley of Shirley Temple songs. Mostly, though, her concept of an album of movie songs "came from my past, from my experience. A lot of them, as you see, from my youth," she explained. (Newman, 2003)

Streisand worked with a handful of masterful arrangers on the album: Johnny Mandel, Jeremy Lubbock, Jorge Calandrelli, and Robbie Buchanan. "Smile" and "Moon River," the first two tracks, are arguably the best known songs on the album. Barbra relates in her liner notes that she recorded "Smile" after her dear bijon frise dog, Sammy, passed away, giving emotional subtext to Charlie Chaplin's lyric. Did you know Sydney Chaplin, Barbra's costar in *Funny Girl* on Broadway was the son of Charlie? She had sung "Moon River" back in 1961 on Mike Wallace's talk show. Here she gives it a proper studio arrangement and vocal.

"Wild Is the Wind" is the standout track on the album, oozing angst and cinematic strings. Barbra reached back to her teendom for this song because she loved the 1957 George Cukor film starring Anthony Quinn, Anna Magnani and Anthony Franciosa, whom she had a crush on. In her liner notes, Streisand wrote: "I associate movie songs with a kind of orchestral lushness . . . and was delighted with arranger Jorge Calandrelli's wonderful chart for this one . . . emotional and romantic."

"More in Love with You" had to be converted into a song by Streisand and her team. It began as a movie theme by André Previn for Vincente Minnelli's 1962 dramatic film *The Four Horsemen of the Apocalypse*. Streisand loved the melody so much she chose to play it as she and James Brolin walked down the aisle on their wedding day. But for the album, Streisand was determined to make it a song. She didn't care about commercial considerations; she told Previn to think of it as an "art song" rather than a pop song. Because she also wanted it to convey the hopefulness of a married couple, Barbra engaged Marilyn and Alan Bergman to craft lyrics for the piece. Ultimately, when she recorded "More in Love with You," she spent a lot of studio time fine-tuning Jeremy Lubbock's orchestration, and she was left with only three takes on her vocal. All the work that went toward creating this song paid off, because the track is unforgettable. As the Bergmans wrote, "More in Love with You" is "wonderful, impossible and yet it's true."

Even though Stephen Sondheim is one of Streisand's favorite Broadway songwriters, he doesn't have a large résumé of screen songs. Streisand could have recorded "I Never Do Anything Twice," a bawdy song he wrote for the 1976 film *The Seven-Per-Cent Solution*. She also could have performed any of the tunes Sondheim contributed to 1990's *Dick Tracy* movie. Those songs, which were specifically crafted for Madonna's femme fatale character, were brassier than what Streisand usually gravitated toward.

Instead, she chose the melody Sondheim wrote for Warren Beatty's 1981 movie about the Russian Revolution, *Reds*. The song has an interesting backstory: Sondheim admits he based the tune on the former national anthem of the Soviet Union, "The Internationale." Beatty wanted costar Diane Keaton to release the song as a single, so Sondheim added words, but it was never released. Sondheim confessed the song was "an instrumental, not a vocal, and its tessitura (the preeminent areas of its range) was very wide; Diane couldn't handle it comfortably—nor could many

singers, without noticeably awkward shifts from head voice to chest voice." (Sondheim, 2011)

When Streisand recorded "Goodbye for Now" for *The Movie Album*, she wrote in her liner notes, "I love singing Stephen's songs, because they tell a story. They give the actor a chance to play a character. In this case, one that is in the middle of a conversation. Very original."

Patti Austin and James Ingram introduced the Michel Legrand/Bergmans song "How Do You Keep the Music Playing?" in the 1982 film *Best Friends*. Barbra recorded it in 1983 for her *Emotion* album but didn't use it. In 2003, Robbie Buchanan produced it with Barbra. "Sometimes she asks for a key change down, which is a cool thing too," Buchanan told me in 2003. "Like in 'How Do You Keep the Music Playing?'—on that I put a modulation down into the last verse. So when it modulates up through the end of the song, it's actually back up to the original key. So it sounds like it's going up." (Howe, 2003)

Barbra loved the melody of "Emily," but it was a man's song (unless she suddenly wanted to perform it as a same-sex love song!). Streisand asked Johnny Mandel for "a little verse to set it up so that it could be sung by a woman. And he looked at me funny, and said, 'Well, I don't think you can do that.' So I called Marilyn and Alan, and they happened to be on the Johnny Mercer estate board [the song's lyricist]. So I said, 'Well, you can only ask. They can say no, but will you write the melody for it if they say yes to the lyric?' And they did say yes to the lyric." Barbra asked the Bergmans for a line something like "Wouldn't it be wonderful if somebody could whisper in my ear 'Emily'?" "And they would write that line, better than I just said it, but that was the concept, and I'm able to sing 'Emily,' and probably a lot more women will be able to sing it," she said. (Newman, 2003)

Barbra visits other musical genres on *The Movie Album*, including a sexy bossa nova on "I'm in the Mood for Love," a torchy "But Beautiful," and a jazzy "The Second Time Around." Two songs ("Calling You" and "How Do You Keep the Music

Playing?") feature an electric keyboard sound but still rely on the orchestral instruments.

The final song, "You're Gonna Hear from Me," is a throwback to Barbra's sassy youth when she sang songs like "You Wanna Bet," "I Can See It," and "Don't Rain on My Parade"—which is quoted at the climax of the track. *Inside Daisy Clover*, the 1965 movie it was from, somehow never played on cable TV in my youth, and I'd never seen it. The material is a perfect match for Streisand and a great way to close the album.

The Movie Album debuted at number five on the *Billboard* charts and was Barbra's highest-ranking album since *A Love Like Ours*. It probably helped that she made a rare appearance on Oprah Winfrey's daytime talk show to promote the album and sing "Smile."

Columbia released the album as a special collector's edition deluxe Digipak (#CK 90742) that contained the standard CD and a bonus, limited-edition DVD featuring video performances of Barbra recording "I'm in the Mood for Love" and "Wild Is the Wind" and a seven-minute audio-only interview with Barbra speaking about the songs on the album.

The Movie Album was the first Barbra Streisand album released in the SACD (Super Audio CD) format (#CH 90748). Back in 2004, I had an SACD player and speaker system, and I played *The Movie Album* on it. The experience was lush and immersive. Sony Music included an informative insert with the SACD that said, "With multichannel sound, the listener is completely surrounded by the music of the recording." Unfortunately, the SACD technology never really caught on and has gone the way of quadraphonic and other newfangled audio formats.

Barbra received a Grammy nomination for Best Traditional Pop Vocal Album for *The Movie Album*. Guess who won that year? Tony freakin' Bennett . . . again! This is a trend that began in 1994 and continued into the 2010s, with Michael Bublé sometimes beating her instead.

Matt on *The Movie Album*

The Movie Album is one of her most sophisticated, beautifully orchestrated albums in Streisand's entire discography. At the time it was released, some fans complained that it was dull and lacked hit songs, like, for instance, a James Bond theme.

Relieved of the pressure of producing radio hits, Streisand at this time wasn't interested in commercialism. She wanted to sing songs that connected deeply with her artistic sensibilities. Those who were hoping for Disney anthems (see her Disney medley on *The Concert*) or power ballads (why would Streisand sing Celine Dion's "My Heart Will Go On"?) were sorely disappointed but missing the point. *The Movie Album* was carefully curated by Streisand, and if you listen to what she's giving us, it's a very personal album with gorgeous, cinematic arrangements.

Specifically, I'm a huge fan of "Wild Is the Wind"—from the evocative introduction arranged and conducted by Jorge Calandrelli to the strings and horns that support her, Streisand paints a vivid picture with her brooding vocals. "Like a leaf clings to a tree"—can't you just see that image in your mind when Barbra sings it?

"Calling You" is an interesting choice. As a fan of great cinema, I can recommend *Bagdad Cafe*, the West German movie it was written for, directed by Percy Adlon. It's quirky and sweet. "Composer Bob Telson was kind enough to write a new third verse for me," she wrote in her liner notes. "Robbie Buchanan's distant, hypnotic arrangement evokes the wide-open, lonely landscapes I was imagining as I was singing."

When I interviewed Robbie Buchanan in 2003, he told me his soundscape was inspired by a trip to Hawaii. The place his family was staying "had these louvered windows that can open to let air in. Kapalua Bay is very windy. So when they're closed, wind seeps through there and goes 'wooo.' I kept listening to it and I started hearing chords, and it sounded like weird voices going 'wooo' in chords, like a choir kind of thing—but moving around pitchwise." His daughter heard the same thing. "What it was . . . it was Good Friday, and there was a choir rehearsing for a service that night about a half a mile away in Kapalua Bay, and it was coming through with the wind just at that same level. I based that whole arrangement on that sound. It gave me the idea to do it that way."

Does anyone else feel cheated by "How Do You Keep the Music Playing?" I thought the Bergmans would offer an answer to those of us who were questioning. The song is one questioning phrase after another! I'm joking, of course. They do offer some wisdom in their lyrics: "If we can try with every day to make it better as it goes/With any luck then I suppose/ The music never ends."

Guilty Pleasures

Released: September 20, 2005
Produced by: Barry Gibb and John Merchant
Executive producers: Barbra Streisand and Jay Landers
Recorded and mixed by: John Merchant
Art direction: Mary Maurer, Nancy Donald
Photography: Alberto Tolot

Catalog Numbers:
CK 93559 (CD)
CN 94997 (DualDisc)

Tracks:

1. Come Tomorrow (with Barry Gibb)
2. Stranger In A Strange Land
3. Hideaway
4. It's Up To You
5. Night Of My Life
6. Above The Law (with Barry Gibb)
7. Without Your Love
8. All The Children
9. Golden Dawn
10. (Our Love) Don't Throw It All Away
11. Letting Go

Guilty Pleasures DualDisc DVD Side: All eleven songs in PCM Stereo; video interview; music videos: Above the Law (with Barry Gibb), Hideaway, Stranger In A Strange Land, and Letting Go.

Barbra Streisand and Barry Gibb had a huge hit with the *Guilty* album in 1980—it was certified five times platinum, with sales exceeding five million copies in the US and twelve million worldwide.

Streisand stated that "I've always looked back on the *Guilty* album as one of the easiest, most pleasant recording experiences I've ever had. Barry just made the process a delight. Maybe because he's an artist himself, he understands what it takes to be a producer for another singer. For the past two decades, most of my records like *The Broadway Album*, *The Movie Album* or *A Love Like Ours* were made with big orchestras and self-produced, so I thought it would be fun to work on a pop album again, with someone else at the helm. Six months ago, Barry and I spoke about getting together for this project . . . and it happened to coincide with the anniversary . . . so the timing was perfect. It's given our reunion an extra special meaning, but it wasn't something I'd really planned." (Streisand, Guilty Blog, 2005)

Although Robin Gibb had a hand in some of the first few songs that were written, ultimately it was Barry Gibb and his sons Ashley and Stephen who wrote most of the songs around October 2004.

Streisand elaborated: "[Barry] wrote a few songs and sent them to me to see if they'd be something I'd like to record. They were really strong, so I just encouraged him to write more! I told him how much I loved the sound of George Michael's song 'Jesus to a Child' and asked him if he could try to write something in a bossa nova style. The next week he surprised me with 'Golden Dawn', which is one of my favorites on the album." (Streisand, What was Barry's brief for this project? 2005)

Producer John Merchant and musicians produced demos of ten songs, which Streisand loved, so she asked Merchant and Gibb to move forward on the album.

Jay Landers added, "Barry was dealing with some deeply personal issues with his brother Robin, so he was being emotionally pulled in two directions. When it came time to mix the album, I joined him in Miami, mostly just to make sure he was as focused as possible on the work at hand. The obvious difference between *Guilty* and *Guilty Pleasures* is that Barry wasn't surrounded by the same magical team he'd had for so many years—his brothers of course, but also his former coproducers Albhy Galuten and Karl Richardson."

Recording began in May 2005 with Gibb laying tracks in Miami, then traveling to LA at the end of the month to record Streisand's vocals. Streisand, who really wanted to record her vocals at her home, allowed Merchant and Gibb to set up shop at Grandma's House—the guest cottage on Streisand's Malibu property.

"It's really charming," Merchant offered. "The house was built in the 1950s and sits on the cliffs of Malibu. It has beautiful open-beam ceilings, a view of the Pacific, but we had to essentially create a studio." (For Barbra Streisand's Hit Album, Solid State Logic AWS 900 Makes Mixing a Pleasure, 2007)

Merchant rented a Neumann M49 tube mic—the type of microphone that Streisand had recorded with on many past albums. He recorded overdubs and did the mixing with the Solid State Logic AWS 900 Analogue Workstation System.

The original *Guilty* album was well-known for its cover with Barry Gibb and Streisand wearing white outfits against a white background. For the sequel, Streisand, Gibb, and photographer Alberto Tolot went for a black-on-black look. Tolot (who photographed the cover of *A Love Like Ours*) shot Gibb and Streisand on June 9, 2005, at the Barbra Streisand Scoring Stage. They also shot the music videos and interviews that day using the state-of-the-art 24p high-definition video format.

Columbia Records launched an internet publicity campaign for *Guilty Pleasures*. Amazon hosted the world premiere of the video for "Stranger In A Strange Land," Barbra's first single from the album.

"Stranger" was a kinder and gentler political song written by Gibb about soldiers away at war. The song was universal, but also touched on the Iraq war. "I loved the first stanza," Streisand said, "because to me this war is kind of senseless, and I don't know why we're there. It's kind of painful, and I had always imagined just seeing footage of the troops, it's like history repeating itself—here we go again. That was the meaning to me." (AP, Streisand sings anti-war tune, 2005)

Columbia released a CD single of the song and sent it to radio stations; the single was offered as a free bonus disc to people who bought *Guilty Pleasures* at the now-defunct online Sony Music Store. The single was also available at superstores like Target and Walmart.

Back at Amazon, fans who preordered *Guilty Pleasures* online were granted immediate access to an audio stream of three tracks: "Hideaway," "Night of My Life," and "Without Your Love."

On August 23, 2005, Barbra's official site debuted the video for "Letting Go." This beautiful song was written back in 1984, and Barry Gibb has stated he wrote it for Barbra even though it was included on the 1988 soundtrack album of a movie called *Hawks*. It was listed on that album as a "bonus track not featured in the film."

Guilty Pleasures arrived in stores on September 20, 2005. It debuted at number five on the *Billboard* 200 album chart, selling 101,000 units. The album was retitled *Guilty Too* in the UK due to a previous copyright on the *Guilty Pleasures* title.

Streisand did a good amount of press for the album, appearing on *Good Morning America*, ABC *Primetime with Diane Sawyer*, and the UK's *GMTV*. She also sat for a bizarre interview on *The Ellen DeGeneres Show*. A sampling of Ellen's questions:

Ellen: Do you surf?
Barbra: I'm Jewish and I'm from Brooklyn.
Ellen: Does [Jim Brolin] wear briefs or boxers?
Barbra: It's too personal.
Ellen: I guessed boxers.
Barbra: And how about there's another alternative.

A twelve-inch dance single of "Night of My Life" peaked at number two on the *Billboard* Dance chart in October. Columbia Records had commissioned the king of dance club remixes, Junior Vasquez, to work his magic on the Gibb tune. The twelve-inch vinyl single hit stores September 27.

Matt on *Pleasures*

Guilty Pleasures is one of my guilty pleasures! The album was released during an interesting time for American music, when the popular artists of the day included Will Smith, Shakira, Black Eyed Peas, and Kanye West. It wasn't 1980 any longer, and the idea of Streisand being played on popular radio had passed—commercial radio stations had been bought up by media conglomerates, and satellite radio was ascending. Barbra's best chance in that arena was having the original *Guilty* songs played on an oldies station.

Was *Guilty Pleasures* a pop album? The style of Barry Gibb's songs on *Guilty Pleasures* is hard to categorize. Barbra said, "I guess you could say that [the album is] pop or at least 'pop informed.'" (Streisand, Guilty Blog, 2005) Although Barry Gibb and his brothers—collectively called the Bee Gees—are best known for their disco tracks, the songs on *Guilty Pleasures* are less disco than the songs on *Guilty* were. Barry Gibb explained that "Brazilian music and my idols, Burt Bacharach and Hal David," influenced his songwriting for Barbra on this album. (Gibb Chat Transcripts, 2005)

Gibb's songs are slick concoctions—amiable to the ears with impressionistic lyrics, backed by excellent musicians and studio production values. Gibb manages to keep Barbra's oversized voice tamed too. Her singing on *Guilty Pleasures* is measured and warm, with her belt heard only on "Night of My Life."

"All the Children" was originally written as "Children of Israel," but the finished song does not take political sides. It's exciting to hear Barbra sing in its Middle Eastern musical setting.

"Above the Law," a duet with Gibb, never fails to please me. It's buoyant, and she even shares a songwriting credit for the lyrics.

"Golden Dawn" and "Hideaway" are both great tunes for Barbra, sensual and evocative. I often place them on Streisand playlists.

I knew Andy Gibb's original recording of "(Our Love) Don't Throw It All Away"—from listening to FM radio in my youth. It's a catchy song that captures a bit of the *Guilty* magic, with Barbra's voice dancing to Barry's sweet music.

I am delighted when Barbra and Barry play in the musical sandbox together, and that is why *Guilty Pleasures* is such a *pleasure* to listen to.

Live In Concert 2006

Released: May 8, 2007
Produced by: Barbra Streisand and Jay Landers
Arranged and conducted by: William Ross
Recorded and mixed by: David Reitzas
Art direction and design: Mary Maurer @2310 Design
Photography: Kevin Mazur
Mixed at: Larrabee Sound Studios, North Hollywood; Westlake Recording Studios, Los Angeles; and Grandma's House, Malibu
Mastered by: Doug Sax at the Mastering Lab, Ojai, California.
Recording production manager: Janet Weber
Very special thanks to: Michael Cohl

Catalog Numbers:
88697 01922 2
88697 08449 2-BG (Target)
88697 09440 2-BC (Barnes & Noble)

Disc 1/Act 1:

1. *Funny Girl* Broadway Overture
2. Starting Here, Starting Now
3. Opening Remarks
4. Down With Love
5. The Way We Were
6. Songwriting (Dialogue)
7. Ma Première Chanson
8. Evergreen (with Il Divo)
9. Come Rain Or Come Shine
10. Funny Girl (Dialogue)
11. Funny Girl
12. The Music That Makes Me Dance
13. My Man
14. People (Dialogue)
15. People

Disc 2/Act 2:

1. Entr'acte
2. The Music Of The Night (with Il Divo)
3. Jason's Theme
4. Carefully Taught/Children Will Listen
5. Unusual Way
6. What Are You Doing The Rest Of Your Life?
7. Happy Days Are Here Again
8. (Have I Stayed) Too Long At The Fair
9. William Saroyan (Dialogue)
10. The Time Of Your Life
11. A Cockeyed Optimist
12. Somewhere (Dialogue)
13. Somewhere (with Il Divo)
14. My Shining Hour
15. Don't Rain On My Parade (reprise)
16. Smile

Bonus tracks:
Stoney End *
Don't Rain On My Parade *
When The Sun Comes Out †
* Target stores only
† Barnes & Noble stores only

In the liner notes for the album, Jay Landers wrote about this concert tour: "Creatively, [Barbra] saw the shows as an opportunity to revisit some of her rarely performed, celebrated back catalog and a chance to discover new ways of interpreting her well-known standards. She wanted to challenge herself by selecting material she'd never performed live before, like 'Unusual Way' from the Broadway musical *Nine* (with a sublime arrangement by Peter Matz) or the vocally demanding 'Starting Here, Starting Now.'"

Live in Concert 2006 is a record of Streisand's 2006 concert tour. One of the new pieces of material performed by Barbra on this tour was the song "A Cockeyed Optimist," by Rodgers and Hammerstein. In the CD liner notes, Barbra writes: "My personal thanks to Marilyn Lovell Matz for sharing a very special piece of music with me. Marilyn combined and arranged William Saroyan's foreword to his play 'The Time of Your Life' with Rodgers & Hammerstein's 'A Cockeyed Optimist' from *South Pacific*, orchestrated by her late husband Peter Matz. Peter was a gifted composer and arranger who was so important to my musical career . . . and to me." More background on this: Marilyn Lovell Matz, also a performer, was Los Angeles's leading therapist for AIDS patients, all the while fighting her own battle with multiple sclerosis for more than thirty years. In the 1980s and 1990s, she and Peter Matz performed their act in living rooms and concert halls to raise money for AIDS research and treatment.

Jay Landers revealed, "Barbra is keenly aware that people spend hard-earned money to attend her concerts. Besides the tickets, there's the babysitter, parking, food, concert programs, and T-shirts that they are forking over big bucks for. So they want to hear the hits, and Barbra doesn't want to disappoint them. However, like every major artist I've ever met or read about, she's more excited about singing songs she hasn't performed, rather than the ones she's sung over and over again. I want to emphasize we're not dictating the repertoire—it's a completely democratic process, with Barbra taking the lead and Richard Jay-Alexander and I just trying to fulfill her many ideas!"

The Barnes & Noble version included "When the Sun Comes Out" on Disc 2—it was also a bonus video track on the concert's DVD and Blu-ray discs. The Target version included two bonus tracks: "Stoney End" and "Don't Rain on My Parade." This is probably the rarer CD, because Target no longer sells it and Columbia hasn't added the tracks to streaming services like Spotify. "Don't Rain on My Parade" is very rare because Barbra cut it early during the tour; she did not sing it in Florida, so, therefore, it is not on the TV special. It's the entire song, whereas "Stoney End" is just a snippet.

Also, don't forget to embrace William Ross's orchestral "Entr'acte," which begins Disc 2—this is a masterful compilation of Streisand's film music played by this melodious orchestra. Not since Marvin Hamlisch's medleys during the 1994 tour have Barbra's songs been given such fine attention. *Live in Concert 2006* was nominated for Best Traditional Pop Vocal Album in 2008, but Michael Bublé's *Call Me Irresponsible* won that year.

Matt on *Live 2006*

Live 2006 is Barbra's sixth live recording. It's a gorgeous package—great liner notes and photos. This was the first big Streisand concert to feature guest singers. Gratefully, Il Divo, the multinational classical vocal group, appears on just three tracks. Their solo numbers are not included on this album.

Streisand with her long-time codirector Richard Jay-Alexander cement *Funny Girl* as Barbra's legacy in this concert. Not only do they open the show with the Broadway overture, but Act One ends with a suite of *Funny Girl* songs. Then they double down and end the concert with the Broadway *reprise* of "Don't Rain on My Parade"—brilliant!

Back in 2006, when I saw this concert in Philadelphia (opening night!) and DC, I remarked how much the set list was filled with deep cuts. So many of the songs were rarer choices from Streisand's discography and truly surprised me. I don't know how casual fans responded, but this rabid fan loved almost every song choice throughout the evening. "Ma Première Chanson" sung live?? "Unusual Way"??

"Starting Here, Starting Now" was my second-favorite concert opening song, after 1994's opening number, "As If We Never Said Goodbye."

Streisand is in excellent voice on this recording, and it's rich to hear William Ross's fifty-eight-member orchestra accompanying her.

My two choices for best track are: "Unusual Way"—the melody, the emotion, the performance. Chef's kiss!

"My Shining Hour"—little known to me, but I have enjoyed it ever since I heard it. Play it again if you haven't heard it in a while. It's calm and happy and bright.

STREISAND COLLABORATORS

WILLIAM ROSS

I spoke to William (Bill) Ross, Barbra's arranger and conductor, in September 2022. In addition to orchestrating and conducting for Barbra in the studio, he conducted her 2000, 2006–2007, and 2012–2013 concert tours. Barbra said that "when I'm at the microphone, I know Bill has my back." (Momentum RLP, 2016) Ross started out in jazz and classical piano, but dreamed of being an arranger for either Frank Sinatra, Aretha Franklin, or Barbra Streisand ("I never got to work with Frank," he told me—but his other two dreams came true.)

"Barbra isn't a perfectionist; she wants to try things until she gets perfection."

Matt Howe: When you're at a recording session with Barbra, how much is preparation versus inspiration that happens in the moment, while you're recording?

Bill Ross: What a fabulous question that leads to part of the confusion that has surrounded Barbra for years. Barbra's style is experimental; she wants to try things. *What about this? What if we did this?* She's not saying, "'I hate what you did, I want to do something different." She's saying, "Come with me, I want to try something." The challenge with that is that you have to be able to think on your feet. Barbra and I have never had a single cross word, never had a single argument about anything. I respect her right to try things, and she respects that I'm trying. She does like to move quickly, so you can't sit there and take as much time as you would like sometimes. That's part of the massive confusion around Barbra Streisand. She doesn't claim to know exactly what she wants; she claims to say, "I'm going to keep trying until I find it."

Howe: Barbra said in a video tribute to you that "Bill follows me so intensely that he actually breathes with me, and that's so liberating." (Momentum RLP, 2016) How do you learn to breathe with Barbra, and then, on top of that, get the fifty-eight or sixty members of the orchestra to follow along?

Ross: Breathing with Barbra is a delight. First of all, she's extremely musical—her breathing is musical. She's easy to follow, but you have to be ready, because it's never going to be the same. I can tell if she's tense or if she's relaxed just by the way she breathes. I get [an audio] monitor right next to my ear—it's as though Barbra were standing right next to me. That monitor has no reverb, so it's literally like she's there. In order to have the orchestra where it needs to be, or where I think it needs to be, or where she would like it, I have to hear her breathe so that I can put the orchestra right where the note comes out. If I wait for the note, the orchestra will be behind. When Barbra says, "You breathe with me," that's what I think she means.

"When Barbra learns a song, the first thing she seems to do—she doesn't even care about the melody. It's the words. She goes over the words like they're a poem. If there's one word that doesn't feel right, whatever it is, she challenges it."

Ross gave me an insight into "variable clicks" ("which I've spent a lot of time developing," he said). This is a recording technique to add an orchestra to a previously recorded track. He explained that he will add "click, click" to the track, which assists in knowing when the orchestra comes in.

Ross: Sometimes what I'll do with Barbra is she will come out and sing in the [recording] booth, and I'll just follow her. We get a track that feels good to her. And then she'll go home, or on her own time, and she'll keep singing until she gets the vocal the way she wants it. We've done that, and we've done the opposite, where she sings with a pianist and gets it to where "I love this, I love the vocal, I love the piano, now put the orchestra in." And that's where we find clever ways to use click tracks, so that it feels like it was all done together."

The secret to being successful in recording is preparation. So we spend a lot of time making sure the arrangement is the way we want, and then we go to the studio and we dive in. We plan for about an hour per song. Nowadays, we can mock up an arrangement using synths—they sound reasonably close, so that you can tell if you like the string parts. What that has done is saved a lot of time in the studio.

Howe: Do you have memories of your concert tours with Barbra?

Ross: I've had the best time with Barbra on stage. She's something else. Conducting with Barbra is a treat. It's a pleasure, because she's so musical. You never know what she's going to do. She starts talking about something and you might have planned for eight bars for her to talk, and you realize there's no way she's going to finish. We had all ways and clues I would communicate with the orchestra.

Barbra taught me what the word "artist" was. Before I was working with Barbra, I never really used that term. I liked the term "craftsman" better. We were doing a dress rehearsal in Philadelphia. On "I Stayed Too Long at the Fair," I started feeling these chills. What is going on? I looked over at her. She had both hands on the mic, looking up, and just kind of swaying to the music. I thought, *Where is she?* Richard Jay-Alexander came out to give her a staging note. He has a job to do with staging. I remember watching her. When she opened her eyes, I really got the feeling that she was so lost in that song. That willingness to be vulnerable, that's what I took in. That's what an artist is. Somebody who is willing to be vulnerable. I really applaud her for that. She's a genuine artist, no question about it. Barbra is a great actress who happens to have a great voice."

Released: September 29, 2009
Produced by: Diana Krall
Coproduced by: Tommy LiPuma
Executive producer: Barbra Streisand
Recorded by: Al Schmitt and Steve Genewick
Mixed by: Al Schmitt
A & R: Jay Landers
Recorded and mixed at Capitol Studios, Hollywood
Photography: Firooz Zahedi
Sammie and ocean photo: Barbra Streisand
Design: Michael Lau-Robles
Liner notes: Diana Krall, Jay Landers, Barbra Streisand

Catalog Numbers:
88697 43354 2 9 (orchestrated version)
88697 48283 2 7 (deluxe edition—2-disc version w/ orchestrated and quartet versions)
*88697 57150 2 2 (Starbucks edition)**
*88697 433541 (LP/vinyl album—2 LPs)***
** The Starbucks CD was a mix of orchestra and quartet versions of the songs.*
*** 2 LPs; heavyweight 180g vinyl; gatefold cover with printed inner sleeves containing photos, liner notes, and album credits.*

Tracks:
1. Here's To Life
2. In The Wee Small Hours Of The Morning
3. Gentle Rain
4. If You Go Away (Ne Me Quitte Pas)
5. Spring Can Really Hang You Up The Most
6. Make Someone Happy
7. Where Do You Start?
8. A Time For Love
9. Here's That Rainy Day
10. Love Dance
11. Smoke Gets In Your Eyes
12. Some Other Time

Bonus track: You Must Believe In Spring

The Canadian jazz pianist and singer Diana Krall was pregnant with twins when she and Streisand first connected. "I was at a small dinner party where Barbra was also there. She was just about to start a tour, and she said, 'I need some inspiration. I need some song ideas.' And, you know, I like to make mixed tapes, so I sent her some songs that I thought might be interesting for her." (Ryan, 2008)

Krall attended Barbra's 2006 concert at Madison Square Garden, and Streisand picks up the story: "She was sitting next to Alan Bergman, who said, 'I always wanted Barbra to do a jazz album,' and Diana just said, 'I'll produce it.' And then he told me about it and I thought, *Well, that might be interesting, 'cause I usually produce many of my own albums*. And I thought it would be interesting to work together. I've always admired her musicianship and love the way she sings." (*Love Is the Answer* Exclusive Video, 2009)

Krall recruited an A-team to create the album, including eighty-four-year-old arranger Johnny Mandel and producer Tommy LiPuma, who had worked with Barbra back in 1973. Mandel explained the process: "Barbra first got together with Diana and went over the songs she wanted to do and the keys in which she wanted to sing them. Then Diana and I spoke about the approach." (Myers, 2009)

Krall convinced Streisand to record this album differently than her others. First, Mandel arranged the songs for Diana's quartet of musicians (piano, bass, guitar, and drums). Then, Krall recorded Streisand's vocals as she sang live with the quartet. Next, Mandel created orchestral arrangements around the quartet tracks. Lastly, the orchestra was recorded at a separate session, and the tracks were combined seamlessly. "David Foster records that way, where you do the tracks first," said Streisand. "I don't particularly like it. I love the inspiration of the orchestra. But it brought me back to the way I started, so there is something very pure about it, not innocent but young and youthful—nostalgic." (King, 2009)

"The trick for me on the orchestration side," Mandel elaborated, "was to elegantly surround the arrangements I wrote for Diana's quartet. You don't want to hear the quartet accompanied by the orchestra, or first the quartet and then the orchestra. I hate that sound—hearing one and then the other. Barbra has never recorded an album like this before, with a jazz quartet plus orchestration. She had mixed feelings about it, mostly over concern that just the sound of a quartet might be too spare for her sound. Which was perfect for me, since I like when a quartet and orchestra overlay are completely integrated as one." (Myers, 2009)

Columbia arranged an exciting promotion for the album too. Streisand would sing a selection of songs from the new album on September 26 at New York's jazz club the Village Vanguard. Fans entered a sweepstakes on her official site to win free tickets to see Barbra perform.

When *Love Is the Answer* was released, Columbia put out a deluxe edition—two CDs that contained both the quartet and the orchestrated tracks. Streisand wrote in the liner notes: "As much as I love the fully orchestrated versions of the songs we recorded, these 'unplugged' takes have their own special intimacy. We've included them here to give you an idea of the basic tracks."

Streisand's vocals are exactly the same on both versions except for "Smoke Gets in Your Eyes"—on the quartet version, Barbra sings a different final note on "eyes." Streisand has great success with the "up-tempo" songs on this album too. I use quotes because the speediest tempo we get on the album is on the breezy bossa nova songs "Gentle Rain," and "Love Dance."

"If You Go Away" is poignant, because Barbra mines thematic material that had endeared her to us years earlier with "My Man" and "I Had Myself a True Love." Unrequited love is the perfect subject for torch songs, and "Ne Me Quitte Pas," the French translation of the song, is an instant Streisand classic on this album. Streisand pleads with her lover in the song and claims she would have been "the shadow of your shadow" if he would have kept her. That was a lyric change, by the way. Rod McKuen's original lyric was "I'd have been the shadow of your dog," but he rewrote the lyric in the 1960s for the singers who covered it. For instance, Dusty Springfield's 1967 version used "shadow of your shadow," whereas Frank Sinatra sang "shadow of your dog" in 1969.

Streisand said, "I remember thinking, No, I don't think I would ever be anyone's shadow of a dog. The shadow of your shadow is actually lower than a dog. But it's more poetic to me, the shadow of your shadow." (*Love Is the Answer* Exclusive Video, 2009)

David Foster's 1993 arrangement of "Smoke Gets in Your Eyes" for the album *Back to Broadway* is not good. Streisand didn't like it either. As for the new recording with Diana Krall, I prefer the orchestrated version of "Smoke." The clarinet and flute at the top of the song is wonderful, and the strings give the song forward motion. Streisand really impresses with her vocals on this song—such long lines! Does she breathe? Listen to "tears I cannot hide . . . so I smile and say," all with one breath as she bends the note on "hide." Wowza!

Streisand gave press interviews and participated in television promotion for the album by appearing in the UK on *The Jonathan Ross Show* and in the US on Oprah's talk show. Side note: I attended the taping of the Oprah show, where Barbra sang "Make Someone Happy" and "Evergreen." Since I assisted with some photos for the show, one of the producers arranged tickets for me. What I recall most is that Oprah's taping ran like a fine-tuned machine, with no time wasted. I also recall my jealousy: if you were female and wore bright colors, you were chosen to sit closer to the stage! The Harpo Studio in Chicago wasn't big, and Barbra's voice filled the space so beautifully. When Barbra's interview aired, she shared the hour with Jay-Z (whose segment was taped separately). I recall that Barbra and Oprah spent a little more time during the taping talking about Barbra's house and showing photos of food from her travels. What an adventure! I'll never forget it.

Love Is the Answer was Streisand's ninth number-one album on the *Billboard* 200 chart, initially selling 180,000 copies, according to Nielsen SoundScan. In its second week, Barbra's album went from number four to number one in the UK. *Love Is the Answer* also charted at number two for three weeks in a row on *Billboard*'s Jazz Album chart.

Love Is the Answer was nominated in the category of Best Traditional Pop Vocal Album at the 2011 Grammy Awards. Since Tony Bennett was not nominated that year, Michael Bublé won instead for his album *Crazy Love*. Unbelievable! She was robbed. Of the two versions, the quartet CD is my favorite. Somehow, the quartet songs strike me as the "legitimate" ones, since they were recorded first. The players are tight, and Streisand achieves an intimacy with the microphone on her vocals.

Matt on *The Answer*

I'm not a technician, but it even sounds like Diana Krall somehow managed to record Streisand differently too. Her voice is very present on the tracks, giving the impression that Streisand is cuddled up to the microphone. Barbra hardly belts on this album. She achieves her high notes effortlessly and intimately.

"A Time for Love" is my favorite track. Streisand sings long musical lines here, almost like a spring breeze rustling the leaves in the trees. She renders a striking sound picture in my mind's eye when she repeats the phrase "the willow bends and so do I." It's genius when she takes the one-syllable word "bends" and actually *bends* it vocally into a three-syllable word ("be-e-ends")—which gives me chills.

And just to make sure we've got it, when she sings the phrase the last time, she adds what voice teachers call "vocal fry" to "bends"—that's that creaky, breathy, almost weary sound she endows the word with.

DECADE 00 ENCORE

Barbra released four studio albums in the 2000s along with two live concert albums—both two-CD sets. There were three hits albums as well.

The decade ended with what I believe is one of her best albums ever—*Love Is the Answer*. On that album, Barbra went back to her nightclub roots by collaborating with Diana Krall, and the results are outstanding. I'm still very disappointed that Barbra did not win the Grammy for that album. Maybe it was the publicity? Columbia could have dialed up the hype a bit more and really hit home in the press that *Love Is the Answer* was Barbra's comeback album. Streisand's most excellent work on that recording stands for itself, though. Kudos to Miss Krall for producing such a tasteful and tuneful collection of standards.

Coming off the nineties, with commercial radio practically dead and satellite radio on the rise, Barbra Streisand was free to record the style of music she really excels at. The Grammys classify her category as Best Traditional Pop Vocal, but Barbra's singing milieu really is the American songbook, with some Broadway and movie music thrown into the mix, and that's what she gave us in the 2000s. The *Guilty Pleasures* album is the outlier of the decade, but it was guided by Barry Gibb's tuneful ear, and most of his songs ended up sounding like Tin Pan Alley counterparts.

It's difficult to summarize the music Barbra recorded in the 2000s because we must assume our idol was happiest being Barbra Joan Brolin. After finding love and marriage with Jim Brolin, Barbra surely was less interested in recording, let alone publicizing, a bunch of albums. Barbra also seemingly embraced her status as a cultural icon in the 2000s, accepting lifetime achievement awards from the Golden Globes, the American Film Institute, and the Kennedy Center Honors and revisiting her entire career by answering hours of questions from James Lipton on *Inside the Actors Studio*.

Barbra's discography in the 2000s reflects her legendary status too. Columbia put out *Essential*, *The Collection*, *Duets*, and *Super Hits*. Barbra lent her legendary voice to Tony Bennett's big duets project, while her own *Duets* album merely collected previously recorded songs, plus two new ones.

The good news is that fans could see Miss Streisand sing live more than ever before in the decade of the 2000s—thanks to *Timeless*, a handful of political concerts, and the 2006-2007 shows, there was an abundance of concert-attending opportunities. It almost seemed as if Mr. and Mrs. Brolin undertook concertizing to fit in some travel in between shows! First, they toured Australia, where Barbra dazzled fans with four stadium shows before moving on to New Zealand. Mid-decade, Barbra trekked to sixteen North American cities, then winged to Europe for gigs in seven burgs. In Zurich, Vienna, and Paris, she scheduled enough days between shows so that she and her hubby could explore the local scenery—and eat some delicious food.

Streisand celebrated her sixtieth birthday during the decade, and although her musical output wasn't as prolific as in, say, the 1970s, she did reward us with a handful of great albums and concert tours.

THE 2010S

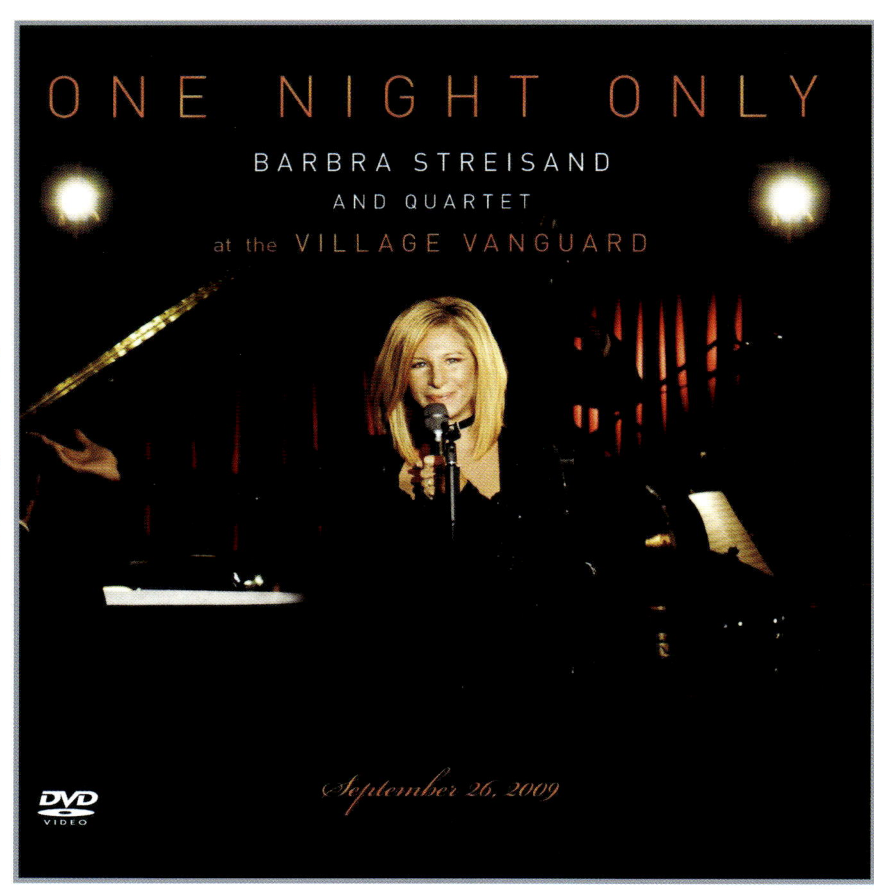

Released: May 4, 2010
Mastered by: Doug Sax at The Mastering Lab, Ojai, California
Executive producers: Barbra Streisand and Martin Erlichman
Produced by: Richard Jay-Alexander and Scott Lochmus
Recorded and mixed by: David Reitzas
Music supervision: Jay Landers
Art direction and design: Fusako Chubachi
Photography: Kevin Mazur

Catalog Numbers:
88697 68411 9 (CD and DVD)

Tracks:

1. Intro
2. Here's To Life
3. In The Wee Small Hours Of The Morning
4. Gentle Rain
5. Spring Can Really Hang You Up The Most
6. If You Go Away (Ne Me Quitte Pas)
7. Where Do You Start?
8. Nobody's Heart Belongs To Me
9. Make Someone Happy
10. My Funny Valentine
11. Bewitched, Bothered And Bewildered
12. Thank You's And Introductions
13. Evergreen
14. Exit Music
15. Some Other Time
16. [Encore] The Way We Were

To promote *Love Is the Answer*, Barbra Streisand sang a one-night-only gig at New York's famed jazz club the Village Vanguard. "It's hard to have stage fright when there's practically no stage!" Streisand joked at the outset of the concert at the Vanguard, which seated about one hundred people. The September 26, 2009, evening performance was recorded by Columbia Records and videotaped as a TV special. Columbia bundled Barbra's intimate club show as a DVD/CD combo pack.

Dave Reitzas, who recorded and mixed the live sound, told MixOnline he used an Audio-Technica AE5400 handheld condenser mic for Streisand's vocals. The mic's wire ran from inside the club to the All Mobile truck outside. In these days of wireless mics, using a wired one was actually "part of re-creating the 1960s ambience of the club," said Jim Flynn, who provided the recording equipment for the evening. (Daley, 2009)

To promote the DVD/CD, Barbra's codirector, Richard Jay-Alexander, appeared on the cable shopping channel QVC with host Shawn Killinger. QVC offered the DVD by itself as well as the DVD/CD package, which included a bonus poster of Barbra onstage at the Bon Soir. Almost a year after Columbia released the DVD/CD album, *Live at the Village Vanguard* aired across America on PBS stations.

Matt on *Village*

With the historic New York nightclub the Bon Soir extinct by 2009, Barbra staged her homecoming performance at the Village Vanguard, which had opened in 1935 and played host over the years to such giants of jazz as Miles Davis, Sonny Rollins, Anita O'Day, and Charlie Mingus. Even though Barbra had never played the Vanguard back in the sixties, the club was intimate, old school, and a part of New York City nightlife lore.

This recording definitely gives us a "you are there" vibe. Streisand's vocals aren't particularly her best, but it's cool to hear her patter and the audience's chatter.

The very lucky people who were able to attend this show also responded glowingly to her rendition of "If You Go Away."

"Gentle Rain" was one of my favorites when I first heard her live version of it. It's also nice that Barbra allows the amazing Tamir Hendelman to play his soothing piano solo uninterrupted.

Although Barbra's set list drew heavily from *Love Is the Answer*, it's great to hear some of her older material done here, like "Nobody's Heart," "My Funny Valentine," and "Bewitched."

It's hilarious that in her introduction to "Some Other Time," Barbra admits she got confused by the song order and walked off the stage one song too soon.

Ultimately, *One Night Only* works best as a TV show. The pleasure is watching Streisand in such close quarters with her dewy skin as she interrupts almost every song to say something to the audience, seeing Nicole Kidman and Sarah Jessica Parker craning their necks to watch her, and viewing the adoring audience glowing from the sepia lights.

What Matters Most

Released: August 23, 2011
Produced by: Barbra Streisand
A & R: Jay Landers
Recorded by: Armin Steiner and Dave Reitzas
Mixed and mastered by: Dave Reitzas
Arranged by: William A. Ross
Arranged by: Patrick Williams ("That Face" and "Nice 'n' Easy")
Cover photo: Russell James
Sydney Pollack photo by: Camilla Morandi/Rex Features
Piano image: Christie B. Thomas
Art direction: Dave Bett and Kristin Lum

Catalog Numbers:
88697 86257 2 (10-track CD)
88697 94057 2 (20-track Deluxe CD)
88697 94194 2 (13-track Starbucks CD)
88697 95565 9 (22-minute QVC DVD)

Tracks:

1. The Windmills Of Your Mind
2. Something New In My Life
3. Solitary Moon
4. Nice 'n' Easy
5. Alone In The World
6. So Many Stars
7. The Same Hello, The Same Goodbye
8. That Face
9. I'll Never Say Goodbye
10. What Matters Most

"What matters most is friendship and love," Streisand stated about the title of her album of songs by Alan and Marilyn Bergman. "And I love the Bergmans and we've been friends for almost half a century. I thought it was a good time to sing more of their songs that I love that I just haven't gotten around to singing." (Sony Music, 2011)

The idea to record an entire album of Bergman songs was born in May 2009 when Streisand participated in a tribute to her friends at the Academy of Motion Picture Arts & Sciences in Los Angeles. "Knowing how she dislikes appearing in front of a lot of people, we were all the more appreciative of her participation," the Bergmans wrote in the album liner notes. "And when she said, 'My next album is going to be a tribute to you guys,' we were speechless."

Streisand's process of approaching this album was simple; she asked them to send her tapes of all their songs she hadn't recorded yet. Then she picked her favorites. Work began on the album with orchestrator Bill Ross deciding on arrangements with Streisand and her friends. Jay Landers revealed on the CD insert that "the orchestra tracks . . . took a mere three days to record. . . . The actual studio process was reminiscent of the 'old days' (early 1960's) when she used to record and mix an entire LP faster than it takes most engineers to get a good drum sound these days."

The CD, packaged in a jewel box or Digipak (depending on which version you bought), contained a beautiful twenty-four-page booklet that Streisand revised until the printers got the peach color on some of the pages absolutely right. The deluxe version of the album contained a bonus disc with ten previously released but iconic Bergman songs recorded by Streisand: "The Way We Were," "What Are You Doing the Rest of Your Life?," "You Don't Bring Me Flowers," "Papa, Can You Hear Me?," "Pieces of Dreams," "The Island," "The Summer Knows," "How Do You Keep the Music Playing?," "After the Rain," "A Piece of Sky."

Publicitywise, Amazon ran a video of Streisand discussing the album, and Richard Jay-Alexander appeared on the cable shopping channel QVC, which offered the deluxe edition with a bonus DVD containing interview footage of Streisand and the Bergmans as well as footage of Streisand from the MusiCares concert singing "The Windmills of Your Mind" and "I'll Never Say Goodbye."

Columbia Records promoted the album by streaming her segment of the MusiCares concert at Starbucks stores during August 2011.

Streisand wrote in the liner notes: "The main reason I've made this album is that I want to thank Alan and Marilyn for a lifetime of love. Not only have they provided me with many beautiful songs to sing, but also as important, they've nurtured my soul and spirit." Incidentally, Barbra and Marilyn and Alan dedicate the album to their friend Sydney Pollack, the director of *The Way We Were*, who had passed away in 2008.

Jay Landers told me, "As Barbra was recording 'The Same Hello,The Same Goodbye' she kept hearing one note that sounded odd to her. The conductor checked the score and confirmed that the musicians were playing exactly what was on the page. Barbra seemed to let it go, but the truth is, she never really lets anything go! While she was in the vocal booth, an assistant found me in the control room and said, 'Steven Spielberg's out in the lobby, and wonders if he could pop in for a brief hello.' I stepped into the lobby and sure enough, there he was! I walked him into the inner sanctum of the control room, where he greeted the Bergmans and Marty Erlichman while Barbra was singing. He asked about the song and I told him it was something the Bergmans had written with John Williams four decades ago. Steven lit up and said, 'You're not going to believe this: I'm working right next door with John on the score to my next picture *Lincoln*. Do you think I could bring him over?' Two minutes later, just as Spielberg returned with John Williams, Barbra was just completing her vocal take. She came out of the vocal booth and was delighted to see her friend standing there. I then said to Barbra, 'I'd like you to

meet Maestro John Williams.' Instead of saying 'hello' or 'nice to meet you,' Barbra said, 'John, let me ask you something. There's a note in this score that's driving me crazy!' Without missing a beat, John said, 'Well, I haven't heard the song in about thirty years; let me take a look at the chart.' Someone brought the chart into the room, John examined it and, pointing at the sheet music, said, 'Well, I see the copyist wrote down the wrong note here.' Everyone broke into laughter because no one other than Barbra, and now John, had noticed the error! It was a fantastic moment, and a great way of illustrating Barbra's impeccable ears and innate musical genius."

What Matters Most was nominated for two Grammy Awards: Best Traditional Pop Vocal Album and, for Bill Ross's arrangement of "The Windmills of My Mind," Best Instrumental Arrangement Accompanying Vocalist(s). Barbra lost in both categories to—well, this is getting ridiculous—Tony Bennett's *Duets II* album. Do the Grammys hate Barbra? Or is it simply a boys' club? I will reiterate that I totally respect Mr. Bennett, his legacy, and his talent. But after all these decades of him collecting Grammy after Grammy . . . and Streisand not being awarded one since 1987 . . . surely something else is going on behind the scenes with Grammy voters.

Matt on *Matters*

By honoring the Bergmans, Barbra Streisand gave us an elegant album. The arrangements by Bill Ross and Patrick Williams ("That Face") are superb. Commercially, the album isn't a home run—although it did peak on the chart at number four, which isn't bad. The joy of this album is in the care and love so obviously poured into the recording. Streisand's curation of the Bergmans' works is instructive and expanding: we get to hear, beyond their collaborations with Michel Legrand, some well-crafted songs with melodies by composers like John Williams, David Shire, Dave Grusin, Jerry Goldsmith, and Lew Spence.

The album opener, "The Windmills of Your Mind," is sublime, and one of the best cuts Streisand has recorded in years. I knew the song as sung by Dusty Springfield, but when I heard Barbra's version I thought: *Yes*! *That's the Barbra way to do it*. It was written as the opening credit song for the original *The Thomas Crown Affair* (1968), but Barbra's version is "like the mechanical clockworks of your mind," Streisand explained. Added Marilyn Bergman "As she walked into the [recording] booth, she said something like, 'Oh, this is a descent into madness.' Exactly. That's exactly what we were using when we wrote the song." (Sony Music, 2011)

Since the Bergmans are well-known and aptly awarded film music lyricists, it's no surprise that five of the ten songs on the disc are themes from movies.: "Windmills," "Something New in My Life" (*Micki & Maude*), "Alone in the World" (*The Russia House*), "I'll Never Say Goodbye" (*The Promise*), and "What Matters Most" (*The Champ*).

"Solitary Moon," with music by Johnny Mandel, is a voluptuous song with a sexy saxophone solo by Dan Higgins and beautiful strings surrounding and supporting Barbra.

I also like "Alone in the World," which contains a trumpet solo by Chris Botti. It's an affecting song from a movie I remember with

Sean Connery and Michele Pfeiffer—although I didn't remember the song! I really admire the Bergmans' words: "Sleep inside my arms/Kiss the world away/Let tomorrow come/Let me face the day with you."

By now you must know how much I admire Barbra's "acting songs," and "The Same Hello, the Same Goodbye" is a standout for me on this album. It has such an interesting backstory too. John Williams (*Star Wars*, *Indiana Jones*, and *Harry Potter* scores) wrote the song with the Bergmans for Ol' Blue Eyes himself, Frank Sinatra, who intended to record it but ultimately did not. It wasn't until 2008 that singer, pianist, and Ambassador of American Songbook Michael Feinstein uncovered this gem when recording it for his *The Sinatra Project* album. He explained its history: "One day [the Bergmans] got a call from Frank asking if they could write what he called a 'performance piece' for him. So they got together with John Williams and wrote this four-section piece. When they finished, Sinatra told them to come to Palm Springs. There was Williams at the piano and Alan singing, and when they finished Sinatra was sobbing. He said, 'Jesus, how do you know so much about my life?' and Marilyn laughed and said, 'As if your life is a closed book!' Sinatra kept saying, 'I'm going to learn that thing, it's fantastic,' but he never did. So, when I was putting this recording together, I called Alan and Marilyn and asked about the piece. Alan was a little cagey about it. They kept me on tenterhooks [but] I kept after them, and finally Alan said, 'Come over.' They'd extracted one of the songs. I sat down and read through the lead sheet and was deeply moved by it. About three weeks later, I recorded it with Alan in the studio to make sure I did it to their satisfaction." (Concord, 2008)

The other "acting song" on this album also happens to feature a dynamic and passionate vocal performance by Barbra. I have always imagined Barbra singing "I'll Never Say Goodbye" as if she were playing Juliet from Shakespeare's play. "I'll Never Say Goodbye" is the balcony scene between Romeo and Juliet, is it not? Barbra has never said that's what she's acting during this song, but for me this is exactly the scene she's playing when she sings it. That is why "I'll Never Say Goodbye" is yet another classic, perfect performance by Barbra. WOW!

I confess that I had to carefully consider the lyrics to "What Matters Most" several times because I didn't quite understand them. I do that often; sometimes I even transcribe lyrics so that I can see the sentence structure and the words on the page. I wanted to understand what the Bergmans were saying with this song and why Streisand chose it to close the album with her very sensitive vocal. "What Matters Most" makes me weep because it's so simple yet profound. The lyrics work two ways too: if you've been in a long-term relationship or if you are processing the deep feelings around a breakup. Many of the song's stanzas begin with the words "It's not." I believe that the Bergmans are wisely telling us that the way we sometimes measure a relationship (time, seasons, and displays of affection) aren't what matters the most; rather, it's the fact that we loved at all.

The Bergman songwriting partnership ended when Marilyn passed away in 2022. Alan continued to write until his death in 2025, but their beautiful words will be with us for the ages. It's moving to know that in "What Matters Most" they wrote: "It's not how far we traveled on our way, but what we found to say." They said it very well.

STREISAND COLLABORATORS

THE BERGMANS

Lifelong F.O.B.s (Friends of Barbra), the Bergmans are brilliant lyricists who met while writing lyrics separately for songwriter Lew Spence. Marilyn was Spence's afternoon lyric writer, and Alan was his morning lyric writer. Once Spence introduced them, the rest was history. The first bona fide hit together was "Nice 'n' Easy," which was recorded by Frank Sinatra (who called them "the kids").

"We were writing a show in New York [*Something More* with Sammy Fain], and Jule Styne took us down to the Bon Soir to hear a girl," Marilyn remembered. "He said, 'You have to hear this girl.' And we had been in casting sessions all day listening to girls. The last thing we wanted to do at the end of the day was go to hear another girl singer, but he said, 'No, no, no, you must come.' So reluctantly we went. Little did we know . . . She walked out and sang one note and I remember starting to cry, and I never stopped crying the whole show. I remember saying to her, 'Do you know how wonderful you are?'" (Howe, Interview with Marilyn and Alan Bergman, 2007) Streisand and the Bergmans became very close friends, and in the 1970s Barbra began recording many of their songs. This friendship and affinity for music climaxed with the score of *Yentl* in 1983. Marilyn Bergman explained why they chose Michel Legrand to write the music for *Yentl*: "We felt that *Yentl* was a story of Middle Europe at a particular time. They happened to be Jews—but really it was an interior monologue of this young woman, and a great deal of it was very romantic, and I think we decided that what would make it more accessible—we probably did have accessibility in mind—was a composer who wrote European, romantic music." (Pogrebin, 2022)

The Bergmans won Academy Awards for "The Windmills of Your Mind" (from 1968's *The Thomas Crown Affair*) and their score for *Yentl*. They also won four Emmys, two Golden Globes, and two Grammys, including Song of the Year for "The Way We Were." They were also behind some of television's best theme songs, having written the words to *Maude*, *Alice*, and *Good Times*.

Marilyn Bergman died at age ninety-three in January 2022 after serving as the chairman and president of the American Society of Composers, Songwriters, and Performers (ASCAP) from 1994 to 2009. After Alan died, aged ninety-nine, Barbra wrote on social media: "I like to think he's again in Marilyn's warm embrace and I'm sure they have started collaborating again on another song! I will miss them both."

The Bergmans' songs recorded by Barbra Streisand and the name of the person who wrote the music:

Yentl 40th Anniversary (2023)
All music by Michel Legrand
Where Is It Written? (demo)
Papa, Can You Hear Me? (demo)
The Way He Makes Me Feel (demo)
Several Sins a Day (demo)
No Wonder (demo) with Marilyn Bergman
Tomorrow Night (demo)
Will Someone Ever Look at Me This Way? (demo) with Michel Legrand
The Moon and I (demo)
A Piece of Sky (demo)
Papa, Can You Hear Me? (studio)
Several Sins a Day (studio)
Where Is It Written? (with Rabbinical chorus)
Papa, Can You Hear Me? (single)
This Is One of Those Moments (reprise)

Release Me 2 (2021)
One Day (A Prayer) - Michel Legrand
Once You've Been In Love - Michel Legrand

Walls (2018)
Walls - Walter Afanasieff

Encore: Movie Partners Sing Broadway (2016)
Fifty Percent - Billy Goldenberg

Partners (2014)
The Way We Were (w/Lionel Richie) - Marvin Hamlisch

Release Me (2012)
Mother And Child - Michel Legrand
If It's Meant To Be - Brian Byrne
What Matters Most—Barbra Streisand Sings The Lyrics of Alan And Marilyn Bergman (2011)
The Windmills Of Your Mind - Michel Legrand
Something New In My Life - Michel Legrand
Solitary Moon - Johnny Mandel
Nice 'n' Easy - Lew Spence
Alone In The World - Jerry Goldsmith
So Many Stars - Sérgio Mendes
The Same Hello, The Same Goodbye - John Williams
That Face - Lew Spence and Alan Bergman
I'll Never Say Goodbye - David Shire
What Matters Most - Dave Grusin
Love Is The Answer (2009)
Where Do You Start? - Johnny Mandel
You Must Believe In Spring - Michel Legrand
The Movie Album (2003)
Emily - Johnny Mandel; lyrics by Johnny Mercer with additional new lyrics by Alan and Marilyn Bergman
More In Love With You -André Previn
How Do You Keep The Music Playing? - Michel Legrand
Christmas Memories (2001)
A Christmas Love Song - Johnny Mandel
Christmas Mem'ries - Don Costa
Timeless (2000)
The Clicker Blues/Simple Pleasures/
Everytime You Hear Auld Lang Syne - Marvin Hamlisch
A Love Like Ours (1999)
The Island - Ivan Lins and Vitor Martins
Love Like Ours - David Grusin
Wait - Michel Legrand
Higher Ground (1997)
Leading With Your Heart - Marvin Hamlisch
The Mirror Has Two Faces (1996)
All Of My Life - Barbra Streisand and Marvin Hamlisch
It Doesn't Get Better Than This* - Barbra Streisand and Marvin Hamlisch
*Unreleased but used by director Streisand at one of the early screenings of the film.
The Concert (1994)
Ordinary Miracles - Marvin Hamlisch
The Prince Of Tides (1991)
Places That Belong To You - James Newton Howard
Just For The Record (1991)
If I Close My Eyes - Billy Goldenberg
Between Yesterday And Tomorrow - Michel Legrand
Can You Tell The Moment? - Michel Legrand
The Way We Weren't (live) - Marvin Hamlisch
The Moon And I (demo) - Michel Legrand
Till I Loved You (1988)
On My Way To You - Michel Legrand
Why Let It Go? -Alan Hawkshaw and Barry Mason
Two People - Barbra Streisand
Yentl (1983)
Where Is It Written? - all music by Michel Legrand
Papa, Can You Hear Me?
This Is One Of Those Moments
No Wonder, (Part Two), and (Reprise)
The Way He Makes Me Feel
Tomorrow Night
Will Someone Ever Look At Me That Way?
No Matter What Happens
A Piece Of Sky
Wet (1979)
On Rainy Afternoons - Lalo Schifrin
After The Rain - Michel Legrand
Songbird (1978)
You Don't Bring Me Flowers - Neil Diamond
A Star Is Born (1976)
I Believe In Love - Kenny Loggins
Lazy Afternoon (1975)
A Child Is Born - Dave Grusin
The Way We Were (1974)
The Way We Were - Marvin Hamlisch
What Are You Doing The Rest Of Your Life?/Summer Me, Winter Me/Pieces Of Dreams - Michel Legrand
Life Cycle Of A Woman Sessions (1973)
The Smile I've Never Smiled (unreleased) - Michel Legrand
Barbra Joan Streisand (1971)
The Summer Knows - Michel Legrand
What About Today? (1969)
Ask Yourself Why - Michel Legrand
Color Me Barbra (1966)
That Face (excerpted as part of the circus medley) Music by Lew Spence and Lyrics by Lew Spence and Alan Bergman

Vinyl released: September 25, 2012
CD released: October 9, 2012
Album produced by: Barbra Streisand and Jay Landers
Remixing and tape restoration: Brian Malouf
Original masters recorded and mixed by: John Arias, Armin Steiner, Don Meehan, Glen Kolotkin, David Reitzas
Remixed at: Cookie Jar Studios, Los Angeles
Tape restoration at: Iron Mountain, Hollywood
Mastered by: Stephen Marcussen at Marcussen Mastering, Hollywood
Research assistance: Matt Howe
Liner notes: Jay Landers
Creative direction: Dave Bett
Art direction and design: Kristin Lum
Album cover photo: Firooz Zahedi
Vault photos: Jay Landers

Catalog Numbers:
88725 45855 1 (LP)
88725 45855 2 (CD)

Tracks:

1. Being Good Isn't Good Enough
2. Didn't We
3. Willow Weep For Me
4. Try To Win A Friend
5. I Think It's Going To Rain Today
6. With One More Look At You
7. Lost In Wonderland
8. How Are Things In Glocca Morra/Heather On The Hill
9. Mother And Child
10. If It's Meant To Be
11. Home

Release Me is the first collection of unreleased tracks from Barbra Streisand's vaults since *Just for the Record* in 1991. Jay Landers wrote in his liner notes for the album that upon entering Barbra's storage vaults, "the first thing you'll notice are the floor-to-ceiling shelves with tape boxes from every era of her recording career—*People*, *Color Me Barbra*, *A Star Is Born*, *The Bon Soir*, Daniel Ellsberg Fundraiser, *Judy Garland Show*, The Hungry-I, McGovern Concert, *Guilty*, . . . on and on . . . ."

Barbra and Jay spent many hours reviewing over one hundred previously unreleased recordings to select the tracks for this album. Landers told *All About Barbra* magazine, "For at least two months, every other day, I went to this vault to unearth the gems which Barbra had either recalled from her various lists, or to find something that I'd heard about but never actually heard." (Landers, 2012)

Jay likened the gathering of Streisand's unreleased material to Indiana Jones searching for the lost ark. "On more than a few occasions, I'd find myself standing on the uppermost rung of a ladder with a heavy tape box in one hand and my cell phone in the other, talking with Barbra aficionado Matt Howe. Matt would try to help me identify certain mislabeled titles . . . or remind me if there were multiple unreleased versions of the same title . . . then he'd help me figure out which one I was barely holding on to at the moment!"

I can tell you, taking one of Jay's calls is exhilarating! "You're in THE VAULT now?!" was my reaction as my head exploded from the realization that he was digging through Streisand history. On one of Jay's calls, he was searching for "Didn't We." I reminded him it was recorded for an abandoned album called *The Singer*, probably around 1970. He found the box.

The Larry Gatlin song "Try to Win a Friend" was recorded in April 1977 for the *Superman* album (1978) but put aside for over thirty years until Barbra included it on *Release Me*. Gatlin taught Streisand the song at her house all those years ago—she was considering it for *A Star Is Born*. For *Release Me*, Barbra and Jay sent the master recording to Nashville producer Fred Mollin, who added John Hobbs on pedal steel guitar, Paul Franklin on piano, and Jaime Babbitt providing background vocals.

Irish composer Brian Byrne wrote and recorded the newest song on *Release Me*: "If It's Meant to Be," with lyrics by the Bergmans. Upon the first few months of moving to America, he was introduced to the songwriting couple. "I recorded it live with her, conducted the orchestra. This was happening in the same three weeks as I was working on [the film soundtrack to] *Albert Nobbs* and the song 'Lay Your Head Down' and doing arrangements for Katy Perry." (Tubridy, 2012)

Streisand had only ten minutes of studio time to record Byrne's song. "I had to change some of the orchestration at the moment . . . it was panic time. But I liked it. It was left off of *What Matters Most* because we had enough. And I thought it would be interesting for people to hear something that was left off in 2011, since everything else [on *Release Me*] is so much older. 'If It's Meant to Be' sounds like it comes from a stage play. I can feel the theatricality in it. It would be very good in a musical on stage." (Barbra Streisand YouTube Channel, 2012) Streisand and Byrne recorded vocals with piano after sending the musicians home . . . just in case!

Release Me's striking cover was created by graphic designer Kristin Lum. "I worked with Barbra directly to interpret her vision for *Release Me*," Lum wrote. "After many hours on the phone with her and searches through her image archives, I created this package with a classic, timeless look and feel." (Lum, 2012) Collier Strong was Streisand's makeup artist on this photo shoot, which was lensed by photographer Firooz Zahedi.

"Mother and Child," an outtake from the *Life Cycle of a Woman* album sessions, is fun to finally hear. It's technically perfect, with Barbra singing counterpoint melodies with herself.

Matt on *Release Me*

Release Me was particularly thrilling for me to hear because of my partiality toward Barbra's unreleased material. I was also delighted to be included in the project (in my small way). Still, I was surprised to see such tracks as "If It's Meant to Be" and "Lost in Wonderland" included.

Does it really matter that "Wonderland" is not a perfect vocal? I don't think so. We don't know how many takes Barbra did, but it's a complicated, dense lyric sung in rhythm. What we hear on *Release Me* is practically perfect, and that's good enough for me.

I listened to the original (bootleg) unreleased recording of "Home" again, and the new accompaniment is better—Streisand decided to rerecord the drums, bass, and piano in 2012 for *Release Me*, and it's a big improvement. What's more amazing is that she managed to get the original three musicians to repeat their parts on the update! For me, the *Release Me* track is more urgent and rhythmic and better than the original.

"Being Good Isn't Good Enough" is magnificent. Wow, what a vocal! I also think Barbra showed courage and a lack of vanity by singing it months later in concert using a lower key. Her 2012-2013 tour came twenty-seven years after that original recording, so there's no shame in admitting her voice had lowered. Barbra obviously still connected with the song's meaning, despite what key it was sung in.

Jay actually played this song over the phone for me when I was helping out on the album, and I was gobsmacked.

"Being Good" was meant to be the opening track of *The Broadway Album*, but Barbra went another way when she recorded "Putting It Together" for that spot instead. It's hard to believe that "Being Good" was cut! The song also encapsulates Streisand's internal drive to be good—even though, at the same time, she has insecurity about whether her best is good enough for the audience. The song from *Hallelujah Baby* was written for a Black character who was singing about the hurdles she had to overcome in order to succeed because of her skin color. But Streisand interprets it her way, making it a soaring ballad that, really, is a more melodic version of the determination in "Don't Rain on My Parade." She sings, "Gotta fly and if I fall, well, that's the way it's gotta be, there's no other way for me." In her live performances of this song, she doubles down by adding an extra "The best! The best! Or nothing at all."

"Try to Win a Friend" is lovely too. Streisand has an easy way with this song, and the sentiment behind it is truthful: "Though you've lost a lover, try to win a friend."

"How Are Things in Glocca Morra"/"Heather on the Hill" is expertly performed. I love hearing her sing Harburg and Lerner's song, especially when she asks about the brook: "Does it still run down to Donny cove? Through Killybegs, Kilkerry, and Kildare?" Those words are as delicious as a Guinness beer!

Matt on *The Vault*

Barbra Streisand and Columbia Records have given the fans two volumes of *Release Me* albums that collected rare, unreleased songs from Barbra's vaults. And in 1991, they blessed us with the amazing *Just for the Record* box set, which included many never-before-heard tracks. Then in 2023, they gave us the *Yentl* deluxe release. I've mentioned several unreleased songs in the previous chapters, so this list is not complete. But what's wrong with wanting more?

The RCA Records Demo—Streisand recorded nine songs on a twelve-inch acetate as an audition for RCA Records in March 1962. Accompanied by piano, Barbra sang: "A Sleepin' Bee," "Have I Stayed Too Long at the Fair," "When the Sun Comes Out," "A Taste of Honey," "At the Codfish Ball," "Lover Come Back to Me," "Bewitched," "I Had Myself a True Love," and "Soon It's Gonna Rain."

The hungry i Performances—A few years ago I was contacted by a person who inherited the original recordings made by audio engineer Reice Hamel. He had restored and digitized those tapes of Streisand singing at the San Francisco club. They sound great, although Barbra's repertoire there closely resembled her songs at the Bon Soir.

A Very Informal History of the American Musical Theater: 1926-1966—Recorded live in London at the US Embassy, Streisand sang "Where Am I Going?" and an amazing (and long!) medley of songs from *Porgy and Bess*, plus "People."

An Evening with Barbra Streisand 1966—Columbia recorded the Philadelphia performance.

1967 Hollywood Bowl Concert—We know it was recorded because Columbia used Barbra's monologue from that evening on the *Central Park* album. But wouldn't it be cool to hear the whole show?

The Belle of 14th Street Soundtrack Album—There are studio recordings of the TV special's songs including "I Don't Care," "Put Your Arms Around Me Honey," and (my favorite!) "Everybody Loves My Baby."

"Think About Your Troubles"—Barbra's 1971 recording of this Harry Nilsson tune, I imagine, would be lovely, especially since Richard Perry produced it.

"Better"—Written by Ed Kleban and Marvin Hamlisch, this is a catchy, up-tempo song that Barbra recorded at least three versions of in the 1970s. Also unreleased from those sessions: a sexy song titled "Do Me Wrong, But Do Me."

"The Smile I Never Smiled"—The only song from the 1973 Bergman/Legrand sessions that hasn't been released.

1973 Daniel Ellsberg Fundraiser—Streisand sang with Marvin Hamlisch and a small combo of musicians. This performance deserves its own deluxe album release, with photos (John and Ringo of the Beatles attended!), and liner notes explaining the importance of the evening and the context of what Mr. Ellsberg was raising funds for (Google "The Pentagon Papers"). Songs sung that evening include: "I Don't Know Where I Stand," "I'll Get By," and "Long Ago and Far Away."

For Pete's Sake Theme Song—"Don't Let Him Down" isn't particularly feminist, but it's a fun ditty that has never appeared on an album.

The Broadway Album Outtakes—We can hear some of the jazzy "Can't Help Lovin' That Man" on the TV special. Let's hear the whole thing! I've also heard a snippet of "Show Me" from *My Fair Lady*, and I thought it sounded great. That one too, please!

Back to Broadway Outtakes—From the Rupert Holmes sessions, we still haven't heard "On My Own," "A Funny Thing Happened on My Way to Love," "Moonfall," and "Make Our Garden Grow."

"I Have a Love/One Hand One Heart"—The orchestrated version of the Mathis and Streisand song, please.

"It Doesn't Get Better Than This"—an alternate version of *The Mirror Has Two Faces* theme song that played during one of the movie's previews over the end credits. Sure it's a little less formed than the song that was released, but still sounds great.

The Unreleased Singles—That's my suggested title. Columbia could compile a collection of all the 45s that are rare or have never been on an album, all remastered for the digital age. Some of the tracks the label could include on this collection:

- The early 1962 singles with alternate arrangements
- "Funny Girl" (the 1964 up-tempo song) and "I Am Woman" (solo)
- "I Like Him," "Our Corner of the Night," and "He Could Show Me" ('60s singles that have never appeared on an album)
- "Look" and "Les enfants qui pleurant" (two singles from the *Je m'appelle Barbra* sessions not on any album)
- "Funny Girl" and "I'd Rather Be Blue" (movie singles with Peter Matz arrangements)
- "Frank Mills" from *Hair*
- "Before the Parade Passes By" (Matz arrangement)
- "On a Clear Day" (Matz arrangement)
- "Evergreen"—French, Italian, and Spanish versions
- "Ordinary Miracles" (studio version—Grammy nominated!)
- "Let's Start Right Now" and "Just Because" (outtakes from *A Love Like Ours*)
- "Come Rain or Come Shine" (Live, Australia)
- "Night of My Life" (12 inch)

Released: November 25, 2013
CD produced by: Barbra Streisand and Jay Landers
Recorded, edited, and mixed by: Dave Reitzas

Catalog Numbers:
88843 00758 9 (DVD/CD deluxe edition)
88843 00195 2 (CD-only Digipak)

Tracks:

1. I Remember Barbra #1 2. As If We Never Said Goodbye 3. Nice 'n' Easy/That Face 4. The Way He Makes Me Feel 5. Bewitched, Bothered And Bewildered 6. Didn't We 7. Marvin Hamlisch Intro 8. The Way We Were/ Through The Eyes Of Love 9. Jule Styne Intro 10. Being Good Isn't Good Enough 11. Rose's Turn/Some People/ Don't Rain On My Parade 12. I Remember Barbra #2 13. You're The Top 14. What'll I Do?/My Funny Valentine (with Chris Botti) 15. Lost Inside Of You (with Chris Botti) 16. Evergreen (with Chris Botti) 17. Jason Gould Intro 18. How Deep Is The Ocean? (with Jason Gould) 19. People 20. Here's To Life Intro 21. Here's To Life 22. Make Our Garden Grow 23. Some Other Time Intro 24. Some Other Time

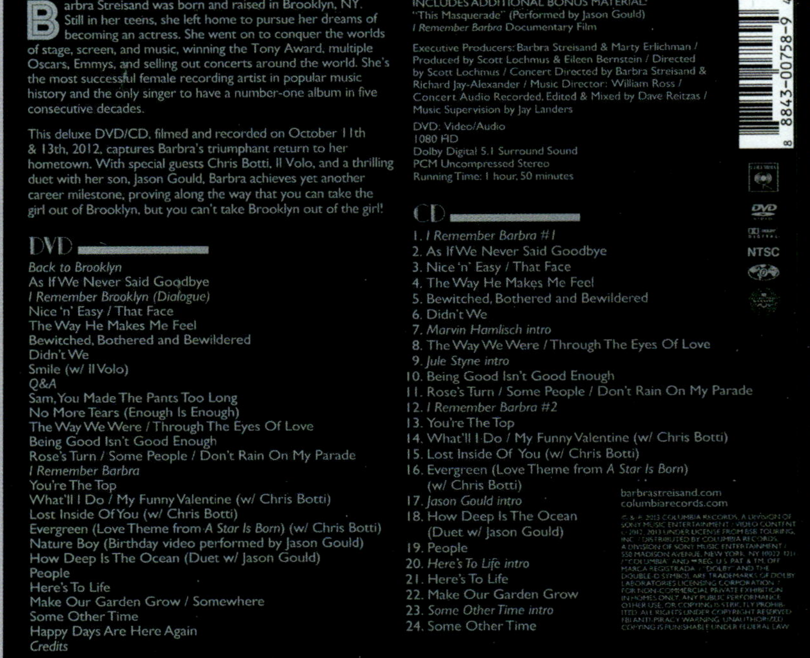

Barbra was booked at Barclays in Brooklyn. That very alliterative sentence describes why her 2012 concert tour, the fourth she had undertaken since 1994, was titled *Back to Brooklyn*—Barbra was returning to her hometown to perform for the first time since she used to sing on the stoops with the neighborhood children. The Barclays Center was the borough's fancy new 19,000-seat sports and entertainment venue located at the intersection of Atlantic and Flatbush Avenues. Barbra's October 11 and 13 shows were recorded by Columbia for this album and filmed as a TV special.

I have many misty watercolor mem'ries about this show and this tour, but first we'll discuss the actual CD, *Back to Brooklyn*. The full-color CD booklet contained a great layout with photos of Barbra's youth that honored the history and love for Brooklyn with quotes from famous authors about the borough. Jay Landers provided an excellent essay about working with Barbra, Marty Erlichman, and Richard Jay-Alexander assembling the show. "The conversation flowed," he wrote, explaining how they talked and ate food that Renata, Barbra's assistant, cooked. Streisand was "creating a Valentine to the people and places that helped shape her early worldview."

Columbia sold a deluxe edition of this album that contained the CD plus a DVD of the television special. The DVD contained two standout bonus features—Jason Gould's solo performance of the classic Leon Russell song "This Masquerade" and a documentary entitled "I Remember Barbra" featuring interviews and anecdotes with people who remembered Barbra as she was growing up in Brooklyn. Excerpts from the video were seen on the TV special, but also heard twice on the CD. By the way: if you buy the *Back to Brooklyn* TV show on iTunes, both videos are included at the end, after the credits.

This CD is an exceptional record of Barbra's 2012-2013 concerts. Since both the CD and DVD were recorded in Brooklyn, the only tracks missing from the audio recording is the duet with Il Divo ("Smile") and Barbra's "snippets" from the Q&A section—"Sam, You Made the Pants Too Long" and "Enough Is Enough." Also, Barbra's last song, "Happy Days," is not on the CD. You can see those on the DVD, though. Essentially, the video is one hour and fifty minutes; the CD is one hour, nineteen.

Matt on *Brooklyn*

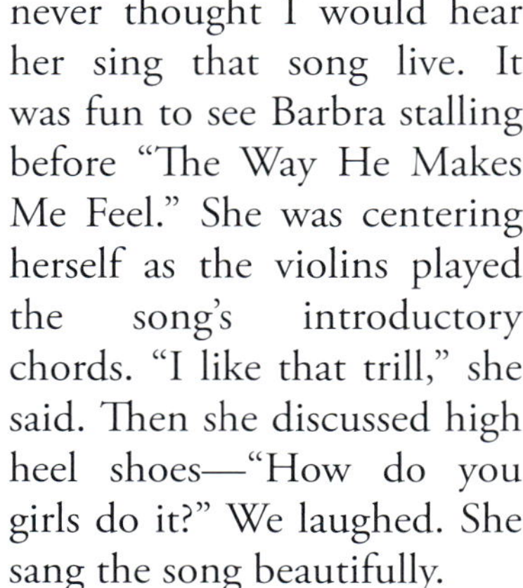

The North America and Europe 2012-2013 tour was a great time to be a Barbra Streisand fan. But it's the afternoon of October 5, 2012, that I will never forget. I was invited to Barbra's "friends and family" dress rehearsal, which took place in Philadelphia at the Liacouras Center, Temple University. There, Barbra's set and lights were assembled and her orchestra rehearsed. About eight hundred of us were invited, and I'll never forget hanging out with Broadway legend Donna McKechnie—I was her hero when I ran into the auditorium and managed to snag seats in the center, three rows from the stage. I have a background in theater and have participated in many dress rehearsals, so this one was not very different. Our job as an audience was to provide an honest and supportive response to Barbra and Richard Jay-Alexander's new show. They had conceived and rehearsed it for weeks, but now they needed to show it off to a real, live audience.

Almost immediately we witnessed a dress rehearsal snafu—the big Kabuki curtain that surrounded the orchestra failed to release and fall away during the overture. "Like I said, it's a rehearsal," Richard Jay-Alexander announced to the audience. "It worked fine yesterday," he said, and we all laughed. The truth is, we loved it! It was such a thrill to be eyewitnesses to this early version of Barbra's show. By the way, the Kabuki curtain was included only in the first few concerts and was dropped shortly after.

Barbra took the stage looking simply amazing and sang like a bird, even though I was told she had a sleepless night, worrying about the show. We heard the special Brooklyn lyrics to "As If We Never Said Goodbye" for the first time and laughed. I hope Barbra didn't hear me, but one word I kept saying out loud during the entire rehearsal was "Wow!" I was paralyzed by "Didn't We"—I'd never thought I would hear her sing that song live. It was fun to see Barbra stalling before "The Way He Makes Me Feel." She was centering herself as the violins played the song's introductory chords. "I like that trill," she said. Then she discussed high heel shoes—"How do you girls do it?" We laughed. She sang the song beautifully.

One of my most precious memories is that Barbra answered my question during the dress rehearsal Q&A! My "Ask Barbra" question was "Chocolate ice cream or angel food cake? Which one?" Barbra's answer: "Angel food cake with chocolate ice cream!"

Guess what my reaction was when the orchestra started vamping the intro to "Rose's Turn" from *Gypsy*? Oh, wow! I didn't think it was possible that Barbra would ever perform songs from her long-gestating movie version of the musical *Gypsy*. But here she was in Philadelphia performing it for us. Oh, wow.

Barbra sang "Bewitched" in the second act for this rehearsal, right after "You're the Top." It was charming when she sang the line "Couldn't sleep . . . " and rolled her eyes. "That's true," she said

Barbra came back onstage a beat late after Chris Botti's musical set. "Sorry, that was a very hard costume change! We may not be able to do it, but whatever," Barbra confessed. "It better be worth it, right? I was gonna try to curl my hair a little . . . forget it!" If I remember correctly, Barbra changed into a black version of the second-act gown. She was unable to fasten her sleeves and fussed with them on stage. "So we'll have to have hooks and eyes, girls, the old-time hooks and eyes," Barbra said aloud to her costumers who were backstage, referring to the simple, secure closure used on clothing.

We all knew "Make Our Garden Grow" was coming, because we heard the Brooklyn Youth Choir rehearsing as we waited outside the theater before the show started. It was a feat for Bill Ross to syncopate the choir with the orchestra, and they didn't get it right until the Brooklyn shows.

When it came time for opening night at Philadelphia's Wells Fargo Center, Barbra had already shuffled her set list, and opened the concert with "Being Good." My jaw dropped and I said out loud, "Wow."

Flash forward to the June 10, 2013, concert in Amsterdam at the Ziggo Dome. I was invited to attend this concert and meet Barbra backstage, so I made the travel arrangements despite my crazy schedule—wouldn't you? She opened with "On a

Clear Day" and knocked me out with her amazing voice. "Caffeine and cannabis, what a menu!" Streisand exclaimed about Amsterdam's coffee shops.

Afterward, I was taken backstage to meet Barbra. Robin Lipman was there—for those who don't know her, Robin attends every concert or live appearance that Barbra makes. Besides being so sweet, Robin has a zealous dedication to Barbra, and the term superfan describes her well. It was Robin's first time meeting her idol too, so we bonded backstage. After watching the show for a few hours, I needed a "bio break," so I used the bathroom in the green room. But it was a weird setup: one room had a toilet; another room had a sink. So shortly after closing the door, I heard Barbra come into the room and say, "Where's Matt?" Well, I was in the toilet. I stuck my head out the door. "Hi, Barbra!" There she was in person, so pretty! My god! "Did you wash your hands?" she asked, comically. Well, I had not washed them . . . there was no sink. I took a few steps into the sink room and washed up. Barbra made her way through the room, speaking to Robin and the people from the Anne Frank house, which Barbra had visited while in Amsterdam. Then it was my turn. She took my hand and thanked me for my website. She was so professional, beautiful, and warm. I was in heaven. And, frankly, tongue-tied. It's a lesson I learned the hard way—when you meet your idol, plan what you want to say. My in-the-moment wit failed me. So I will confess that I was not charming and was probably awkward. But Barbra is a lady and very sweet (and has met adoring fans for years), so it was all wonderful. "There are moments you remember all your life" is a lyric that applies here. I'll never forget my eighteen hours in the "Venice of the North" and finally meeting Barbra Streisand.

Columbia Records would never have been able to exhaustively record every performance to make a definitive recording of the entire tour, so it's worth mentioning what songs we *didn't* get after the Brooklyn shows.

- Barbra's sister, Roslyn Kind, joined the tour after Brooklyn and ended up singing duets with her at the other shows on "Happy Days" and "Smile." For those who wonder why Roz is not on the CD—she wasn't in the show yet!
- In Montreal, Barbra sang "If You Go Away (Ne Me Quitte Pas)."
- In later shows, Barbra and Richard Jay-Alexander added "My Man" as the act-two opener, preceded by a video clip from *Funny Girl* in which Fanny says goodbye to Nick.
- In Europe, Roslyn Kind joined Barbra onstage for a segment called "Diana's Daughters" in which they played an audio recording of their mother, Diana, singing the serenade from *The Student Prince*; then Roz and Barbra dueted.
- In Cologne and Israel, Barbra sang the complete "Woman in Love"; in Berlin and Israel she sang "Send in the Clowns."
- In Israel, Barbra sang "Hatikva."
- Yes, the Israel show was filmed as a possible television special.

My favorite part of the *Back to Brooklyn* concert is Barbra's opening set before Il Divo comes out. It's five songs, and it's almost a perfect Streisand miniconcert, so satisfying. She opens with "As If We Never Said Goodbye," then gives us living-legend vibes with the "Nice"/"Face" medley, followed by a "deep cut"—the first time she ever performed "The Way He Makes Me Feel" live! Then she tops that with a classic performance of "Bewitched" and hits it out of the ballpark with "Didn't We."

I'll also mention "Some Other Time," which has become one of my favorite newer songs of Barbra's. Video editors putting together an interview or clip package of Streisand's amazing career should remember this song as performed in Brooklyn. She holds the last note so long and so purely; it's a great way to end a video edit.

Back to Brooklyn was not only a career highlight for Barbra, but also a couple of years of great memories for me.

CD and vinyl released: September 16, 2014
Produced by: Kenny "Babyface" Edmonds and Walter Afanasieff
Executive producers: Barbra Streisand and Jay Landers
Recorded and mixed by: David Reitzas
Orchestra arranged by: Walter Afanasieff and William A. Ross
All songs conducted by: William A. Ross
Engineered by: David Retizas, Tyler Gordon, and Paul Boutin
Orchestras recorded by: Armin Steiner and Tommy Vicari
Art direction: Barbra Streisand and Gabrielle Raumberger/eposinc.com
Design: Teresa Kim
Cover photo of Ms. Streisand and inner photo of Ms. Streisand and Sammie: Russell James

Catalog Numbers:
88843 09114 2—CD
88875 00807 2 S1—deluxe Target CD
C-110615/88843 09114 1—LP (2-disc vinyl)
88875 01640 2—European deluxe CD

Tracks:

1. It Had To Be You (Michael Bublé)
2. People (Stevie Wonder)
3. Come Rain Or Come Shine (John Mayer)
4. Evergreen (Babyface)
5. New York State Of Mind (Billy Joel)
6. I'd Want It To Be You (Blake Shelton)
7. The Way We Were (Lionel Richie)
8. I Still Can See Your Face (Andrea Bocelli)
9. How Deep Is The Ocean (Jason Gould)
10. What Kind Of Fool (John Legend)
11. Somewhere (Josh Groban)
12. Love Me Tender (Elvis Presley)

Deluxe CD—Target Bonus Disc:
1. Lost Inside Of You (with Babyface) 2. I've Got A Crush On You (with Frank Sinatra) 3. I Finally Found Someone (with Bryan Adams) 4. I Won't Be The One To Let Go (Radio Version) (with Barry Manilow) 5. Guilty (with Barry Gibb)

Oy! This album! For months, there were "fake news" leaks, and fans were whipped into such a frenzy that Facebook looked like a frothy cappuccino. Insiders proclaimed Barbra will sing with Bette Midler! Beyoncé! Lady Gaga! Adele! I bit my tongue and practiced restraint because I knew that Barbra and her team had decided to make an album of duets with *men*.

"Everyone we asked was . . . busy," Streisand said. "[Beyoncé] had her people try to do a track of one of the songs from my movie *A Star Is Born*, and it just, we didn't have the time to finish it, to get it right," she said. "We had to release the album. Maybe someday we'll do a duet, because she's so great." Streisand added: "I'd love to sing with Rihanna, Adele. But I don't know all the other girls." (ABC News, 2014)

So Barbra went with the men singers who were available. "It took a long time to get it done," said Kenneth "Babyface" Edmonds, a coproducer on the album, three months before the album was released. "It's a beautiful, beautiful record. She's singing amazingly well, and it's been a fun project to do." (Graff, 2014)

Barbra chose Babyface because she liked the producing job he had done on the album *Waiting to Exhale*, the soundtrack to the movie with Whitney Houston. "Barbra said that she loved the songs, she loved my voice, and she'd like to do a duet with me one day," Edmonds said. (Barbra Streisand Official, 2014)

"Kenny is an amazing vocal arranger," Streisand explained. "Plus," said coproducer Walter Afanasieff, "he's added his own background vocals. Kenny has this famous background vocal sound; it just works so perfectly." (Barbra Streisand Official, 2014)

Afanasieff added: "We basically thought that it would be great to take her most famous songs that she's done and try to reinvent them, sort of, in new arrangements that fit a duet setting." (Barbra Streisand Official YouTube, 2014)

Edmonds created several demos for the reimagined Streisand standards going back to 2012. For Barbra's *A Star Is Born* song, "Lost Inside of You," Edmonds sang the male part on the demo, and Barbra ended up using his vocal as a bonus track on the Target version of the album.

Barbra recorded vocals for a duet with country artist Willie Nelson in 2012, and Jay Landers traveled to Pedernales Studio in Spicewood, Texas, to capture Nelson's vocals. Their song, "I'd Want It to Be You," was written by Steve Dorff, who admitted that he did rewrites because Barbra "wanted the song to be rewritten in more of a 'friendship' tone, as opposed to the traditional love song that it initially was intended to be." (Dorff, 2017)

So why did Blake Shelton end up singing the song on the final album? Dorff explained the whole story about Willie Nelson to CNN's Larry King: "It was a song that Barbra and her producer Jay Landers loved of mine. They asked me to rewrite it for a duet with Willie Nelson. The song was terrific. It just wasn't in Willie's wheelhouse." (Larry King, 2017)

Despite what Dorff said, Willie's and Barbra's recordings were finally combined on *Release Me 2*, and the result is lovely, with Willie providing some tender vocals.

Another track recorded for possible inclusion on the album was "When You Wish Upon a Star" with Mary J. Blige. After Barbra and her producers settled on the duets-with-men theme, the duet was dropped, and Blige included it on her 2013 holiday album, *A Mary Christmas*. *Billboard* hinted at this when it reported that "their pairing marks the first time Streisand has allowed a duet to be released first on the other artist's project." (Mitchell G., 2013)

The publicity for this album was relentless, and it was nice to see Columbia go all out for *Partners*. By August 2014, iTunes was giving fans an advance download of "New York State of Mind" with Billy Joel and "The Way We Were" with Lionel Richie if they preordered the album digitally. *Parade* magazine streamed an online preview of "Love Me Tender," Barbra's duet with Elvis Presley. After some rabid Elvis fans complained about the digital duet of Barbra and the King, the Presley estate posted a statement on the Graceland website stating, "Other fans see [the digital duet] as a welcome adaptation of a classic, made new again and shared with future generations of fans."

SiriusXM thrilled fans when it announced the launch of a Barbra Streisand Channel to air for almost a month starting in September 2014. Streisand even recorded special intros and promos for the channel.

Barbra's appearance on Jimmy Fallon's *Tonight Show*—her first guest spot on a late-night TV show since the 1960s—also probably assisted in hitting the sales of *Partners* out of the ballpark. Indeed, the album debuted on the *Billboard* 200 chart at number one, making Barbra the first act to achieve number-one albums in each of the last six decades. *Partners* sold 196,000 copies in the week ending September 21, according to Nielsen SoundScan. *Partners*, Streisand's tenth number-one album, recorded the largest sales week for a female artist in 2014 and chalked up Streisand's biggest sales numbers since *Higher Ground*, which had sold 402,000 units in a similar time frame. (Robinson, 2014)

On her official website, Barbra posted thanks, writing: "Being told that I've had #1 albums in six consecutive decades makes me feel truly blessed and grateful to have such loyal fans. I feel you rooting for me and I so appreciate all of your energy and support."

With over 500,000 units sold, the album was certified gold by the RIAA, Streisand's fifty-second gold award. "Barbra is the most recognized female in the history of gold and platinum album awards," said Cary Sherman, RIAA chairman and chief executive officer. "What an incredible feat. It's no surprise that she's returning to the top of the charts and earned yet another gold album. We congratulate Barbra on her continued extraordinary success." (RIAA, 2014)

Then, on January 20, 2015, the RIAA certified *Partners* platinum, with over one million units sold. Again, this was a milestone: Streisand's thirty-first platinum album—the most for any female recording artist in RIAA history. (Columbia Records, 2015)

Matt on *Partners*

The concept of Streisand reinterpreting her classic songs with male duet partners was not very exciting to me, I must admit. After hearing the album, I felt there were some home runs and some misses.

Home runs: "It Had to Be You" with Michael Bublé, "Come Rain or Come Shine" with John Mayer, "The Way We Were" with Lionel Richie, "I Still Can See Your Face" with Andrea Bocelli, "What Kind of Fool" with John Legend, and "Somewhere" with cutie-patootie Josh Groban.

There is sheer joy in "It Had to Be You" with the eager Bublé. We don't get to hear Barbra in a big band soundscape very often, so this track is most welcome, and most played by me. By the way, Bublé puts on an enjoyable concert and is a joy to see live.

Just a few months after their duet debuted, Barbra taped an appearance on Bublé's Christmas TV special. They sang the song again, but this time with special holiday lyrics that Jay Landers penned. Barbra intoned: "*Winter dreams like I've always had could be . . . should be . . . makin' me glad. Color me blue; Here without you Christmas day.*"

John Mayer and Barbra Streisand? It shouldn't have worked, but it did. It's one of the best tracks, with Barbra giving us some soulful singing. I'll throw in my two cents again too: Mayer is a wonder to see live. He's one of the best guitarists playing these days. I even sat through his gig with Dead & Company—the band comprising former Grateful Dead members Bob Weir, Mickey Hart, and Bill Kreutzmann, with Mayer playing guitar and singing some of the vocals. That music is not my favorite, but I was impressed to see such guitar virtuosity by John Mayer. Wowza. Barbra and John create magic on "Come Rain or Come Shine." They even seem a little turned on by each other, which is sexy and totally comes through on the track!

"The Way We Were" with Lionel Richie is probably my favorite on the whole album. This is a track that is a remake of a classic but works as a complete rethinking of the song and its arrangement. It doesn't stray too far from the original, but it elevates the song to a different level. First, there's Richie's vocals, which recall such earlier hits as "Endless Love" and "Hello." Then there is Babyface's arrangement, which is so fresh! Barbra even comes up with some new vocal lines to surprise us, especially on "whenever weeeeeeee remember" at the end of the song. "The Way We Were" with Richie is so good, I just can't stop listening to it.

"I Still Can See Your Face" stands out to me as an underappreciated track that I should be playing more often. Bernie Herms, Charlie Midnight, and Jay Landers wrote this one, and it's a beautiful, bespoke song crafted for two amazing talents who had wanted to sing together for many years. The song combines classical sensibilities with pop music refinement. "I close my eyes and realize I've never let you goooooo," Barbra and Bocelli sing.

John Legend's vocals on "What Kind of Fool" are impeccable, and the whole redo is spectacular. I won't forget Barry Gibb's vocals on the original, but Legend brings a modern sensibility to this song that I appreciate. Afanasieff and Babyface have given the song an orchestral introduction that plays like a flashback in a movie—very cinematic! "Their mutual respect was evident from the start," Kenny Edmonds said about Legend and Streisand. "When Barbra heard the passion in John's vocal performance, it truly inspired the way she shaped her own vocals. As a record producer, sitting in the studio hearing these two magical voices playing off each other, pouring through the speakers, was an incredible feeling. There really are no words to explain the kind of emotion you feel when you realize you're capturing that kind of lightning in a bottle." (Boilen, 2014)

"Somewhere" on *Partners* is my new favorite version of the song. Streisand has stunned most of us over the years when she belts this song out in concert or in a music video. But the 2014 "Somewhere" is sensitive and subtle, with Barbra and Josh Groban giving us beautiful harmony and thoughtful vocals. It's kinder and gentler, this "Somewhere."

Now, as for the misses: I hate the patter at the end of "New York State of Mind" with Billy Joel and Barbra discussing Chinese food. I don't like that Barbra begins the song with "Well" either. Those are two edits I would have made from the start. After those, we must discuss the multiple key changes. Joel and Streisand do not sing this song in the same key, and some of the modulations during the song are too obvious. I do like Afanasieff's Gershwin-esque piano during this song, however.

The Elvis duet was manufactured in the editing room . . . and I can't get over that. Presley died in 1977, and there have been over forty years of impersonators and tribute shows. Barbra delivers some beautiful vocals on this duet, but the magic trick of resuscitating the dead by using technology doesn't work for me here.

"People" is fun, and Barbra even sang a bit of this bossa nova remake during her 2019 concerts, but she and Stevie Wonder just don't click for me. Again, I hear more modulations to account for the different keys these two singers sing in.

It was exciting that Barbra had such a big hit with *Partners*, even though she's made better albums before and since. She followed a template laid out by singers like Frank Sinatra and Tony Bennett, who, late in their careers, released similar albums pairing them with vibrant duet partners. Barbra gave it her own twist but stayed in the middle of the road as well.

CD and vinyl released: August 26, 2016
Conceived and directed by: Barbra Streisand
Produced by: Walter Afanasieff and Barbra Streisand
Arranged by: Walter Afanasieff, William Ross, and Barbra Streisand
Recorded and mixed by: David Reitzas
Dialogue written and adapted by: Barbra Streisand
A & R: Jay Landers
Cover photo: Russell James
Art direction: Barbra Streisand
Photo research: Kim Skalecki

Catalog Numbers:
88985 33975 2—CD
88985 35096 2—deluxe Target CD
C-173343—Barnes & Noble LP (lavender-colored vinyl)
C-173337—LP (regular vinyl)
88985 35355 2—European deluxe CD

Tracks:

1. At The Ballet (Anne Hathaway and Daisy Ridley)
2. Loving You (Patrick Wilson)
3. Who Can I Turn To? (When Nobody Needs Me) (Anthony Newley)
4. The Best Thing That Ever Has Happened (Alec Baldwin)
5. Any Moment Now (Hugh Jackman)
6. Anything You Can Do (Melissa McCarthy)
7. Pure Imagination (Seth MacFarlane)
8. Take Me To The World (Antonio Banderas)
9. I'll Be Seeing You/I've Grown Accustomed To Her Face (Chris Pine)
10. Climb Ev'ry Mountain (Jamie Foxx)

Deluxe CD: Target and European Version (solo tracks): I Didn't Know What Time It Was, Not A Day Goes By, Fifty Percent, Losing My Mind

For her follow-up to the very successful album *Partners*, Streisand went back to Broadway for a third time. Streisand compiled theater songs that she would integrate with original dialogue to set up the songs—a concept that ultimately played like listening to a Broadway cast album.

Walter Afanasieff was back producing *Encore* for Streisand. Shortly after demos were created, David Reitzas recorded the dialogue for the songs at Grandma's House on Streisand's California property. "That was the early stages of creating a kind of dialogue road map," Reitzas explained. "She performed all the parts of the female vocals, and Walter or her husband [James Brolin] did the male vocal parts."

The recording of final vocals began on February 12, 2016, at Woodshed Recording. Many of the promotional videos and interviews for this album were filmed at the craftsman-style studio, situated on a picturesque piece of property in Malibu, California. Jamie Foxx and Streisand recorded "Climb Ev'ry Mountain" first on February 17. "At the Ballet," "Loving You," "Pure Imagination," "Losing My Mind," and "Who Can I Turn To?" followed.

The virtual duet with Anthony Newley, who died in 1999, was Streisand's idea. "I've heard that David Bowie was very influenced by Tony Newley," Streisand stated. "I was doing *Funny Girl* and he was doing *The Roar of the Greasepaint*, and I met him that year and thought he was fantastic. Then we became friends." In her memoir, Streisand was less coy; she and Newley had an affair. Newley even wrote a song about Streisand called "Too Much Woman." When Streisand was reminded about it, she said, "I'm proud of that song. I'm proud that he wrote it for me." (Iley, 2016)

Daisy Ridley, the star of *Star Wars: The Force Awakens*, was in town for the Oscars, so she recorded her duet with Streisand on Saturday, February 27. They also discussed the role of Gypsy Rose Lee in Barbra's then-in-development movie of *Gypsy*.

Alec Baldwin and Hugh Jackman were recorded at MSR Studios in New York; Chris Pine's vocals were done at Angel Studios, London; and Antonio Banderas worked at AIR Studios, London.

In early April 2016, ten of the songs' final arrangements were recorded at the Barbra Streisand Scoring Stage in Culver City, California, with Bill Ross conducting the orchestra using movie streamers to keep in time with the score. (For "Anything You Can Do," the team kept the original orchestral mock-up from the demo.)

Recording *Encore* wasn't always a high-tech effort—sometimes the iPhone Voice Memos app was used! "There were a couple of times where [Barbra] had a vocal idea that she had recorded into her iPhone," Reitzas told *Sound on Sound*. "I would put these ideas in the session as markers so we could later record those ideas properly on her microphone, but when we later tried to re-record some of those ideas, she was like: 'No, I like my reading of what I did on the iPhone better, so let's just use that.' So you have to make it work. Obviously, you use things like EQ and compression, or maybe you put a cymbal roll right before or after to try to trick the ear into not noticing or focusing on the sonic difference of the part I am trying to keep in there from the phone recording." (Tingen, 2016)

Another surprise surrounding this album was the May 16, 2016, announcement that Streisand would do a small, nine-city concert tour that would include songs from *Encore: Movie Partners Sing Broadway*. "Every ticket purchased online includes a CD of Streisand's new album," it was announced.

Meanwhile, Streisand and Reitzas worked together at Grandma's House to complete the final mixes of the songs. Final mastering was done at Gateway Mastering in Maine.

Columbia had other exciting promotions for the album: SiriusXM's Streisand Channel returned from September 6–October 3, 2016; Streisand appeared with Alec Baldwin on Jimmy Fallon's *Tonight Show*, singing the Sondheim duet "The Best Thing That Ever Has Happened"; NPR streamed the album on its website; Streisand did an interview with NPR; Patrick Wilson interviewed Streisand onstage in New York for a special SiriusXM town hall; and Streisand did a handful of television interviews.

Superfans should note that a solo version of "Loving You" was released as a digital bonus track to customers who bought Streisand concert tickets on the StubHub website. Its orchestration and vocal differ from those on the album's duet with Patrick Wilson.

Encore: Movie Partners Sing Broadway was Barbra Streisand's *eleventh* number one album on the *Billboard* 200 chart. In this era of digital downloads, Streisand is still a big "physical media" seller—126,000 of the 148,000 albums sold were CDs and LPs (aided by Target's exclusive edition with bonus tracks). Also, some of *Encore*'s album sales were bundled with her concert tickets. *Billboard* noted: "Only those albums that are actively redeemed by a customer count towards the charts."

Encore was nominated for a Grammy in the usual category: Best Traditional Pop Vocal Album. Willie Nelson's album of Gershwin songs won that year.

Matt on *Encore*

The version of this album to own is the Target Deluxe CD (or one of the Europe discs that contained the same tracks). On the Target CD, we're rewarded with four solo tracks by Streisand, and each one is iconic and timeless.

"I Didn't Know What Time It Was," a Rodgers and Hart tune, is exactly what Streisand should be singing at this point in her career. She managed to incorporate it into most of her concert tour too. It's one of my new favorites.

"Not a Day Goes By" is from one of my most cherished Stephen Sondheim musicals, *Merrily We Roll Along*, which tells its protagonists' story backward, starting when they are adult and cynical about their lives and ending with them as their young, idealistic selves

What Streisand has wisely done on this record is choose the *other* version of "Not a Day Goes By," which is rarely recorded. I am most familiar with Bernadette Peters's interpretation of "Not a Day Goes By"—but she's singing the sad, breakup version of the song that appears early in the show. By the way, Bernadette always slays me when she sings this song. Tears! So moving!

Back to Barbra. Her "Not A Day Goes By" comes from *later* in the show, because Sondheim is telling the story *backward*, ya know what I mean? So, in *Merrily*, the second act "Not a Day Goes By" is a love song, sung with idealistic longing. It was a dream come true for me to hear Barbra finally record this song.

Then there's "Fifty Percent." Many fans thought she'd record it for her Marilyn and Alan Bergman album—the Bergmans wrote it with Billy Goldenberg for a show called *Ballroom*.

"Losing My Mind" is the fourth solo track on the Target CD, and it's a Sondheim classic from *Follies*. Again, I'd always wished to hear Streisand sing this song, and she did us one better: she included it live in her concerts against a moody, red theatrical curtain backdrop.

As for the duets on *Encore*, I cannot resist "Loving You" with Patrick Wilson, who is just so darn handsome . . . and kind! When I went backstage after the Miami concert in 2016, I was chatting with Jamie Foxx and Barbra and noticed Patrick Wilson in the corner. I became bold as we were taking photos. "Patrick Wilson, I love you!" I called across the room to him. We invited him over, and now I have a photo of me, Barbra, Jamie Foxx, and Patrick Wilson!! As we chatted between camera snaps, I told Patrick and Barbra that I didn't know the melody of "Loving You" very well, but that it had now become my favorite song. And yes—Patrick and Barbra sang "Loving You" live at that show, which was taped for Netflix. There was a technical snafu at the beginning of the song, and there was no time for retakes, so that's most likely why it wasn't included.

I was blown away when I learned that the opening song of the album was "At the Ballet" from *A Chorus Line*. What?!? Now, this was a song I never suspected Barbra would sing. We all know Oscar winner Anne Hathaway can sing (and she sounds lovely here, while being majorly pregnant at the time of recording), but Daisy Ridley is lovely as well, with a throaty singing voice. I enjoy Barbra's notes on "At the Ballet." I know that song backward and forward from the Michael Bennett original Broadway cast album, so it's nice that Barbra gives us the melody and then some. Need I point out that Barbra's character in the song, Sheila, is auditioner number twenty-four?

I also love to sing along with "The Best Thing That Ever Has Happened," her duet with Alec Baldwin from Sondheim's last produced musical, *Road Show*, which was formerly titled *Wise Guys*, then *Bounce*.

At first, I felt Chris Pine's vocal on the duet "I'll Be Seeing You/I've Grown Accustomed to Her Face" was affected and "put on" and I didn't like that. But I've grown accustomed to Pine's voice. The truth is, I didn't really know what Chris Pine sounds like singing, but I now accept his moody, stylish vocal. Also, the medley is so well-crafted; these songs belong together and tell a dramatic story. And who doesn't enjoy a bossa nova beat, which comes in on "I've Grown Accustomed to Her Face"?

Hearing Jamie Foxx and Barbra discuss achieving dreams is better than any self-help seminar or silly Tony Robbins speech. Then they knock the wind out of us with their dynamic and passionate singing on "Climb E'vry Mountain." Of course, everyone who saw Jamie join Barbra on stage in LA, Brooklyn, and Florida was dazzled by him. Barbra obviously adores him and enjoys singing this song with him. Fantastic!

I don't have a lot of criticism for *Encore*. It's a very well-produced album and more likable than *Partners*. I would aim any criticism at "Anything You Can Do" with Melissa McCarthy, who is adorable. I just hate the synthesized orchestra, which you can hear from the first digital toots of the trumpets. Also, there's something about the notes or harmonies on "Take Me to the World" that are not pleasant to my ears. I may be too biased by the Bernadette Peters and Mandy Patinkin recording, which was the only good recording of that song for years.

Seth MacFarlane can certainly sing, but I like Barbra's live, solo version of "Pure Imagination" better. Sorry, Seth!

My last complaint is simply that the title and concept of this album are so convoluted! *Encore: Movie Partners Sing Broadway* is a mouthful, but I get it—these movie stars helped sell this album. I'm sure Barbra enjoyed assembling the actors and being a director on these tracks, which are quite theatrical.

For my money, though, the Target CD is the one to own. Get it!!

Released: December 8, 2017
Produced by: Barbra Streisand and Jay Landers
Recorded and mixed by: Dave Reitzas
Recorded at: American Airlines Arena (Miami) (December 5, 2016)
Art direction: Barbra Streisand
Design: Jeri Heiden, SMOG Design, Inc.
Liner notes: Jay Landers
Photography: Russell James, Kevin Mazur, Don Hunstein, Steve Schapiro, Richard Corman, Dave Hogan
Mastered by: Eric Boulanger at The Bakery (Culver City, California)
Management: Marty Erlichman

Catalog Numbers:
19075803512 (deluxe 2-CD—Digipak)
19075803502 (1-CD)

Tracks:

DISC 1: ACT I

1. People Overture (Entrance) 2. The Way We Were 3. Introductory Remarks 4. Everything 5. Being At War With Each Other 6. No More Tears (Enough Is Enough) 7. Evergreen 8. You Don't Bring Me Flowers 9. Being Alive 10. Directing Movies 11. Papa, Can You Hear Me?

DISC 2: ACT II

1. Pure Imagination 2. Making Encore 3. Who Can I Turn To? (When Nobody Needs Me) (with Anthony Newley) 4. Losing My Mind 5. Isn't This Better? 6. How Lucky Can You Get? 7. Don't Rain On My Parade 8. People 9. Climb Ev'ry Mountain (with Jamie Foxx) 10. Happy Days Are Here Again 11. Jingle Bells? 12. With One More Look At You 13. I Didn't Know What Time It Was

Bonus tracks:
By The Way, Children Will Listen,
Everything Must Change

Barbra: The Music . . . The Mem'ries . . . The Magic! is Barbra Streisand's ninth live album for Columbia Records. It is also the album of record for Streisand's triumphant concert tour of the same name in 2016. This collection captures Barbra culminating her thirteen-city tour in Miami on December 5, 2016. It was hard for some of Barbra's fans to understand the Netflix concert deal! To date, this concert is still streaming on Netflix, with no physical media planned for release (DVD or Blu-ray). The only way to see it is to subscribe to Netflix—or go to eBay and order one of the thousands of DVD screeners that were sent to Emmy voters and are up for sale. (Ssshh! You didn't hear that here.)

Devotees were grateful, then, when Columbia announced a CD audio version of the Netflix show. It was released as a one- or double-disc version. The deluxe CD had a sticker that touted "5 extra tracks." Those five tracks, which do not appear on the standard CD, are "Jingle Bells?," "With One More Look at You," and the three bonus tracks: "By the Way," "Children Will Listen," and "Everything Must Change." It should be noted that these last three were performed in Miami but not included on the Netflix show. The deluxe CD also includes three talking tracks that are not on the one-CD version: "Introductory Remarks," "Directing Movies," and "Making Encore." *Barbra: The Music . . . The Mem'ries . . . The Magic!* was nominated for a Grammy Award in 2018 in the category Best Traditional Pop Vocal Album. Willie Nelson's album *My Way* was the winner that year.

Matt on *The Music*

This album is all about Richard Jay-Alexander and his work with Barbra to create this amazing amalgamation of songs that somehow manages to appeal to her most ardent fans as well as those who pay the high-ticket prices to hear Barbra's hits. The concert's theme was based on Barbra revising music history books by becoming the only recording artist with number-one albums in each of the last six decades—the sixties through the twenty-tens. The set list for these shows was practically perfect, pleasing almost everyone.

Yes, of course! Open the show with "The Way We Were," a song that becomes the theme of the entire evening. "Everything" from *A Star Is Born* is somewhat of a deep cut but was an audience favorite at all the concerts I attended. If the audience didn't know "Being at War with Each Other," then it definitely responded to its immediateness. Fun concert story: at all the concerts I attended, there was a fan stage left in the bleachers who shouted out every time Barbra sang "Everything" something like, "Thank you, Barbra, for singing 'Everything!'" The one time she didn't yell this out was at the Netflix taping. Dammit.

I'm happy we got a solo version of Streisand singing "Pure Imagination," and it's a solid vocal too. I'm not dismissing Seth MacFarlane, who sang it with Barbra on *Encore*. I just prefer Barbra singing it solo.

It's miraculous that Barbra even recorded the Sondheim classic "Losing My Mind." But then she went further and included it as a major number during her concert tour.

For me, this entire concert was elevated because Richard Jay-Alexander managed to finally work in *Funny Lady* songs. The movie sequel, with original songs by Kander and Ebb, is totally unappreciated. There's some amazing acting, singing, and production in that film. Anyway, Richard Jay-Alexander felt that "How Lucky Can You Get?" was Streisand's "Rose's Turn," and he had wanted her to sing it in previous tours. When she added "Isn't This Better?" from *Funny Lady*, I was *verklempt*!

"Isn't This Better?" is a simple but complicated song written for the character of Fanny Brice, who is confused about her easy relationship with Billy Rose versus her complicated and emotional romance with Nick Arnstein. As I listen to the track right now, I am grateful I was able to hear Barbra sing this song live several times, including this recording. I honestly thought "Isn't This Better?" was a song she'd never sing live. What a gift! Cabaret singers should note this song for their acts. It's really such a well-written, simple, but melodic song. And then Barbra transitions into "How Lucky Can You Get?" from *Funny Lady*.

My mind was blown. How was this possible? My geekiest Barbra Streisand wish came true. She sang this theatrical powerhouse of a song that I had admired for ages live in concert, sounding strong and sassy.

Readers should know that *The Music* is the only Barbra Streisand album to have an E rating (for explicit) on Apple Music. During her patter for "How Lucky," Barbra says that being famous is "fan-fucking-tastic." This was her ninth live album released over the past seventeen years.

CD and vinyl released: November 2, 2018
Executive producers: Barbra Streisand and Jay Landers
Recorded and mixed by: Jochem van der Saag
Orchestra recorded by: Shawn Murphy, Obie O'Brien, JC Monterossa ("Lady Liberty"), Steve Churchyard ("Don't Lie to Me" and "The Rain Will Fall")
Engineering: Tyler Gordon, Adrian Bradford, Dmytro Gordon, Keith Gretlein ("Don't Lie to Me" and "The Rain Will Fall")
Mastered by: Vlado Meller
Art direction: Barbra Streisand
Design: Jeri Heiden, Smog Design, Inc.
Photography: Russell James

Catalog Numbers:
19075895482 (CD)
C217765 (LP)

Side One:

1. What's On My Mind
2. Don't Lie To Me
3. Imagine/What A Wonderful World
4. Walls
5. Lady Liberty

Side Two:

6. What The World Needs Now
7. Better Angels
8. Love's Never Wrong
9. The Rain Will Fall
10. Take Care Of This House
11. Happy Days Are Here Again

"It's always a challenge to find songs that tick all the boxes for Barbra," Jay Landers shared. For *Walls*, Jay and Barbra discussed "how few artists today were making political statements through their music." Jay was referencing recording artists like Bob Dylan and Marvin Gaye—Gaye, of course, was an amazing performer who sang about "What's Going On" (literally). Jay liked that Barbra said, "I should do an album about what's on my mind" and thought that would be a great song title, if not the album's title. Eventually, Barbra, Jay, Carole Bayer Sager, and Jonas Myrin wrote the song "What's on My Mind," which ended up opening the album.

Walls is an album I find myself listening to more often than I thought I would. For starters, Barbra sounds amazing at seventy-six years old. It's easy to nitpick "the voice," but there are so few examples of singers still producing such beautiful tones over the age of seventy. I can think of Johnny Mathis and the late Barbara Cook—both delivering beautiful vocals into their eighties.

The songs of *Walls*—both newly written for the album and some covers—grew on me. *Walls* did not do well on the charts, selling fewer units than usual for Streisand.

Once Columbia released the single "Don't Lie to Me" ahead of the album, the publicity narrative got out of hand, and there was no going back. In a divided and emotional America, *Walls* was being touted as "Barbra's anti-Trump album." I would argue that it's so much more.

First, there's the obvious fact that Streisand is a lifelong Democrat and liberal. No matter where you fall on the political spectrum, America's forty-fifth president was a polarizing figure. And *Walls* was no more a "protest album" than *Higher Ground* was a "spiritual album."

The expression "the whole is greater than the sum of its parts" applies to *Walls* (and, frankly, most of Streisand's albums!). If you want to talk about anti-Trump songs, only two address him specifically: "Don't Lie to Me" and "The Rain Will Fall." Both quote Trump's pithy media soundbites. Streisand pointed out in a couple of interviews that "Rain" could also be interpreted as "Reign."

You must acknowledge that once the media jumped on the "anti-Trump" album wagon, even Streisand's staunchest fans balked. Some fans simply want to enjoy Streisand singing and not have to digest her politics. Others, who agreed with her politics, were already burned out by the political theatrics in this country and didn't want to listen to Streisand sing about them too.

But here's where the adage "Don't throw the baby out with the bathwater" applies to this album. There are nine other tracks to enjoy on *Walls* that aren't specifically political. In fact, Streisand cowrote three of the album's new songs, and four new songs were commissioned from songwriters Carole Bayer Sager, Desmond Child, Steve Dorff, and others.

"Better Angels" is a typical power ballad produced by David Foster, and Barbra belts her heart out, singing strong and delivering the powerful message of the song. It's hard to blame David Foster here: "Better Angels" is fantastic! The lyric was inspired by President Abraham Lincoln's inaugural address in 1861, and Jay told me that for a while it was considered as the title song but made the album sound like it would be like *Higher Ground*, an album of spiritual songs. "The lyric credit for the song really should go to Carole Bayer Sager, Jonas Myrin, Jay Landers . . . and Abe Lincoln," said Jay.

Desmond Child's "Lady Liberty" is a perfect statement for Streisand. Child wrote an inspiring and yet complicated melody for Streisand to sing, including some age-defying high notes that Streisand hits with aplomb. Child is most known for his rock songs: "Livin' la Vida Loca," "You Give Love a Bad Name," and more. But for Streisand Jay said Desmond "was thinking about Barbra going past the Statue of Liberty in *Funny Girl*. He had the idea of looking at the tablets—'give me your weak, your tired,' and all that."

Desmond Child wrote in his memoir, *Livin' on a Prayer: Big Songs Big Life*, that he saw the *Funny Girl* movie while he was young in Ecuador. "I swooned as she sang 'Don't Rain on My Parade' from the helm of a tugboat passing the Statue of Liberty. The son of an immigrant, I was moved by that symbol's aspirational attitude."

Desmond [pictured to the right] told a charming tale in his book of presenting the demo of "Lady Liberty" to Barbra at Grandma's House. He wrote: "We discussed the key and decided that the body of the song would sound best a half step down from the demo. At the same time, a challenging D flat above high C in full voice was required on the last syllable of the word 'remember.' When she expressed concern, I said that singing at the top of her range would give the song the dramatic angst it needed. I reminded her that in her 'People' she had sung the high notes in full voice two half steps higher. She laughed and said, 'Yes, but I was twenty years old!'"

On the day they recorded the song, he wrote: "She immediately sang through the entire song a few times. She had it down. She then decided to concentrate on perfecting each section at a time. She did so in no more than four takes. With anyone else, I'd require dozens of takes and be forced to spend endless mind-boggling days piecing those takes together into a reconstituted vocal. Not with Barbra."

Streisand moved us all with the "Imagine/ Wonderful World" medley. "Lyrically these two songs could be complimentary for each other," Jay said. One problem, however: as the musicians waited onstage to record the songs, Jay didn't have the rights. Yoko Ono, John Lennon's widow, "is known to be extremely litigious about the misuse of John's songs." Although one would think Ms. Ono would be excited that Barbra wanted to record their song, Jay had to write her a letter explaining the medley and use of it. According to Jay, Yoko gave permission for Barbra to record the song because she and John Lennon loved *The Way We Were*. On top of that, John and Yoko were impressed when they heard Barbra had been kind enough to reach out to a colleague's dying daughter. For those reasons, Yoko Ono granted the rights for Barbra to include "Imagine" on this album.

Matt on *Walls*

Whoever brought "Take Care of This House" to Barbra's attention should be applauded. It manages to check so many boxes for a Streisand album: obscure Broadway musical; political sensibility; iconic American composer and lyricist. "Take Care" comes from a 1976 musical called *1600 Pennsylvania Avenue*, which was a flop, playing only thirteen performances. The Leonard Bernstein and Alan Jay Lerner musical told the story of the first one hundred years in the White House through the eyes of its presidents and staff. Streisand stressed, "The lyrics articulate the obligation that every occupant of the Oval Office has to uphold the values of our nation." (Streisand, Take Care of This House [Behind the Song], 2018)

"Take Care of This House" continues the tradition started decades ago of Streisand choosing obscure and interesting material over just recording well-known, popular songs. William Ross's arrangement deserves praise as well. His work with Streisand is always tasteful and cinematic.

The remake of "Happy Days Are Here Again," another inspired William Ross orchestration done in tandem with Streisand, is a curious choice to close the album considering she's sung it (mostly live) about eight times before on recordings. Those recordings are mostly positive, happy takes on the song. But on the *Walls* version, Barbra does not shirk dark emotions; "Happy Days" is a dirge. "I wanted a kind of symphonic story of dread," she said about the arrangement. (Bruner, 2018) It sounds like she weeps at the end of the track.

One can only assume that much thought went into whether to remake this chestnut for *Walls*. Streisand's choice was to include it, stressing the dramatic and mournful. *Walls*, the album, does not have a happy ending, but it certainly makes you think about things.

STREISAND COLLABORATORS

WALTER AFANASIEFF

Walter Afanasieff (called "Walter A." by his friends) is a Grammy-winning, Oscar-nominated record producer who's worked with amazing singers like Idina Menzel, Lionel Richie, and Mariah Carey. Afanasieff has produced, performed, written, or cowritten some of the most iconic tunes of all time, including songs for Whitney Houston, *Aladdin*'s "A Whole New World," and *Titanic*'s "My Heart Will Go On."

With that background out of the way, it's obvious that Barbra is a Walter A. fan, considering how involved he's been in her recent recording projects. "He's very gifted," Barbra stated, calling him a "beautiful melody writer." (Lynch, 2021)

Afanasieff began working with Streisand in 1994 when he produced and arranged both "Ordinary Miracles" and the then-unreleased classic "Sweet Forgiveness." Next, Walter A. cowrote and produced "Tell Him" for Streisand and Dion with Linda Thompson and David Foster. Afanasieff clarified his different way of recording artists: "He has a way of being the boss in the room," Walter said about David Foster. "I have a more gentle approach with my artists. I'll never push them, I'll never fight with them, I'll never argue with them, I'll never have any of that. Sometimes, David has that sort of approach and I'm not really a fan of that. I'm not going to make something out of frustration or anger. Artists are very, very temperamental. What they're doing into that microphone is going to be their legacy for the whole, entire course of time." (Hot Takes & Deep Dives, 2020)

He next worked with Streisand on the songs "The Island" on *A Love Like Ours* and "I Won't Be the One to Let Go," the duet with Barry Manilow on *Duets*.

Afanasieff slid into the driver's seat, however, when he coproduced Barbra's 2014 album, *Partners*, with Kenny "Babyface" Edmonds. *Partners* sold over one million units and put Barbra in the history books for having a number-one album in each of the last six decades. *Partners* was not only popular, but also something of a late-career triumph for her saleswise. Afanasieff came back again to produce *Encore: Movie Partners Sing Broadway*, but it's his work on *Walls* that is exemplary, with Afanasieff producing many of the tracks and even cowriting one of the songs.

"Her powerful knowledge of herself, her artistry . . . Nobody knows better than she knows," Afanasieff stated. "It's such a hoot working with her because to this day I still pinch myself." (Hot Takes & Deep Dives, 2020)

DECADE 10 ENCORE

"Where has the time all gone to? Haven't done half the things we want to. Oh well…"

I'm left with "scattered pictures" of the 2010s, which seemed like a decade that went by quickly. As for Barbra in that decade:

Ten albums: two studio solo albums, three live recordings, two collections of new duets, two "hits" collections, and one from the vaults. She sang a single line in an all-star recording of "We Are the World 25 for Haiti." Meanwhile, the American-Canadian DJ duo Duck Sauce released a hot dance track with the title and repeated chorus"Barbra Streisand." Barbra sang at the Grammys and the night before at the MusiCares event. Using outtakes from the original recording sessions of "Somewhere," Barbra contributed a duet with Jackie Evancho to her album *Dream With Me*. Meanwhile, also during the tens, Barbra's contract with Columbia Records was up for renewal, and Marty told *The Hollywood Reporter*, "I'm not peddling Barbra. I will stay with Columbia unless I can't make a deal, then I'll go elsewhere." (They made a deal, and Columbia signed Barbra again in 2012). Willie Nelson told the press he wanted to record with Barbra (then, about four years later, he did, but it wasn't released until seven years later). Barbra told the press at an event with Sting that she'd like to duet with him. "I think our voices would go well together," she said. (They sang together fourteen years later). Barbra commenced a ten-city North American concert tour, then went abroad for a five-city European (and Israel) tour. There was some sadness this decade when several of Barbra's musical collaborators passed away this decade, including Marvin Hamlisch, Phil Ramone, and Mort Lindsey. Several of Barbra's movie projects passed away too, as she was unable to secure funding for productions of *Gypsy, Skinny and Kat*, and *Catherine the Great*. But on a high note: several of Barbra's songs were featured in the hit Amazon Prime TV series *The Marvelous Mrs. Maisel*; and two of Barbra's 2010 albums went to number one on the charts.

What stood out for me in this decade was the care that went into recording the two solo studio albums, especially *What Matters Most*, which sounded sumptuous with the orchestra. Also, I'm grateful for the abundance of live recordings (and the fact that she did so many tours and one-off concerts). As of 2025, Barbra has not done a live performance since Chicago in August 2019. Finally, I'm enormously fond of *Release Me* because I'm the guy who maintains the Barbra Archives website, and I was waiting for years to hear those tracks.

THE 2020S

CD and vinyl released: August 6, 2021
Executive producers: Barbra Streisand and Jay Landers
Art direction: Barbra Streisand and Gabrielle Raumberger
Cover photo design: Barbra Streisand
Package design: Gabrielle Raumberger
Barbra Streisand Archivist/Production Supervision: Kim Skalecki
Mastered by: Jochem van der Saag and Paul Blakemore
Special thanks: Richard Story, Rob Stringer, Matt Howe, and Richard Jay-Alexander

Catalog Numbers:
19439863402 (CD, red)
19439863411 (LP, red)
19439876472 (Target CD, pink)
19439876451 (Target LP, pink)
19439876431 (Barnes & Noble LP, green)
19439876441 (Spotify LP, blue
19439884071 (Prime Europe LP, purple)
19439876421 (Official Store LP, hot pink)

Side One:

1. Be Aware
2. You Light Up My Life
3. I'd Want It To Be You (with Willie Nelson)
4. Sweet Forgiveness
5. Living Without You

Side Two:

6. One Day (A Prayer)
7. Rainbow Connection (with Kermit The Frog)
8. Right As The Rain
9. If Only You Were Mine (with Barry Gibb)
10. Once You've Been In Love

Target bonus track: When The Lovin' Goes Out Of The Lovin'

The second *Release Me* album simply carried the number 2 in its title to distinguish it from the first album of unreleased songs. This sequel featured less in-studio chatter before the tracks than the first one did, but the gems included on it are just as impressive! Columbia went color happy on the promotion, releasing the album in several different colors, with colored vinyl as well. The very rare Spotify edition (blue cover) ended up being sold on eBay for over $800! *Release Me 2* included several of my "bucket list" Streisand songs that I longed to hear. I was most surprised by "Sweet Forgiveness" and most impressed with "You Light Up My Life."

I'd heard bootleg rehearsal tapes of Barbra singing "You Light Up My Life" for years but never heard the actual studio recordings. The song, as reconfigured on *Release Me 2*, is a revelation! "Somehow the track wasn't sitting quite right," Streisand explained about the original, 1974 recording. "I hired Neil Diamond's piano player to do an arrangement, and I didn't like it. It didn't support my vocal. It was too dull." (Dwyer, 2021) So she asked engineer Jochem van der Saag to record congas to augment the original recording. The result is so fresh and lively I play it often for an energetic lift.

Again, I'd heard "Once You've Been in Love" only as a muffled bootleg recording. I knew it was a gem, but I was desperate to hear an official release. Fans should know "Love" has been edited for *Release Me 2*—its original musical introduction is left off this album. Michel Legrand originally recorded a cacophonous orchestral introduction, similar to what he did on "Alfie" back in 1968. The original intro was jarring but very dramatic. On *Release Me 2*, Barbra and Jay Landers simply fade the song in on the orchestra's downbeat, which is more pleasing to the ears. Barbra recorded this song in 1973 standing amid the orchestra—no isolation booth to preserve her vocals or the separation from the orchestra for mixing later. It's truly a one-and-done performance and is amazing.

For the record, "Rainbow Connection" was recorded as a solo song for Barbra's album *Wet*, in 1979. The idea to pair her with Kermit the Frog was all because of *Release Me 2*, and it involved negotiations with Disney, which now owns the Muppets' intellectual property. Jay and Barbra were able to use Jim Henson's original Kermit vocals and match them to Streisand's solo recording to create this duet. Kermit is ageless and—literally—evergreen, but let's not forget that it's entirely possible that adding Kermit's vocals may have saved this song from collecting dust on the shelf. Based on my interview with Gary Klein, who produced this song, the original recording just wasn't working. "Barbra called me into the studio, moved in close to me, and said, smiling, 'Why the fuck are we recording this song? Can we go home now?'" Klein recalled. "I thanked everyone and said goodnight."

"Right as the Rain" was confusing for a few Streisand fans who emailed me about it. Historically, it's a very important recording that none of us had ever heard. Yes, Barbra included the same song on *The Second Album*. But this recording was made nearly a year earlier with a different arranger and producer. It's the only song from those October 16, 1962, recording sessions that had never been released. And now it has.

Matt on *Release Me 2*

Release Me 2 is all about the song "Sweet Forgiveness," which arrived completely unannounced and is, for me, immensely moving. "Two lives, one heart" and the note held on "heart" . . . so unbelievably beautiful.

"Sweet Forgiveness" is a master class in recording and performance, and according to Barbra and her team, it was recorded in probably one take due to a lack of time. I'd like to think that I had a small part in bringing the song out of the vaults—I'd heard Walter Afanasieff (who wrote the song with John Bettis) mention it on a podcast—my ears perked up because I had never heard of this song! So I added it to my website's list of unreleased songs. Et voilà! Jay Landers found it in the archived sessions for "Ordinary Miracles," circa 1994. The song is a testament to Barbra's exemplary talent. Can you imagine Barbra doing take after take of "Ordinary Miracles," then finding that the session was about to end? If she insisted on continuing, every musician in that room would get double or triple pay and blow the recording budget. What probably happened is that in just a few minutes, she and conductor Jeremy Lubbock listened to the orchestra run down the song, made what adjustments they could with the clock ticking away, then—"Sweet Forgiveness: Take One!" And Barbra nailed it.

The song follows a recent trend in an ABCABCDC song form, which I find fascinating. It may look like alphabet soup to you, but it has a logic. Follow along:

- Section A is the parts of the song that begin with: "4:00 a.m." and "I need you."
- Section B is "Tell me why . . ."
- Section C is what most would consider the chorus: "You and I, two

lives, one heart."

- Then D, which could be considered the bridge, is "Walls, we built these very walls."

At the end, we repeat section C: "You and I, two lives, one heart." One thing I learned from "Sweet Forgiveness" is that songs affect different people in different ways. Several fans emailed me about how they found the song disappointing and underwhelming. Personally, I was emotionally devastated by the song, especially after my recent breakup. "Sweet Forgiveness" does have a repetitious cadence, but the joy is in Streisand's idiosyncratic acting of certain words and phrases until the bridge. The lyric is laid out like the singer is writing a letter, so try listening to the argument that her character is presenting to her lover. "Why does this love we're in stay just out of reach?" she asks. For me, the heartbreak of the song is the line "When did passion turn to pride?" It's a question I've asked often, trying to pinpoint that moment in the wreckage of the relationship.

"Be Aware" is another beautiful remixing of a rare song that sounds so modern and important on this album. I love that Barbra and her engineer have literally turned up the knobs on some of the instruments to give them a louder voice.

Oy, another Randy Newman song! "Living Without You" received a complete audio makeover for this album (it was originally recorded with a New Orleans-styled arrangement). Barbra has stripped the song down, accompanied by a piano, and it's just fine . . . even though it's by Newman, not a favorite of mine.

"If Only You Were Mine" has a casualness that is infectious. This is one of the songs Jay Landers played over the phone for me back on the first *Release Me* album, and I was immediately attracted to it. It has a Tin Pan Alley vibe to it, which is probably why it didn't make the pop-oriented *Guilty Pleasures*. I've heard Streisand fans complain about getting

Barry Gibb only "bum-bum-bumming" on the track, but they seem to have ignored that it's two minutes and thirty-four seconds of Streisand singing this really catchy tune!

Another breakup song! Oy! "Once You've Been in Love" slayed me as much as "Sweet Forgiveness." If you follow the lyric, it's just devastating, as the singer tries to understand how to live life without the love of their life. They pose many questions, suggesting that pretending or forgetting might help them get through the pain. Then they arrive at the final question: "But with so many memories, where do you begin, once you've been in love?" It's a hot, raw dump of emotions, this song—without a solution either. Barbra's vocal is impeccable, and the Legrand arrangement brings tears. Just perfection.

"When the Lovin' Goes Out of the Lovin'" is another perfect track, unfortunately exiled to the exclusive Target LP and CD. I hope Barbra's fans have had a chance to hear this one. The song has undergone more revisions, like several others on this album. If you compare it to the bootleg I've heard, you'll notice that one of the choruses has been cut down and the arrangement is reimagined which downplays the background singers, who can still (barely) be heard. Beginning the song with the plaintive plucking of a guitar is a brilliant change! Bobby Whiteside was responsible for the original arrangement, in 1984, for the *Emotion* album. The magical Jochem van der Saag contributed additional production for the *Release Me 2* version.

CD released: November 4, 2022
SACD released: December 2022
Vinyl Released: March 2023
Album produced by: Barbra Streisand, Jay Landers, and Martin Erlichman
Mixed by: Jochem van der Saag
Original recording supervisor: Mike Berniker
Research & Bon Soir images: Courtesy of Matt Howe
Memorabilia: Courtesy of Eliot Hubbard, Lou Papalas
Liner notes: Jay Landers & Barbra Streisand
Liner notes editor: Todd Sussman
Barbra Streisand archivist/production supervisor: Kim Skalecki
Product manager: Chris Pappe

Catalog Numbers:
19658713762 (CD)
856276002435 (LP)
856276002749 (SACD)

Tracks:

1. Introduction/My Name Is Barbara 2. Much More 3. Napoleon 4. I Hate Music 5. Right As The Rain 6. Cry Me A River 7. Value 8. Lover, Come Back To Me 9. Band Introductions 10. Soon It's Gonna Rain 11. Come To The Supermarket (In Old Peking) 12. When The Sun Comes Out 13. Happy Days Are Here Again 14. Keepin' Out Of Mischief Now 15. A Sleepin' Bee 16. I Had Myself A True Love 17. Bewitched, Bothered And Bewildered 18. Who's Afraid Of The Big Bad Wolf? 19. I'll Tell The Man In The Street 20. A Taste Of Honey 21. Never Will I Marry 22. Nobody's Heart Belongs To Me 23. My Honey's Lovin' Arms 24. I Stayed Too Long at the Fair

The Bon Soir nightclub, in Manhattan's Greenwich Village, was the spot where Barbra's career took off. She met Marty Erlichman there; she enchanted her early fans there, and she recorded her first album there. The 2022 CD includes every song title Barbra performed on November 5, 6, and 7, 1962; the best performances were chosen for the CD.

Why wasn't this released? Why sixty years later? The original technicians recorded the shows on three tracks (piano and drums to the left side, guitar and bass to the right, and Barbra's voice in the center), but that didn't solve the sound problems that were created by that subterranean nightclub.

Jochem van der Saag, the 2022 album's mixer, wrote in the liner notes, "The moment we played the tapes through modern state-of-the-art speakers, it was clear what the original engineers had faced. The club's acoustics were obviously not designed for recording, and there was a lot of leakage from the instruments into her vocal mic. If we wanted to lower the volume of the piano, for example, the vocal volume would decrease, too. To give listeners 'the best seat in the house,' we used cutting-edge, spectral-editing technology, clarifying the true artistry of Barbra and her band."

At the Bon Soir, Barbra sang with the "house band." Streisand posted about her 1962 musicians on her official TikTok: "Tiger Haynes and the group were always so warm and loving and supportive. We had a wonderful comradery. I think you can hear that on the record, actually. They would talk back to me, you know, if I hit a particularly good note, [they'd say] 'Oh, sing it girl!' you know. It was just an amazing support system for me."

Streisand explained, "They were fabulous veteran musicians as well. And we always seemed to be in sync with each other."

The rarest track on this album is "Napoleon" by Harold Arlen. Barbra recorded an unreleased studio version of this song, but the live track on the *Bon Soir* CD marks its long-delayed official debut. It's a witty and rhythmic song from the songwriters of *The Wizard of Oz*.

Eight tracks from the *Bon Soir* recordings were already released on *Just for the Record*. Columbia recorded four of her shows over three nights. How does the 2022 CD differ from 1991's *JFTR*?

"Value" has a different spoken intro than from *JFTR*, but the same vocal. Then there's "I Hate Music," "Keepin' Out of Mischief Now," "Lover, Come Back," "Nobody's Heart"—these are all the same on both CDs even though the *Live at the Bon Soir* tracks possess improved sound fidelity. The *Bon Soir* CD version of "Big Bad Wolf" contains a short aside by Barbra ("Lord!") that was edited from the *JFTR* track. It's also neat that the *Bon Soir* CD includes the introduction of Barbra by Columbia's Dave Kapralik, whereas *JFTR* uses MC Jimmie Daniels from one of the other nights recorded.

On iTunes, the *Bon Soir* tracks are titled with their performance dates too. Tracks one to thirteen were performed on November 5, tracks fourteen to nineteen on November 6, and the rest on November 7.

It's so funny to hear Barbara tell the audience on track nine ("Band Introductions"): "I feel like saying I'll pick up all your checks! But I won't."

Matt on *Bon Soir*

I love hearing Dave Kapralik, Barbra's Columbia Records A&R man, telling the audience on this recording, "For me and for everyone at Columbia she's a singular artist; you can't put her in any category…"

I've listened to low-quality bootleg recordings of the Bon Soir shows for years. And many rabid fans like me put up with this: we watched VHS tapes that were duped 300 times so that all clarity was wiped away; we also listened to mono, horrible copies of tapes of tapes of rare songs. We were grateful to hear and see these offerings. But we wished: "What's wrong with wanting more (quality) ?"

So, Live at the Bon Soir was an excellent gift to the fans and a celebration of Barbra's longtime association with Columbia Records.

Marty Erlichman, Jay Landers, and Barbra are credited as producers for this album, which makes total sense. Marty was probably right there in 1962, smoking a cigarette and protecting Barbra's interests.

Barbra was raw, young, and exercising her beautiful gift of song at the Bon Soir. Her song repertoire would be duplicated in the studio for her first three albums, but it's emotional to hear these musical prototypes, sung live for an adoring audience.

What I like best about the Bon Soir recording is how intimate it is. It feels as if we were placed in this subterranean nightclub and are listening to this new, unique vocalist. Don't be confused by the technology that was used to resurrect this recording … this is what it sounded like when you were seated at one of the Bon Soir's tables. Can I order another drink?

Evergreens: Celebrating Six Decades on Columbia Records

CD Released: October 27, 2023
Produced by: Barbra Streisand and Jay Landers
Art Direction/Design: Gabrielle Raumberger
Cover Photo: Russell James
Back Cover, Back of Booklet Photo: Courtesy Barwood Archives
Booklet Photo: Matthew Rolston
Product Manager: Chris Poppe
Archivist: Kim Skalecki
Liner Notes Editor: Todd Sussman
Research: Matt Howe
Album Title Inspiration: Richard Jay-Alexander

Catalog Numbers:
19658820072 (CD)
196588200915 (Target pink vinyl)

Tracks:

1. I'll Tell the Man in the Street
2. Bewitched (Bothered and Bewildered)
3. Absent Minded Me
4. The Shadow of Your Smile
5. Where or When
6. Ma Première Chanson
7. I Don't Know Where I Stand
8. I Never Meant to Hurt You
9. Letters That Cross in the Mail
10. Answer Me
11. Tomorrow
12. Can't Help Lovin' That Man
13. Two People
14. Some Enchanted Evening
15. I Believe
16. Isn't It a Pity?
17. Moon River
18. Here's to Life (Orchestra version)
19. The Windmills of Your Mind
20. Who Can I Turn To (When Nobody Needs Me)
21. Lady Liberty
22. Evergreen (2023)

The total length of the tracks prevented Jay Landers from including twenty-four songs on this album (Barbra's lucky number, of course). But twenty-two tracks is close enough. Jay explained: "The concept of this album was to take a deeper dive into her illustrious catalog and intentionally *not include* any of her greatest hits or signature songs that had been on other compilations. This was to encourage old fans and new fans to listen to the songs that sometimes get overlooked and that she feels strongly about."

After Jay gave Barbra track lists (minus the big hits), he asked her to choose two songs from each album—"I just wanted her visceral reaction," he explained. That's how they arrived at these twenty-two songs.

Evergreens's subtitle ("Celebrating Six Decades on Columbia Records") was important, too, since Streisand signed with the record company back in 1962. It was released on the same day as the *40th Anniversary Deluxe Edition of the Yentl* soundtrack, and together these two albums also created a synergy around Barbra's long-awaited memoir, *My Name is Barbra*, released the next week.

None of the tracks on this album are new save the remix of "Evergreen"—Barbra's vocals are the same as on her 1976 recording. "I Believe," by the way, is the single version released on a Europe EP and also included on the CD *Hurricane Relief—Come Together Now* (RIAA, 2005). There is an orchestrated outro on this track (which instead segues into "You'll Never Walk Alone" on *Higher Ground*).

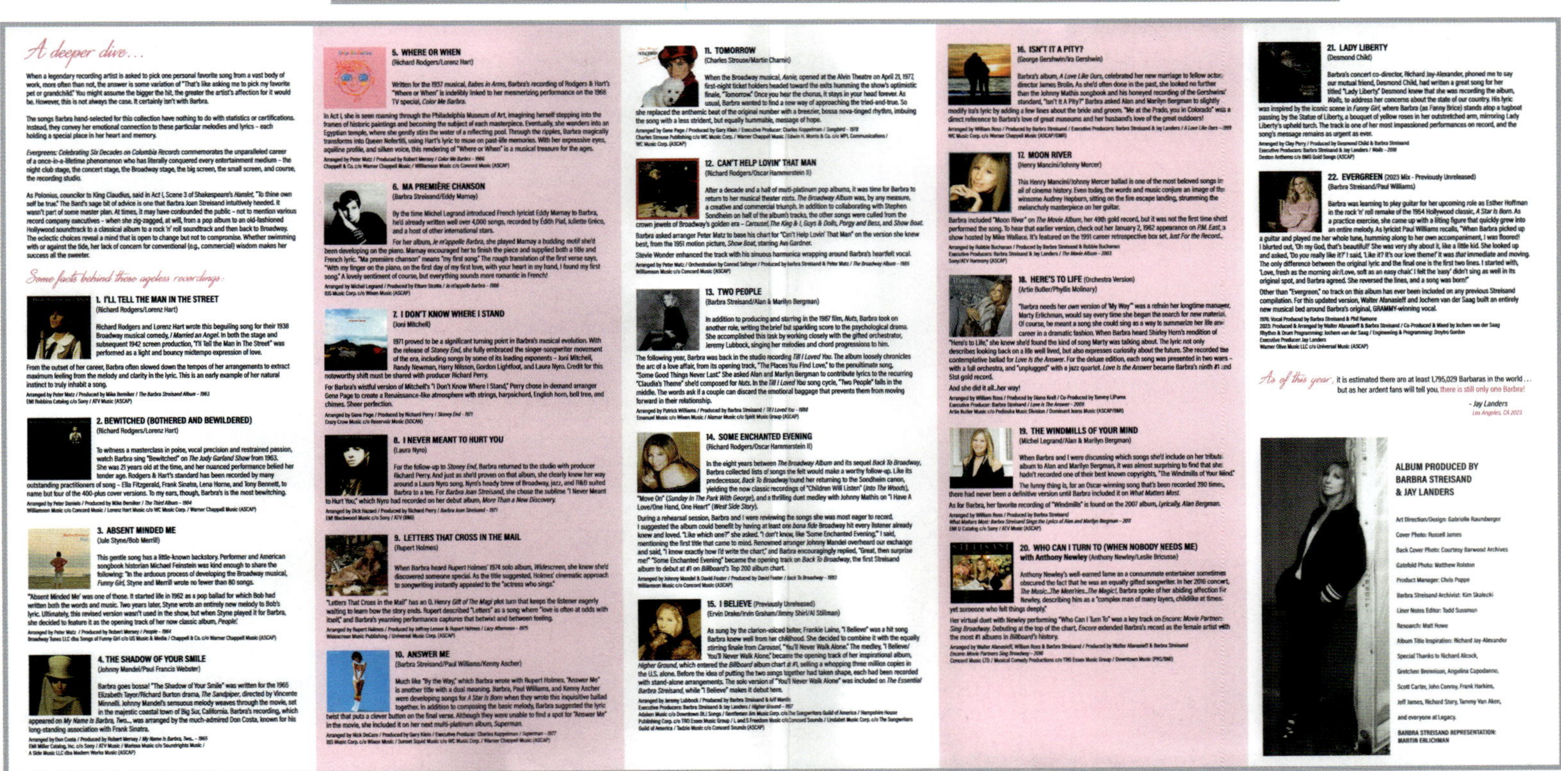

A deeper dive…

Some facts behind these ageless recordings

1. I'LL TELL THE MAN IN THE STREET
2. BEWITCHED (BOTHERED AND BEWILDERED)
3. ABSENT MINDED ME
4. THE SHADOW OF YOUR SMILE
5. WHERE OR WHEN
6. MA PREMIÈRE CHANSON
7. I DON'T KNOW WHERE I STAND
8. I NEVER MEANT TO HURT YOU
9. LETTERS THAT CROSS IN THE MAIL
10. ANSWER ME
11. TOMORROW
12. CAN'T HELP LOVIN' THAT MAN
13. TWO PEOPLE
14. SOME ENCHANTED EVENING
15. I BELIEVE
16. ISN'T IT A PITY?
17. MOON RIVER
18. HERE'S TO LIFE
19. THE WINDMILLS OF YOUR MIND
20. WHO CAN I TURN TO (WHEN NOBODY NEEDS ME) with Anthony Newley
21. LADY LIBERTY
22. EVERGREEN

As of this year, …

ALBUM PRODUCED BY
BARBRA STREISAND
& JAY LANDERS

CD released: October 27, 2023
Vinyl Released: March 2023
2023 DELUXE EDITION
Executive Producers: Barbra Streisand and Jay Landers
Engineering & Mixing by Jochem van der Saag
Art Direction & Design: Gabrielle Raumberger
Photography: Hulton Archive / Getty Images
Illustrations by Richard Amsel
Tape and Photo Archivist: Kim Skalecki
Liner Notes Editor: Todd Sussman
Research: Matt Howe and Richard Jay-Alexander
Product Manager: Chris Poppe
Special Thanks to Richard Alcock, Gretchen Brennison, Angelina Capodanno, Scott Carter, John Conroy, Frank Harkins, Jeff James, Richard Story, Tammy Van Aken, and everyone at Legacy.

Catalog Numbers:
19658800712 (CD)
19658800721 (LP)

Tracks:

CD disc one: Original Motion Picture Soundtrack
CD disc two: AUDITION TAPES & MORE
(Tracks 1-9: Barbra Streisand accompanied by Michel Legrand)

1. Where Is It Written? (demo)
2. Papa, Can You Hear Me? (demo)
3. The Way He Makes Me Feel (demo)
4. Several Sins A Day (demo)
5. No Wonder (demo) with Marilyn Bergman
6. Tomorrow Night (demo)
7. Will Someone Ever look At Me This Way? (demo) with Michel Legrand
8. The Moon and I (demo)
9. A Piece of Sky (demo)
10. Papa, Can You Hear Me? (studio version)
11. Several Sins A Day (studio version)*
12. Where Is It Written? (with Rabbinical chorus)*
13. Papa, Can You Hear Me? (single version)*
14. This Is One of Those Moments (reprise)*
15. End Title (instrumental medley)*

*CD only

As I explained to Jay Landers during our November 4, 2023 YouTube video interview, being credited on this album for "research" was truly a full-circle moment for me. *Yentl* inspired me in 1983 to follow Barbra Streisand's amazing career. Then, flash-forward to the *Yentl* deluxe CD in 2023, and there's my name listed in the liner notes as a contributor. If that doesn't blow your mind, then what does? ("There are moments you remember all your life.")

My "research" credit involved me making a list for Jay of all the *Yentl* tracks that I thought should be included on this anniversary album. Then we chatted about what would make a good anniversary album. Jay, of course, went to Barbra's archives where, he explained, there is a wall of master tapes for *Yentl*. "Every single take, every single outtake . . . I actually listened to everything," Jay said.

Although *Yentl*'s tagline is "Nothing's Impossible," for this anniversary release, Jay was limited by budget, licensing costs, etc. "My original plan," he told me, "was to have a three-disc set." Those discs would have been the original LP, the demos, and the Legrand score. "That proved to be too unwieldy."

What we got is still pretty amazing. The standout track is "Several Sins a Day," a musical number that was cut and never filmed. Jay found a fully orchestrated track of this song and, even better, Barbra's notes on the box, so the editor could shorten the instrumental interludes.

I am very happy my suggestion of "Where Is It Written (with Rabbinical Choir)" was included. This is an extraordinary track, unused in the film, but with a great vocal by Barbra, accompanied by those spiritual men's voices.

Jay was also excited to find the "Papa, Can You Hear Me" pop version arranged by Dave Grusin. Supported by keyboards and strings, this version has a surprisingly emotional performance by Barbra—probably not very commercial as a radio single. But all these years later, it's incredible to hear this unreleased version.

Three of the *Yentl* demos were included on *Just for the Record*, and on that collection, they sounded sped up. Jay told me that engineer Jochem van der Saag agreed. "I don't know if it was a mastering error or if the cassettes were wildly inaccurate. They weren't recording these songs with the intention of putting them on albums." Jochem went to the piano and hit a middle-C note and said, "You see, it's playing too fast."

So the first and best thing van der Saag did was pitch-correct the demo recordings. Next, he muted the extraneous room noise that was captured on these crude home recordings. "There's something about these demos that have an immediacy to them that I love," Jay stated. Jay and I were most disappointed to learn that Dave Grusin's pop/single version of the finale, "A Piece of Sky," did not exist. Before his death, Phil Ramone told me that he had produced that pop version. I've listed it on my Streisand website for years. "We looked high and low, and we could not find any version with Barbra's vocal on it," Jay confirmed. Jay was able to recover a recording of a musician's jam session . . . with no vocals by Barbra. Frankly, it's hard to find the melody of the song in this session. It was a musical idea that never coalesced and was never finished.

I was very surprised to hear "Tomorrow Night (Demo)." Never heard on the bootlegs from the eighties, this is an earlier version of the song with a completely different melody in the middle. I've never heard this version before! It includes more narration by Yentl than on the later versions, which truncate the narration.

There is actually one demo that is not included: a solo vocal by Michel Legrand of "Tomorrow Night (Reprise)." After hearing Barbra's narration on this new CD, I believe that Legrand's demo vocal was the song the women were to sing to Hadas in the bathhouse as she was being cleansed for her wedding night.

Finally, it's fun to hear Barbra admit on the demo tape that "A Piece of Sky" is "still a work in progress. It's not quite finished." (But it sounds GREAT!).

Released: June 27, 2025
Produced by: Walter Afanasieff & Peter Asher
Executive Producers: Barbra Streisand & Jay Landers
Mixed by: Jochem van der Saag
Vocal Recording, Programming, and Sound Design: Jochem van der Saag
Orchestra Conducted by: William Ross
Orchestra Arranged by: William Ross & Walter Afanasieff (except "Letter to My 13 Year Old Self" and "Secret o' Life," arranged by: David Campbell)
Liner Notes: Jay Landers
Liner Notes Editor: Todd Sussman
Art Direction: Barbra Streisand
Design: Gabrielle Raumberger
Cover Photo: Kathryn Boyd Brolin

Catalog Numbers:

19802889652 (CD)
19802889661-S1 (Blush Vinyl)
19802889671-S1 (Cream Vinyl—Amazon exclusive)

Tracks:

1. The First Time Ever I Saw Your Face (with Hozier)
2. My Valentine (with Paul McCartney)
3. To Lose You Again (with Sam Smith)
4. The Very Thought of You (with Bob Dylan)
5. Letter to My 13-year-old Self (with Laufey)
6. One Heart, One Voice (with Mariah Carey & Ariana Grande)
7. I Love Us (with Tim McGraw)
8. Secret O' Life (with James Taylor)
9. Fragile (with Sting)
10. Where Do I Go From You? (with Josh Groban)
11. Love Will Survive (with Seal)

Several days after Barbra's eighty-third birthday, Columbia Records announced that her new studio album, *The Secret of Life: Partners, Volume Two*, would be released on June 27. Even better, the first song and lyric-video from the album were also released that day: "The First Time Ever I Saw Your Face" with Irish singer-songwriter Hozier (full name: Andrew John Hozier-Byrne). In the promotional YouTube video for the duet, Hozier accurately described the song as "impossibly intimate at the same time as it's cosmically large."

Hozier also said, "Barbra Streisand is one of the most enduring and iconic vocalists of our time, and somebody who defined an era with the sheer force of her voice, her talent, charisma, and vision. To be asked to join her on a duet was a huge honor and came as a wonderful and welcome surprise."

Songwriter Ewan MacColl's "The First Time Ever I Saw Your Face" has been heavily associated with the late Roberta Flack. Barbra, of course, gave us a new, indelible "take" on the song with her singing of the first line.

"I've always loved singing duets with gifted artists. They inspire me in unique and different ways . . . and make our time in the studio a joy," Streisand said in a statement.

For this new album of duets, English producer Peter Asher had a hand (an ear?) in blending the notes and voices. Finding the partners wasn't hard, though. "Everyone says yes," he laughed. "That's the amazing part. What singer could possibly get all these people to say yes without any questions? Barbra Streisand."

The eighty-year-old Asher explained that Jay Landers "had this idea of putting myself and producer Walter Afanasieff together on the project. Then it was just going through lists of songs and lists of people, assembling the right mixture. We had great arrangers. Barbra's singing is extraordinary. She's older than me, and she totally nailed it."

The second song released ahead of the album featured Barbra and a Beatle. "My Valentine" was a "jazz noir" song, at once both somber and mysterious (like love can be). It was written by Sir Paul McCartney, another Englishman. Barbra has recorded the Beatles and variations of the Beatles in her discography over the years; she's sung three songs written by Lennon/McCartney, two Lennon-only songs, and one Lennon/Ono-penned song. This is the first McCartney-only-composed song she's recorded.

McCartney's "My Valentine" was first released in 2012, a single from his fifteenth solo album, *Kisses on the Bottom*. He wrote the song for his wife, Nancy Shevell, on a rainy day in Morocco when the couple had to stay in their hotel to keep dry. Paul said that the rain "led me towards a kind of minor-y type thing and the sentiment of you know, oh it's raining."

McCartney wrote the song on a "slightly out of tune [piano] in the foyer of the hotel." The nostalgic tune was inspired by "this lovely Irish guy who knew so much old stuff, like 'Beautiful Dreamer,' 'If You Were the Only Girl in the World' . . .. Again, stuff from my dad's era. I used to enjoy listening to him, and he put me in mind of that genre."

As for working with Streisand on the song, McCartney said, "I think the session was about three hours . . .. But it started off with a big forty-piece orchestra on the Sony lot, which is one of the old Hollywood film studios; it's very impressive. And we were on 'The Barbra Streisand Scoring Stage,' so no pressure there!"

McCartney explained that there was a key change in the song to deal with. He said, "They'd arranged it so that it had to go in Barbra's key and then in my key. So to get from Barbra's key into mine was kind of difficult, and I had to launch in not knowing what key I was in. Mine was lower, hers was higher."

McCartney ultimately praised working with Barbra in the studio. "I didn't realize how rounded she is creatively. They were filming the session, and as soon as we went in, she said, 'Who put that camera there? That shouldn't be there. Bring it over here. And what about those lights?' I thought, *Wow, you're directing it!* But then I suddenly remembered she's directed three big movies. She's a smart cookie."

The duet with country music star Tim McGraw was probably inspired by a video he and his daughter Gracie recorded for YouTube that went viral. Driving in a car, they sang together to Barbra and Barry Gibb's hit song, "What Kind of Fool."

Steve Dorff and Bill Anderson wrote the song, and Anderson posted online: "I can hear you saying, 'But she's not country!' And you're right. But she has recorded it with somebody who is . . . Tim McGraw!" Anderson concluded that "I've never heard Barbra or Tim sound any better than they sound together on this amazing recording."

Bob Dylan and Barbra go back to the 1960s, when they both were signed to Columbia Records. Barbra said, "I remember him sending me flowers and writing me a card in different-color pencils, like a child's writing: 'Would you sing with me?' I thought, *What would I sing with him? How could we get together on this?* I couldn't understand it at that time. But it sure was wonderful to have picked a song, 'The Very Thought of You.' Bob loved that song. He's very shy, like I am. But he was wonderful to work with. I was told that he didn't want any direction. But when I talked to him about things that I suggested, he was so pliable—he was so open to suggestions. Everything I heard about him just went out the window. He stood on his feet for three hours with me."

Peter Asher told the Boston Globe: "One thinks Dylan and Streisand come from different worlds, and they do, but those worlds have a degree of similarity. And clearly, they're mutual admirers."

In a promotional video for "Letter to My 13 Year Old Self," Jay Landers said, "When we played Barbra the song, she instantly related to it. Then, she called her assistant and said, 'Bring me my diary that I wrote when I was thirteen years old.' It turns out she had written the dreams she had had for herself. It was like Laufey wrote the song for her." The video showed the diary, which is placed below with a picture of Barbra as a youth. Sony released the song as a single on Friday, June 6, to promote the album,

and it immediately went to Number 1 on the iTunes Song chart.

There's something beautifully generational about the duet with Laufey. The Icelandic singer-songwriter's name is pronounced LAY-vay, by the way. On this song we get "Gamma" Barbra and young Laufey, twenty-six years old when this was recorded. Their voices merge in a beautiful choreography of harmony. Laufey explained that Peter Asher was the person who played her song for Barbra, "and she immediately related to it and was down to sing it, and on top of that she said, 'Why don't you sing it with me?' Hearing my voice with hers is something I thought I'd never be able to do. We recorded separately, but I've gotten to speak to her, and it's really cool."

Barbra had wanted to sing with Sting for years. For *Partners Two,* he wrote a new coda to his song "Fragile" to accommodate her. On this recording they sing, "On and on . . . in every human heart some rain is bound to fall," then end the song with "We're too blind to see how fragile we are."

The Lambily and the Arianators (Mariah Carey's and Ariana Grande's fans respectively) were just as excited as the Streisand fans were to hear their new trio on "One Heart, One Voice." Jay Landers explained on Facebook that "Walter Afanasieff, Charlie Midnight, and I initially conceived it as a 'theme' for Barbra's Women's Heart Center at Cedar Sinai Hospital in Los Angeles." He continued: "When Barbra heard the demo, she made many critical suggestions that encouraged us to expand the lyric into a declaration and celebration of female empowerment—that could be sung by three generations of strong-willed women united in one life affirming message." Ariana Grande confessed in a promotional video that she went to see Barbra's 2006 tour and a picture of her in the audience made it onto the DVD.

Barbra did a smattering of interviews to promote *Partners 2*, including a great podcast with Marc Malkin from *Variety*. But she did not participate in any television interviews and only released four behind-the-scenes videos on YouTube. Perhaps this is why the album underperformed on the *Billboard* charts? *The Secret of Life* debuted at Number 31, which was surprising. Even *Walls* performed better, coming in at Number 12. Even *Release Me 2* did better, debuting at Number 15 on the *Billboard* 200 list.

Billboard's post about her new album was encouraging, reminding its readers of several facts: she extended her record for "the most top 40 albums among women in the history of the chart." Compared with other solo-acts, Barbra has the "second-most top 40 albums," behind Elvis and Frank Sinatra, who are tied at fifty-eight each. Finally, *Billboard* stated that "Streisand also continues to be the only woman with top 40-charted albums on the *Billboard* 200 in every decade from the 1960s through the 2020s."

Matt on *The Secret*

Another album of duets? I was dubious. But the assembled talent and choice of songs on this one exceeded past efforts.

What comes to mind each time I've played *Partners Volume Two*: harmonies. I don't have a way of measuring the minutes of harmonies on this album compared with *Partners* or *Encore*, but the impression this album left with me was how gorgeous (and often) Barbra harmonized with her new duet partners.

The harmonies with Laufey and on the songs "I Love Us" and "Where Do I Go from You" are echoing in my head.

I was lucky enough to see the video of Barbra singing "The Very Thought of You" for Marty at his eightieth-birthday party. Dear Marvin Hamlisch was tickling the ivories that night, and friends and family were there, including Jason Gould, Don Rickles, Phyllis Diller, Jay, and Richard Jay. There was a special moment when Barbra, accompanied by Marvin, underneath the trees and lights on her Malibu property, sang this treasure for Marty. . .. It was magical. Since it's Marty's favorite song, I have always assumed that someday . . . somewhere . . . Barbra would record it. I just didn't expect she'd do it with Bob Dylan. There are a lot of key modulations on this recording to accommodate these two singers, but frankly, I can dine on Barbra's vocal at the 1:25 minute mark. "The mere idea of you/the longing here for you/you'll never know how slow the moments go till I'm near to you." (Again, at eighty-three, she has amazing breath control.) And doesn't Grégoire Maret sound amazing on harmonica on this track? I could have sworn it was Stevie Wonder until I read the album insert.

The duet with Seal on "Love Will Survive" is a lovely upgrade from the original solo version Barbra had already released. Their voices go together very well—it's that combination of butter and grit that Barbra exploited before with singers like Kim Carnes and Neil Diamond. Now Barbra's vocals on the duet are note for note from the solo recording released in April 2024 (I compared the songs). The only new vocal I can hear is in the middle of the song at the climax. Barbra seems to have recorded a new "answer line" to Seal: "I'll walk beside you."

That brings up a "lost media" problem with the original, solo "Love Will Survive." You can't buy it anywhere except as a digital download. There was a very rare and expensive vinyl of the soundtrack to *The Tattooist of Auschwitz* television series released from AtTheMoviesShop.com that included the track. Otherwise, the Emmy- and Grammy-nominated song is not on any physical media. I was hoping Columbia Records would add the single as a bonus track to this album . . . until I found out that the song had been remade as a duet with Seal.

"Where Do I Go from You" was written by Desmond Child and Davitt Sigerson for a Broadway-bound musical they're developing called *Beba's Mambo*, previously known as *Cuba Libre*. Desmond wrote on his Facebook page that it is based on "my beautiful aunt Beba, who became the mistress of the Cuban dictator, Fulgencio Batista, before the revolution." Child told another outlet that the musical will be "the true story of my mother's two extraordinary younger sisters caught up in the 'conga line of history' before and after the turbulent aftermath of the Cuban revolution. One became the mistress of the dictator Fulgencio Batista and the other the lover of Fidel Castro."

That explanation may give us some context for this dramatic duet. It's a little odd that Josh Groban has only two solo lines in this song. The rest of the time he and Barbra sing in harmony—that sweet harmony I mentioned earlier that seems to be the theme of this album. By the way . . . this is Josh's third duet with Barbra—lucky him!

"Where Do I Go from You" is a Broadway power ballad perfect for Barbra, in the style of "With One Look" and "Loving You." Barbra sounds great here, in full Diva Broadway Belt mode.

My favorite song on the entire album is "To Lose You Again" (which could have been titled "I'm Done with Singin' the

Blues"). I must have played it three hundred times as I'm writing this. With its catchy chorus and key modulation (after "can't you seeeee?"), "To Lose You" is so sing-alongable. And it's more than a breakup song; it's a "we're not good for each other" boundaries song. "Don't fuel the fire," Barbra sings. Then, at the end, she adamantly sings, "I am *not* gonna love you." I love it!

Then there's the Diva Goddess anthem "One Heart, One Voice" with Ariana Grande and Mariah Carey. Barbra sings to us: "In countless stories since ancient time the poets spoke of it in verse and rhyme . . .." This song has a "We Are the World" vibe, but with a feminist point of view. My favorite part is the bridge ("There are no excuses left to make/The ancient rules are ours to break").

The title song with James Taylor is easy-breezy Barbra. Again, she's sounding so young and happy—as is Taylor.

This album was Barbra's first venture back into the recording studio in over six years, since *Walls* was released, and she sounds great, her voice defying her years on this planet. *Partners Two* surprised me too; a duet with Laufey?! A trio with Ariana and Mariah?! And the bluesy "To Lose You Again" with Sam Smith?! Now these were thinking-outside-the-box choices and excited me much more than the 2014 *Partners* album, in which Barbra pulled a Frank Sinatra and sang her old songs with others. It's a pleasure to hear her creating such beautiful harmonies with these new singing partners. My only complaint about the album is that it never really kicks in to high gear; there's a sameness to most of the tracks. I believe the respective fandoms of the women's trio expected another "Enough Is Enough" . . . but on "One Heart, One Voice" we instead got a sort of mellow anthem.

One last note on the LP versus the CD: if you own both, you'll notice that "A Note From Barbra" is different on each insert. The CD contains photos which are not on the LP, and a warm, six-paragraph note from Barbra about her beloved granddaughters and how the album's cover photo was captured. The LP has a one-paragraph note, mostly containing thank yous to her team and her granddaughters, but with a different photo. That means that a very limited amount of the vinyl records were printed with this discrepancy; the newer versions will match the CD notes and photos.

DECADE 20 ENCORE

As I'm writing in 2025, Barbra still has some recording to do. Barbra wants to record those two Michel Legrand songs that Alan Bergman put words to. She also mentioned she's considering a *Streisand Sings Sondheim* album.

Then there are songs and albums in her vaults that could be released. (Lately, I've been obsessed with the unreleased *Belle of 14th Street* soundtrack. That was her 1967 TV show that had amazing arrangements by Mort Lindsey and some great turn-of-the-century songs we should all hear. Sure, there's one lone DVD version of it that came out in 2005, but I'd love to finally listen to the studio recordings, one of which they put out on *Just for the Record*.)

The 2020s began with *Release Me 2*, which (hard to believe) thrilled me more than the first *Release Me* nine years earlier. I'm a sucker for anything from the vault when it comes to Barbra's music. Give me *Release Me 3*, *4*, and *5*!

Finally hearing those Bon Soir tapes in pristine condition was another dream come true. After the fortieth of *Yentl* and the compilation album *Evergreens*, Barbra finally went back into the recording studio to produce *The Secret of Life*—her first studio recording since 2018's *Walls*. I knew she was still sounding good when she released her single "Love Will Survive" mid-2024, from the Sky/Peacock series *The Tattooist of Auschwitz*.

Now we're only halfway through the 2020s, and there's so much more music she could release in the next five years to round out the decade. I'm on pins and needles waiting for what's next.

STREISAND ALBUMS REMASTERED BY COLUMBIA RECORDS OVER THE YEARS

Compact discs and CD players first appeared on the consumer market around 1983. The CD was created to be the successor to vinyl LPs, which scratched easily, could sometimes ship warped, and melted if left too long in a hot car. At first, audiophiles complained about CD technology—they argued that the sound from the discs was not as warm as that of a vinyl LP played on a turntable. In the matter of only five years, however, CD sales surpassed LPs, making the digital format the most popular on the market until the advent of digital downloads and streaming.

It was in the 1980s that the Society of Professional Audio Recording Services (SPARS) created a three-digit code to alert consumers as to how a CD was recorded, mixed, and mastered. For Streisand CDs, the SPARS code was AAD: recorded onto analog tape, mixed analog in the studio, and mastered digitally. The early Streisand CDs have the SPARS code printed on the front cover.

Phil Ramone, who engineered the sound for some of Barbra's live concerts and also produced records for her, did a great job explaining CD versus LP technology in his book *Making Records: The Scenes Behind the Music*:

"When we cut records thirty years ago, they sounded good in the control room, but it was hard to channel that sound onto an LP. Session tapes underwent a lot of tweaking during their transposition to vinyl, and the compromising to compensate for vinyl's deficiencies began in the mixing phase and ended in mastering.

"In mastering a tape for LP, you had to cut back the bass, crank up the mid-range and high end, and use compression to make it sound pleasing on an average record player. There was a complex physiology behind groove width and depth, and the width of the grooves changed as you got toward the end of the record. The last track on an album was the most problematic; if you didn't master the tape and cut the disc properly it would sound distorted. You could have the most dynamic mix in the world, but it would sound awful if you couldn't squeeze it into a record's grooves."

Ramone surmised that "with the CD, groove physiology is no longer a factor. But since digital recording's high resolution can magnify a mix's flaws, mastering becomes even more critical in the digital domain."

To further explain why remastering is important, engineer Andy Walter (who worked on converting the Beatles albums) told Abbey Road Studios: "Remastering and the use of 'state of the art' technology allows us to polish and remove the gremlins of both time and the recording medium such as analog tape. We can reduce background noise and hum, enhance and expand

frequencies, improve analog tape edits, remove unwanted electrical clicks and other extraneous unwanted noises—as well as better capture, at a much higher resolution, the magic of the original recording to any medium."

Walter stated: "It's both a preservation job as well as a future-proofing enhancement of the catalog!"

The first Barbra Streisand album released on a CD was *The Broadway Album*. It hit the stores on LP and cassette tape in November 1985, and the compact disc version (with a bonus track added—"Adelaide's Lament") was in stores by February 1986. *One Voice* was the next compact disc released by Columbia Records in 1987. To entice consumers to buy the new format, Columbia added Barbra's live performance of "Send in the Clowns" as a bonus track on the CD; it did not appear on the LP version.

As compact discs started selling, Columbia dipped into Streisand's catalog and began issuing older albums in the format. It released *The Barbra Streisand Album* (catalog #8807) and *The Second* (#8854) and *The Third Album* (#8954) on CD for the first time in 1987. These discs, however, suffered from the mastering problem mentioned by Phil Ramone above—the original analog production masters were used. "They were the worst sounding CDs I ever heard," said Victor Bisio, a California-based recording engineer. "They were screechy and distorted. When she hit the high notes, it just shattered your speakers."

Now, I own the 1987 *Second Album*, and although I do not think it is the worst sounding CD I've ever heard, there is a considerable difference between it and the 1993 remaster by John Arrias, a recording engineer and record producer. The 1993 CD sounds great, and the slight distortions on the high notes that you can hear on the 1987 disc are not present at all.

John Arrias is a name you'll see on many Streisand albums over the years. He is also responsible for remastering most of Barbra's album catalog. He was instrumental in preparing the audio for the box set *Just for the Record*. Those tracks were sourced from "a hodgepodge of analog equipment," he told me. Arrias created the CAP System to do this. "It was all put in a rollaway rack and labeled CAP for simplicity. It stands for Complete Audio Preservation. It included equalizers, limiters, compressors, and audio restoration equipment."

Arrias did his work at B & J Studio, which was constructed on the first floor of Lion Share Studios in Beverly Hills, California, in 1986. Arrias confirmed B & J stands for Barbra (Streisand) and John (Arrias).

"After we released *Just for the Record*, I was approached by Columbia Records to prepare Barbra's first three albums for CD release," Arrias recalled. "It went so well that they just kept sending me more recordings that had never been released on CD. The condition of some of the tapes were so bad that it soon became an archival project. I am proud to say that Barbra's entire catalog is now digitally preserved and in the vaults. It was a great honor and so much fun. All of the recordings were first directly transferred, with their original sound, onto digital tape; no equalizers or filters were used. I then went back and used my CAP system to create the remastered CDs."

Next: "When possible, I made new mixes from the original masters to a half-inch analog tape using the CAP system. I then took the final mixes to Bernie Grundman Mastering in Hollywood, where Bernie and I put the final touches on the mixes using his analog console. The new mixes were then transferred for CD release," Arrias said.

John was very impressed with Barbra's first three albums, recorded in 1963 and 1964 on three tracks. "When I finally located a three-track head assembly, I began playing back the recordings. The split was: Track 1 was orchestra left, Track 2 was Barbra's live vocal, Track 3 was orchestra right. That's it. So simple, yet the balances were remarkable. These recordings were originally released in mono."

Columbia Records began rolling out eleven remastered CDs in 1993. The sales sheet, sent to retailers, said: "The objective with each album was to restore the tapes to the quality of the original master recording. To do this in some cases, 30 years of noise had to be eliminated. In each case great care was taken to maintain the integrity of the original albums. The packages were recreated using original art or printing film. Many of the packages have extensive liner notes that are reproduced in their entirety."

Speaking of packages … Many of you will remember the CD long boxes of the 1980s. Because CDs still had to compete with

LPs in record stores, the labels were afraid the smaller CDs would be lost in the record bins. So the album art was reformatted into a twelve-by-six-inch box—the same height as an LP. All of the Streisand CDs were sold like this, and you'll see some of the long boxes pop up for sale on eBay occasionally. Long boxes were phased out by 1993, however, when artists and consumers complained about the wasteful use of materials. By then, record stores had proper CD bins anyway.

Streisand's 1993 CD titles came with a gold sticker on the front cover that read: "Digitally Remastered and Restored from the Original Master Tapes." Eight of the eleven albums had never appeared on CD before. All of them carried the credits "restored by" John Arrias and "remastered by" Bernie Grundman on the back covers. The eleven albums were: *I Can Get It for You Wholesale*, *Pins and Needles*, *The Barbra Streisand Album*, *The Second Barbra Streisand Album*, *The Third Album*, *Harold Sings Arlen* (now out of print), *What About Today?*, *On a Clear Day You Can See Forever*, *The Way We Were* (Original Soundtrack), *A Star Is Born*, and *The Main Event* Soundtrack (out of print).

Then, between 1994 and 1998, Columbia Records issued remastered versions of twenty-four more Streisand CDs. This packaging had a white sticker affixed to the jewel box that read: "Digitally Restored From The Original Master Tapes/Digitally Remastered."

During this period, the Streisand remastering program encountered an issue. Columbia was releasing new, remastered discs, but they were inside the older CD packaging. But where it got confusing was when fans discovered that Sony Music's manufacturing plants had inadvertently placed the older, nonremastered CDs in the jewel boxes containing the newly remastered white stickers. Sony's Quality Management Department helped fans exchange the old CDs for remastered CDs. This was all sorted out by June 1998.

Sometimes fans reach out to me concerned they may not have the correct, remastered CDs. Today, this is simply not a problem to worry about. The old CDs are completely out of circulation, and the only reason you should question what you have in your collection is if you bought a used CD sitting in a bin since the 1990s.

In January 2002, five popular Streisand albums were remastered by Stephen Marcussen, mastering engineer. These 2002 CDs replaced the previous Arrias editions in stores. Each disc had specially designed, brand-new packaging, restoring original LP artwork and notes. The Marcussen discs were assigned new catalog numbers, and the CD itself was the classic red Columbia label. The five CDs were *People*, *Funny Girl* soundtrack, *The Way We Were* studio album, *A Star Is Born*, and *The Broadway Album*.

Since 2002, a few more remastered CDs have been released:

- *Guilty: The 25th Anniversary Edition*—released in 2005 in Dual Disc format (remastered audio on one side; video content on the other).
- *Classical Barbra*—remastered in 2013 (with the addition of two bonus songs).
- Capitol Records's limited edition of *Funny Girl: Original Broadway Cast Recording*, remastered in 2014.

CT/CK 47014
What About Today

CT/CK 52722
Harold Sings Arlen (With Friend)

CT/CK 53020
I Can Get It For You Wholesale (Original Broadway Cast Recording)

CT/CK 57374
The Barbra Streisand Album

CT/CK 57375
A Star Is Born (Original Soundtrack Recording)

CT/CK 57376
The Main Event (Original Soundtrack Recording)

THE SINGLES

Seven-inch, 45 rpm, twelve-inch singles, dance mixes, CD singles, etc.—here is a complete list of Barbra Streisand's US singles with catalog numbers.

To refresh those older minds and maybe those of the kids who weren't around for vinyl records, seven-inch singles had two sides. The A-side was the featured song that the record company hoped would be played on the radio and become a hit. The B-side (a.k.a. flipside) was a secondary song that usually, though not always, appeared on the same album. Once the 1990s arrived, Columbia Records moved into the digital age and released singles on compact disc.

One more caveat for this list: These are the US singles, although there are some instances where I discuss or note the European versions.

After Barbra's commercially released singles are listed, I have included two more categories:

"Hall of Fame" Singles: Columbia rereleased some of its artists' singles through its "Hall of Fame" series. Columbia clarified any confusion about first and later pressings by giving "Fame" singles a unique label and a new catalog number.

Promotional or Demonstration Singles: These Streisand singles were never meant to be sold to fans in stores. Instead, they were circulated by Columbia Records' publicity department to radio stations or music magazines.

1960s Singles

Happy Days Are Here Again/When The Sun Comes Out #4-42631, released November 1962
As mentioned previously, these songs have different orchestrations and vocals from the versions that appear on Barbra's first album.

My Coloring Book/Lover, Come Back to Me
#4-42648, released November 1962
Again—different orchestrations and vocals from Barbra's first album.

People/I Am Woman
#4-42965, released January 1964
"I Am Woman" exists only on vinyl; it has a different arrangement, lyric, and vocal from the Broadway cast album.

Absent Minded Me/Funny Girl
#4-43127, released August 1964
"Funny Girl" exists only on vinyl; it has a different melody and lyric from the same-titled movie version of the song.

Why Did I Choose You?/My Love
#4-43248, released March 1965
"My Love" exists only on vinyl; it is a different version of "My Pa" on *My Name Is Barbra*.

My Man/Where Is The Wonder?
#4-43323, released June 1965

He Touched Me/I Like Him
#4-43403, released September 1965
"I Like Him" from the Broadway musical *Drat! The Cat!* exists only on vinyl.

Second Hand Rose/The Kind Of Man A Woman Needs
#4-43469, released November 1965

Where Am I Going?/You Wanna Bet
#4-43518, released January 1966
For years, "You Wanna Bet" was available only on vinyl until Barbra included it on *Just for the Record.*

Sam, You Made The Pants Too Long/The Minute Waltz
#4-43612, released April 1966

Non C'est Rien/Le Mur
#4-43739, released July 1966

En Français
#EP 6048, released July 1966.
7-inch EP released in France/Europe only by CBS Records
Side One: 1. Non C'est Rien, 2. Les enfants qui pleurent
Side Two: 1. Et la mer, 2. Le mur

Free Again/I've Been Here
#4-43808, released September 1966

Sleep In Heavenly Peace/Gounod's Ave Maria
#4-43896, released October 1966

Stout-Hearted Men/Look
#4-44225, released June 1967
"Stout," the single, has a different vocal. Barbra does not do her Mae West impression.

Lover Man/My Funny Valentine
#44331, released October 1967

Our Corner Of The Night/He Could Show Me
#4-44474, released February 1968
Both songs remain vinyl only. There has not been a digital release to date, nor have these tracks ever appeared on a Streisand album.

The Morning After/Where Is The Wonder?
#4-44532, released April 1968

Funny Girl/I'd Rather Be Blue Over You (Than Happy With Somebody Else)
#4-44622, released July 1968
Both songs here are alternate recordings with different orchestrations from the movie. Peter Matz did the arrangements.

My Man/Don't Rain On My Parade
#4-44704, released November 1968

Frank Mills/Punky's Dilemma
#4-44775, released February 1969
"Frank Mills," from the musical *Hair*, is vinyl only. It's never been released on an album or digitally.

Little Tin Soldier/Honey Pie
#4-44921, released July 1969

What Are You Doing The Rest Of Your Life?/What About Today? #4-45040, released October 1969

Before The Parade Passes By/Love Is Only Love
#4S-45072, released December 1969
"Parade" is a dynamic arrangement by Peter Matz, vinyl only, and completely different from the 20th Century Fox soundtrack version. Streisand used to sing this arrangement in Las Vegas.

"HALL OF FAME" SINGLES

Happy Days Are Here Again/My Coloring Book
#13-33078, released March 1965
Contains original November 1962 versions of both songs.

People/Second Hand Rose
#13-33092, released 1966

Funny Girl/I'd Rather Be Blue Over You (Than Happy With Somebody Else)
#13-33154, released May 1969
Contains same songs released July 1968.

My Man/Don't Rain On My Parade
#13-33161, released June 1969
Contains same songs released November 1968.

PROMO-ONLY SINGLES

Miss Marmelstein/Who Knows? (Marilyn Cooper)
#JZSP 57067, released April 1962
From *I Can Get It for You Wholesale*. The label spells Barbra's name "Barbara."

I'm All Smiles/Autumn
#JZSP 79183, released 1964

Hello, Dolly! (mono)/Hello, Dolly! (stereo)
#6714, released December 1969 (20th Century Fox Records)
The song was an edited version of movie soundtrack song with an alternate vocal section.

1967 CHRISTMAS SINGLES

Jingle Bells?/White Christmas
#4-44350, released November 1967

Have Yourself A Merry Little Christmas/The Best Gift
#4-44351, released November 1967

My Favorite Things/The Christmas Song
#4-44352, released November 1967

The Lord's Prayer/I Wonder As I Wander
#4-44354, released November 1967

1970s Singles

The Best Thing You've Ever Done/Summer Me, Winter Me
#4-45147, released April 1970
"Best Thing," although mostly like the album version, has an extra section and alternate vocal by Streisand.

Stoney End/I'll Be Home
#4-45236, released September 1970

Time And Love/No Easy Way Down
#4-45341, released February 1971

Flim Flam Man/Maybe
#4-45384, released April 1971

Where You Lead/Since I Fell For You
#4-45414, released June 1971

Mother/The Summer Knows
#4-45471, released September 1971

Space Captain/One Less Bell To Answer/A House Is Not A Home
#4-45511, released November 1971

Sweet Inspiration/Where You Lead/Didn't We
#4-45626, released May 1972

Sing/Make Your Own Kind Of Music/Starting Here, Starting Now
#4-45686, released August 1972

Didn't We/On A Clear Day (You Can See Forever)
#4-45739, released November 1972

If I Close My Eyes/If I Close My Eyes (Instrumental)
#4-45780, released January 1973 (PS)
The theme song from Barbra's movie *Up the Sandbox.*

The Way We Were/What Are You Doing The Rest Of Your Life?
#4-45944, released September 1973
Barbra Streisand's first No. 1 single. As mentioned previously, the single has a different vocal section from the album version. The album version has become the one used on most Streisand hits compilations.

All In Love Is Fair/My Buddy/How About Me?
#4-46024, released March 1974

Guava Jelly/Love In The Afternoon
#3-10075, released December 1974

Jubilation/Let The Good Times Roll
#3-10130, released April 1975

How Lucky Can You Get?/More Than You Know
#AS 0123, released April 1975 (Arista Records)
From the movie *Funny Lady*. The single version of "How Lucky" differs from the soundtrack. The Arista *Funny Lady* CD included this single version.

My Father's Song/By The Way
#3-10198, released August 1975

Shake Me, Wake Me (When It's Over)/Widescreen
#3-10272, released December 1975

Evergreen—US and foreign singles:
US #3-10450, released November 16, 1976* No. 1 single
French #5101 (De rêve en rêveriere), released February 1977
Italian #5062 (Sempreverde), released February 1977
Spanish #5866 (Tema De Amor De "Nace Una Estrella"), released February 1977

My Heart Belongs To Me/Answer Me
#3-10555, released May 1977

Songbird/Honey Can I Put On Your Clothes?
#3-10756, released May 1978

Love Theme From "Eyes Of Laura Mars" (Prisoner)/ Laura & Neville (Instrumental)
#3-10777, released July 1978

You Don't Bring Me Flowers (duet with Neil Diamond)/ You Don't Bring Me Flowers (Instrumental)
#3-10840, released October 1978 * No. 1 single

Superman/A Man I Loved
#3-10931, released March 1979

The Main Event/Fight (short version)/The Main Event/Fight (Instrumental)
#3-11008, released June 1979

No More Tears (Enough Is Enough) {duet with Donna Summer}/Wet
#1-11125, released October 1979 * No. 1 single

No More Tears (Enough Is Enough) {duet with Donna Summer}
NBD 20199, released October 1979 (Casablanca Record & FilmWorks) {12-inch, picture sleeve}

Kiss Me In The Rain/I Ain't Gonna Cry Tonight
#1-11179, released December 1979

"HALL OF FAME" SINGLES

Stoney End/Time And Love
#13-33199, released August 1971

The Best Thing You've Ever Done/What Are You Doing The Rest Of Your Life? #13-33207, released May 1972

The Way We Were/All In Love Is Fair
#13-33262, released November 1974

Evergreen/My Heart Belongs To Me
#13-33365, released 1979

You Don't Bring Me Flowers (duet with Neil Diamond)/Forever In Blue Jeans (Diamond)
#13-33382, released 1979

PROMO-ONLY SINGLES

On A Clear Day (You Can See Forever) {mono}/On A Clear Day (You Can See Forever) {stereo}
AE-24, released July 1970
Arranged and conducted by Peter Matz and produced by Wally Gold, this is a completely different recording from the *On a Clear Day* soundtrack version (that album was arranged and conducted by Nelson Riddle).

The Way We Were
No serial number; released September 1973; Alternate arrangement and vocals by Streisand (Columbia Pictures, promo-only)

Shake Me, Wake Me (2:52 short version)/Shake Me, Wake Me (4:55 long version)
#3-10272, released December 1975 (white label, promo-only)

Shake Me, Wake Me (When It's Over) Stereo/Mono
#AS 217, released December 1975 (Columbia Disco Series—12-inch promo-only)

The Main Event/Fight
#AS 625, released June 1979 (12-inch promo-only—11:42 minutes)

1980s Singles

Woman in Love/Run Wild
#1-11364, released August 1980 * No. 1 single

Guilty (duet with Barry Gibb)/Life Story
#11-11390, released October 1980

What Kind Of Fool (duet with Barry Gibb)/The Love Inside #11-11430, released January 1981

Promises/Make It Like A Memory
#11-02065, released April 1981

Promises/Make It Like A Memory
#43-02089, released May 1981 (12-inch)

Comin' In And Out Of Your Life/Lost Inside Of You
#18-02621, released November 1981

Memory/Evergreen
#18-02717, released February 1982

The Way He Makes Me Feel (studio version)/The Way He Makes Me Feel (film version)
#38-04177, released October 1983

Papa, Can You Hear Me?/Will Someone Ever Look At Me That Way?
#38-04357, released January 1984

Left In The Dark/Here We Are At Last
#38-04605, released September 1984

Make No Mistake, He's Mine (duet with Kim Carnes)/Clear Sailing
#38-04695, released November 1984

Emotion/Here We Are At Last
#38-04707, released February 1985

Emotion/Emotion (Instrumental)
#44-05167, released February 1985 (12-inch)
Remix of Barbra's song by John "Jellybean" Benitez

Somewhere/Not While I'm Around
#38-05680, released November 1985

Send In The Clowns/Being Alive
#38-05837, released February 1986

The Main Event/Fight/Promises (12-inch)
#44H-06920, released 1987 (Columbia Mixed Masters Series)

Till I Loved You (duet with Don Johnson)/Two People
#38-08062 released October 1988

Till I Loved You (duet with Don Johnson)/Two People—CD3 single
#38K 08062, released October 1988

All I Ask Of You/On My Way To You
#38-08026, released December 1988

What Were We Thinking Of?/Why Let It Go?
#38-68691, released February 1989

We're Not Makin' Love Anymore/Here We Are At Last #38-73016, released October 1989

"HALL OF FAME" SINGLES

No More Tears (Enough Is Enough)/Wet
13-68710, released March 1989

Woman in Love/Run Wild
13-68711, released March 1989

You Don't Bring Me Flowers (duet with Neil Diamond)/Forever In Blue Jeans (Neil Diamond)—CD3 single #13K 68640, released 1989

The Way We Were/All In Love Is Fair—CD3 single #13K 68660, released 1989

PROMO-ONLY SINGLES

Memory #AS 1610, released 1982 (demonstration; 12-inch; same track on both sides)

The Way He Makes Me Feel (studio version)/The Way He Makes Me Feel (film version)
#38-04177, released October 1983 (different picture sleeve, white label)

The Way He Makes Me Feel (studio version)/The Way He Makes Me Feel (film version) #AS99-1791, released November 1983 (12-inch picture disc)

Left In The Dark (With Spoken Intro-5:42)/Left In the Dark (Without Spoken Intro-4:58)
#AE7-1938, released September 1984 (white label)

Till I Loved You (Short Version: 4:14)/Till I Loved You (Long Version 4:48) #CSK 1312, released October 1988 on CD. NOTE: the 4:14-minute version was included on the 2002 Streisand album *Duets*

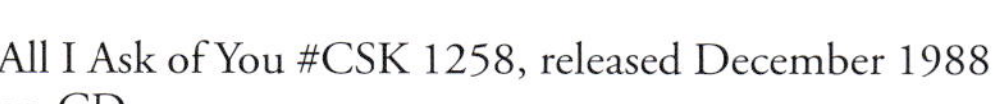

All I Ask of You #CSK 1258, released December 1988 on CD

Someone That I Used To Love # CSK 73099, released 1989; promo CD

We're Not Makin' Love Anymore (Single Version: 4:28) and (Album Version: 5:32) #CSK 1816, released October 1989; demonstration CD

1990s Singles

As If We Never Said Goodbye—UK 3-Track CD:
Guilty/No More Tears (Enough is Enough) # 660357 2; released Summer 1993; UK only

The Music Of The Night/Children Will Listen:
#659738 7, released on CD January 1994, UK only

With One Look—UK 3-Track CD:
Memory/All I Ask Of You
#659342 2; released 1993, UK only

Ordinary Miracles CD/Vinyl:
Ordinary Miracles (Studio Version)
Ordinary Miracles (Live Version)
38-77533 and # 44K 77534, released May 1994

I Finally Found Someone CD Single:
I Finally Found Someone (3:42) Let's Make A Night To Remember (6:19) [Bryan Adams] Evergreen (Spanish Version) (3:06) [Barbra Streisand]
38K 78480, released November 1996.
Note: First and only digital release of "Evergreen" in Spanish.

Everything Must Change (Streisand)/Where Is The Love (Dion)/Tell Him (duet with Celine Dion)
#665205-2; released October 1997, Europe only

If I Could 4-Track CD:
At The Same Time/I Believe (single version) /Evergreen (French version) # 665522-2; released February 23, 1998; Europe only. Note: First and only digital release of "Evergreen" in French.

I've Dreamed of You (4:45)
#38K 79211 CD Single released June 22,1999

If You Ever Leave Me (Duet with Vince Gill)
#CSK-42713, Demonstration CD Single

If You Ever Leave Me 4-Track CD:
Just Because/Let's Start Right Now/At The Same Time #667801-2, released September 13, 1999; Europe only. Note: "Just Because" and "Let's Start Right Now" are outtakes from *A Love Like Ours* and only appear on this CD.

PROMO-ONLY SINGLES

Places That Belong To You #CSK 4257, released 1991, CD

For All We Know #CSK 4507, released 1992, CD

The Music Of The Night (Edit: 4:17) and (Album Version: 5:37) # CSK 5429, released summer 1993,

Children Will Listen (spoken intro—4:19)
Children Will Listen (album version—4:07)
CSK 5288; released 1993, CD
Note: Barbra speaks the intro to this song, singing "Rockabye Baby" as she did at President Bill Clinton's Inauguration.

Speak Low #CSK 5580, released 1993, CD

Frank Sinatra—*Duets*: DPRO-79316
I've Got A Crush On You (duet with Frank Sinatra/Streisand) Edit and LP Version on Capitol Records; released November 1993; Promotional CD single contains short version (2:50) of Frank Sinatra—*Duets* track, omitting the instrumental intro.

Evergreen (Live)
CSK 6602; released 1994; Promotional CD Single

Tell Him (duet with Celine Dion)
Radio Edit (4:52)
Album Version (4:50)
#BSK 3469, released October 7, 1997; Promotional CD Single

2000+ Singles

Come Rain Or Come Shine (live)
#CSK 16130, released September 19, 2000
Included as a bonus disc with the Barnes & Noble edition of Timeless.

Stranger In A Strange Land
#CSK 17286, released September 1, 2005

Night Of My Life (12-inch vinyl single)
44-80392, released September 27, 2005

Come Tomorrow (duet with Barry Gibb)/Night Of My Life (Love To Infinity Master Mix) # 82876 771472, released December 19, 2005; UK only

In The Wee Small Hours Of The Morning
Digital single, released September 1, 2009
Streisand's first digital single, available online only for download at iTunes and at Amazon.com.

We Are the World 25
Digital single, released February 12, 2010 (video) and March 2, 2010 (single)
"We Are the World 25 for Haiti" was a charity single recorded by music superstars in 2010 (Barbra sang one line).

Don't Lie to Me (Dave Audé Remix)
Digital single, released October 20, 2018
Debuted on the *Billboard* Dance Club Songs chart November 24, 2018, at #46, then climbed, reaching #8 on January 12, 2019, charting for 11 weeks.

Sweet Forgiveness—J's Remix
Digital EP, released July 23, 2021
Mixed by Release Me 2's mixer Jochem van der Saag, this 1994 song was released as a digital EP with a 4-minute and a 3:33-minute "Radio Remix" version.

Love Will Survive (from *The Tattooist of Auschwitz*)
Digital single, released April 25, 2024

God Bless America
Digital single, 2024 Columbia de-coupled this promo-only CD single from *Christmas Memories*.

FINALE

I have listened to Barbra Streisand's music for over forty years. At this point her voice is omnipresent in my life, singing in my headphones, the car, or on the household audio system. So it's difficult to elucidate why I love her so much—"Still?" as Barbra asked on the *Forum* album.

And how do you describe a voice, let alone "the voice" that is Barbra Streisand? On YouTube, some of the commenters try: "Pure, unadulterated talent," wrote one about Barbra. "This woman sings like a bird," typed another. Stephen Holden, of the *New York Times* eloquently called Streisand's voice "singularly compelling" in his 2012 review of her concert. Duet partner Michael Bublé said, "God kissed her throat and she's blessed with this beautiful voice. But I think what makes people fall even more in love with her is her ability to tell a story. And I guess that's the actress within her." Even pianist Glenn Gould wrote that Barbra's voice was one of the "natural wonders of the age, an instrument of infinite diversity and timbral resource." (Mach, 1980)

The best interview with Barbra about the mechanics of her singing style was in 2009. Anthony Tommasini wrote: "Her singing is uncommonly intimate and exposed . . . she had a way of reaching the peak of a phrase and sustaining a pitch with such focused vibrato and pulsating tone that she seemed to be soaring effortlessly." (Tommasini, 2009)

Although others have been more articulate about her singing, I will try to describe why I love Barbra's music so much.

Barbra is practically incapable of singing a bad note (even when singing live). Technically, she sings in tune, on pitch. Then there's the innate actress that she is—the way she phrases a song on a record as if she were standing center stage in a spotlight. She is elegant and precise with the lyrics she's intoning, voicing long, open vowels. And, oh, those vowels! "Starting Here, Starting Now" is a perfect example of Barbra singing, wide open, "love, here, now, allow" then meticulously popping the *t's* and *k's* at the end of the words.

She never sings a song the same way twice. She has confessed she gets bored singing her hits over and over, so she experiments and plays with the melody. And that is why Barbra, to this day, still surprises me. I keep coming back for more because she constantly revises her songs and imprints her uniqueness on song standards.

Despite her lack of schooling in music theory, and despite the fact that she does not read music, Barbra has an instinctive musicality—that's where those wild, unexpected notes come from. Sure, she'll sing the first verse of a song as written so that the writer's melody is expressed as they intended. Then she'll sing the notes she hears in her head to elaborate the tune. I'm thinking of Barbra's "Unusual Way" or "Losing My Mind." Nobody has sung those songs with those alternate notes like Barbra has!

Everything she sings is definitive, emotionally explored, fully committed to—and sometimes she will throw in a bit of vocal "jazz hands" to show off. Her only flaw is a tendency to fall behind the beat on rhythm songs.

Why did Barbra ascend to her status as a world-renowned vocalist?

Her voice is a gift, passed down to her from her mother. "Mine was a singing family," Diana Streisand Kind recalled. "My father was a tailor who also served as a part-time cantor in the neighborhood Jewish Temple . . . At home, we'd sing a lot. Barbra would like nothing better than to sit on the stoop of our house and sing loud enough for the neighbors to open their windows, listen, clap and ask for more." (*TV Radio Mirror*, 1965)

Barbra is an untrained singer; she's never taken a lesson. But with her natural talent and the hours and hours of practice she accumulated before she turned twenty-one years old, Barbra became the celebrated singer we all love today.

The trajectory she took to becoming our greatest singer surely began with her public school music education. Barbra attended Erasmus Hall High School in Brooklyn, where she sang in the choral club, practicing several times a week (if not every day). At eighteen, she was singing live into a microphone several nights a week at small New York nightclubs. Then, just a few years later, she was on Broadway belting twelve songs at each performance, eight shows a week (Sundays off). Barbra sang the *Funny*

Girl score over one thousand times. Also, let's not forget her staggering output of records in the first two decades of her career. All that time in the recording studio developed her voice more. You can hear the raw brashness on the *Funny Girl* cast album versus the maturity that can be heard in her voice on the *People* album, or on *Je m'appelle Barbra*. Then, in the Seventies, Barbra developed a superior microphone recording technique, sounding less like a Broadway belter and more like the iconic diva we know her as now.

Barbra Streisand's longevity is because she is also timeless, with a recording career over sixty years long. Because she chose to record song standards most of her career, she's hardly gone out of style. As she said herself about showtunes and standards, "This kind of music will never be out of date." That being said, Barbra has dabbled in music trends—everything from disco to classical to rock.

I know there is a contingent of Barbra's fans who get frustrated with her song choices. The truth is that she always wanted to be unique, never singing other people's songs. Back in 1961 on the TV show *PM East* (and the very beginning of her career), she humorously confessed: "They all ask me, where do I get [my songs] from? My songs are all written by reputable people, you must understand this. Cole Porter, Harold Arlen, you know what I mean? It's not like I go around digging them up in ash cans."

Perhaps *Funny Girl*'s composer, Jule Styne, stated it best at the 1964 opening of that show. "She's unique, original," he said about Barbra. "Unfortunately, a lot of singers copy one another and fall into a trap. This girl has marvelous musical taste and naturally she's going to survive a lot of people who have bad musical taste." Styne's proclamations about Streisand were prophetic. "This girl is unique," he continued, "Honest. No fake. Honest. She's one of the greatest singers of my time, and I've heard them all." (WNEW Radio, 1964)

I am glad I was alive in the twentieth century so I could experience the career of Barbra Streisand, especially as her legacy reaches into the twenty-first century.

I am grateful Barbra loves to make albums—from those amazing and iconic covers to the carefully chosen songs.

I am always surprised and touched that I've met and corresponded with so many fans who have been affected by this woman's voice. Thousands of us have been in arenas around the world perched at the edge of our seats listening to her magnificent voice, sometimes moved to tears, sometimes simply in awe that we finally made it into the same room as her!

Barbra says in concert, "We're all here because of the music, right? Music can transcend all of our differences."

Thank you, Barbra, for being the conduit . . . the channel that's brought all the world together listening to your music.

"Sing, sing a song
Make it simple to last
Your whole life long
Don't worry that it's not
Good enough for anyone else to hear
Just sing, sing a song"

SPECIAL THANKS:
ON MY WAY TO YOU

I've maintained Barbra-Archives.info for over twenty years, which makes me think—*where has the time all gone to*? Writing this book challenged me to become adept at writing about *music*. I am *not* a musician, and like Barbra, I don't read music. Although I've dabbled in the cabaret scene (I've sung and written and directed shows), it was challenging to write here about instruments, arrangements, keys, tempos, modulations, and more. I hope I haven't committed any major music faux pas. I thank my sister, Pam, a musician and singer, and her husband, Chris (otherwise known as Phatty, because he plays a *phat* bass!), for confirming modulations and identifying instruments on Barbra's records. And for their love and support.

I'd like to give special thanks to the "two Jays" for their amazing support of this project.

Not only did Jay Landers agree to write the foreword of this book, but he elaborated about his work on the albums and songs he produced with Barbra via email and on camera for our YouTube series. His input elevated this book to a new level, and I am very grateful for the time he spent clarifying and explaining. Thank you, Jay, for being so kind and meticulous. The readers, too, have benefited from your contributions.

Richard Jay-Alexander is an energetic source of inspiration. He (literally) can talk about Barbra and her discography for hours and is such a fan, which makes him so appealing. His work with her reflects the obvious joy he feels for her movies and albums. He also gives great advice, which I appreciate. Thank you, RJA!

Richard hooked me up with Bill Ross, and I'm so glad that happened. Thank you, Bill, for your time and the information you shared. As I told you on the phone, I'm a *Star Wars* geek, and although we "talked Barbra," I could have had a whole other conversation with you about your work with John Williams and the galactic saga. I'm such a fan.

Allison Waldman, who died in 2013, would have loved this book. We were friends, talking on the phone about Barbra often, and connecting in person at the Streisand concerts. I will never forget her ferociousness at the 2012 concerts, presenting her just-written book to Barbra herself.

Thank you to Barbra's associates who, over the years, have granted me interviews about their work with her: John Arrias, Alan and Marilyn Bergman, Robbie Buchanan, Rupert Holmes, Mark Radice, Gary Klein, and the late, great Phil Ramone.

Mark Iskowitz curated The Barbra Streisand Music Guide website for years, and in a way he is responsible for Barbra Archives. Mark encouraged me to make my website different from his, so I went down the "archive" path of Barbra's career. Thanks, Mark!

Then there's Team Barbra, which has been so cool and sweet to interact with: Tracy, Grace, and Kim. You're the best!
Marty Erlichman—thank you for your support over the years! You're an icon and a gentleman.

Chris Poppe—thank you SO MUCH.

You'll never know just how much I love you: Todd Sussman, Craig Hall, Matt Amato, Jeffrey James, Joseph Marzullo, Greg Stewart, and Bob Scott.

I spent two afternoons with Edmund La Fosse watching Streisand bootleg videos back in the nineties. He is to blame for all of this (and I say that with love).

Then there's my sweet Barbra bud Matt Clinton, whom I met in London during the Hyde Park concert; the OG Streisand fan and fanzine writer Chris Nickens; Rafe Chase; Craig Dickson; Silvio Palmieri (I miss him so!); Lynne Pounder (*All About Barbra* magazine); and the DC Streisand crew: George Shubert, Brett Fox, and Kevin Hall.

Also: Paul Katz (we had great bootleg times!), Lou Papalas (it took us a while to meet, and when we did, you were amazing), and the late James Spada, who wrote those great books about Barbra.

There are many others who have corresponded with me over the years—it's been fun chatting, and I always enjoy receiving your emails and DMs even if I don't respond immediately.

I have my sources, but I could not maintain the exclusive information on the website (and in this book) without the contributions of generous fans. A big THANK YOU to all of you who have shared tapes, files, and CDs . . . you know who you are. As Harold Arlen wrote: "I'm gratulant and grateful and an indebted idolater."

Thank you, David Bushman, for editing the book and catching everything, including *affect* versus *effect*.

My editor, Scott Ryan, was a saint putting up with my edits and revisions. I knew that every word and fact had to be impeccable. Thank you for encouraging me to share my opinions and thank you for believing in the entire prospect. Scott is obsessed with *The Concert* too, so that sparked many discussions!

Finally, there's Barbra Streisand herself—thank you, Barbra! What more can I say? I've written a whole book about your recording legacy. Your music means so much to so many people . . . and to me. Although I've written at length about songs, songwriters, recording techniques, CDs, LPs, and all the topics that surround your albums, when it comes down to it: you touched me . . . I felt a sudden tingle when you touched me . . . a sparkle, a glow.

I look forward to your *next* album.

PHOTO CREDITS

2: albums photo by Matt Howe
13: Barbra in Central Park, 1962 by Michael Ochs
29: Barbra on the Chicago beach by Don Bronstein
34: CBS-TV "My Name is Barbra" candid and slide
39, 40: "Color Me Barbra" full color album insert
45: Streisand and Eddy Marnay (courtesy eddymarnay.com)
46: Columbia Records advert for "Je m'appelle Barbra"
49: "Simply Streisand" insert; ten-page foldout
50: CBS-TV, photo: James Moore; Holland picture sleeve
54: Various "Christmas Album" releases, including: Alternate CD cover; the Barnes & Noble white vinyl 2024 remaster; "The Christmas Collection" CD, containing the 1967 and 2001 holiday albums; "Season's Greetings from Barbra Streisand" featured Barbra's 1967 Christmas songs on side one.
55, 57: Streisand in "Funny Girl," Columbia Pictures 1967
61-63: CBS-TV "A Happening In Central Park"
66: Streisand and Matz in the studio; courtesy of Wally Gold
69: "Hello Dolly's" parade; courtesy 20th Century Fox
70: Philips CD magazine ad (left); 20th Century-Fox (right)
72: "A Star is Born" promo photo; courtesy First Artists
78: Alternate cover photo by Barry Feinstein;
79: Streisand in the recording studio, from the back, with Richard Perry. Photographer unknown.
82: Streisand recording; photo by Ed Thrasher
86: Barbra singing at the Forum. Photo by Jim McCrary/Redferns
87: "Forum". Kirn Vintage Stock/Alamy Stock Photo
90: Ray Charles and Barbra harmonize on her "Other Musical Instruments" TV show; photo by CBS TV.
94: Photo by David Bailey
100: Photo by Ed Thrasher
101, 103, 108, 114, 148: gatefold LPs
104: "Funny Lady" courtesy Columbia Pictures
105: Streisand and Jon Peters; Scavullo (condenaststore.com)
109: Streisand at microphone by Steve Schapiro
115: French picture sleeve for "Evergreen."
121: Ralph Dominguez/MediaPunch
122: Alternate photo by Steve Schapiro
123, 125, 126: Alternate "Wet" photos by Mario Casilli
140: Greg Gorman photo
144: Alternate "Guilty" photo by Mario Casilli
147: "Yentl" UK picture sleeve for "Papa"; United Artists' publicity photo; UK picture sleeve for "No Matter What Happens."
152: Streisand from the music video for "Left in the Dark."
153: "Emotion" 12-inch remix
154: Back cover of "Emotion" 12-inch; Sondheim and Streisand; photo by Mark Sennet
155: Sondheim and Streisand; photo by Ebet Roberts
157: Barbra wearing a beret; photo by Richard Corman
158: Streisand and Sondheim; Barwood Films
159: Picture sleeve for "Send in the Clowns" single
160: US Magazine (alternate photo from the cover session by Richard Corman)
161: Streisand recording a song for "The Broadway Album"; photo by Mark Sennet
162: David Foster and Barbra in the studio; photo by Mark Sennet
163: Streisand and her Grammy for "The Broadway Album"; Brompton Photo Library
165: Barry Gibb and Barbra rehearsing "One Voice" duets; Courtesy of the "Bee Gees: How Can You Mend a Broken Heart" (HBOMax)
168: Picture sleeve of "Till I Loved You" single
169: "Till I Loved You" cover outtake; photo by Randee St. Nicholas
170: "The Concert" promotional photo by Matthew Rolston
173: Insert for promotional CD "Selections From Just for the Record"
174-5: Posters promoting "Just for the Record"
184-185: Ticket stub and vinyl courtesy of Scott Ryan
186-187: "Mirror Has Two Faces" photos courtesy TriStar Pictures
190: Poster advertising "Higher Ground" album
193: Rosie O'Donnell and Barbra. Courtesy: KidRo Productions
194: CBS-TV and Reuters/Alamy Stock Photo
199: Barbra and Jim Brolin wedding photo by Deborah Wald
209: Richard, Barbra, and Randy Waldman at piano. Courtesy Richard Jay-Alexander
231: The Bergmans and Barbra at Women in Film Crystal Awards, 1986; photo by Ron Galella
232: Barbra/M. Bergman. Courtesy: Women Songwriters Hof F
233: The Bergmans and Barbra at University of Judaism, 1985
234: Marilyn and Alan Bergman; United Artists
239: Photo of tapes in Barbra's vault. Courtesy: Jay Landers
249-250: with Patrick Wilson, Alec Baldwin, and Daisy Ridley courtesy Barbra Streisand official Instagram
251: Jamie Foxx, Patrick Wilson, Matt Howe, and Barbra Streisand after the 2016 Miami concert; Photo by Manny Hernadez.
255: Streisand and Russell James photographing the cover of "Walls." Photo: Jay Landers
256-257: Top: Courtesy Desmond Child Instagram. Bottom & 257: Russell James "Walls" outtakes
258: Walter Afanasieff and Barbra from williamrossmusic.com
265: Photos of the various "Release Me 2" covers and picture sleeves.
269: The CD and LP gatefolds for "Evergreens."
271: The "Yentl 40th" LP insert
290: Right profile, photo by: Cecil Beaton; Left profile, photo by: Firooz Zahedi

SOURCES

(1965). *TV Radio Mirror.*

20/20 Barbara Walters Interview. (1997, November 14). youtu.be/U0FJ-WD4vC8.

ABC News. (2014, September 16). "Barbra Streisand Talks 'Partners,' the Downside of Fame and Being 'Mad' for Beyoncé." Retrieved from ABC News: https://t.ly/CXpu.

Academy, T. (2021, March 17). Lee Holdridge Interview. youtu.be/AE31qMumOI4.

Associated Press. (1992, December 16). "Streisand to Ink Mega-deal."

Associated Press (2005, October 10). "Streisand Sings Anti-war Tune." Daily Star.

ASCAP (1996, November). "Alan & Marilyn Bergman on Songwriting." tinyurl.com/274hsxs3

Avrich, B. (Director). (2019). "David Foster off the Record" [Motion Picture].

Balliett, W. (1994, June 20). "Showcase Barbra Streisand." *New Yorker.*

Barbra Streisand YouTube. (2014, August 21). Barbra Streisand—Evergreen. youtu.be/mFjehT-_PHI.

Barbra Streisand YouTube. (2014, September 17). "I Can Still See Your Face" official video. youtu.be/iq0Ami5jYd4.

Barbra Streisand YouTube. (2014, September 5). *Partners* trailer. youtu.be/jasozy6wKsI.

Barbra Streisand YouTube. (2012, October 10). "If It's Meant to Be." youtu.be/iw8Yti9ZtyM.

Barry Gibb Chat Transcripts. (2005, September 10). beegees-world.com/bac-chat.html.

Beck, M. (1977). "A Producer Is Born: Jon Peters." *TV Time and Channel.*

Beck, M. (1986, February 10). "Composer Paul Jabara Still Looking for His Cut of Streisand's 'Broadway' Album." *Courier Post.*

Beck, M. (1999, September 7). "Streisand's New Album Echoes Her Wedding." *Sacramento Bee.*

Bergman, M. A. (2013). "The Way We Were: Looking Back." (T. T. Video, Interviewer).

Berk, P. (1985, November 30). "Barbra Streisand: Taking Time to Look Back, Ready to Move Forward." *Cashbox.*

Bethany, M. (1994, June). "Barbra Streisand Shares the Album of the House She Called Home for 20 Years." *In Style.*

Betts, S. L. (2015, July 14). "Songwriter Spotlight: Kim Carnes." Retrieved from *Rolling Stone.* t.ly/llaU.

Blank, E. (1991, December 15). "The Way She Is." *The Pittsburgh Press.*

Bliss, P. (1996). My "Emotion." *The Barbra Streisand Music Guide.* tinyurl.com/25be89a7.

Bobbin, J. (2001, February 11-17). "'Timeless' Barbra." *Chicago Tribune.*

Boilen, B. (2014, September 8). "Barbra Streisand and John Legend Together." WNYC. t.ly/zaTJ.

Brenner, M. (1975, January 24). "Collision on Rainbow Road." *New Times Magazine.*

Bruner, R. (2018, September 27). "Barbra Streisand Takes a Stand Against Trump on New Song." *Time.*

Budge, D. (1974, March 23). *Insight & Sound.* Cash Box.

Campbell, M. (1978, September 22). "Streisand's 'Discovery' Sidetracked Holmes." AP Newsfeatures.

Carpenter, B. (1993, May 28). "How Johnny Mathis Keeps the Music Playing." *Goldmine.*

Carr, J. (1991, December 22). "Of Time and 'Tides.'" *Boston Globe.*

CBS-TV (2004, June 22). "AFI's 100 Years 100 Songs." youtu.be/UR9R4pq1F3o.

Christensen, P. (2007, December 11). "Song Story: Holy Ground by Geron Davis." *Alive Worship Experience.* t.ly/2kk5.

Cliporama. (1997). "Celine Dion on Barbra Streisand." youtu.be/Dfl8zcYyeqM.

Columbia Records. (2015, January 20). "Barbra Streisand Goes Platinum Making 31st Time with 'Partners.'" *PR Newswire.* t.ly/8VvN2.

Concord. (2008, August). Michael Feinstein Interview. Concord.com. concord.com/artist/michael-feinstein.

Considine, S. (1985). *Barbra Streisand: The Woman, the Myth, the Music.* New York: Dell Publishing.

Cox, J. (1974, March 17). "But He Won't Rat It." *Cincinnati Enquirer.*

Crowe, C. (1976, September). *Playboy.*

Daley, D. (2009, November 1). "Streisand at the Vanguard." Mix Online. t.ly/fOPY.

Danton, E. R. (2018, March 16). "Fanny Lives: Inside the Return of the Pioneering All-Female Rock Band." *Rolling Stone.* t.ly/jPW4.

Davis, C., and A. DeCurtis (2013). *The Soundtrack of My Life.* New York. Simon & Schuster.

Davis, P. F. (1968, September 29). "Music Director Says of Barbra 'She's Stubborn, but Talented'." United Press International.

Dennen, B. (1997). *My Life with Barbra: A Love Story.* United States. Prometheus Books.

Deseret News. (1998, February 23). "Arethat Franklin Still Calls Michigan Town Her Home." t.ly/hwop.

Dion, C. (2001). *Celine Dion: My Story, My Dream.* United States. Harper Collins.

Dorff, S. (2017). *I Wrote That One, Too.* Wisconsin. Backbeat Books.

Dorsey, T. (1978, September 28). "A Record-Making Hit for a Mrs." *The Courier-Journal.*

Doyle, T. (2004, July). "Arif Mardin: Producer." *Sound on Sound.*

Drake University. (2007). Drake University Admissions. t.ly/6FZcQ.

Dreifus, C. (1997, November 11). "Love Soft as an Easy Chair (Cue the Violins)." *New York Times.*

DrumStories. (2010, January 17). William Ross Interview. youtu.be/nZtWCgZkDOI.

Dwyer, M. (2021, July 29). "Barbra Streisand: 'I Don't Understand a Lot of Today's Music.'" *Sydney Morning Herald*. t.ly/4TuG.

Eder, S. (1974, October 22). Column. *Detroit Free Press*.

Edgar, K. A. (1991, November 26). "Sax Man Whalum Plays a Mean Balancing Act as Well." *Star-Telegram*.

Farber, J. (2018, March 1). "Fanny: Behind the Reunion of a Groundbreaking All-Female Rock band." *The Guardian*. t.ly/zVLL.

Feather, L. (1963, September 22). "Barbra Streisand Cut the Gimmicks and Made It Big." *Minneapolis Sunday Tribune*.

Fink, M. (2000, July 31). *New York Daily News*.

Fishbein, E. (1977, January 19). "Coordinated Promo Campaign Behind the Merchandising of 'Star Is Born,'" *Variety*.

"For Barbra Streisand's Hit Album, Solid State Logic AWS 900 Makes Mixing a Pleasure." (2007, March 25). JohnMerchant.com. t.ly/Zj_X.

Foster, D. (2008). *Hitman*. New York. Pocket Books.

France, P. (2014, November 17). "Front & Center: CoFounder & Lead Guitarist of Fanny." June Millington. WiMN. t.ly/tx-X.

"Frank Laico. Anatomy of a Session Pt 1." (2008, December 16). (D. Mortensen, Producer, & AES Pacific Northwest Section). youtu.be/KJbhGHmY_UA.

Gahan, J. (1962, February 13). "'I Can Get It for You Wholesale' Opens." *Philadelphia Daily News*.

Gallin, S. (2016, April 12). *Radio Andy*. (A. Cohen, Interviewer).

Goldstein, P. (1991, August 11). "30 Years of Memories Cross Pages of Streisand's Mind." *Los Angeles Times*.

Graff, G. (2014, June 26). "Barbra Streisand Duets Album Almost Finished, Says Babyface." *Billboard*.

"Grammy Record Nominee." (1981, February 28). *Billboard*.

Grein, P. (1979, July 14). "Getting the Fit: Hit Maker Says Not Every Artist Should Attempt Disco." *Billboard*.

Grein, P. (1986, February 15). "Erlichman Back as Streisand's Manager." *Billboard*.

Grein, P. (1986, March 1). "Producer Enjoys 'Broadway' LP's Success." *Billboard*.

Guilty—Multi-Platinum Certification. (1989). Retrieved from RIAA website.

Gundersen, E. (2001, December 12). "Streisand's Christmas Offering." *USA Today*.

Haber, J. (1974, June 25). "Barbra's 'Butterfly Album Untracked?" *Los Angeles Times*.

Haber, J. (1974, June 27). "Streisand 'Happiest She's Ever Been'." *Los Angeles Times*.

Haber, J. (1975, April 3). "The Goings-on of Jon and Barbra." *Los Angeles Times*.

Hall, C. (2005). "BarbraNews Talks to Ann Hampton Callaway." Barbra News.com. barbranews.com/annhamptoncallaway.htm.

Hall, C. (2005, December 10). "BarbraNews Talks to Jay Landers." BarbraNews.com. barbranews.com/landers.htm.

Hall, C. (2007). "Barbra News Talks to Richard Jay-Alexander." BarbraNews.com barbranews.com/rja.htm.

Hamlisch, Marvin and Gardner, G. (1992). *The Way I Was*. Michigan: C. Scribner's Sons.

Hammerstein, R. (1985). Esty Rehearsal Tapes [Recorded by B. Streisand]. Los Angeles.

Harold Arlen Centennial Celebration. (2005). Harold Arlen 2005: HaroldArlen2005.com.

Harry (2017, January 30). Harry Connick, Jr. Interview. "Patrick Wilson Sings with Barbra Streisand." youtu.be/PhSoHpM7xT8.

Heater, B. (2020, September 10). "Recorded Music Revenue Is Up on Streaming Growth, as Physical Sales Plummet." TechCrunch.com. t.ly/02jv.

Hilburn, R. (1997, November 20). "From 'Funny Girl' to One of the 'Luckiest People.'" *Los Angeles Times Weekend*.

Hochman, S. (1994, September 11). "Streisand, Pure and Unsweetened." *Los Angeles Times*.

Holden, S. (1985, November 10). "Barbra Streisand: 'This Is the Music I Love. It Is My Roots.'" *New York Times*.

Holden, S. (1988, November 6). "Barbra Streisand and the Showstopper Syndrome." *New York Times*.

Holden, S. (2005, September 19). "Critics' Choices: New CD's; Barbra Streisand. *New York Times*. t.ly/1BD-.

Holmes, R. (2021, November 18). "JPC Extra: Rupert Holmes". (J. P. Podcast, Interview).

Hopkins, C. (1974, November 24). "How to Get Ahead in Hollywood." *Independent Press Telegram*.

Horowitz, S. (2017, July 21). "Laura Nyro: A Little Magic, a Little Kindness—The Complete Mono Albums." PopMatters. t.ly/PR_p.

Hot Takes & Deep Dives. (2020, December 21). "Interview w/ Mariah's 'All I Want for Christmas Is You' Cowriter Walter Afanasieff." Hot Takes Podcast. t.ly/nadA.

Housman, S. M. (2003, October). "Barbra Speaks." Genre.

Howe, M. (2003, October). Interview with Robbie Buchanan. Barbra Archives. t.ly/H0lX.

Howe, M. (2003, August). Rupert Holmes Interview. Barbra Archives. t.ly/a-7l.

Howe, M. (2005, February). Phil Ramone Interview. Barbra Archives. t.ly/kqoP.

Howe, M. (2007, May). Interview with Marilyn and Alan Bergman. Barbra Archives. t.ly/qC76.

Howe, M. (2011, September). Interview with Gary Klein. Barbra Archives.t.ly/RHFa.

Howe, M. (2012). Streisand Remastered. Barbra Archives. t.ly/p75w.

Hunt, D. (1978, February 12). "Pop News." *Los Angeles Times*.

Hunt, D. (1986, February 9). "Maurice White Still Has the Fire at 44." *Los Angeles Times*.

Hunt, D. (1993, March 11). "Q&A with David Foster." *Los Angeles Times*.

Hurwitz, M. (2013, May 31). "David Foster's Versatility Makes Him a Top Session Musician." *Variety*. t.ly/NjiL.

Iley, C. (2016, August 21). "The Way We Were—Streisand on Her Extraordinary Life and Lovers." *Sunday Times Magazine*.

Jacobs, D. (2003). "The Michel Legrand Story." BBC Radio 2.

Kashad, M. (2022, April 20). "Why the New Girls Can't Sing." youtu.be/psIowaNEZuQ.

Kawashima, D. (2006, March). "Top A&R Exec Jay Landers Has Great Success with Barbra Streisand, Josh Groban and Hilary Duff." Songwriter Universe. t.ly/bZOD.

Kaye, E. (1975, April). "Barbra: The Superstar Who Wants to be a Woman." *McCall's*.

Kimbrell, J. (1989). *Barbra: An Actress Who Sings*. Boston. Branden Publishing.

King, Larry. (2017, November 24). "Songwriter Steve Dorff on Working with Barbra Streisand." youtu.be/fM4ADUqef_Y.

King, S. (1994, August 21). "Her Music Man: Marvin Hamlisch." *Los Angeles Times*.

King, S. (2009, August 31). "Streisand Unchains Melodies. *Los Angeles Times*.

King, S. (2012, August 14). "Harmonious Is the Way They Were." *Los Angeles Times*.

Konder, G. C. (1995, Spring). *Show Music*.

Kruth, J. (2021). *Hold On World: The Lasting Impact of John Lennon and Yoko Ono's Plastic Ono Band, Fifty Years On*. Maryland. Backbeat Books.

Landers, J. (2012). "Sweet 'Release.'" *All about Barbra*.

Laurents, A. (2000). *Original Story by: A Memoir of Broadway and Hollywood*. New York. Applause Theatre Books.

LeBlanc, L. (2021, May 24). "Interview: A&R Exec Jay Landers." Celebrity Access. t.ly/zNhf.

Lewis, D. (1973, October 28). "Now, Here's Barbra." *Sunday Record*.

Lewis, G. (1971, June 24). "The Jeaning of Barbra Streisand." *Rolling Stone*.

Lightman, I. (1993, June 12). "Big Col Blitz Backs Barbra's 'Back to B'way.'" *Billboard*.

Live Nation. (2007). *Live in Concert 2006* Blu-ray. "The People Behind the Scenes" (interview with Richard Jay-Alexander).

Lobsenz, N. (1963, November). "Only Two A's in Barbra." *Pageant Magazine*.

Love Is the Answer Exclusive Video. (2009, August 12). youtu.be/39zHAeEnM-c.

Lukowski, A. (2018, July 4). *Time Out*. timeout.com/london/theatre/the-king-and-i-review.

Lum, K. (2012, September). Kristin Lum. t.ly/wkO5.

Lynch, J. (2021, August 6). "Barbra Streisand Talks Diving into Her Archives." *Billboard*. t.ly/9lA4.

Mach, E. (1980). *Great Contemporary Pianists Speak for Themselves*. New York. Dodd, Mead and Company.

Magness, C. (2020, December 30). Episode 295.

Malkin, M. (2018, February 1). "Barbra Streisand Explains Why She Allowed 'Marvelous Mrs. Maisel' to Use Her Songs." *Hollywood Reporter*. t.ly/mbsp.

Marinucci, S. (n.d.). "Carol Kaye on Bass, Brian and the Beach Boys." t.ly/DQ7k.

Marmorstein, G. (2007). *The Label—The Story of Columbia Records*. Thunder's Mouth Press.

Matre, L. V. (1981, March 4). "Barry Gibb Stretches Out." *Detroit Free Press*.

McClintick, D. (1993, December). "Sinatra's Double Play." *Vanity Fair*.

McKuen, R. (1986, February). "Barbra Streisand Stages a Hit." *Digital Audio & Compact Disc Review*.

McMillen, M. (2015). "5 Ways Not to Sound Old." *AARP*. t.ly/r-Sl.

MGM/UA Entertainment. (1983). *Yentl* press packet. Ladbroke Entertainments Ltd.

Michel Legrand Anthology (liner notes). (2013, October). EmArcy.

Mitchell, G. (2013, September 3). "'A Mary Christmas' Fall Music Preview 2013." *Billboard*. t.ly/xYQh.

Mitchell, S. (1996, November 7). "Barbra In One Take." *Los Angeles Times*.

Momentum RLP. (2016, December 21). "Barbra Streisand on Working with William Ross." youtu.be/JfoFnh-1FSw.

Morgenstern, J. (1983, November 13). "Streisand's Rite of Passage". *Los Angeles Herald Examiner*.

Morning, C. S. (2016, August 28). "Barbra Streisand, With a Little Help from Her Friends."*CBS Sunday Morning*.

Muir, F. (1969, April 5). "Nomination Was for Real, No Nightmare." *The Odessa American*.

Myers, M. (2009, October 15). "Johnny Mandel on Streisand." JazzWax. t.ly/meqU.

Newman, M. (2003, September 26). "Streisand Readies New 'Movie.'" *Billboard*.

News, M. (1991, October 18). "Oy, the Vaults." *Entertainment Weekly*.

Niles, R. (2021, April 14). Arif Mardin Interview. youtu.be/exDLh13ca7g.

O'Donnell, R. (2007). *Celebrity Detox*. New York. Grand Central Publishing.

Orange, J. (1976, May 10). "A Superstar Is Born Again." *Woman's Day*.

Orr, J. (1999, July 29). "Shufflin' Right Along." *The Tennessean*.

Page, M. (2016, August 11)." Throwback Thursday: Barbra Streisand." Facebook.

Paley, M. (1970, January 30). "The Funky Madonna of New York Soul." *Life*.

Parker, M. (2010, November 28). Richard Page Interview. *Smashing Interviews*. t.ly/RYFZ.

Paulson, D. (2015, January 10). "Story Behind the Song: Evergreen. *Tennessean*. t.ly/0QEr.

Pener, D. (2012, May 18). "How Donna Summer & Barbra Streisand's Famous Duet 'Enough Is Enough' Came Together." *Hollywood Reporter*. t.ly/rCqY.

People Etc. (1986, July 6). *Arizona Republic*.

Perry, R. (2005, May 4). "The Richard Perry Story." BBC Radio 2.

Pietroluongo, S. (1999, July 10). Hot 100 Singles Spotlight. *Billboard*.

Pogrebin, A. (2022, January 11). "Marilyn and Alan Bergman on 'Yentl,' Israel, and What It Means to 'Feel Jewish." *Tablet Mag*. t.ly/5fA5.

RIAA. (2014, November 2). "Barbra Streisand Goes Gold for Groundbreaking 52nd Time with 'Partners.'" RIAA. t.ly/4U65.

Ramone, P. (2007). *Making Records: The Scenes Behind the Music*. Hachette Books.

Reich, H. (2006, November 5). "Barbra Today." *Chicago Tribune*.

Reich, H. (2019, July 24). "Barbra on Barbra: Streisand Riffs on Music, Anti-Semitism and How Chicago Has Always Brought Her Good Luck." *Chicago Tribune*.

RIAA. (1997, December 22). "Higher Ground Certifications." Recording Industry Association of America. t.ly/qxJ1X.

Robertson, S. (1989, November). "Far Too Heathen." JimSteinman.com. jimsteinman.com.

Robinson, J. (2014, September 24). "Barbra Streisand Just Outsold Chris Brown and Made Billboard History." *Vanity Fair*. t.ly/at8b.

Rolontz, B. (1964, May 16). "The Making of an Artist." *Music Business*.

Rosky, N. (2020, August 14). "Liz Callaway's New Single, 'The Morning After,' Now Available!" *Broadway World*. t.ly/k-gr.

Ross, Jonathan (2006, December 17). "Don Johnson BBC 2006." youtu.be/GRPa0rvjrEg.

Ruber, K. (1979, October). "Music." *Orange Coast Magazine*.

Ryan, D. (2008, December 20). "Home at Last." *The Vancouver Sun*.

Ryan, L. L. (2004, October 7). "Radio Facing Music of Change." *Chicago Tribune*.

Sager, C. B. (2017). *They're Playing Our Song: a Memoir*. New York: Simon & Schuster.

Sandiford-Waller, T. (1997, November 8). "Hot 100 Singles Spotlight." *Billboard*.

Santon, C. (1962, September). "Light Listening." *Audio Magazine*.

Schifrin, L. (2008). *Mission Impossible*. United States. Scarecrow Press.

Schnee, B. (2021). *Chairman at the Board: Recording the Soundtrack of a Generation*. Lanham, MD. Backbeat Books.

Shultz, Larry. (2013). "Working for Jon Peters and Barbra Streisand." lawrenceshultz.net.

Shalit, G. (1967, February). "What's Happening?". *Ladies' Home Journal*.

Shuman, E. (2013). *Excerpts from Songs for Sale: The Story of a Songwriter*. United States. Cerro Chato Publishing.

Siegel, T. (2017, January 12). "'I Am the Trump of Hollywood': The Reclusive and Outrageous Jon Peters Is Still Rich. Really Rich." *Hollywood Reporter*. t.ly/sdy8.

Singersroom. (2008, October 27). "Siedah Garrett: The Woman in the Mirror." *Singers Room*. t.ly/JiCF.

SiriusXM. (2014, 2016). Barbra Streisand Channel Interstitials.

Skipper, R. (2021, May 28). "Richard Skipper Celebrates Richard Jay-Alexander." youtu.be/mYCkmhfiXTc.

Sondheim, S. (2011). *Look, I Made a Hat* Collected Lyrics (1981-2011) with Attendant Comments, Amplifications, Dogmas, Harangues, Digressions, Anecdotes and Miscellany. United States: Alfred A. Knopf.

Sondheim, S. (2010, July). *Sunday in the Park with George* commentary. Image Entertainment.

Sony Music. (2011, June 25). *What Matters Most—Behind the Scenes* DVD. USA.

Spada, J. (1983, December 10). "The Legend of Barbra Streisand." *Billboard*.

Staff, T. T. (1978, May 12). "Listen." *Los Angeles Times*.

Stewart, Z. (1991, December 1). "You'll Place the Tune if Not the Name." *Los Angeles Times*.

"Streisand & Summer Team Up for a Duet of Disco and Egos." (1979, November 13). *Us Magazine*.

"Streisand Album Set." (1974, June 15). *Desert Sun*.

"Streisand Catalog Overhauled." (1995, January). ICE: The Monthly CD Newsletter.

Streisand, B. (1970, January 9). "Who Am I Anyway?" *Life*.

Streisand, B. (1991). *Just for the Record* liner notes. Columbia Records.

Streisand, B. (1999, February). "A Wedding Planned with a Director's Eye." *In Style*.

Streisand, B. (2005, August 19). "Guilty Blog." BarbraStreisand.com. tinyurl.com/4bs8w3zy.

Streisand, B. (2023). *My Name Is Barbra*. United Kingdom: Penguin Publishing Group.

Streisand, B. (2009, October 3). "The Way I Am." BBC Radio 2. (P. Gambaccini, Interviewer).

Streisand, B. (2018, November 3). "NPR Weekend Edition Saturday." (S. Simon, Interviewer).

Streisand, B. (2018, November 27). "Take Care of This House (Behind the Song)." youtu.be/7QtphDz4FHk.

Streisand, B. (2019, April 11). (T. L. Congress, Interviewer).

Studio Star. (1975, January 13). *Newsweek*.

Summer, Donna (2008). *Ordinary Girl: The Journey*. United States. Villard.

Sussman, T. (2018, January 4). "In Tune with Marsha Malamet." *Windy City Times*. t.ly/cScv.

Sutel, S. (2005, February 26). "Radio Boom Times a Thing of the Past." *The Seattle Times*. t.ly/dmnx.

Sutherland, S. G. (1978, August 19). "The Coast." *Record World*.

Swenson, K. (1986). *Barbra, the Second Decade*. United States. Citadel Press.

Syme, R. (2018, November 4). "Barbra Streisand Can Hear Herself Again." *New Yorker*.

Syndicated. (1963). "Young Singer Follows Idea 'Be Yourself.'"

Taylor, J. (1986, March 31). "The Multi-Talented Peter Matz." *Daily News* (Los Angeles).

The Today Show. (1983). 1983 Interview. youtube/1G96pIMVVRU.

Time. (1964, April 3). "On the Rue Streisand." *Time*.

Tingen, P. (2016, November). "Inside Track: Secrets of the Mix Engineers: David Reitzas." *Sound on Sound*.

Touzeau, J. (2009). *Artists on Recording Techniques*. Course Technology.

TriStar Pictures. (1996). "Roundtable Interview with Streisand." *Just Like Buttah #9*.

Tubridy, R. (2012, November 3). "First Encounters." *Irish Times*.

Twentieth Century-Fox (1969). *A Special 30-Minute Musical Radio Show with the Stars of Hello, Dolly!*

Vance, K. (2017, September 17). Facebook. t.ly/4vN6.

Verdugo, L. (1979, Spring). "Spinning Gold." *Barbra*.

Vincentelli, E. (2017, November 10). "Natalie Dessay Finishes What Barbra Streisand Started." *New York Times*.

Walters, G. (2020, September 20). "Barbra Streisand's 'Guilty' Turns 40." *Albumism*. t.ly/avBW.

Warner Bros. (1997, November 24). "Show Tops Its Previous Ratings Records." PRNews wire.

White, M. (2016). *My Life with Earth, Wind & Fire*. New York. Harper Collins.

Wikane, C. J. (2017, April 24). "Where the Heart Is: An Interview with Multi-Grammy Winner Kim Carnes." *Pop Matters*. t.ly/XZJFJ.

Williams, J. (1997, November 21). "Streisand Lives Up to O'Donnell's Dreams." *USA Today*.

Wilson, B. (1972, December 22). "Barbra Discovers Business Matters Loosen Her Tongue." *Philadelphia Inquirer*.

Wilson, E. (1965, May 10). "Stella Seeks an Identity." AP.

Wilson, J. S. (1964, May). "A Kook from Madagascar." *High Fidelity*.

Wiser, C. (2007, June 1). "Paul Williams." *Song Facts*. t.ly/oNbl.

Wong, C. M. (2013, January 18). "Culture & Arts." *Huffington Post*. t.ly/60cn.

Zadan, C. (1986). *Sondheim & Co*. New York. Harper & Row.

Zinsser, W. (2001). *Easy to Remember - The Great American Songwriters and Their Songs*. New Hampshire. David R. Godine.

Zulaica, D. (2012, April 11). "Soundspike Interview: Drummer Jim Keltner." *Jim Keltner Discography*. t.ly/CKNS.

Zutell, I. (2000, October 9). "Barbra Streisand: The Farewell Interview." *Us Magazine*.

imagine murder
A JOHN LENNON MYSTERY
DEAN THOMPSON
with Thom Moon & Victoria Hallerman
BROOME ST

The Dreamer's Path
Twin Peaks and David Lynch the Actor
Brent Simon

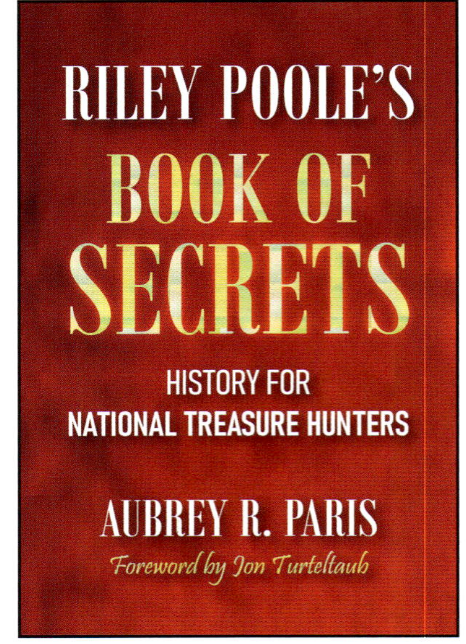
RILEY POOLE'S
BOOK OF
SECRETS
HISTORY FOR
NATIONAL TREASURE HUNTERS
AUBREY R. PARIS
Foreword by Jon Turteltaub

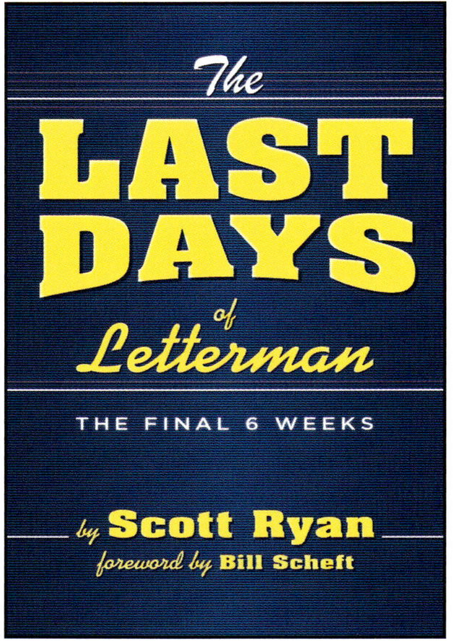
The
LAST
DAYS
of
Letterman
THE FINAL 6 WEEKS
by Scott Ryan
foreword by Bill Scheft

TUCKER
DS
PRESS

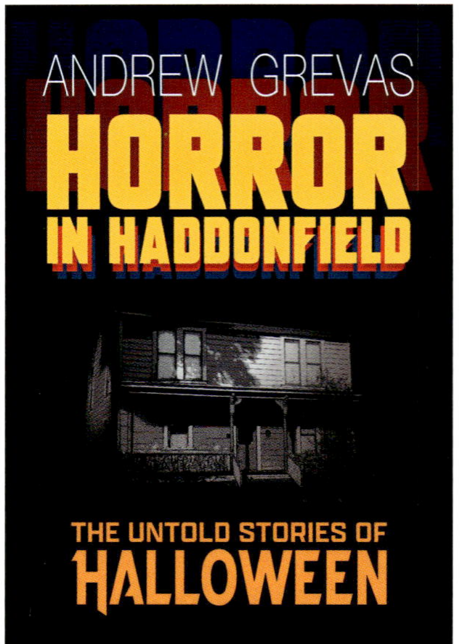
ANDREW GREVAS
HORROR
IN HADDONFIELD
THE UNTOLD STORIES OF
HALLOWEEN

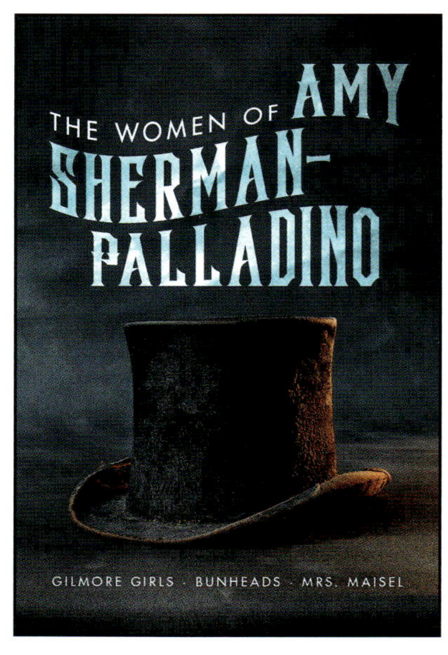
THE WOMEN OF AMY
SHERMAN-
PALLADINO
GILMORE GIRLS · BUNHEADS · MRS. MAISEL

COMFORT SEQUELS
THE PSYCHOLOGY OF MOVIE SEQUELS
FROM THE 80'S AND 90'S
Emily Marinelli

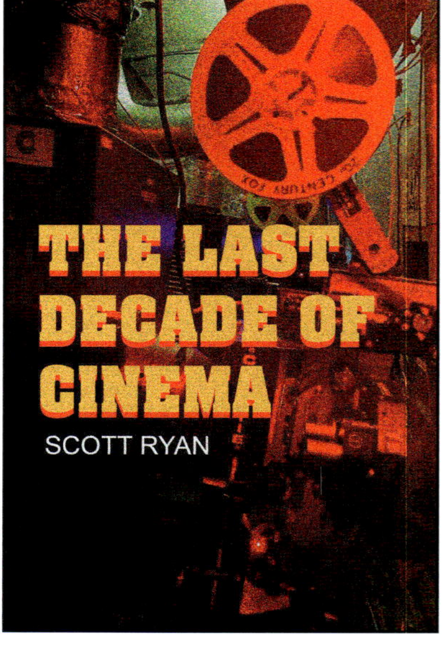
THE LAST
DECADE OF
CINEMA
SCOTT RYAN